CIVIC CENTER

By Dammit, We're Marines!

Veterans' Stories Of Heroism, Horror, And
Humor In World War II On The Pacific Front

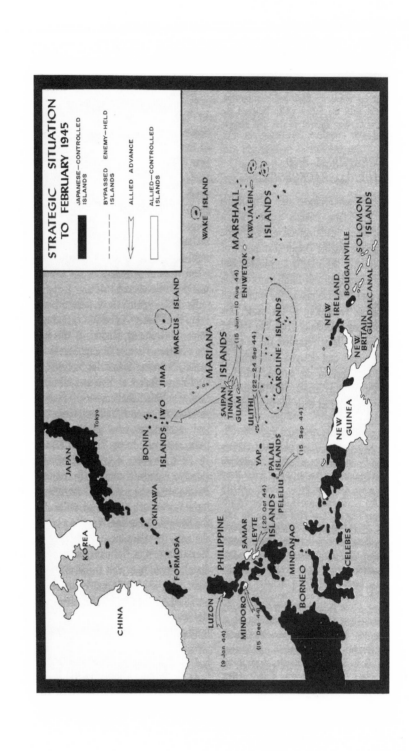

By Dammit, We're Marines!

Veterans' Stories Of Heroism, Horror, And
Humor In World War II On The Pacific Front

Methvin Publishing
3225 Lower Ridge Road
San Diego, CA 92130
Telephone (858) 205-2600
http://www.methvinpublising.com

ISBN-13: 9780977903948
ISBN-10: 0-9779039-4-X

Library of Congress Control Number: 2008929133

Printed and Bound in the United States of America

Cover Design: Robert S. Jones

10 9 8 7 6 5 4 3 2 1

SAN: 8 5 0 – 5 4 3 8

ACKNOWLEDGMENTS

My father was a Marine on Bougainville, Guam and Iwo Jima. He served in HQ Company, 2nd Battalion, 9th Marines, 3rd Marine Division. He also served in Iceland before the war and wore a polar bear patch on his uniform.

For my father's participation in the three major battles against the Japanese, Major General G. B. Erskine signed a Meritorious Service Commendation citing that Sergeant John M. Methvin's "devotion to duty and his exemplary conduct under adverse conditions were an inspiration to his comrades."

I wish I knew more about my father's wartime service. He died when I was 15 years old and more interested in the Beatles' invasion than the invasion of Bougainville. He never spoke about his wartime experiences and I never asked. His war stories are lost forever.

Through my interviews with the 52 veterans in this book, I came to understand and appreciate my father's time in the Marines. For that, I will always be in their debt and cannot thank them enough for sharing their time and their memories.

I know these men only as fathers and grandfathers, but as they told me their stories, I could picture them as young men. My two daughters are the same ages as these men were when they witnessed the horrors of war and the mother in me wanted to reach back in time to protect them. The daughter in me hung on every word my 'band of fathers' said. We shared tears and laughter but most of all we shared a first-hand look at history that will be lost when this generation of Marines falls in for final formation.

Ten of these veterans have died since their interviews. I am honored to have known Edgar Steinau, Frank McCarthy, Joe Parrish, Charles Goe, Joe Kratcoski, James Francavilla, Marold Miller, Earle Davis, John Herman and Henry Koellein. Sadly, my mother also passed away before this book went to print. She enjoyed hearing these stories and reminiscing about the home front.

Personal thanks go to Paul McLellan whom my husband and I met years ago at the annual Iwo Jima Commemorative Banquet held at Camp Pendleton. His anecdotes about Bougainville and Iwo Jima inspired me to put this book together. Thanks to Mike Mervosh, a legend in the Marine Corps, for his fatherly encouragement and advice. Thanks also to Joe Garza who searched his private papers and found my dad's name in the minutes of the first regional meeting of the Third Marine Division Association dated 8 May 1950 that they both attended.

It is indeed a small world. Thanks to Russ Silverthorn for sharing the books of archival photos taken on Iwo Jima during the battle and presented to his father, Lt. Gen. Merwin H. Silverthorn, Assistant Commandant USMC 1950-1952.

This endeavor could not be possible without the support of my husband, Alan, and my daughters, Chelsea and Emma. Thanks to Brandi Morann for her encouragement; to Eddie Carter for his computer expertise; and to my editor, Mary Ellen Barnes. Thanks also to Robert S. Jones for his assistance in producing this book.

Most important, my everlasting thanks to all the Marines, sailors, soldiers, airmen and coast guardsmen who served their country during World War II and to those who continue that proud legacy today.

Photo of the author's father, John Manning Methvin,
after returning from Iceland in 1941

Table of Contents

Introduction

America's strength comes from her citizen soldiers, ordinary men and women called upon to do extraordinary things during wartime. History books tell of the strategies and tactics of war; but the real war stories, the stories of heroism, courage, personal sacrifice and loss can only be told by those who were there on the front lines. The oral histories of these few veterans, both enlisted and commissioned, serve to honor and represent the many whose stories will never be told. Each man's life is a short story in this book, for war and its warriors cannot be described in just a few paragraphs.

For most of these veterans, the story begins on December 7, 1941, when the Japanese attacked not only Pearl Harbor but also Wake Island, the Philippines, Malaya, Guam, Midway, Thailand and Shanghai. The next day, President Franklin D. Roosevelt declared war on Japan.

The unprovoked attack on Sunday morning so shook our nation that by afternoon lines had formed outside military recruiting offices in cities and towns across America as men enlisted in record numbers. Full of patriotism, selflessness, courage, and admittedly unprepared for what they would later encounter, these farmers, city kids, high school dropouts and college graduates answered the call to war. Many lied about their age and enlisted as boys of 16; and others, 'old' men of 25. Given a choice of branch of service, they chose the Marines.

Within months of the attack on Pearl Harbor, the Japanese invaded and controlled a swath of territory from the Korean Peninsula to New Guinea and all the island nations in between. Hong Kong, the Dutch East Indies, the Mariana Islands, Palau, the Gilbert Islands, the Marshall Islands, the Caroline Islands, Wake Island, Burma, Siam, French Indo-China and the Philippines all fell like dominoes to the powerful Japanese Army and Navy. The Japanese dominated these island nations for years but proved no match for the counter invasions by the U.S. military.

"There is one thing the Japs always made a mistake about," recalls John Holle of the 14th Marines. "They'd let us land before they opened up on us, and once we are on land, we aren't going to leave."

When ordered to secure another Japanese-held island, these Marines grabbed their M-1 rifles, climbed down rope ladders into the waiting landing craft, and hit the beaches. They faced not only an embedded, well-equipped enemy, but also flesh shredding coral reefs, malarial and dengue fever-ridden jungles, mosquito and crocodile infested swamps, and a noxious moonscape sulfur island.

1

Success in seizing the Japanese homeland territory of Iwo Jima would be a defining moment in Marine Corps history, but to the veterans who landed on the morning of February 19, 1945, it was just another island invasion in a series of them. Bougainville, Guam, Roi-Namur, Saipan, Tinian, Iwo Jima: unfamiliar places that seared unforgettable memories for those who fought there.

Through their personal narratives, these insightful octogenarians are transformed into invincible teenagers during World War II. Born at the end of World War I, their fathers had fought in the Great War, the war meant to end all wars. It didn't. Less than two decades later, this Greatest Generation of young men would answer their nation's call. Their war, the Good War, ended but planted seeds of discontent and rebellion in other nations and these young men again took up arms in Korea, the Forgotten War. Their sons would serve in America's longest war, Viet Nam, and their grandsons and granddaughters would fight in the Gulf War and the Global War on Terror.

Technology changes with every war but the universal human experience of combat remains the same. Marines and soldiers from the battlefields of Valley Forge to the streets of Fallujah understand patriotism, fear, death, loneliness, and the humor that helps them through the rough times. Separated from family and loved ones, each generation of combatants knows that their mental and physical survival depends upon the camaraderie they share. In essence, young men enlist to safeguard their country, but they fight to safeguard their friends. "The guy next to you knows you are going to be there and you know damn well he's going to be there and it really isn't much beyond that," recalls Bill Swanson, a corporal on Iwo Jima. "Our world was just us. It's kind of hard to think you could really separate yourself from the rest of the world that way but you can." With an average deployment during World War II of 33 months, it is not difficult to understand that thinking.

Their stories also offer a literary archeological dig of sorts into 1940's culture and technology. Body armor was a canvas shirt with a metal covered copy of the Bible in the breast pocket. Camouflage clothing was do-it-yourself burlap suits stippled with Max Factor women's make-up. Cutting edge medicine was sulfa tablets to treat infection and blood plasma shipped in glass bottles to field hospitals. Canvas hammocks stacked eight to ten high served as bunks aboard overcrowded ships. They used salt water soap for salt water baths and were issued OPA tickets, V-mail, C-rations, K-rations, and helmets that served as sinks and saucepans. Creating the safest foxhole took some ingenuity and a few discarded tank parts.

By Dammit, We're Marines!

Most of the veterans interviewed in this book are Marines, but war is a collaborative effort. Marines were transported by the Navy, relieved by the Army, and most of the time their job was to secure airfields for the Army Air Corps. No story of the Marines would be complete without hearing from those branches of service. There was rivalry but also respect. "I owe my being alive to the Marines who took Iwo," said Vic Chalker of the Army Air Corps whose B-29 made three emergency landings on Iwo Jima.

Chaplain John Wolf on the USS Frederick Funston told the Marines of the 2nd Division how his shipmates felt about their fellow passengers. "When all is said and done, we give you a lot of credit for landing on that beach [Saipan] while we remain relatively safe on our ship. We would never admit it, of course, but we do admire you for the part you will play in the final victory and we will be only too glad to take you home again whenever you finish your job."

In less than four years, the Greatest Generation had indeed finished their job. They returned home to take advantage of the new G.I. Bill, find a good woman, and live in peace. Many of the men in this book have never spoken about the war until now when the safety of six decades makes their memories easier to bear. "What you find among these veterans is that they really don't want to talk to others about it. They don't believe you can comprehend it. It was so violent at the time and it numbed their minds in a lot of cases," Lt. General Lawrence F. Snowden explained.

Nearly 20,000 Marines were buried at sea and in cemeteries throughout those hard-fought Pacific Islands. On Iwo Jima, near the base of Mt. Suribachi, Rabbi Roland Gittelsohn delivered a timeless, almost prophetic eulogy at the dedication of the 5th Marine Division cemetery on March 21, 1945. It is reprinted in its entirety in the chapter entitled "Remembrance."

These veterans tell their stories in their own way using their own words. For many, remembering the names of their friends and events came easier than remembering exact dates and specific locations. I've footnoted when possible, but long forgotten details will not change the power of their stories. To learn more about the war in the Pacific, a bibliography at the end of this book offers a few suggestions.

These men are proud of their Marine Corps service and continue to think of themselves as Marines. They do not call themselves heroes; they are too humble to seek glory or fame. They offer their stories as a part of our historical record with the hope that battles like Saipan, Bougainville, and Iwo Jima will never happen again.

3

ATTEN-HUT!

by Sgt. Major Mike "Iron Mike" Mervosh USMC (Ret.)

Our Greatest Generation is thinning out and fading away at a rapid rate. This great generation, hell, all they ever did was save the country and the world by knowing how to fight and win battles then proceed to rebuild the nation in those post war years. Of all the battles that have been fought and won during World War II that added to those illustrious chapters of our Marine Corps history and heritage of our country, I would like to take one example of many, never before or since equaled.

Iwo Jima is recorded as the most demanding, toughest, fiercest, and bloodiest battle in the history of the Marine Corps. What's least known by the American public is that it was also a perfect battle on a perfect battlefield, a defender's dream. The battlefield resembled the moon with its lunar landscape, bombed-out craters and washboard terrain. Not one single structure remained above ground. There wasn't any collateral damage assessed on civilian areas, not an innocent female or child or civilian killed because there weren't any civilian areas. It was strictly fighting man against fighting man; kill or be killed. It's the only battle of its kind in the history of the Marine Corps, our country, and possibly the world.

There were so many unselfish and unrelenting acts of bravery, courage and heroism that occurred routinely on a daily basis as a true and keen sense of duty that it was taken for granted, unrecognized and most of it unaccounted for. The battle for Iwo Jima brought forth this inspirational message from Admiral Nimitz that will live on forever:

"Among the men who fought on Iwo Jima, uncommon valor was a common virtue."

Admiral Nimitz could have very well meant that message towards the enemy as they also performed in a brave and courageous manner. We Marines experienced this many times in their fanatical and suicidal ways as each and every one of the enemy on Iwo Jima was ordered by his Commander to kill 10 Marines before he made his defensive position his gravesite. Iwo Jima had to be the toughest and most demanding assignment of my lifetime and I'm one of the few infantrymen who didn't miss a day of that battle, even though a good many of us were the walking wounded at its end.

4

By Dammit, We're Marines!

On D plus 4, our Marines finally seized and secured our primary objective and raised the American flag on Mt. Suribachi. The flag-raising on Mt. Suribachi was not the culmination of the battle as it was just getting started with many more deadly objectives to follow. Casualties occurred on both sides for an additional 32 days in the likes of Hill 362, Hill 382, the Amphitheater, Turkey Knob, the Meatgrinder, the Quarry, the Boat Basin, Bloody Knoll, Cushman's Pocket (that's where your dad was, Gail), Kitana Point, and Airfields Number 1 and 2, just to name a few.

There was no place for us to hide or to take cover. The enemy was well prepared to fight in well-entrenched, concealed, underground fortifications. The enemy did not fight on Iwo Jima, they fought 'in it' which made them the unseen enemy. Over 800 pillboxes, blockhouses, and gun emplacements were connected by miles of tunnels and caves several tiers below the surface; every square yard of that island was covered with intense interlocking fire supplemented with enemy mortars, artillery, and rocket fire. Both anti-tank and anti-aircraft fire were used on us ground Marines. Of course, at that particular time there was no high tech weaponry or we could have possibly secured the island as predicted in 4 or 5 days. We were without those guided laser missles, unmanned flying drones, bunker busters, good old smart bombs, robots to search out the enemy and explosives, night vision goggles, or even flak jackets. All we had was a Marine utility jacket while being armed with our deadly rifle and bayonet, hand grenades, demolition charges, flamethrowers and greatest of all, sheer determination and guts.

Did we run? Hell yes, though impossible at times in that ankle deep volcanic ash, but we did it the good old Marine way by being ever so aggressive. We forged ahead to attack and assault, time and time again, until we won ultimate victory.

That victory brought forth another inspiring message from then Secretary of the Navy, James Forrestal. "The raising of that flag on Suribachi means a Marine Corps for the next 500 years."

Thank God, our Marine Corps has survived 63 of those 500 years. Therefore today's Marines cannot afford to be complacent or rest and live on past sentiments, glories, laurels, and accomplishments. What they must do, and what I tell them to do, is to face that challenge and strive to be a hell of a lot different and a hell of a lot better than any military organization in the world. They must be committed to continue and to maintain our 232-year legacy as the finest, the proudest and the fightingest Marine Corps possible.

* * *

5

Gail Chatfield

Christmas at the Front

By Pvt. William Swanson
2nd Platoon, C Company, 9th Marines, 3rd Division

The Battle for Bougainville, a long and bitter jungle campaign, is finally winding down, or so the rumors are saying. The latest hot scoop being the Army will relieve us in a few days. Beautiful news to put it mildly, and having just been on patrol, we figure we have it made and with a little luck, we should be able to ride it out.

Then, just as we had the thing all planned out, in our dreams of course, orders come down for my platoon to get our gear on and prepare to move out. Our protestations that we had just been on patrol bring the usual response, the sergeant's retort being something like, "Tell it to the Chaplain" only not in those exact words. This little outing is to be no run of the mill patrol but a serious effort to locate a rumored large enemy force building up for a counter attack against our lines.

Taking a moment to put this little tale into some sort of perspective, the jungle and its many miseries has taken considerable toll on us footsloggers. We are tired, beat down is more like it, and weary of the elements, the jungle itself, the mosquitoes and flies, the insects of all kinds, the cotton mouth of thirst, the never knowing what will happen next and whether you will be around to see it. More or less constant fear, over time, simply grinds one down.

Our dungarees are tattered and torn by almost two months of rain, swamp and hard use and, if all that not be enough, we are sick with one thing or another most of the time and not helped at all by an almost constant state of exhaustion. We haven't been eating too well either. A real meal is just a distant memory. Still and all, we hold onto the old Gyrene feeling of camaraderie along with the spirit, though sorely tested, of doing what has to be done and a little, in truth a hell of a lot, of griping and cursing notwithstanding.

Another unit had originally been chosen for this trek but shortly after leaving the front lines, they set off a land mine—one of those damned "Bouncing Bettys" which seriously wounded several men. We somehow manage again to draw the short straw and were selected to take their place. The odds, those damn odds—how quick they change. We, of course, put any concerns we might have aside and do as ordered. Our gear consisted of full cartridge belts and canteens, first aid kits, rifles or B.A.R. as the case may be, a couple of grenades and, for most of us, a sheath knife of some sort. There would also be a few machetes scattered about the group.

Then, as we get ready to move out, my platoon, down to only seventeen or eighteen at this point, is joined by a small group from Regimental Headquarters—reconnaissance experts we are told. This brings the patrol up to perhaps the short side of twenty-five instead of our usual four or five, and only reinforcing that earlier assessment of a change in the odds.

Taking leave of the front lines, we move carefully down the steep trail, watching closely for trip wires or anything else that looks out of place. Our first chore is to set an ambush, hoping that some Japanese patrol would accommodate us by walking into our little trap. A couple of hours are spent in this endeavor but there is no such accommodation and we proceed with our primary mission. Valuable time has been used up, however. Time that will be missed as the day wears on.

Moving in a single file, we make our way through dense jungle and swamp, ford a river or two and by early afternoon are out beyond our normal patrol zone. The farther we go, the spookier it gets and we strain our senses, trying to look everywhere at once while at the same time listening for the slightest out of place sound. The point man always has the worst of it as he must keep our compass course while going over and around the many obstacles and, of course, living with the ever present thought that, when something happens, it will no doubt happen to him first. This being such a delightful job, we all (us Privates, that is) get a turn at it. The more the afternoon wears on, the more we get the uneasy feeling of walking into some dark, alien world, unsure of what to expect, yet expecting the worst.

Now, our quite regular late afternoon rain begins and it is a veritable downpour, adding more misery to an already miserable day. In addition, we should be thinking about heading back, instead, we begin to see trails and other signs of enemy activity and so are ordered to continue. We do this with extreme caution, hoping to see without being seen. However, as we pass more and more of these trails, the inescapable conclusion is that there are a lot of Japs around here and the report of a large buildup is apparently all too true. Along with this comes a growing awareness that we are completely on our own and no cavalry will come should we run into trouble.

Although sure that our enemy is close by, we have seen none yet; then, *Son of a bitch, there's one over there.* Sure enough, in a small clearing to our left, a lone sentry is sitting down, trying to heat his dinner in the pouring rain. The poor bastard looks almost as miserable as we feel.

There is a small discussion about killing him now but it is finally decided to leave the S.O.B. to his dinner, at least for the time being.

Leaving the Jap to his troubles, we push on slowly and carefully until the patrol leader decides some of us should scout a few of the trails. I get "lucky," of course, and am ordered to check a faint path angling off to the right. After a few steps, I lose sight of the others and am immediately gripped by deep fear. A small, steady fear has been with us all afternoon but this is different. I find that being alone in the jungle, in the midst of the enemy, is a special kind of terror. Without a doubt, misery does love company.

Now, rather thankful for the rain, I move as quietly as possible and worry over each step. The foliage is extremely dense along the path, providing much cover for those who would do me in and, even though wishing to hell I was somewhere else, I manage to check the thing out as ordered. I see no Japs on this little stroll but am nevertheless struck with the uncomfortable feeling they are nearby. Turning back, I have an almost overpowering urge to take off running and it takes all my will power just to keep a somewhat normal pace...the miserable expectation of a knife in the back doffing each step. The patrol is a welcome sight and I allow my back muscles to relax just a bit.

With the many signs of recent activity, we wonder about not seeing more of the enemy and finally decide the downpour must be keeping them in their foxholes. Perhaps the rain is a blessing even though we are soaked to the skin. We continue to move cautiously, most of us hoping we can see what we came to see and then get the hell out. It wasn't to be.

All of a sudden comes *bang-bang, rat-o-tat-tat* from up ahead.

Dirty son of a bitch, we're in for it now!

We immediately hit the deck or try to as firing erupts all over the damn place. As I go down, my foot gets stuck between a couple of big roots and I wind up laying over another one with my rear end sticking high in the air. Then, before I can free myself, an arm rises out of some nearby bushes and a grenade comes sailing my way.

Holy Christ, I'm gonna get it for sure. Help me God!

The grenade lands about ten feet away while I quickly try to cram as much of me as possible into my helmet and wonder how bad it will be. Fully expecting the worst, the damn thing explodes and, to my great surprise, nothing...not even a scratch.

Thanks, God. Hardly able to believe my good luck, I waste no time getting untangled and then take cover in those same roots. It takes no prompting for us to realize how serious our situation is, although we take some comfort in the fact that the Japanese are probably even more confused than we are.

As expected by some at least, we have apparently stumbled into a fair sized enemy force. From the look of it, they are at least battalion strength, no doubt preparing to hit our lines, and they are damn sure not going to let us get back if they can help it. And now, added to the fact that we are outnumbered to beat hell, it is getting late and we are a long way from "home." Meaning, it will be dark soon and our merely difficult situation will be a desperate one.

It isn't really hard to figure out that the longer we stay in this exposed position, the more chance the Japs have of getting organized and wiping us out. However, there have been no orders to fall back or to do anything else for that matter. The reality of this jungle war being what it is, we are quite often left to battle it out on our own and, in our present situation, we really have no choice but to hold to the bitter end no matter what that may be.

Meanwhile, grenades pop along with automatic weapon and rifle fire as both sides try to find targets, thick brush and heavy rain allowing few clear shots. This lack of visibility, though somewhat to our advantage, is nevertheless frustrating. As a matter of fact, I feel damn lonely when I look around and see only the two men on either side of me and it is not much help that they are some five yards away, barely visible in all this greenery. It is even more discouraging when we realize what a downright mean and dangerous situation we are in and, for the first time, I begin to feel that this might be the end of it—that I might well be killed here in this stinking, God-forsaken piece of jungle. Surrender, by the way, is really not an option for us. To begin with, the Corps does not look kindly on giving up for any reason. Added to that is the terrible reputation the Japs have when it comes to prisoner treatment; rumors of bayonet practice during the Guadalcanal Campaign still fresh in our minds. It may be understood then, that some of us have vague thoughts of saving a last cartridge.

The rather uneven battle in the jungle and in the rain continues for, I'm damned if I know how long, and we begin to wonder what in the hell the plan is. Do we stay and fight it out for whatever time we can? (Not a very good option we think.) Or do we try to let go this tiger's tail and get the hell out? (A better idea we think.)

Darkness soon is no help and then, just as we thought the damned thing couldn't get any worse, it does. The patrol leader, no doubt figuring he had seen all he needed to see, apparently ordered a withdrawal—but, in the confusion of rain and jungle battle, some seven or eight of us did not get the word and were left behind. A revolting development of the very first order---bad, bad news. Fear tugs hard as the grim reality begins to sink in.

It was important, of course, that someone get back and report this heavy enemy buildup, the whole idea of this little excursion, so we can hardly fault the patrol leader for not coming back for us. However, by now our desperate plight is a first priority—other considerations, of necessity, taking a back seat. And, to be perfectly honest, if the patrol had attempted a rescue, the probability is that we would all have been killed in the attempt.

We worry and wonder about our fate as we try to put up a good fight and then, at it's blackest, a bit of good news. Someone has taken charge, thank God, and the orders are to slowly break off and try to get together a few yards to our rear. Halting our firing one at a time, we crawl back hopefully away from Japanese positions. The downpour continues, a life saving deluge perhaps, and we slip away.

Getting together some twenty yards back and feeling lucky as hell to have gotten this far, we decide to make a run for it and hope for the best. Time, though, is a very real problem and there is none to spare. We move out in a single file, taking a compass heading that should get us back but thick jungle prevents us from seeing anything in the way of landmarks. Running at a trot whenever possible, we pass through a number of enemy positions, fully expecting to be cut down at any second. The whole thing is unreal as hell and we just cannot believe that our luck can continue. Rain, keep coming — the harder the better.

Then, right in front of us, a God-damn swamp. *Dirty, no good son of a bitch!* No time to look for a way around so we just plow into the stinking slime. We have spent our share of time in these rotten places, usually griping and cursing as we struggle through the murky waters, always relieved to feel somewhat dry ground. Today is different, however, and as we become more engulfed and hidden in the heavy brush, we dare think that maybe, just maybe, we might get out of this damn thing yet. Funny, but I never realized, until now, just how lovely a swamp could be. Our luck, or is it luck, seems incredible. Rain and now swamp, maybe He is helping us.

We eventually plow our way out of the foul smelling waters and look warily over our shoulders for any sign of our pursuers. Seeing none, and being pleasantly surprised I might add, we quickly get on our way. We are thankful to be out of the swamp but it is still rough country and we must climb trees occasionally to check our bearings. Then, it is here, the last river, and we feel relief in getting this far. However, the open water is worrisome and we feel much like sitting ducks as we wade across—still expecting the Japs to open up at any time.

By Dammit, We're Marines!

The rain has slowed somewhat as we move into the last stretch of jungle but our precious daylight is fading fast. That brings us to other problems and we are reminded of the rule that considers any movement after dark to be the enemy. It would be another revolting development if our own troops should fire on us but, hopefully, they are aware that we are still out. Then, as we get close to the lines, land mines and booby traps become yet another threat. What a stinking shame if, after all this, we manage to set one of those damned things off.

It turns dark as we reach the bottom of the hill but the frontlines are now only a couple hundred feet above us. *Just a little more God, just a little more.* We call out the password and our unit number as we take one last uneasy look over our shoulders. There is a momentary silence and then the words we have been waiting for: "Come on home, all is forgiven." The short wait while a guide is sent down to get us through the mines is hard, but then it is up the hill and into the front lines. What a feeling. We are home, back in our muddy foxholes and it is Christmas Eve. *Thanks, God.*

We learned the main part of the patrol got back earlier and alerted the front lines to watch for us before passing the word on Japanese positions back to artillery. The big guns held their fire, allowing us time to get in the clear. Now, however, the Long Toms open up with a hellish barrage. Lying in our foxholes, we listen to the outgoing shells with a certain satisfaction yet, at the same time feeling just a bit sorry for the poor bastards out there....they are catching all kinds of hell. This time it is them. Next time it will no doubt be us.

* * *

Officers

Lt. General Lawrence F. Snowden, USMC (Ret.)
Captain, Commanding Officer, F Company,
2nd Battalion, 23rd Marines, 4th Division

Lawrence Snowden, wartime photo.

In high school I had a family dentist who served in the Marines in Nicaragua in what we called the old Corps. He used to tell me about his experiences and he'd always say when he finished, "You wouldn't be able to handle that." He gave me a challenge that I later used as a recruiter. The Marine Corps still uses the challenge today.

"What makes you think you are good enough to be a Marine?"

It doesn't say you are going to be an Army of One; it says, the Few, the Proud, the Marines, and that kind of pride is just drilled into them hour after hour when they get to recruit training at Parris Island or San Diego. The fundamental core product of a Marine recruit is pride at what he accomplished in the way of self discipline, confidence in his team mates because battlefield takes teamwork, and genuine pride in having survived what he survived. After the Crucible, which is the last few days of recruit training, the drill sergeant shakes each one's hand and presses that Marine Corps emblem into it and says, "Now you can be called a Marine."

By Dammit, We're Marines!

During World War II, many were draftees, but they served equally well with the volunteers because in those days everybody wanted to get into the war. An unprecedented 16 million men and women served in the military during World War II. There were a few protestors, there always are, but they amounted to nothing. World War II is a classic example of what you can do if the nation is with you and behind you.

World War II did a lot of things to change this country. First of all it brought women into the labor force in numbers like never before seen in our history. Rosie the Riveter proved that women could make a significant contribution in the labor force. It's the first time in our history the labor force became mobile. Farmers from Connecticut went to Detroit to help build tanks. From all over, men and women went to ship yards to build those liberty ships and build all those landing craft, too. When the veterans came home, the G.I. Bill provided an opportunity to go to school and buy a house. To look back at it, the social change brought on by World War II had a lot more impact in this country than the fact of our winning did overseas. We won it, clearly, no question about it, and as the most generous people in the world, we helped rebuild the countries that we helped tear down through the process of war.

The Marines were right for the Pacific war going from island to island up the Central Pacific to Japan. The 4th Marine Division was the first division in the U.S. to sail directly from port of embarkation in San Diego straight to Roi-Namur in the Marshall Islands for our first combat experience. In terms of the operations that followed on Tinian, Saipan, and Iwo Jima, Roi-Namur was a simple operation because the atoll itself was pretty small. It did not have a very heavily defended force so we got our own way quickly. We had enough casualties to instill in all of us that this was serious business. No matter what kind of operation it is, when you see some of your friends die it takes on new significance on what it means to be there and to fight for your life. We went back to Maui where we had our base camp and we prepared to go to Saipan. After Saipan we simply went overnight on LSTs and landed on Tinian the next morning.

There is more to that overnight story to me than to most people. When I finished officer school, I stood number 18 in a class of about 300. At that time, the Marine Corps policy was to offer commissions into the regular Marine Corps to the top ten so I figured I didn't get that chance. We are in the middle of the fighting on Saipan and a runner from battalion came up and said, "Headquarters Marine Corps wants to know if you are still interested in a regular commission."

My friends, most of whom were reserves like me, asked, "You've got to be kidding. You're not going to answer that question are you?"

"Yes I am. Tell them 'yes'," I said.

When we went aboard the LST that night, I was sworn into the regular Marine Corps and I didn't look back for another 37 plus years. I retired on 31 May 1979 as a lieutenant general. I also served as Chief of Staff for the Marine Corps.

I was a lieutenant on Saipan and by the time we got back from Tinian, I was promoted to captain. As we redistributed officers in the battalion and the regiment, the whole 4th Division started to build up for the next battle. Reassigned, I took command of Fox Company, 2nd Battalion 23rd Marines, the unit I commanded when we landed on Iwo. Tom Brokaw coined the expression "The Greatest Generation" and I've said that since then because I had a first hand look at these young men and I can guarantee you that they earned that title.

On Iwo Jima in particular, many of those young men are alive today because they were more skilled with the K-bar knife than the Japanese adversary. It was a tough war, eyeball to eyeball in so many places. In hindsight, several writers said the problem was that the Japanese were "in" Iwo and we were "on" Iwo. They were right. They had 17 miles of tunnels on that island of only 8 square miles. If there was one major intelligence error, in hindsight, it's the intelligence people didn't appreciate what that soft volcanic ash would be for the troops and for vehicles. To go up a slope, we'd take a step up and slip back, but we kept trying. My own tractor was supposed to go about 700 yards inland and we got 50 yards and couldn't tract it any more so we jumped out. In those days, LVTs didn't have any cover on top, it was open, so we bailed out over the sides. I did what everyone did, locate the first bomb crater I could find and jump in it. I jumped and nearly landed on one of my sergeants, Len Ash, with his leg almost off. Len's leg looked so bad that I thought surely he would not be able to keep it.

"Captain, you've got to help me," he said.

"Len, I'll give you a shot of morphine, but I've got to move." I had it drilled in me that as an officer commanding troops, and I had 200 troops, I cannot devote my time to an individual Marine.

I turned back and yelled, "Corpsman."

"On the way," a corpsman answered.

"Len, help is coming. I'll see you," I said.

I didn't see Len again for 25 years until I went to make a speech in Daytona Beach and there was Len Ash walking on two legs. He had 20 operations on his legs so he could walk and play a slow game of golf.

By Dammit, We're Marines!

On D-Day plus six or seven, I caught some fragments from a 362 mm mortar weapon. The 362 mm is as big as a five gallon garbage can so when you hear it leave the launcher, it made a big squealing noise that pierced your ears. We'd look up and see it coming and we'd hold a finger up over it to cover it. If the mortar was either side of your finger, you didn't worry about it because it was going to go someplace else. But if it stayed behind your finger for more than a couple of seconds, you knew you had to move. Well the one you didn't see is usually the one that will get you. I had shell fragments in the back of my neck and on my hands and I looked like a bloody mess but I really wasn't badly wounded. Between the shock and blowing out my ears and the shell fragments, I was evacuated to the beach and put aboard a hospital ship and went overnight to Guam to Field Hospital 115. With the clean up they did on the ship and at the hospital, I said to the first doctor who came to see me that I'm really not that hurt and I want to go back and join my company.

"I think the Marine Corps policy is not to send anybody back.," he said.

"Is there a Marine Command here?" I asked.

I went to the forward headquarters and luck was with me, one of my former classmates in officers' school was the adjutant and I told him what I wanted to see the colonel about. While I talked to the colonel, in came another captain, John Alden, from the artillery unit who had the same situation. He looked bad but was OK. I knew the colonel's son in the 14th regiment, so we talked about him.

I finally got around to saying, "Colonel, I would like to go back to Iwo Jima, and let me assure you I'm not a hero but that is my family up there."

I hadn't seen my wife or infant son for about two years by that time, but my family now was on Iwo. I told him that I didn't want to become some faceless number in some replacement center over there on Oahu.

"Well," he said, "that's not our policy."

I told the colonel that I was also asking for an exception to policy for John Alden who would like to go, too.

"I'll tell you what, tomorrow morning we are sending our first flight of blood plasma and mail to Iwo," the colonel said. "You go down to the airstrip and find the pilot and if he agrees that you can get on, I'll let you go."

We saw the pilot and he told us that it was going to be pretty cold and there were no seats. It's all blood plasma and mail, but we could lie down on top of the mail sacks. And that's what we did. We got back and

I rejoined my company immediately. Twenty four hours later, a round hit and blew my ears out again, but this time I only went back to the regimental aid station overnight. In that overnight time there was a very serious counter charge by the Japanese. My company fought them off, and I wasn't even there to help them. The next day I went back up, joined them and stayed there until the operation was over. It was a unique experience but I missed some of it by God's divine hand, I suppose. I have no other way to account for it.

Iwo Jima wasn't just a small island, it was a piece of the mainland under the administration of the Tokyo Prefecture. It was a psychological blow to the Japanese for us to take it away from them. More importantly from an aircraft standpoint, they had two workable airfields and a third one they had under construction. There were 2200 B-29s that made emergency landings on Iwo that could not have returned to Tinian or Saipan or Guam because of the damage to the aircraft. That meant 24,000 air crewmen's lives were saved by the availability of Iwo Jima. Does that make it worth the cost? It depends on where you sit in the equation. If you lost your husband or your brother or family some way out there, that's a pretty high cost. But in the best interest of the United States in advancing the war and giving a clear signal to Japan that they could not win, we had them by the throat when we got Iwo. It was the right decision to make.

If we had to invade Japan with the plan I was familiar with, a lot of Army and all six Marine Divisions would have participated. I think we would have suffered a million casualties trying to dominate those islands that constitute the mainland of Japan. Weighing the casualties on both sides, it was the right decision to drop the bombs. I have been at Hiroshima on the 6th of August when they have a ceremony to remember the dropping of the bomb on that city. Some of the people who show up in the streets bear the scars of the burns. I regret that, but unfortunately, war being what it is, you just can't escape that. One of the trials and tribulations we face in fighting international terrorism is that they use civilians as shields and hide in the midst of them dressed like they are. They hide in the mosques and churches of every kind with no compunction. It means nothing to them that they are sacrificing women and children as we try to get them. That's a tough barrier for most Americans; we don't do business like that.

I considered myself a professional Marine from the moment I accepted that regular commission. I was dedicated to the job I was to do and it was not my business to be personal about things. Be professional; take it head on as you get to it to solve the problem. I didn't realize that I was serious about that until I went back to Japan during Korea. I got on a train and a man of my height was about four to five inches taller than the Japanese. I looked over the sea of black hair and I asked myself, what are you doing? Why are you in this place? The superb treatment I received from the Japanese whom I met there made me realize that they are just like we are. They are trying to do things for their families, trying to get ahead in life. I had nothing to do with going to war on Iwo Jima. I had nothing to do with Pearl Harbor. I am an innocent bystander and suddenly the government says this is what you've got to do.

Why was I so intensely against them? I know why. I was caught up in the propaganda in the U.S. before going to war against Japan. Pictures were published of an American flyer on his knees, hands tied behind his back, and a guy with a samurai sword ready to cut his head off. That influenced me to say, "I gotta get those *%&#*, and I'm going to go fight them as soon as I can."

That's why I went down to enlist the day after Pearl Harbor. But I realized later that they were different. I say this on Iwo and I say it every year and I will say it next March at the Reunion of Honor: those of us here in 1945 had nothing to do with why we were here. We were here because our national leaders and our military leaders said go and do it. So we came and we did it. One side won, the other side lost. And here we are now to celebrate the men who gave their lives in the battle of Iwo Jima.

The Japanese keep a team of five or six people there constantly searching for caves and tunnels they don't think they have found yet. When they find remains, a bone or two, they have a ceremony there and then fly the remains with great dignity to Tokyo for another ceremony and burial with Buddhist rites. Reunions of Honor held in March are a great experience for the Japanese who can't get to the island any other way. It's a military base as far as the government is concerned and they don't allow ordinary people on military bases. The Japanese are very eager to get there and worship their ancestors at the places where they were lost. The Iwo Jima Association of Japan works with me and others to prepare these Reunions of Honor. It's a very touching service for the U.S. survivors and for the Japanese. There are only a few survivors who come down there because there are not very many left. When they make it there for the first time and step off that airplane onto the black sands of the island again, it's a tremendous emotional experience. In my own case, and I have been there a number of times, when I get off that airplane and get on that island, I can almost hear those rounds going off, seeing the bodies, and asking, "Why God, why them? Why not me?" I'm sure you know that many a Christian was born in foxholes and battlefields.

I tell these Marines today they missed some valuable experiences. For example, you can't take a helmet these days and do what we did. We cooked in ours, we bathed in them, everything in a helmet. Later on when half the battle was over and we finally got some food ashore, we got these big cans of Dubuque bacon. How did we cook it? On the back of a shovel. We would take some sand and get the back of the shovel fairly clean and light little fire sticks. On the back of that shovel, we fried good bacon. And did you ever make a stew in a helmet? No, you can't do that these days.

The food was adequate but not great so anything that made it feel different, we did it. We dumped out common rations in a helmet and got it all boiling over for a little time and then scooped out a hot canteen cup full and away we went.

When I was in training as a 2nd lieutenant, my drill instructor kept saying, "Where you guys are going to go, water is going to be a precious commodity so you ought to learn to do without it." So I did. I carried two full canteens on my belt every day and I never touched a drop of it. The net result was I left the Marine Corps thinking I didn't want to drink water. It was only until recently that doctors persuaded me to drink more fluids, so I forced myself to drink more. Then I began to have heart problems and the doctor said, "You're drinking too much water. Don't drink so much, just drink it more often." That's what I do now.

I couldn't have had a more supporting wife and I want to give her full credit. We would have been married 64 years before she passed. Our first son was born in Oceanside on Nov. 10. After the birth, I said, "Good work, honey," and with that I left her because I had to go and participate in the Marine Corps Birthday parade at Camp Pendleton. That son retired as a Marine Corps colonel after 28 years of service. Our second son is a teacher of Old Castilian Spanish at a linguistic institute and teaches English to Japanese and Koreans. I have 12 grandchildren and 16 great-grandchildren.

* * *

Colonel James Shelton Scales USMCR (Ret.)

Major, Battalion Commander, A Company, 1st Battalion,
23rd Marines, 4th Marine Division

Col. Scales shares the battle of Iwo Jima
with elementary students.

I was born 28 April, 1917, in Stokes County, North Carolina, in a little farming community called Sandy Ridge. I graduated the University of North Carolina at Chapel Hill in June of 1940. Our government had set a date in October for all men 18-35 to register in preparation for a peacetime draft. It was the first time we had ever drafted men in peacetime. Europe had been at war over a year and I guess we were getting ready just in case. I heard about the Marine officer training at Quantico for college graduates so I went down to Raleigh and enlisted in the officer candidate class. They cut my orders and I reported to duty the first day of November 1940.

I went through the 13 weeks of basic officer candidate training and was commissioned a 2nd lieutenant in February 1941. We then enrolled in a reserve officers course for three months where they told us how to be platoon leaders with all the intended subjects of map reading, command presence, and so forth. We were then supposed to go to a regular Marine unit and serve another six months. This is all in peacetime. I finished this course in May of 1941 and I was assigned along with three of my classmates back to the candidates class as instructors. I had the rare experience of going back to the same company I had been in three months before as a private first class and now I am a shaved-tail lieutenant. The NCOs who gave us such a hard time are now saying, "Aye Aye, Sir!" I enjoyed that immensely. I stayed there and was promoted to 1st lieutenant in April of 1942 and then by golly on August 7, 1942, three things happened that I will always remember. I was notified that I was promoted to captain, I was given command of an officer candidates company, and I learned the 1st Marine Division landed on Guadalcanal.

I stayed at Quantico until July of 1943 and then a number of us in the Marine Corps schools were ordered to Camp Pendleton, California, to join the then forming 4th Marine Division. A buddy and I drove across country. It was a long trip and everything was rationed. I figured the tires on that '37 Plymouth coupe my buddy owned were as smooth as a baby's butt. They gave us these OPA, Office of Price Administration, tickets that were good for one filling of the gas tank. My buddy got 20 and the old Sergeant Major at Quantico gave me 20 although I didn't have a car. I said to my buddy, Bob Davidson, that since we're using his car, we'll use my tickets to get the gas. "Oh no," he says, "I'd be using them even if you didn't go." He only used 8 of the 20 to get to California. Now I'm stuck with these 20 OPA tickets. After about a month I realized since they checked them out to me, they are going to wonder what happened to them. I found out where the ration office was there at Pendleton and went down and an old salty Marine gunny was on duty. I walked in and showed him these tickets and said these were issued to me in Quantico but I rode with a buddy, I didn't need them, and I don't have a car so what should I do with them? He looked right and left and looked at me and said, "Put them in your *@#% pocket and get the hell out of here!"

I bought a car soon after that. My wife came out in September of 1943. When I went overseas in January, she stayed on with a friend for about a year. Our daughter, Judy, was six months old when I left. My wife took the car back to the dealer in Los Angeles who was the father of one of my Marine buddies. He gave her exactly what I paid for it a year before, so we had the use of a car for one year at no cost plus those 20 gas tickets. I would wean that car down to the last drop so I could get a full tank. I ran out of gas a couple of times and my wife was ready to wring my neck. I'd have to get out and hitchhike to get gas and come back to get her and Judy and then off we'd go.

By Dammit, We're Marines!

When I first joined the 23d Regiment in Pendleton in late July 1943, I was a captain and assigned to A Company of the 1st Battalion. Most of my men were 17 or 18 years old. Some had conned their mother or father to sign the papers and came in at 15, 16 years of age. You'd run across an old sergeant who had been in 10-15 years and they were the backbone of the unit. They knew the ropes and taught the new men what to do.

We trained at Pendleton and left for overseas on January 13 heading for the Marshall Islands. We made our first landing at the northern end of the Kwajelein atoll, at Roi-Namur, which were two small islands. Our regiment was assigned to take Roi Island, that's a French word meaning king. We took it the first day, happily. Roi was the first landing after Tarawa which was a terrible battle and almost didn't come off. We were very nervous that we were going to get into a battle similar to or even worse than Tarawa, but it turned out that we had it easy. I had in my company two men killed and seven or eight wounded. It was bad of course for the seriously wounded and certainly for those killed but it was a cakewalk compared to what we encountered later on. Roi was mainly a Japanese airfield. By the time we landed, the hangars and service buildings were all busted up by bombing and naval gun fire. Most of the Japs on Roi scooted over that causeway to Namur where there were trees and underbrush and where they had a much better defensive position. A lot of the Japanese committed suicide when they saw they were going to be overrun and maybe captured. The Japs were indoctrinated since birth, I guess, never to be captured under any circumstances and they would frequently kill themselves when capture was imminent.

Morale was good after that success. We then came back to Maui in Hawaii for our base camp which was about 1500 feet up that extinct volcano, Haleakala. We trained there until the end of May at which time we loaded up again and headed to Saipan. We landed there the 15th of June and it took about a month to take Saipan, an island 12 miles long by about 5 to 8 miles wide. That's where Army Major General Ralph Smith was relieved of his command by General Holland Smith, a Marine. That thing still rankles to this day, I think.*

The 2d and 4th Marine Divisions landed on Saipan on D-Day and the 27th Army Division was held in reserve to land on order when they were needed. We needed them pretty quick and they came in and went into the middle of the island with the 4th on the right and the 2nd on the left heading north going up the island. The Army just simply couldn't do their job. They lagged behind and General Holland 'Howlin' Mad Smith finally just relieved the Army general and put some other general in there. That stirred up a hornet's nest. The very idea of a Marine of all people relieving a major general of the army. We heard about this and were surprised. We heard of lieutenants and captains sometimes getting the boot, but not a general.

After we took Saipan, they gave us a week to get ready to land and retake Tinian three miles south of Saipan, which we did. I happened to land on my wife's birthday. We would have celebrated 65 years of married life but my wife passed away the 6th of November 2006.

We went back to our camp in Maui and trained until New Years Eve. I was given command of the 3rd Battalion and landed on D-Day on Iwo Jima and was there the entire battle. When we landed the beaches got crowded. General Kuribayashi, the Japanese commander, gave the order to commence firing the artillery and mortars and they just walked it up and down the crowded beach, getting five, six, or seven Marines every time a shell landed. When you'd advance you'd get shot at and you'd wonder where the bullet or shell came from. That's what I landed into, and I had to go up and down that crowded beach raked with enemy fire for about an hour trying to get my men up and move them inland, get them spread out. Why I wasn't hit during that foray there, I'll never know. It wasn't my time. I lost a lot of men that first day.

I didn't see the flag going up. I was busy trying to do my job along the front lines. My runner, the Marine assigned to me as CO, stayed with me the whole time. He was my gofer, valet, foxhole digger, chow-getter, whatever needed to be done, he would be right there. We were about two miles north by that time when he looked back towards Suribachi. "What's that up on Suribachi?" he asked. When I looked, I saw a flag but at that distance we couldn't be sure whether it was a Jap flag or an American or what. I got my binoculars out of the case and when I focused in and saw the colors rippling in the breeze, I told them it was the second most beautiful sight I had ever seen in my life. The most beautiful sight was my bride on my wedding day. It didn't get any prettier than that.

My battalion was the first one to tackle Hill 382, the second highest level on the island. We had men on top of 382, and I thought we had it made but the Japanese drove us off with heavy casualties. We got chewed up pretty badly. We were pulled back and another battalion tried it, and then another one. It took about four or five tries before we took 382. I saw maybe four or five live Japs above ground during the 36 days I was there. Pilots flying over the island said they could see the Marines all the way across the island but it was rare that they ever saw a Japanese above ground.

By Dammit, We're Marines!

Our success was due to the excellent training the Marines give their officers and men. You just have to concentrate on doing your job and black out the bad parts and just keep going. That's what kept us all from going crazy I think. Occasionally, something funny would happen, crazy, improbable, something to get everybody relaxed and laughing and that helped a great deal.

I'll give an example. When you are on the rifle range shooting at the targets 200, 500 yards down the range and you miss the whole six foot square target, they examine it and wave a red flag that means you missed the whole target. You know what we call that red flag? Maggie's drawers.

Well, one time on Iwo there was a big ridge off to my right front. All at once machine gun fire started hitting right inside my command post kicking up sand. Everybody dove into the foxhole and crouched down hoping it didn't come in and get them in there. There was this Jap gunner way up firing at the men on that ridge, and some of it was clearing the top of that ridge and impacting in my area. I looked back and a Marine had a red bandana handkerchief waving on the end of his rifle giving the Jap gunner Maggie's drawers! It got everybody laughing although one or two of my men were hit, not too badly wounded, but enough to get them a Purple Heart, certainly.

You wondered whether you were going to see the sunset that day or the sunrise after a bad night or wonder if the shadows you see out there were Japs crawling in trying to infiltrate our lines. They did that. They were good at that. The ships offshore fired the star shells that explode over the island and that big, luminous light would light up the countryside almost like daylight as it came down on the parachute. It would hit the ground and go out then we'd call for some more. Every outfit didn't want to endure that darkness too long because that would give the Japs some time to get right in the lines with us.

Time and again the Japs infiltrated our lines. There was a lot of hand-to-hand fighting. One unit was moving up and getting situated when a Jap officer came bolting out of a camouflage cave entrance nearby with a sword. He ran at one of my sergeants who threw his left hand up to ward off the blow and it almost cut his hand off. He was grappling with the Jap and one of his buddies right there with him tried to get a shot at the Jap, fired and hit the sergeant in the shoulder. Finally they did kill the Jap and got this sergeant evacuated, but I understand he lost his hand.

There is only one word to describe Iwo Jima that I have ever found in the English language and that's "carnage." Carnage on both sides. There were 6,821 killed on our side. There were 19,000 wounded and something like 2,000 were combat fatigued who were just losing it, screaming, crying. You had to get them off of the front line and get them back where they could relax and get a hold of themselves. They'd come back and go on out again. We had several men sneak off to the hospital ship offshore and come back to join the outfit. I'm convinced that every man has his breaking point sooner or later. You can't keep day after day after day seeing your buddies killed or wounded, seeing these horrible things knowing that it's coming to you sooner or later if you keep at it. Some of the men just fold under that pressure. Many of them were able to overcome it and return to the line. I don't think there was too much stigma because the men who they left realized that they may be teetering on the brink of it themselves. It wasn't unique to Iwo. It happened on Saipan. Some men are closer to breaking up than others; it's a matter of the individual. I think the good Marine training we had plus all these practice landings and such, we had it down to a pretty good degree and that helped. That helped me because I knew what my job was. I just lowered my head and tried my best to do it and rule out these things I can't control.

We overwhelmed the Japanese. We landed something like 70,000 men. Even with heavy casualties, my battalion got replacements three different times. New men coming in to take the place of those killed and wounded. Most of the replacements did not have experience, unfortunately, and it was tragic. Some of them got killed before we could get them assigned to their unit or company. It was tragic; it really was. That's why I say war is insanity. Absolute madness. The whole premise is I'm gonna kill you before you kill me.

When it was over, I wanted to wave that damn place good bye. The most poignant experience of my life, I guess, took place about two days before we left the island. The 3rd Division cemetery and 4th Division cemetery which were pretty much together were dedicated. Word came down that half of the command would be able to go to attend the dedication ceremony. About half of my officers and I went down and we walked along the rows of crosses seeing the good men and good friends we had trained with for about two years. At the ceremony, the general spoke and the chaplain pronounced the benediction and then the bugler played Taps. I don't think there was a dry eye in that whole crowd. It was a very heart-rending procedure.

It was the end of March when we left Iwo Jima and we hit the International Date Line on the 1st day of April which happened to be Easter Sunday. That of course was also D-Day on Okinawa. We continued to train on Maui and in July we were given the objective of retaking Wake Island. Major Devereux was commanding the Marine detachment on Wake Island when the Japs took the island. Major Devereux and the others were taken prisoner from late December 1941 until the war was over in 1945 and they were released. The Japs had the island that whole time and the 23rd and 24th Regiments were ordered to go land there the first day of October 1945 and retake it. At first I wondered, why the hell do we need that thing up in the northern Pacific way out in nowhere, but we were getting ready to invade the home islands of Japan and we needed that airfield for refueling stops on the way to Japan. The war ended in August and happily we didn't have to do that and even happier we didn't have to go into those home islands. It would have been the father of all battles.

When the war was over, I came home and had to bite my tongue time and again to keep from cussing. We would go for months and months, day after day, and it was just Marines and the four letter words got to be in the majority practically.

I went back to Iwo Jima in 1995 on a military tour. They put us up in a first class resort hotel in Saipan about 500 yards down the beach where we landed 50 years before. We went down to that beach. Then they flew us up to Iwo Jima where the pilot flew us all around the island and then came in and landed.

We walked down on those quiet, serene landing beaches thinking about what it was like coming in with the shelling, with the dead and wounded, and the terror. It was rather heart tugging. I got a bottle of that black coarse volcanic sand that gave us so much trouble down around Suribachi. I went in the tunnels into a Japanese hospital. I had to damn near crawl in those tunnels because they are only 5 foot high and I'm 6'3". I never imagined it was that intricate. They could shift whole groups underground.

I was a battalion commander on Iwo. I wasn't on the front line. I was up near it a lot, checking on my company commanders and seeing what they needed. The men on the front line endured so much day after day, losing their buddies, seeing shadows at night thinking there's a Jap crawling up to cut their throats. Many of them still today are affected by those horrors. That's why I think war should be outlawed.

The Marines seemed to be special. I have never regretted being involved with the Marine Corps, although I wouldn't want go through that Pacific harangue for all the money in Ft. Knox not knowing if I'd come through it like I did.

*The Army's 27th Division was a New York National Guard outfit that was transferred to Marine command for the Saipan invasion. For the big attack northward on Saipan, Marine General Holland Smith ordered the 27th to move up between the 2nd and 4th Marine Division. The 27th was an hour late getting started and had barely moved when the advance began. Gaps opened between the stalled 27th and the fast moving Marines. The attack came to a halt. The Marine general said that if the 27th's General Ralph Smith did not move his division forward the next day, then the Army general should be relieved. The division did not budge the next day so the Army general was relieved of duty. Twelve days later, there was a 300-yard gap between two of the 27th's battalions when the Japanese made their last banzai charge. The 27th was overrun partly because their own 3rd battalion did not shift over to help stop the charge. Marine Corps artillerymen and a reserve Army infantry regiment finally halted the attack at the cost of over 1,000 U.S. casualties. Howlin' Mad pulled the 27th out of the line and never let them do any more fighting on Saipan and the Marianas.

* * *

Lt. Col. Paul F. McLellan, USMC (Ret.)
Captain, G Company, 2nd Battalion, 9th Marines, 3rd Division

Navy Cross recipient, Lt. Col. Paul McLellan

I was in the Army ROTC at South Dakota State University. As a requirement of the state before the war, every able-bodied man was required to take two years of military training. When you got out of the program, you could go on if you wanted to for the next two years and get a commission. I stayed on and got through my third year. The war in Europe wasn't looking too good and besides, I didn't have any money. We went to camp in Minnesota for six weeks of field training. I was there for 5 weeks and 3 days, and they pulled me out and said I was all through. I didn't pass the physical. They said I had sinus problems and nasal polyps. I don't have sinus problems to this day, but nevertheless that's what they said. I went to the infirmary and had the nasal polyps removed and was sent home. I talked to the ROTC Colonel about it, and he suggested the V-12 program as a way of getting a Reserve Commission in the Navy. I would also be able to finish college. About six of us went to Sioux Falls for our physicals and we passed.

We went to Omaha, Nebraska, for more evaluations, and they said five of the six of us had bad hearts. I was one of them. Sinus, nasal polyps, and now a bad heart. It upset me so much since I played basketball, football, baseball all in high school and never had a problem. I said I'm going to enlist in the regular Navy, but they said, "No way; that old ticker may stop at any time." I ran into the ROTC Colonel at the Student Union back at college and he took me to the Marine recruiter for the officer candidate class. I passed that physical, but then they found out that I was too old. I was 25. When I graduated from high school, it was during the Depression so I stayed home for three years and helped my dad on the farm. A few weeks after I was told I was too old, the Marines changed the age limit and they swore me in. That's when my time in the Marine Corps started, April 4, 1942. I graduated from college in June and went to Quantico in July for training.

After officer training, we were shipped overseas. New Zealand, Guadalcanal, Bougainville, Guam, Iwo Jima. The men in my company were quite young. The first sergeant I had was an older guy, he had been a gunnery sergeant but the rest of them were just young men. I'd been executive officer of a company on Guam and I got to know a lot of the men there. On Guam we took about 70% casualties. Our battalion was on Fonte Ridge which was the Japanese last stand. For four or five days we were under heavy attack and were trying to advance. We were short on ammunition. It was touch and go sometimes. There were banzai attacks and you could hear the enemy getting ready to attack as they got liquored up. You knew it was coming. But you stand pat, set up your defenses and get ready to put out all the fire you can…mortars, artillery if they are far enough away. We suffered a lot of casualties, a lot of hand to hand combat, but we took the Ridge.

I was wounded on Guam and sent to the hospital. I had my front teeth broken off by shrapnel, and I couldn't speak plain so I was ordered back. The reason I couldn't talk was because I had shrapnel stuck up under the gum. They pulled out the shrapnel and I could talk, but the doctor thought I had a broken jaw and sent me back to the field hospital. I spent the night there, and I'm telling you I got out of there as fast as I could. Nobody went to bed without a rifle at their side. A few nights before, which I wasn't aware, the Japanese broke through someplace and went through the hospital killing people. The Japanese were trying to get to the beach and tear up our communications but they were stopped.

For the battle of Iwo Jima, the 3rd Division was held in reserve, with the 4th and 5th Division being the first to land. We heard about the high casualties. After four or five days, they called for two regiments of the 3rd Marine Division, the 9th and 21st, to go ashore. We went in on big boats but the tide was so high there that it was almost impossible to get down a net. We couldn't hold onto the nets and our boat would rise up about 12 to 15 feet then drop back down again. The beach was supposedly secure; it wasn't. Shells were falling on the beach. Our company went in and got in position. We were in there that night, and the next day we relieved another unit. The 21st Marines were on the left of us, and the 5th Marine Division was on the left side of them. The 4th Marine Division was on the right side. The 3rd Marine Division went up the middle. The artillery barrage that the Japanese had put down on us was accurate and heavy. They had been there for so many years and they had every place pinpointed. They could put artillery down on any place they wanted to. The artillery was underground and we couldn't see it to knock it out. Their riflemen were expert shooters. Many Marines got shot in the head. After the first day, we made a little bit of progress. The next morning the company commander was killed, and we had a lot of other casualties. I took over the company immediately, and we just inched forward. The main way to move was to put out an artillery barrage of our own and try to get out underneath that and advance. Those Marines just kept inching forward in spite of the heavy casualties.

I always think it's amazing how these men handle situations so calmly. I was talking to a sergeant on the walkie-talkie when the enemy shot the phone out of his hand and shot his finger off. The corpsman bandaged him up and he was back on the walkie-talkie. He was later evacuated. You just kept going. You think about the danger. You can't help but think about it, but you have a job to do and you just keep moving forward.

I think it was on the third day when we took out a stronghold. The guns were holding up a couple of Divisions, and we knocked that out and moved on from there. The men had to literally blow up these pillboxes with dynamite to seal them. We moved up across the second airfield then up towards the third airfield and got across there but we had taken many casualties. We lost practically all our platoon commanders, lieutenants, and platoon sergeants so all we had were corporals and sergeants leading the platoons.

Replacements were trained but had no experience and some of them forgot their training. I had a staff sergeant I'd given a platoon to and I remember when I assigned him.

"I'm a demolition man," he said. "I've never commanded a platoon or anything like that, but I'll get the job done."

A couple hours after the attack started some replacement had a BAR that jammed and didn't know how to take care of it so the staff sergeant ran over to help him and got killed.

We used those big craters where the bombs had dropped or naval gunfire had hit for some of our forward command posts. I stayed close behind the troops where I could see them. We'd dig foxholes on the inside of the crater in that hot volcanic sand. I had to put a blanket or a poncho down in the foxhole a couple of nights to keep from getting burned. We would place our C-ration cans in the volcanic ash and they would be heated in a short time.

I had sergeants and corporals out on the line as platoon commanders and could see where they were. They'd have had three or four men they were in charge of, maybe six or seven, but not a platoon. I could talk to them on my walkie-talkie, but I thought I should go out and talk to them personally. I called them and told them I was coming out. I don't know how some of these men kept a sense of humor, but they did. I brought a messenger out with me because he carried a walkie-talkie and I could talk to my executive officer, if needed. The messenger was a young man from south St. Louis. We ran fast and jumped in their foxhole. I talked to the platoon commanders and told them they were doing well and to do as they had done before—they just had a few more men to control. We ran back and jumped in our crater hole.

My messenger then said to me, "Lieutenant, if my mother knew where you just got through taking me, she'd be madder than hell at you."

"We made it this time," I said. "The good Lord willing, we'll make it tomorrow."

Two days later he was killed.

We'd always run a telephone wire when we moved up so we could talk to our rear command post. We had moved forward to a new position, and it was kind of rough terrain. We no more than got there when the enemy had us pinned down with a heavy artillery barrage and cut the telephone wire we'd run. We couldn't get in communication with anyone. I was in a foxhole in the crater as was the first sergeant and the messenger. We had forward observers with us and they carried communications so they could call in the artillery and naval gun fire and tell them where to place it. They were sitting down in the bottom of the crater facing forward. A shell landed on the edge of the crater and it broke apart. There was a jagged edge of one piece that flew down in the bottom of the crater and took off the arm of one of the men there and went through his heart. After about six minutes, the artillery barrage stopped. Since we had no communication with anyone, the messenger was sent to the rear command post with a message to call in to the battalion commander as to our location and that our communications were out at the time but we would get them back in a while. The messenger was shot in the back by the enemy on the way. He made it to the rear command post but died there.

By Dammit, We're Marines!

We finally got pretty well up the island and then hit a stronghold we could not penetrate. We just couldn't make headway. We were taking heavy losses. Today, they call this place Cushman's Pocket, named after our battalion commander. We bypassed it on each side and some of us were able to move forward. We were on the front line for four to six days and then a company would relieve us. We would come out of the lines at night and be off for a day or two so the men could get cleaned up, clean their weapons and do things like that. We suffered severe casualties. I had gone back out on the line one night at 10 o'clock and about 3 or 4 o'clock in the morning Colonel Cushman called me to his CP.

"I'm giving an order that I don't like to give," he said. "The order is a pre-dawn attack. They move out under the cover of darkness."

Lt. Wilcie O'Bannon was probably the best friend I had. He led F Company and I led G Company at this time. They moved out, but when dawn came, his company was caught between enemy foxholes. They were trapped and taking casualties. He had his small command pinned down in foxholes; they didn't dare lift their heads up. Others in his company managed to get back through our front lines. I had communication with him. I was the only one, in fact. We'd come up on the radio every hour on the hour to check on any changes in their status.

That day at noon I received the order from my Battalion Commander, Colonel Cushman, to rescue the surrounded group. It was hopeless because we didn't know where they were and we couldn't put artillery out there to help us. We started to make a move and immediately received casualties. I called Colonel Cushman and said, "I request that you delete that order. I haven't really got started and I am taking many casualties. I would stand a better chance of rescuing the group if I would personally lead a group of volunteers out that night with stretchers for the wounded."

"OK call it off," he said.

O'Bannon somehow or another got in communication with our tanks. He could tell where the tanks were and called them in his direction right in over their foxholes. The men were pulled up through the bottom of the tanks. A lot of the enemy artillery that could have taken out the tanks had been knocked out by this time The tanks brought the men out of there.

I then received orders to move my company immediately to the rear and side of this pocket and attack. It was rather rough terrain and pretty hard keeping any kind of a line. We were going through hedge fences and suddenly found ourselves up against block walls. The Japanese threw grenades over the block wall at us, the First Sergeant, the communications man and me. We kicked the grenades to the side so as to get them down into a trench.

We finally sent the first sergeant back for the bazooka. As evening went on, we pulled back some, organized, and got our lines straightened up. We still had people unaccounted for. One or two came back through the line that night. They had had their packs and canteens cut off and were left there for dead. The next day we consolidated our position and I had two new lieutenants who had been there just a few days. One was killed that night. The next evening the other one called on the walkie-talkie and said there was a big gap between his unit and the 21st Marines and he had moved as far as he could and didn't have the men to move any farther.

"I'll take care of it," I said. So I told my messenger, "We're going to move fast and run across the gap to the unit on our right, the 21st Marines, to see if they could stretch their lines."

We did and came up behind the front line of the 21st. I asked where the company commander was and that's when I got hit by a bullet. I thought an artillery shell had landed near me as I had pains in my stomach.

My messenger knew it was a bullet and reached down and grabbed me by the collar and said, "Get the hell out of here before you get hit again."

He helped me get behind a big boulder. The unit called for a corpsman to give me first aid. They got me over to a field ambulance that had come for the 21st Marines. While being patched up by the corpsman, I called my executive officer and advised him that he had the company and good luck to him.

I was privileged to command such great fighting men and to have outstanding Navy corpsmen and doctors with us. We lost several corpsmen with the company. We tried to have one corpsman with each platoon but at the end on Iwo Jima, I had one corpsman for the whole company. I was told from higher up that if I lost that one, I didn't get any more because there weren't any more.

There were four of us on the field ambulance, and it was slow going to the field hospital because of the rough terrain. I believe the corpsman called down to the hospital and said the worst wounded has a belly wound, because when we arrived, they came running out.

"Where's the man with the belly wound?" they asked.

They took me in and cut my clothes off and I was in surgery. The next morning about 9 o'clock I awakened. The doctor came by and said, "McLellan, I wouldn't have been surprised to have seen you dead this morning."

"Doc, that's the best night's sleep I've had in a long time, I feel great!" I said.

I think I was there one night in the tent. The hospital was right on the beach and the next evening they loaded three of us on a boat. The boatswain knew the ship each one of us was to go to. He backed off the beach but went up on a sand bar so we had to spend the night out under the stars which I was used to doing. The next morning when the tide came in he backed the boat off and we went to our respective ships.

It was a troop ship but they had a hospital compartment with about 20 people in it. I was there for about a week when I commenced to get a high fever, 103-104.

"You know when we get in cooler weather away from here, you'll be all right," my doctor said. The night before we left, we took a medical battalion aboard the troop ship to go back to Hawaii, and there was a doctor from that battalion who had a friend on board so he came down to see him. I was just inside the door and he stopped and asked, "How are you doing?"

"Fine, my temperature gets pretty high sometimes but the doctor said when we get to cooler weather I'll be all right."

He looked at me and asked the corpsman to get my file. He looked at it and didn't say anything to me. Then he left and went up to talk with my doctor. My doctor came down the next morning as the ship was just getting underway and asked me if there was any pain as he pressed my abdomen.

"Yes," I said. Within an hour I was under the knife. I had a large abscess.

The day after I was wounded they called the island secured. When they call the area secure, there is still a lot of fighting going on. It only means the enemy's back is broken and they can no longer launch a big attack. We still lost a number of people in our company while completely securing the island. The Japanese on Iwo Jima fought almost to the last man.

It is to the great fighting men of G Company, 2nd Battalion, 9th Marines, 3rd Marine Division that I give credit for the award of my Navy Cross.

The enemy was entrenched in concrete pill boxes underground. My men could not see them, but carried the battle forward as the gallant men they were. I was the fortunate one to lead them.

* * *

Lt. Colonel McLellan retired from the Marine Corps in 1968. The citation for his Navy Cross reads:

"For extraordinary heroism as Executive Officer of Company G, Second Battalion, Ninth Marines, Third Marine Division, in action against enemy Japanese forces on Iwo Jima, Volcano Islands, from 26 February to 15 March 1945. On 26 February, when his Company Commander was killed during an attack against strongly fortified positions, Captain McLellan immediately assumed command and, in the face of intense hostile fire, skillfully led the attack and permitted his company to overrun an enemy strong point near the second airfield and annihilate the Japanese who had previously held up the advance of three Marine Divisions. Again directing his company in an attack against hostile defense near the third airfield on 2 March, he continually braved intense small-arms fire as he moved from one platoon to another to coordinate the attack and, by his daring leadership and tactical ability, aided materially in destroying forty enemy pillboxes and over two hundred of the Japanese. Throughout this period, he continued to lead his company effectively until seriously wounded on 15 March. His strategic ability, initiative and courageous devotion to duty reflect the highest credit on Captain McLellan and the United States Naval Service."

* * *

Lt. Col. Russell Silverthorn USMC (Ret.)
2nd Lt., Rifle Platoon Leader, 2nd Platoon, K Company,
3rd Battalion, 21st Marines, 3rd Marine Division

Silverthorn family, top row, left to right, brothers Robert,
Merwin, Jr., and Russell. Seated are parents Marie and Merwin.

I was born at Marine Barracks, Quantico, Virginia. There were four of us in the Marine Corps …. my dad, two brothers and myself. We were all career. I enlisted in 1942 and retired as a Lt. Colonel in 1968. I was a student at the University of Maryland when I joined the V-12 program in March of 1942. We were activated about a year later, and I became a 2nd Lieutenant on the 12th of April 1944.

We set sail from San Diego in August of '44 and arrived in Guam about three weeks after the Commander, III Amphibious Corps, declared organized resistance over. My dad was in that campaign. He was Chief of Staff, III Amphibious Corps, the force that recaptured the island with the 3rd Marine Division, the 1st Marine Provisional Brigade, and the 77th Army Division. They landed on the 21st of July 1944, recaptured and secured the island by 10th of August. After Guam was secured, my dad returned to headquarters back on Guadalcanal when I landed about three weeks later. We were still mopping up Japanese on Guam at the rate of about 25 a day after that, but the organized combat was over. This was not my first visit to Guam. As a child I lived there for two years when my dad was stationed with the Marines in 1930-32.

To look older, I grew a moustache in preparation for leading my platoon on Iwo Jima. My mother always said that I looked younger than my age. At 22, I was three to four years older than most of the men in my platoon with the exception of my platoon sergeant; however, I didn't look that much older. I grew the moustache to make me look older, but I'm not sure that I fooled anyone. Without a doubt, I was well trained. Iwo Jima was my first operation where I qualified for a battle star on my campaign ribbon. I didn't earn the battle star for the Guam mop up, but I gained a lot of experience and got some good training for future campaigns.

We departed Guam about the 16th of February. It took a couple of days to get to Iwo Jima. We were expecting success, as is the Marine mindset. There was no doubt that we would accomplish the mission to capture and seize Iwo Jima. We didn't expect an easy success; but a real tussle. We knew the island was fortified but we didn't know the details like we do now. We got the word that there had been a couple of months of air bombardment and that there would be at least three days of Navy gunfire. What we didn't know was that most of the Japanese were deep underground in formidable fortifications. They weren't affected all that much from the bombardment. Consequently, the best tactic was to move fast and be very aggressive in the assault. That is why amphibious warfare has such high casualties for the days that they are actually engaged in combat. Overall you actually save personnel when you move out aggressively and drastically shorten the conflict.

As we approached the combat area at sea in preparation of the landing, the doctor aboard the ship told us we'd better all remove our rings from our fingers. In case of a kamikaze plane attack, fire would probably burn our fingers. If we couldn't get our rings off, it could have meant amputating our fingers. Those of us who had rings took them off and put them in the belongings we planned to carry ashore. We carried everything ashore, of course. I put my ring in my dispatch case. That's the last time I saw my ring until about three months later. After I had been hit, my dispatch case was left on the battlefield with the ring inside. Someone later on during the campaign found it and brought it back to Guam where we reassembled after the operation. After I returned from the hospital, I married up again with the case and in there was my ring. I have worn that ring to this day. It's a University of Maryland ring. I removed my fraternity sign and put the Marine Corps emblem on there because the Marine Corps was more meaningful to me.

One thing that sticks in my mind is how seasick I was as well as half the other men when we hit the beach in our landing craft. Because of the combat situation on the beach, they kept us afloat for five hours in rough seas in a ready position for immediate commitment. The situation was so intense on the beach they decided not to land us and brought us back on the ships where we re-embarked. The second day, due to the combat situation, we repeated the same thing; five hours in rough seas again getting very seasick. I have never been that seasick in all my life and never since. It was so miserable all I wanted to do was to get off the landing craft, even if that meant landing on Iwo Jima.

We landed about 2 o'clock in the afternoon on D+2. Not only were we queasy when we got to shore, but I didn't have the strength to wear my helmet or my knapsack. I literally dragged them behind me as I attempted to lead my platoon off the ship. We were not receiving a lot of direct fire from the enemy as the beach was fairly secured at that time. We remained within several hundred yards from where we disembarked from our landing craft. I recall Iwo as very gloomy, rainy, chilly and foreboding. We went into an assembly area right on the beach and prepared for our imminent commitment. I remember the beach master, a naval officer who is what you might call a traffic cop, telling small boats where to land, where to dump their loads on the beach and where to assemble. Using a big bullhorn, he told us where to assemble. He also told us to beware of Japanese suicide swimmers who would come in on the beach behind us. Apparently they were there but fortunately I didn't run into any. Your training and responsibility seem to take over more than fear. You do things by habit; it becomes second nature to react as you were trained. Sure, when you see your first combat casualty, it's a jarring experience and fear has a window in there. What I think is stronger than fear is the fact that you have so much confidence in your unit; you know you are going to be successful. Also, you have just as strong a feeling that you are not going to let your buddy down. Those two things keep you going and that comes directly from Marine Corps training and Marine Corps history.

In the late morning of the 23rd, we got our orders to saddle up because we were going to move out in an hour or so. I remember looking around, and I'll never forget seeing our national flag on Mt. Suribachi. We all felt inspired. With our flag prominently displayed on the highest point of the island, it confirmed that the Marines were in control and we would be victorious as in past battles.

We had orders to move out and relieve the 1st Battalion, 21st Marines. They'd been held up due to heavy fighting just short of Motoyama Airfield No. 2. They fought their way up there the day before and suffered many casualties. We moved out about noon in the approach march and went across Motoyama Airfield No. 1 which had already been secured by 1st Battalion. We didn't have to fight our way up but we had to be observant and move out in a formation that limited casualties from enemy artillery. There was a minimum of enemy resistance getting up to the Motoyama No. 2 and we sustained no casualties. When you are in a platoon, you are channeled as far as your overview goes. You don't get the full picture and only watch the 45 men in your platoon, the terrain, and enemy in your limited sector. We got to Motoyama No. 2 in the late afternoon of the 23rd and were told to dig in just short of the airfield. We planned to jump off the next morning to pass through the 1st Battalion's lines and relieve them. I was looking after my troops as they started to dig in when three mortar shells hit. They started on the left of me and went right down about every 50 yards. I heard one of my men crying out pretty severely, and I was hit in the left foot and right leg moments later, I think by the third shell. Shrapnel had hit my platoon sergeant and two of my runners. When the corpsman came to me, I sent him up to the platoon sergeant who I believed might be severely wounded. The battalion aide station was approximately 400 yards in the rear but I was able to get there on my own power. They treated me there and I was ready to go back to my unit when the doctor said I had to go to the hospital ship because I had shrapnel in my left foot which they couldn't remove at the aide station.

I ended up back aboard ship that same day and went into surgery for my wounds. The doctors couldn't remove the shrapnel in my left foot and it remains there to this day. It doesn't bother me, though. They kept me aboard the ship then sent me back to a hospital in Saipan for a week, did more work on me, and said they were going to send me back to a bigger hospital in Hawaii for better recovery. I was there for a month for more surgery and they put me on crutches. A month later I came back and joined another outfit on Guam with the 3rd Division. This time it was the C Company, 1st Battalion, 21st Marines, the same unit I was sent to relieve on Iwo. Just as a side note, my dad was a personal friend of General Graves B. Erskine who commanded the 3rd Marine Division on Iwo. My dad had asked the general to let him know right away if I became wounded or killed so he could tell my mother first.

I was on Guam training for Operation Olympic--the invasion of Japan, when I heard the war was over. I don't think we even knew what an atomic bomb was at the time even though the B-29 that dropped the bomb took off from Tinian, an adjacent island to Guam. If there was any celebration, it was because we would be going home soon.

Had the war not ended, we were scheduled to land in Kyushu, Japan, with two other Marine Divisions. We hear now and see from TV that the fighters in the Middle East are tenacious, but the Japanese just simply didn't quit. If we were to invade Japan, it would have been intense with high casualties. When I was taken by the landing craft back to the hospital ship, I saw a kamikaze plane attack one of our ships. Of course later in Okinawa there were roughly 300 ships hit by kamikazes and many of the ships sunk. The kamikaze planes were the original suicide bombers. From that pattern I would think that the Japanese would have contested every inch of territory they had the ability to contest.

It was natural for me to make a career of the Marine Corps. My older brother, Merwin, was in five amphibious operations in World War II and retired as a colonel. My younger brother, Robert, served in Korea and was a career Marine for 10 and a half years and was a captain. My dad, Merwin H. Silverthorn, was in every major combat in World War I and was the second most highly decorated lieutenant in that war. During World War II, he was in three amphibious operations on Guam, Peleliu and Okinawa. He later became Assistant Commandant of the Marine Corps, 1950-1952, and retired as a lieutenant general in 1954. He very seldom talked about his involvement in the war. He had to be asked direct questions and he would answer them briefly. With four career Marines in our family, we were quite a drain on the U.S. Treasury. Finally, I recall two things of spiritual nature that provided me comfort in combat. One was the small Marine Corps-issue New Testament with a steel cover that fit neatly in my top left pocket shielding the heart. The second was that a few days prior to my departure from Camp Lejeune for deployment, my mother and I attended church services at the base chapel when the 91st Psalm was highlighted which she claimed as God's promise for me.

* * *

Special Officer Candidates School

By 1944, the war in the Pacific had taken its toll on the Marines especially 1st and 2nd lieutenants. New officers put into combat situations without the experience of training with troops lasted a short time. Desperate for junior officers but lacking the facilities to train them, the Marine Corps convened a Special Officer Candidates School at Camp Lejeune to supplement its regular officer candidate class at Quantico. Brought together from V-12 programs around the country, 400 young men were called to active duty and placed in the SOCS program. It was the only OCS class held outside Quantico. Jack Bradford, Ed Cavallini, Norman Elliott, and Hugh Penton, Sr., were commissioned in September, 1944, and were immediately sent to the Pacific. Iwo Jima would be their first battle as new 1st and 2nd lieutenants.

Capt. Jack Bradford, USMCR (Ret.)
2nd Lt., A Company, 1st Battalion, 23rd Marines, 4th Division

The four officers of A Company, Iwo Jima, March 9, 1945,
(left to right) Lt. Jack Bradford, Lt. Arthur W. Zimmerman, Capt. Bill
Hodge and Lt. Jim Wasson

By Dammit, We're Marines!

The SOCS classes were conducted at the rifle range at Camp Lejeune. This is now the Marine Corps Scout and Sniper training area. We don't particularly know why we were so lucky to be in the SOCS class, but I think it was because we were active in college affairs and most of us were in an athletic program. We were a bunch of go-getters. We were really well-trained for what we did. And did we have morale! There wasn't anything they could do to discourage us.

When you're commissioned, you are supposed to be an officer and a gentleman. We were taught how to be company leaders but nothing about bookwork, being gentlemen, and none of us ever had a pair of dress blues. We just went through company level training because we were going to become the bulk of the rifle company officers on Iwo and Okinawa. The Marines commissioned 400 officers and did it in a very intelligent way. They commissioned alphabetically. They were in a rush at that time. Most of the ones who reported to the 4th Division, the 5th Division, and 3rd Division were more towards the front of the alphabet because the Iwo campaign was coming before the Okinawa campaign. They whipped those of us in the 4th and the 5th Division over to the Hawaiian Islands. The guys going to the 3rd Division went to Guam. We trained at Camp Maui which was on the side of Haleakala, the extinct volcano. Since we went alphabetically, Bill Baker, a friend of mine, was the head of our replacement unit. He knew the spot to most men's hearts was through their stomachs so instead of assigning me to a company right away, I got assigned as the mess officer of the battalion. That isn't very pleasing when you have trained to go in with a rifle company. Each officer wants to get with their unit right away. It is much better to be prepared and to have worked with the guys in your company.

There was a rumor that we were headed to Taiwan. Had we tried that one, we would have all been wiped out. Our destination was to be Iwo Jima. I was just 21 and this would be my first battle.

On Iwo, I was assigned to unload all the LSTs that had brought out our three companies. It took us three days to unload all the materials and supplies on the LSTs and then we were sent in with the guys we had unloaded the LST with. We all reported in the late evening to the battalion operations officer who assigned me to A Company. I didn't get that advantage of previous training with the company I served in. We trained with the replacement battalion so I basically learned on the job. The advantage to me was that I inherited a tremendous platoon sergeant. A Company hadn't gone back into the front lines when I reported in because casualties were so high. Their first night on Iwo a shell hit the whole battalion staff; the colonel, the S-3, the radio officer;

everybody but the S-4, who was the supply officer, was killed. As you can imagine, they had to bring in replacements. There was only one of the eight officers that originally landed with A Company who was still in the company. Everybody else was killed or wounded by then. I was given a platoon that was probably the best trained because the one guy who survived was the platoon leader before me. I thought I was smart enough not to try to get in their way too soon. In the Korean War, you had to spend x number of days observing what the company was doing before assuming command but I think they had a little more time than we had there on Iwo.

The platoon I was to lead started out on Roi-Namur, then went to Saipan and Tinian and Iwo. When I took over the platoon, I think there were something like 18 left out of 46 original guys who started out four operations ago. I brought in replacements with me and from that time on we kept getting replacements throughout the whole campaign. This created a lot of problems because we had a tremendous assault platoon which contained bazookas, flamethrowers, and demolition men. By the time I had been on the line for five days, we didn't have a bazooka man, we didn't have a flamethrower, and we didn't have a demolition man, so we had to try to train their replacements right on the spot. A lot of these guys were basically just out of boot camp with maybe twelve weeks of training afterward. As the campaign went on most of my old timers managed to survive and most of the replacements got killed or wounded and evacuated. I had about 18 guys left when I was wounded and I don't think more than 6 or 7 of them were from the original group.

Our assault platoon was commanded by a platoon sergeant by the name of Fritz Truan, and I think this was his first campaign. He was the world's bronco busting champion.* You can imagine if you have been around horses and broncos, you don't think much about danger. He was a handsome, totally fearless individual. He was killed in action on Iwo. After Iwo, there was a special rodeo in Honolulu as a tribute to him.

We'd spend x number of days on the front lines depending on what casualties we took. We suffered so many casualties that they shipped us back for two days to division reserve that I recall was either by the top of the beach or by the first airfield. We got about 30-40 replacements in those two days. We tried to teach them weapon training but didn't succeed. The reserve area wasn't totally secured because the Japanese could still infiltrate, but I don't think we felt the tension that we normally did. We got reasonably rested. Most of the time we were on the front lines and I think we averaged about two hours sleep a night. You never got tired because you lived on adrenalin. Adrenalin or fright,

I don't know which one. You don't admit to the fright, but you are scared most of the time.

I was on the island when the first flag went up. We could see the small flag. The uniform reaction from those of us who were in the middle of the island was "Thank gosh we won't get shot at from two directions anymore!"

On March 3, we were up at a place called Turkey Knob, where B Company was trying to knock out this gigantic blockhouse when we saw the first B-29 make its crash landing on Iwo. That was more meaningful to us than the flag raising because we suddenly saw the light of day why we were there. The plane was damaged, but it was repaired and flew again. Saved the whole crew.

Before each assault, our Company Commander would call the three platoon leaders together and would ask us what we thought about doing whatever the assignment was. We'd give him our opinion. We'd go back to our NCOs and do the same thing with them. They told the guys on their squad exactly what the assignment was for the next day and they'd try to get the proper weapons for whatever mission we had. I had enough guys who were experienced that they helped me for my first 10 or 12 days. I had 21 days working with one platoon which is more than a lot of guys had during the whole war. They didn't have the continuity we had. Our company really worked very smoothly together. A guy in our company would literally sacrifice his life for his buddy and that's very reassuring. I saw a lot of that.

I think we wore the Japanese down. The Marine Corps will spend three or four days trying to take one place, and we'll keep trying until we finally figure a way to do it even though we are taking terrible casualties.

On February 28, my platoon was the left flank company of the 4th Division right next to the 3rd Division and we were to assault Hill 382, a heavily fortified Japanese position. I took my platoon around the other side of Hill 382 and worked our way around its base, then came up the rear side. By mid-afternoon we had actually taken the hill and the radar installation, but we were pulled off. They were afraid we would be isolated up there and annihilated, and they didn't feel they had enough reserves to cover. But that afternoon I had already talked with the artillery forward observer who planned the lines they were going to fire. I talked with the naval gunfire, and we had the 81 mortars zeroed-in. The company would have a lot of support during the night, but we were pulled back. It was a tragic thing for the platoons that had already lost so many people during the day. Both squad leaders were killed when they were passing out rations. Not only did they have casualties all day but even when they stopped for chow, they got it, too.

On the 10th of March, our company was ordered to go fill in a gap in the line. The 2nd Battalion 23rd Marines were operating ahead of us and they got hit by a banzai the night before. Some of their units were just totally overrun. The lines weren't stable. A runner from somewhere led us to this gap in the lines and told us this is where we were going to defend tonight. So we all asked if this is the gap in the lines, where are the next Marines? There weren't any Marines anywhere near us so we just put concertina wire around our position and we put ourselves in a circular form. We set up trip flares and other warning devices. We were able to get in touch with the Navy and they fired flares over our head all night long. We still thought we were going to get wiped out. The total number killed that night was one Japanese who wandered into our concertina wire. My company commander got this brilliant idea that he wanted to see what a platoon did under those kinds of conditions. He had been the regimental aerial photograph officer and he volunteered to come up after we came back on the 28th from Hill 382.

"Captain," I kept saying, "you need to be at company headquarters to run the rest of the company."

"Oh no," he said, "I think I really need this experience." So he came up and he had a rather fascinating night with us.

I was slightly wounded on March 3 but refused to be evacuated because that's basically the way we'd operate. I was wounded in a major way on March 12. We were planning an envelopment of a machine gun nest we had bypassed that gave us all kinds of heck. B Company and A Company worked on the envelopment, but our company had a special thing we were going to do with our part of it. We met behind a great big rock, 20 feet high, with our maps out and planned our part of the operation. We went around the rock to go back to our squad leaders to tell them how they were going to conduct this operation. Just as we went around the rock, a mortar shell landed probably closest to me than anybody. The platoon sergeant of the other platoon was standing to the right of me and got hit through the back. My runner stood maybe two feet from me and was killed. He was not originally one of my runners. He was originally a rifleman wounded fairly early in the campaign and sent to Guam for hospitalization. I'll be darn, but he came back when we were at Hill 382 and went back for two days in reserve. He said he couldn't stand not to come back to his unit. Now I have been asked over the past 60 something years why would a man do that and all I can say is, that's the way we did it. A Marine who thought he could come back and help, would request to come back. If the doctors in the field hospital out in the Pacific said he could come back, he came back. I made him my runner because I thought I could keep him safe. And I failed. I did the best I could. I never had bad feelings about it except that I had to lie to him when he was injured and tell him he was going to be fine, the corpsman was on the way. I could see he was losing his life. We all knew he was dying from the minute he got hit because he was turning blue.

I got hit through my upper leg and since I was holding my rifle down low, shrapnel went through my arm and severed my artery and my sensory nerve. The corpsman put a tourniquet around my arm and got us in a jeep ambulance. The corpsman evacuated me to the battalion aid station but he got hit by a machine gun. In almost every company the favorite Marine was a Navy guy— the naval corpsman. It was just a love affair. Corpsmen had to stand duty at night and they had to carry weapons because the Japanese didn't adhere to the Geneva conventions.

I was back on Maui when I heard the war was over. I was Assistant Battalion Operation Officer and had learned the plans for the next operation. Two regiments of the 4th Division were loading ships to retake Wake Island when the Japanese surrendered. Had we invaded Japan, we had no way of direct evacuation to the United States of the more seriously injured men. Since Wake Island is about halfway between Japan and the U.S., our planes could land there and refuel. But the war ended.

I became a history teacher after the war and started reading books on the war. My first reaction was, why didn't we do a demonstration atomic bomb drop someplace in an uncivilized part of Japan with observers from other countries to let the Japanese know that there was no rhyme or reason for them to hold on to the war. It turned out that the Japanese leaders weren't really that convinced when we dropped the first bomb. We had to drop a second bomb on Nagasaki before they got the word.

*Fritz Truan was the 1940 World's All-Around Rodeo Champion

* * *

2nd Lt. Ed Cavallini
Rifle Platoon Leader, 1st Platoon, K Company, 3rd Battalion, 24th Marines, 4th Division

I enlisted on December 4, 1942. I was going to USC as an undergraduate. All the various branches of the military had a program for college students as they were looking for officers. I went and talked with all the services to see what the programs were, and I selected the Marine Corps because, and this is very un-heroic, I felt I could stay in school longer if I joined the Marines. Actually, it worked out that I was able to stay for two semesters with the Marine's V-12 program and was able to get my degree.

After SOCS, we were sent on a troop train to Camp Pendleton for more infantry training. During that time, I also got married. You weren't supposed to be married if you were in the V-12 program, although several people were, but they kept it hidden. But as soon as we got a commission, we could get married. I was commissioned on the 30th of September and married Jeanne O'Donnell on the 14th October. We had heard that we were going to get a month's leave after we were commissioned. Jeanne and I had planned on getting married in San Francisco and she even had the wedding announcements made. We had to cancel that because I was sent directly to Pendleton. However, we had a lovely wedding in a friend's home in Beverly Hills. I left for overseas in the later part of November. We had been married only 4 weeks.

I joined the Division in Maui and took over a rifle platoon. Several weeks later, we loaded onto an attack transport ship and headed west. We had no idea where we were going except that it was going to be another operation. Of course, all the Marine operations were attacks on different islands, so that wasn't any surprise. We were given information about Iwo Jima on the way over. I had never heard of Iwo but they said it was very important.

We had bunks in the officers' quarters aboard ship and the guy who had the bunk next to me was Joe Rosenthal who later took the iconic photo of the flag-raising on Mt. Suribachi. He worked for Associated Press based in San Francisco, and I was born and raised there so we had a lot to talk about. We also played a lot of pinochle together after he taught me to play. He was a very quiet, serious gentleman.

I was nervous yet pretty calm because I was going in with the Division. I wasn't going in as a replacement officer. We had several weeks of field exercises that were helpful. I was going in with a unit that had been in three other landings and had a lot of combat experience. The 24th Marines landed on D-Day sometime around noon as a reserve regiment.

It was pretty messy and confusing when I landed. I ran across my friend Matt Carney who had the 3rd Platoon and he was wounded as were our machine gun platoon leader and the executive officer of our company. They were all put out of action the first couple of hours.

"You lucky guy!" I said to Matt.

"If you're lucky enough, you'll be joining me soon!" We had that brief encounter. I was happy for him because I knew that soon he'd be safe and sound.

We had several casualties in our platoon. I remember the first Marine in my unit who I saw dead. It was really tragic. He was the oldest man in the platoon, he was 26, and he was the only one who had any children. It was terrible. That really hit me hard. I was 21. Most of the men in my platoon were younger than me, some were a little older. It's amazing how young we were.

We went in on the far right and headed north. We were waiting for orders to move ahead but we couldn't do much for the first few days because there was so much artillery and mortar fire on the beaches. I didn't feel much stress because I didn't have to do much leading. All we were doing was sitting in place waiting to be called to move up. After we started north a little bit, we had to stop because there were people in front of us who weren't moving. The black sand of Iwo Jima was so fine that typical foxholes could not be dug. Most cover was provided by craters caused by the constant fire of large mortars from higher ground. I think it was the second day there when a Marine sergeant and a war dog were walking by.

A barrage came and he said, "Can I join you?"

"Sure, come on down." I said. It turns out that he was one of my drill instructors at Parris Island when I was at boot camp! We certainly had a different relationship in the foxhole than we did at boot camp. He was a tough DI. We remembered each other. His dog was really scared. In fact, the dog was almost as scared as I was. I felt sorry for the Doberman.

That same afternoon a Marine officer came by and said, "Can I pop in?" and he joined me. This guy was my journalism teacher in high school in San Francisco. He was a captain who was a graves' registration officer. He had the terrible job of validating who everyone was. He was a great prof; it was a really good class. But at that time, this was maybe '39 or something, nobody was talking or thinking about a war.

Gail Chatfield

The next day I was just checking my platoon, going from hole to hole seeing how the men were doing. I was between holes and I got hit by a mortar fragment in the chest. I wound up back in a hole, I don't think it was mine, with a corpsman, one of my sergeants, and a lieutenant who was a forward artillery observer. I got carried down to the beach to a holding area to wait to be taken out to a hospital ship. While I was on the beach, I got hit in the knee with a piece of shrapnel which actually caused me more problems than the one in the heart. I didn't know it at the time but the fragment hit one of my dog tags which probably slowed it down. It wound up embedded in my heart muscle. It's still there because they felt it was more dangerous to remove it since it wasn't moving.

They took us out to an LST, and the whole floor of the LST was made like a hospital ward. They had low cots or stretchers lying on the deck and the nurses and corpsmen were watching over us. By coincidence, the person next to me when I finally came out of it was my battalion commander. His father at the time was the Commandant of the Marine Corps, General A.A. Vandegrift. He was A.A. Jr.; his field name was Archie. All officers had field names. Nicknames. In combat, you don't wear any insignia to show your rank, and you never call anybody captain or so forth in case someone overhears it and picks you out. So instead of calling him colonel, you called him Archie. My name was Count. When we went back to boot camp on Parris Island, all of us from different V-12 schools from all over the country were mixed together. In our platoon, there was a bunch from Southern California, the smart-ass types, and a bunch from Texas and Oklahoma. My name is Cavallini, which is sort of an uncommon name.

So somebody asked one of the ex-UCLA guys, "Tell me about this guy Cavallini."

"He's a Count from Italy who was going to USC and instead of getting drafted, he enlisted in the Marine Corps," he said.

These guys believed it so that became my nickname. When I joined the Division, they said I had to pick out a field name.

"OK, how about Ed?" I asked.

"No, some major has the name Ed."

"How about Count?" and that was it.

I left Iwo before the flag was raised. I was put on the hospital ship USS Samaritan, a big converted liner, and sent back to Saipan. I never heard about the flag raising until I got back to the States. I don't think they realized until later how important the picture was.

Treatment on the hospital ship was good but there was a wounded guy next to me who would moan and groan all the time. They would give him meds; he was in pain, and they couldn't control it. The poor guy finally died about 4 o'clock the next morning. The hospital staff was really upset. They were really good; they really worked hard. I went to the naval hospital back in Saipan for four to five weeks. The Division was supposed to regroup on Saipan, but we got beat up so much they decided to send us back to Maui which was really lucky for us because having liberty in Maui is much better than having liberty in Saipan. Just as we were docking in Maui, we got the word that President Roosevelt had died. It was a shock. Nobody knew anything about Truman, of course.

My rifle platoon had 45 members. After the war looking at the records, we had 104 casualties in my platoon counting replacements. Not that many were killed, but there were that many casualties.

By the time I got back to Maui, I was ready to go back to active duty. We were practicing to land at Honshu, Japan. We were training on the side of Haleakala Crater where it's very rough, rugged volcanic ash except it is red, nasty stuff. We would be out there for a week or so and we'd come back and Matt Carney and I would get a jeep and go to Wailuku which is the largest city on Maui. We found a place run by a nice Japanese family that had steam baths and massage. We'd go in there and get in a steam cabinet for half an hour or so and all the red dust would run off and it would look like blood. We went there one time and were the only two there. We were in our cabinets getting steamed and these are the old fashioned ones where you have just your head sticking out. A couple of sirens went off and everybody ran out of the place. What the hell is going on? All of a sudden, we realize we can't get out of these cabinets, we're getting weak and started yelling. Finally, they came back and let us out. They were really apologetic. The sirens went off because they just announced V-J Day. Our joke was we were almost killed by friendly Japanese on V-J Day!

When they dropped the first bomb, we were out in the field. No one could believe the power of this atom bomb. No one had even heard about it. It's terrible that so many people in Japan got killed, but many, many more people in both Japan and America would have died.

I was sent to Okinawa as a military police officer with the military government section of the Marine Corps. The Okinawa natives were just a lovely, friendly people. They had been occupied by Japan before the war and they weren't treated nicely by the Japanese soldiers at all. Our main job was to protect the facilities like the naval hospital from the Japanese soldiers who still hadn't surrendered. It was pretty easy because they were just hiding out, they weren't a threat to anybody.

I was discharged in June 1946. During the Korean War I was recalled to active duty in June 1951 and spent 16 months as a supply officer with the Training and Replacement Command at Camp Del Mar, Oceanside, California. I was discharged in October 1952 as a captain.

I was in aerospace for 20 years and then went back to school and became a librarian and retired after 30 years. My wife and I have been married 62 years and have four children, three grandchildren, and one great- grandchild on the way.

* * *

2nd Lt. Norman Elliott
K Company, 3rd Battalion, 24th Marines, 4th Division

In the 1920's there was a rash of railroad mail car robberies and mail car clerks who were getting shot. The Commandant of the Marine Corps volunteered the Marines as a policing agency to help with this national problem. Suddenly the robberies stopped. All through the 1930's, the Marines were called on to go in and pacify the situations in Nicaragua, Haiti, Central and South America. The Marines were in the news. We didn't have enough heroes, and the Marines were always doing a good job. When the war came, I enlisted in the Marine Corps V-12 program in the first month or two of 1942.

I was called up on July 1, 1943. The military would select one college in an area and contract with the Defense Department to furnish the infrastructure, housing, etc., for the V-12 training. We got uniforms and were paid $30 a month. We were housed in dormitory rooms that were meant for two people, but they now put four people in there. They were taking recruits by age so I was lucky enough to get through college.

At SOCS at Camp Lejeune, we went through very brutal physical training as well as very simple military training. We graduated September 30, 1944. We'd been promised that after we were commissioned we would get some leave. A lot of us and our girlfriends had gotten the idea we could get married at that time. Instead, they put us on this troop train going from coast to coast under guard. People were quite irate about this. There was a whole covey of disappointed ladies who actually tracked us all the way from the east coast to the west coast, station to station, by automobile and bus and they would be there when the train pulled up. We thought some of these guys were real Lotharios with all the women following them.

We finally got weekend liberty after we got to Camp Pendleton. We were released at noon on Saturday and we were due back at 10 p.m. on Sunday. Not much time, but I think something like 30 of us got married. I married my girlfriend from Occidental College. I left the base at 12 noon, got to LA and was married at 8 p.m. Saturday night.

We were then sent by ship to different staging areas. They sent us out in groups called replacement drafts. I was in the 24th Replacement Draft. As we came ashore on Maui, they allocated us to different units. Our draft's casualty rate for Iwo was 80 percent. The significance is that organized units, companies, regiments, whatever, become ineffective fighting units if they suffer as much as 50 percent casualties. I think the important thing about the Marine Corps is the cohesiveness of the

51

training. We remain effective even when we suffer some very high casualty rates. The 24th Replacement Draft casualties were high, but all the replacements drafts were between 50- 80 percent casualty.

The composition of the company was 7 officers and 235 men. There were four officers already with the company and the three of us newcomers. We had a pretty short time together. We joined the regiment in the middle of November and had from that time until just before New Years when we went aboard ship to go to Iwo.

Iwo Jima was my first combat experience. War is hell. I was in the first wave on February 19th. It was chaotic. There was a pre-landing bombardment and we landed an enormous number of Marines in a very short time on a very difficult beach. You would sink in the sand somewhere between your ankles and your knees. There were crests on the shore that were hard to get up so we were pinned in and then the Japanese started shelling us. We were like flies on a wall. The most terrifying thing in battle is to be the direct object of shellfire and not be able to do anything about it. Just terrifying. A lot of men were wounded right there on the beach. Two of our officers were wounded in minutes as well as a whole lot of the men. I saw my friend Matt and another lieutenant at breakfast aboard ship and never saw them again.

We moved in closer and it was still very nasty. We just squeezed in on a hundred yard strip of beach and we were sitting ducks. A lot of artillery, mortars, and machine guns were giving us a bad time. It was very difficult; there was no cover, no shelter. We really lost track of time. After a while, day after day, everything blurred all together. I remember it was very exciting to see the flag raised. So proud to be an American. That was one moment where you were proud but then you had to get back to business at hand.

The very nature of combat is that you have to move from A to B and men get hurt and you try to make adjustments with the personnel you have. We went on across the island and then turned a right angle and went up the center of the island. I had the mortar platoon, and I had some very competent men. One great thing about the Marine Corps is that they have super non-coms. The best.

We were just a couple of days ashore at the Boat Basin and our extreme right flank was exposed so we now had to look two ways. There had to be a pill box or some kind of a gun emplacement that was firing down laterally at the beach. It was a killer. Different people had different ideas on what to do and it was sudden death if you went right at it. A gunner, who is a commissioned rank in between gunnery sergeant and 2nd lieutenant, was with us as we talked about what to do. He personally found right there on the beach a 37 mm cannon and hand carried it up to where he could get kind of a point blank look at that pill box. He then stood up in plain view shooting this 37 mm cannon at the enemy and silenced that pill box. It was the bravest thing I ever saw. He was just out there in plain view not a care in the world. He should have gotten a medal. You see extraordinary things and the battle goes on and maybe somebody sees it and reports it. Most times they don't.

As we moved up every day, 100, 200 yards, we started doing a little better. We got up to the first airfield, Motoyama No. 1, and I can remember we were told to dig foxholes. We were on the airfield and it was concrete. We had entrenching tools trying to dig through that....but we couldn't do it. The whole time for those first few days until we got to more of the other end of the island there was just no cover at all. I'm surprised that as many people survived as did. We often times had night attacks. That's kind of scary because you see a shape and don't know if it's friendly or unfriendly. You don't get enough sleep because shellfire and machine gun fire goes on all night long.

I think that everything is tolerable but it is cumulative pressure. I don't think I could have gone through two or three battles particularly under shell fire, which is a horrible thing. I saw a lot of combat fatigue. Typically, it was the men who had been in several combat operations and just couldn't take it any more. They were shell shocked, really. It wasn't that common, but it wasn't that uncommon. Some guys did better than others.

We got down to the point where there were three officers left: the Major who was the commanding officer, the Executive Officer 1st Lt. Lou Myers, and me. We were having a strategy tactical meeting one day about March 1st or 2nd in the Amphitheater. The nearest Japanese as far as we could see were 300-400 yards away in this Amphitheater cliff. We had been told that the Japanese couldn't shoot because they had bad eyes. So there we were standing up and a sniper shot the Major, BOOM! We got a stretcher-bearer and got him off. About five minutes later, the Exec Officer and I were standing there and a sniper shot him. So the stretcher bearers take him away. Lou was on the stretcher ready to go out to the rear to the field hospital.

"All right Elliott," he says, "you've got the company. God help us."

A resounding vote of confidence! I was scared to death. I was just barely qualified to be a lieutenant; but I wasn't ready to be a company commander. I was 21 years old.

In the early days of the war, the British had a lot of weapons in the defense perimeter of Singapore. When the Japanese overran the British, they dismantled a lot of them and put them on the islands in the Pacific. There were several eight-inch naval guns that were put on railroad tracks in a cave inside of a hill. At night, when it wasn't visible to the Marines, the Japanese would open the steel doors and wheel the gun out, fire it, and then roll it back in and the doors would close. We were told to keep our eyes opened for these big shells and when we saw one, to take an accurate compass bearing.

The first day we were in the Amphitheater, I wanted to see how the troops were lined up and get an idea where we went from here. I was running laterally along the line of our company seeing where the foxholes were from left to right, and I got out on the right flank a little bit too far. That big eight-inch shell landed about 25 meters away but the concussion was tremendous. You can't imagine the crunch. The concussion knocked me down and disoriented me. I got up and brushed myself off and started running back to what I thought was where I came from, friendly territory. I didn't realize it but I had turned 90 degrees and instead of running back, I was running straight towards the Japanese. After a bit, I started hearing the bullets go by my ears and thought there is something wrong here. It had been awhile since I had seen a friendly face, and I finally put two and two together and realized that they were shooting at me. I was scared to death. I turned and ran back and rejoined my unit. They got about 200 compass bearings for that eight inch gun and plotted them on a map. When the time came, counter battery fire zeroed in on that gun. I commanded the company for a day or two and felt like I was in over my head. After a while they got the word and the battalion sent down a more experienced 1st lieutenant who took over the command.

A few days later, March 4, a big shell came my way when I was out surveying. We were going up the island and I happened to notice some shell bursts that were off to the right hand side. They weren't large; it was obviously a Japanese mortar and he was traversing, 100 yards, 100 yards, 100 yards, a common tactical movement. I shouted and passed the word up and down the line "everybody down."

As I was turning, watching to be sure everybody was taking cover, the mortar dropped on in behind me. I was within the arc of fire as it spreads out so I got shrapnel in my legs, my back, my arms, and my neck, everywhere. I was bleeding all over. I was in pretty bad shape but it wasn't as bad as it looked. The stretcher-bearers cut my dungarees off and put bandages where they could to stop the bleeding. They took me a thousand yards back to an aid station for some more medical care and then back to the beach where they stacked me up next to the dead bodies. I recognized some of the dead. It was a horrible experience. After a while, they got a boatload together and took me out to the hospital ship. From there the ship went to an Army hospital on Saipan where I stayed for a couple of weeks and was flown back out to Pearl Harbor. I stayed three to four months in a Naval hospital there. After all the surgeries, they got everything out except half a dozen pieces that are still around. I had one piece too close to my heart at that time to take out.

I had an uncle who was regular Navy, but at the invasion of Iwo he was a captain in charge of destroyer escorts called DE. They patrolled just off the coast of Iwo and Japan making sure the Japanese didn't send reinforcements or attack the troops that were on the island. When the authorities announced that Iwo Jima was secured, my uncle heard this news and got the idea to have me come to dinner on this flagship. He sent his flag lieutenant on shore to Iwo to invite me which was tantamount to an order. When the lieutenant came ashore, I had already been wounded and evacuated. The lieutenant picked his way to where my unit was still fighting and they told him the truth. When they had seen me last, I was hanging out of a stretcher covered with blood.

"Elliott bought the farm," they said.

That was the message the lieutenant took back to the ship to my uncle who, of course, was disturbed by it. When his ship came into Honolulu several days later, he called his sister, who was my mother-in-law, and reported that I was dead. My mother-in-law told my wife and my mother. Some weeks later I was finally ambulatory, but still in the hospital in Hawaii, when the Red Cross got me a phone line to call home. I had been in this Army hospital on Saipan for several weeks and then flown back to the Naval hospital and was there for several weeks. By the time the Red Cross got me a phone line, it was probably eight weeks after I was wounded. My wife was glad to get the news that I wasn't dead.

I finally got released and had to take a physical exam. They wouldn't certify me fit for active duty so I was reassigned to a military police battalion. I had gone to college and was a pre-law major so I was named as a criminal investigator. My military police battalion was sent up to Saipan to be the island police force. We had traffic cops, regular policemen and I was a detective investigating felonies, everything from homicides down to burglaries. I was in Saipan until February 1946. I was promoted to 1st lieutenant after combat. I was discharged after the war and went to USC law school on the G.I. Bill.

* * *

1st Lt. Hugh Penton
28th Replacement Draft, 21st Marines, 3rd Division

Hugh Penton, wartime photo

I don't really know why I chose the Marines. I had always admired them. They were the best. I liked the prestige of the Marine Corps, certainly. I was never keen on the Navy, and the Army I couldn't care less about. I like to be challenged and am sort of a type A—gung-ho personality. I don't remember what motivated me to drive down to Los Angeles and enlist, but I did and came home and told my family about it. I didn't ask their approval, but I think that they were not too surprised. I was 18 at the time.

I received the monthly newsletters the Marines sent out about the V-12 program. I remember studying at home about barbed wire, barricades, and explosives described in the newsletter. When I went to UCLA, I kept getting this material from the Marines and I finally grabbed their advice seriously. In the V-12 program you were in the service, but unless needed, you could finish college. I didn't get that far. They took us out about one semester before I was supposed to graduate. I went back to UCLA in '46 when I got back and finished up.

I was working at the time as well as going to school. I did a semester and graduated, but stayed in the reserves.

I was a junior at UCLA when they sent all of us from the West Coast to the V-12 program at USC. The Army guys went to UCLA and UC Berkeley. USC became a big Navy school. We lived in dorms, we marched, we had uniforms, but we attended classes, played football, and all the usual things. It was along about December that the Marines started running out of live 2nd lieutenants, so they sent us all to Parris Island in South Carolina for boot camp. We came from all over the country. In our platoon we had four all-American football players. Then they split us into two groups and sent the older ones to Quantico and the younger ones to Camp Lejeune in North Carolina. I lost track of the ones that went to Quantico, but our group stayed in touch and still exchanges newsletters and has reunions. We were all sent to Camp Pendleton and then split up and went to different Marine Divisions. We didn't know where we were going when we shipped out from San Diego. Our 28th Replacement Draft ended up in Guam about 30 days later.

We weren't in Guam very long. It was about 30 days after Saipan was taken and we really didn't get too involved. Our group chased after some of the Japs that were still there in caves, remnants of the Japanese army. I know that we didn't know that we were being prepared for Iwo, and they never told us what was going on. We were just a bunch of young guys waiting for something to happen.

We left Guam on a troop ship and had no idea where we were going until we got there. Iwo was just our next assignment. Our group was really a replacement group. We didn't go in on the first day. We went in on the second or third day, mainly to help land supplies on the beach and empty cargo and duties like that. We'd go back to the ship at night and wait for orders for the next day. It wasn't that exciting because most of the fighting had gone past us at that point. We didn't have any knowledge really of what was going on…clearing up the airfields and such. We had no idea the number of casualties. I was on the beach when the flag went up. I believe that it was the first one, not the one in the pictures. I looked up to the left and there it was. It was not all that emotional. We sort of expected it from the guys who were in the real fighting part at that point. I was just busy on the beach unloading munitions and directing the unloading of tanks. I never kept a diary or took notes or pictures. It was just another day on the beach, and we were not under any big stress or anything. There were some mortar shells thrown at us, but I don't recall being overly worried. We were just young, doing our thing and not paying a lot of attention. The real fighting on the beach had been a few days before.

I was sent to take over a platoon that was just past the Motoyama Airfield No. 2 on the northeast part of the island. I didn't know anybody there. I finally got to know most of them, and we had some activity for a couple of days, nothing too much. The third day was when I got hit. I was bringing my platoon around to take this hill that was kind of like an old volcano. It was about 500 yards from where we were in the valley on the south side of it. I was sitting with my back to the hill with just my head showing. I was talking to my sergeant and busy deploying the platoon to go over the ridge and take the hill. We couldn't see anybody there. It looked pretty bare and desolate, but obviously we were wrong.

There probably were some caves in there that we didn't see because a sniper got me with just the top of my head above the ridge. It was like getting hit with a good left hook, POW! And I was very, very lucky. One fraction of an inch one way or the other and it would have been curtains. I got the bullet through my right cheek, and it came out through the left side of my nose. My head had been turned just to the left, and it was more of glancing blow. My sergeant put a big gauze bandage on it, covering my face and I felt OK. It was just like somebody had hit me hard. My sergeant said that I should go back and see the captain, so I walked back about a quarter of a mile through the valley and up a hill to his headquarters.

The captain had so many casualties that he couldn't afford to send back a guy with just a scratched finger, but he and the corpsman took one look at me with this big bloody bandage covering my face and said to go back for medical attention. I probably looked horrible. The corpsman didn't even want to look under the bandage, and after they took me back on a stretcher on a jeep, nobody else did either. They just sent me out to the hospital ship and to intensive care. I was on the third bunk up, and it was pretty ugly there. There were mostly guys who were very badly injured. I stayed for a day or so. Nobody came around to look at me, and I was just lying there watching all this stuff going on. I got up and took a shower and took my bandage off.

A nurse or a doctor saw me and said, "What are you doing here?"

I just didn't want to lie around and they said I looked pretty good so they sent me from intensive care to a regular part of the hospital ship. The guys there were like I was, shot or shelled, but it wasn't as gruesome as intensive care. I ended up in a hospital in Guam. They didn't do much there either, never sewed me up. I wasn't disabled so I was lucky. Guys were like that, some were lucky, some weren't.

By Dammit, We're Marines!

After a bit I was assigned to another company in charge of a machine gun platoon. That was the 21st Marines. On Guam we were training to invade Japan. We were supposed to be the lead regiment actually under General MacArthur. According to the reports that have come out since, we were going to be one of the first troops to head up the invasion, although we knew nothing at the time. We were on a two day training mission and came back in to camp about 5 o'clock in the afternoon. We were tired and dirty when we heard about the atomic bomb. Wow! Everybody celebrated—the whole camp. We broke out the beer and had a great time. The war was over a few days later. After that we just stayed on Guam, waiting our turn to return home. I never had any stress problems after the war, and rarely ever talked about it.

The Marine experience was a great thing. I learned leadership and how to take orders. I have no regrets, other than missing out on three or four years of normal youth. I was one of the very lucky ones, but I think that we were so young that we didn't ever seem to be worried about how things were going to turn out. I can't recall ever being scared that I would be killed, and I certainly never wrote to my parents about that. And I can't recall any of my friends who ever even brought the subject up.

I got married just before I was to be brought back as a captain to go to Korea, but I flunked my physical due to a bad back. My wife and I were married in 1950 and have three children, plus six grandchildren and one great-granddaughter. I still work, and am not interested in retiring at the age of 83. I still play tennis and walk the golf course, plus work out at the gym 4 days a week. Things could be worse!

* * *

Friends

I met with Mike Mervosh several times at Camp Pendleton in the NCO club named in his honor. The "Iron Mike" Room is filled with memorabilia including the Japanese sword and binoculars he mentions in his interview. Mike is a Marine's Marine.

During our times together, Mike spoke about the men he has known since his early days in the Marines. I met Glenn, Domenick and Peter at the 4th Marine Division reunion in Atlanta a few months later. Over a beer in Mike's hotel room with my tape recorder running, they shared not only their stories of war but of a friendship that has lasted over 63 years.

Peter Santoro was Mike's boxing coach at rest camp in Maui. Glenn Buzzard and Mike were two of the 31 survivors from the 240 men in C Company when the battle for Iwo Jima was over. Domenick Tutalo was the flamethrower attached to their unit.

The 31 survivors of C Company on Iwo Jima, March 1945.
Mike Mervosh top row, seventh from left. Glenn Buzzard
directly behind him.

Cpl. Glenn Buzzard
D and C Company, 1st Battalion, 24th Regiment, 4th Division

Glenn Buzzard, at the end of battle for Iwo Jima

My mother died when I was four during the Depression in 1930. My father made an arrangement with an old maid who kept a summer home near us, and I went to live in Cannonsburg, Pennsylvania, with her. Perry Como cut my hair for eight years. He lived there in Cannonsburg on Murdock Street.

I left high school in my sophomore year and went to work for a couple of months and then joined the Marine Corps. I just went up on Monday and left on Tuesday in August '42. I went in early, at 16. I was illegal. The day I enlisted, I just did it real quick. I decided I was going to do something. Why I chose the Marines, I really don't know. I was about a year behind a guy who went to Guadalcanal when the war broke out in '41, I think he was the biggest influence. They gave me a physical and I was OK that way. I was about six foot tall and only weighed 144 lbs, but I qualified and they said go home and get this piece of paper signed by my dad and the chief of police of the city, Chester, West Virginia, and I did. They said bring my birth certificate and I did. I gave them that piece of paper from the chief of police and my dad but kept the birth certificate in my pocket. Nobody said nothing so I said nothing. We stayed there overnight, I think, and the next day they put us

61

on a troop train to Parris Island. I didn't tell anybody I was 16. One day when we were pretty well through boot camp, the sergeant called me in and I figured, boy, something had happened because sergeants were God. They had new barracks built for us and his room was at the upper end of the barracks, closed off. So I stepped in there.

"Do you want to get out of the Marine Corps?" he asks.

"No," I said.

"OK." And that was the end of it. So I figured the paperwork caught up with him but they didn't say nothing and I didn't either.

We farmed and farmers are a little more advanced on common sense I suppose than most people. I didn't say they are any better but just more advanced on common sense things. That's why I probably didn't have any trouble in the Marine Corps. We had West Virginia guys and we had New York guys and they didn't get along. There was a lot of animosity between them, but it didn't bother me none. Nobody had any trouble with me. Some just didn't catch on as quickly as I did, and they had more trouble in the Marine Corps. If you don't go in there with the right attitude, you are going to have problems. But I didn't have any attitude at all.

We went to New River and we stayed there until they got enough men to make the first separate battalion and then they made the second battalion. Pete Santoro was in that. We went to Pendleton on a troop train and formed the 24th Regiment of the 4th Division.

I was a machine gunner all the way. Mike Mervosh was in C Company to start with and I became attached to him then. Every rifle company had a machine gun platoon, and he was in the machine gun platoon, in the C Company rifle company.

Roi-Namur was my first battle. Carl Cooper and Carmen Ramputi were two of the first killed in our outfit. Ramputi was the company clown. A great big Italian boy into trouble all the time. Cooper's brother was in our outfit, too. Howard Cooper came home after going through it all, but was killed in an auto wreck six weeks after getting home. We also had the Morriston brothers. In those days, it wasn't unusual to have brothers together. If one got killed, the other wouldn't want to go home.

We then went to Saipan where I was wounded by shrapnel. We were up on Mt. Tapochau, and the Japs counter-attacked with a banzai. They dropped mortar stuff in there, and I got hit with a piece of shrapnel, a big long piece. It was spent meaning it didn't have full force when it hit me, but it went up under my skin between the skin and the shoulder blade, the bone part. Adrian De Witt, another rifleman, pulled it out, put sulfa powder on me, and I caught a jeep back to the battalion aid station where they dressed it. I stayed overnight and came back up to the line the next day. The walking wounded.

After I came back up on line, Lt. Alexander Santilli, who was our platoon commander, was assigned to take his platoon to the left side of the skirmish line where we were getting a lot of fire. The Japs had that fortified; it was about 20-30 feet of tree growth right down to the water's edge. Santilli was three year all American football player for Fordham University. We were out in the open in a cane field, and about twenty people came out of those trees. They were women and children and the men were holding up babies, just little babies. That was a distraction and the interpreter was trying to talk to them, you know, 'comono wouna gay' crap. "Take it off," that's one of the Japanese phrases they taught us.

You had to get them undressed because the men would have grenades stuck under their clothes, and as soon as they got a chance, they would throw it at you. Not the women particularly, but the men had it available. Anyway, this was in a cane field and they had piles of cane they were harvesting like farmers do. All at once, one of the piles just opened up and there were men underneath it. They killed Santilli and they killed Sgt. Buller. They were shot within seconds of each other.

I don't know who else was hit but I knew those two personally. Sgt. W. W. Buller, I called him my big brother; not a whole lot older, but then everybody was older than me. I would say he was 24 years old at the time, and I was 17. I met him just out of boot camp. He'd sort of look after me, I'd say. I know I put on some pictures, "This is my brother while I was in the Marine Corps," but that is how I felt about him. He and Santilli were real good friends.

I had my machine gun and we carried it in a sling position for immediate fire; it was a Mickey Mouse thing but it worked. So I just took into that crowd of people and neutralized them, let's say. We eliminated that fire power that was coming at us, and we went back up on line with the rest of the guys and went on up to Marpi Point. That's the way you do it, you just work your way up.

We finished up and that was the end of it. We got to the other end of the island and that's all the resistance there was. We drove them right out into the water, literally. The Japanese soldiers threw the native women and kids over the cliff and jumped over after them. We had loudspeakers set up trying to talk them out of it, but they would get down over that cliff. If they were still alive, a soldier would go right out over the reef, right into the water, and would swim around and drown them. So we tried to kill the soldiers who were doing the drowning.

The Japanese put the fear in the natives that if the Marines get at them, they will rape and murder them. That's how they brainwashed them. It was no big effort for them to jump over and throw their kids over. The Marines who spoke Japanese pleaded with them. That was the end of Saipan. I was 18. We went to the beach where we had landed on D-Day and got aboard the Amtracs. The 4th Division went about four miles over water and made an assault landing on the island of Tinian. We secured the island on August 1, and on August 14 we boarded ship to Maui.

We were on Maui until February 1, 1945, taking on replacements and training them for combat. Twenty-eight percent of our original strength was lost on Saipan and Tinian. These new replacements had no combat experience. We were told when we got on board ship and left Maui that we were just going on maneuvers. We went over to Hawaii and had maneuvers and we then got back on the boat and we started sailing. We didn't know which way we were going, but we sailed for a day or two and then they started telling us we were going to Iwo. Well, where in the hell is Iwo? Nobody knew nothing. So they got the maps out and they showed us. We didn't know what to expect. I mean you never know. They can't tell you that.

I was still a machine gunner and I never deviated off that. We landed in about the eighth or ninth wave, I think. That really didn't make much difference because the first waves were laying there and we just ran over top of them. It was just devastating, that's all there was to it. The only thing that took us on further without being completely wiped out was pure raw guts and the fact that we weren't going to get kicked off there. We did what we had to do to survive, but we didn't take any prisoners. That's one thing that I never saw. Saipan or any place else. There was no room for that. No one wanted to be bothered with that. So we just did what we had to do.

We went to the right to the Quarry and places like that. On March 1, I got shelled again and about 10-12 guys were killed real quick. Otis Boxx was in the hole with me. The only thing left of his head was his lower jaw. That's gruesome but that's the facts. Jack Coutts was out before that barrage came in on us because he was hit in his legs. That's what we were trying to do, get him off this open area and into the hole with us. If we would have accomplished that, he would have probably been killed. We were trying to rescue him, but we were under heavy fire. We had tied canvas machine-gun belts together and threw them out to Coutts to try to get him to take a hold so we could pull him in. And then those shells hit us. The Japs had seen what we were doing and let us have it. Coutts survived and lived up until about a year or so ago in upstate New York.

I was pretty goofy, shell shocked, and I had a lot of their bodies on my dungarees. Somebody cut them off of me and put me in a clean pair that was handy I guess and they got me cleaned up a little bit. I can remember scraping the stuff off me. They took me back to the beach and put me on a boat and put me out on a hospital ship. They got me doctored up and put me in a sack over night, and I got to take a bath. I woke up and the first thing I remember was that I asked a corpsman where in the hell I was. He told me, so I went back to sleep. The next morning when I got up I asked him if I could have some clothes because I was in my skivvies and he gave me a set of dungarees. I went up on deck and they were bringing in more wounded. As they were bringing in the wounded, the boat would go back. I went down the ladder and onto the boat and went back up to C Company.

There was a lot of concussion. You don't hear much of it today but back in those days, concussion was a big thing. A shell goes off and it blows all the air out of an area. If you are in the area, then it blows your eardrums, it blows your stomach, and it blows everything. It was severe enough. I was shell shocked, that's all I was, but then I had shrapnel all up and down my left arm, up and down my left leg. They picked all that out on the boat. I had this finger torn up somehow. They doctored it, wrapped it, and it got to smelling and I wondered what the hell the stink was. Infection! I took off the bandage and I just left it bare open. Deetz the corpsman would dress it occasionally. They dressed us every day if you were wounded. They checked you every day; they'd get behind a stump where you couldn't get shot and looked at you and put sulfa powder on, whatever, and kept us going.

I finished the deal out. We left on the 26th. Thirty-six days we were on there but I was off overnight, that's all. We had a day or so before we went to the rear. I think the Army moved up to the front and was mopping up. We did a lot of mopping up in the back. I was almost 19 when I went home after Iwo. On Iwo, I was a PFC but I made corporal when we went back to Maui. Everybody in the platoon moved up but to make it special they'd fall us out on the parade deck back on Maui and they'd have a ceremony, blow smoke in your ear, you know, and you're a corporal.

I married in 1947 and have been married 60 years. I have five children, 12 grandchildren, and 12 great-grandchildren. That's what the count is now.

I went into farming first and became a caster, that's making sugar bowls, etc. out of liquid clay. It's a trade. I learned that through the G.I.

Bill. I took a course through Ohio State University Agricultural Department called "On the Job Training" for both of them, the farming and the casting. The government paid a portion and the employer paid a portion of my wages. At that time, that was the plans they had.

* * *

Sgt. Major Mike D. Mervosh, USMC (Ret.)
Platoon Sergeant, Machine Gun Section Leader,
C Company, 1st Battalion, 24th Marines, 4th Division

Mike D. Mervosh, wartime photo

My first pay in boot camp was a $20 bill after $10 was taken away for your bucket issue, your toilet articles, things they give you for cleaning up. It was the first $20 bill I ever owned, and I was eighteen years old. I didn't have it more than a day or so and felt I had to send it home. My mother was ever so grateful. While overseas in combat, I was promoted to PFC then corporal and got a few bucks more. When I made sharpshooter that was $3 more a month and a few more dollars I'd send home. I didn't need it, especially overseas. On Iwo Jima, I figured out most of us privates, PFCs were fighting for $1.53 a day. We didn't have hazardous duty pay, separation pay or anything like that. When I came home, I had about $300. With that money, I bought my mother a new stove and a washing machine. I still had money left over and that gave me a chance to marry John Hasara's sister. After the war when we returned home, he met my sister and I met his and we married each other's sisters. My wife always credits me that I saved her brother's life. I probably did on Saipan because I dragged him off that hill when

67

he was wounded by machine gun fire. I made up my mind to stay in the Marines when I got my first pay. Three meals a day, a sack to sleep in, and I got money like this. The Marines were, and years later still are, my life.

When I was a young kid and got into trouble with a broken arm, broken collar bone, my father would say, "Son, at the rate you're going you'll be lucky to reach the age of 21." He remembered that when I was overseas and he was sorry he ever said that. When I came home, he brought that up and said, "Thank God you're over 21 and made it."

Iwo Jima was the battle of all battles as far as I'm concerned. 'Course I was an old warhorse by that time...Roi-Namur, Saipan, Tinian. Our assignment was to land on Iwo on D-Day. Our mission in Charlie Company was to hit Blue Beach 2 which was on the extreme right. We were to head up to Airfield No. 2 to relieve and help out one of the battalions of the 25th Marines because they were getting beaten and battered. It was getting cold and the rains came down. The island hadn't had rain there in years. I think all the shelling brought the rains. We broke out our ponchos. The rain was bone chilling. It wasn't that hot, sweaty, humid, tropical climate like we had on Tinian and Saipan. It was cold and chilly and we weren't too acclimated to that type of weather because Iwo was in the northern Pacific. But that cold rain and the incoming fire kept us awake. That first night, we were hit with Willy Peter, white phosphorus, shells from the enemy. Without those ponchos, we would have had a heck of a lot more casualties. A lot of us did become casualties because the white phosphorus comes down and hits you and goes right through your skin. As we felt those pieces falling on the ponchos we threw our ponchos up to toss them off. It burned through those ponchos but that kind of helped. On the beach, it was all volcanic ash. Moving was so terrible, even us foot Marines were ankle deep in ash. Our vehicles were bogged down to their hubcaps. The tanks and artillery pieces couldn't move. Thank God in a way that we had volcanic ash because the artillery and mortar shells that hit that sand absorbed a lot of that shrapnel. If not, Marines would have taken it in their faces, their backs, legs and arms. In the end, volcanic ash embedded itself in our skin, faces, necks and hands but, hell, that's better than shrapnel.

That next morning, we went to the right flank and cleaned out the Boat Basin. That took several days and from there inch by inch, yard by yard, we ended up at the Quarry and Hill 362. For 36 days that's how it was. You'd gain forty, fifty yards a day, and that was tremendous. Objective areas were kind of erased more or less because of that intense, hectic, heavy enemy resistance. The island was so formidable and their defenses were unbeatable, but beat them we finally did because by dammit, we're Marines.

Our company was pretty well decimated. We didn't have any officers left, they were all casualties. I was the eighth company commander at one point on Iwo. There were no officers and I'm the senior non-com, so I take charge. No one told me to take charge. I took charge. It was a blessing when I got dozens of replacements for each platoon so we can fill up the gaps of the casualties. We had this BAR man and that was a blessing. He must have been on the island an hour or two. I had been there for two weeks and hadn't seen the enemy and they're shooting us all over the place. In mopping up, you always throw hand grenades, WP grenades. I should have used a hand grenade but instead I threw a smoke grenade in this cave entrance and four Japs came running out, choking. I was in a position kind of squatting there, and I caught the first one out. He had a big old saber, and he was going to crank that off right over my head so I shot him right in the face. I found out later on he was a Jap major. I thought I was going to get all four of them but my M-1 rifle jammed.

This replacement who was just a few yards away from me says, "They're Japs, they're Japs!" He had never seen Japs.

"I know they're Japs...kill them!" I yelled.

With his Browning automatic, he wiped them out. "Boy I've never seen any Japs!"

"Son, none of us have seen them on this island. You have got to be glad you've seen them."

"Hot dog!" he says.

He was happy. An hour, an hour and a half later, I lost him. I didn't even get to know his name. I should get to know their names right off but I had a dozen replacements. They tell you their names, but it's so busy and hectic you don't remember. I looked at his dog tags because I had to know who the heck he was because I didn't want him to go MIA. I didn't want any MIAs in my outfit.

The saber from that Japanese officer is in the display case at Camp Pendleton. Of course, I picked up many of those sabers on Saipan and Tinian when we had banzai attacks. We'd get half a dozen rifles and such, and we'd bring them aboard ship and give it to the sailors for a can of pears, a loaf of bread and can of juice.

The sailor says, "I got this on Iwo Jima."

He didn't say nothing about the Marine giving it to him for a can of pears!

On Iwo, I was 21 years old. We were anywhere from 17–21 and a few over 22, 23. You get a guy about 28, 29, 30 and we called him "Pop." And old Gunny Brengle, 40 years of age, he was really a "Pop."

Everyone loved him because he knew so much about tactics and life in general, and he knew his weapons. I remember the remark he made one day on Saipan because of the way we ate and the way we drank dirty water, and the elements and deprivation.

"Mike, if you live to my age, you will be doing great," he said.

"Gunny, if I live to my next birthday," I say, "I'll be doing great!"

We were trained on water discipline, one canteen of water to last you a whole day. I know times it got pretty desperate there. We had this steam condensing can which is a water can for our heavy machine gun. We'd hook up the hose to the jacket of the machine gun and while it's firing it cools the barrel. Of course that steam condensing can has all that cosmoline, a thick, greasy substance, in it. We'd use our dirty hankies to drain that cosmoline, and that water, if you want to call it that, is brown. But it's wet and I know we drank that.

Re-supply on Iwo? I didn't have to ask for water. I didn't have to ask for rations. I didn't have to ask for ammo. You know how we got it? Right off our casualties. After a while the men did it themselves. They didn't have to be told that he didn't need that ammunition, he didn't need C-rations in his pack, he didn't need his canteen, he's evacuated. That's how we re-supplied.

Now his weapon, if it was a better weapon, like a BAR, I'd tell the riflemen, "Right now you're a BAR man, disassemble your rifle, field strip it, bury it in the sand."

We didn't want the enemy to get that rifle, and we didn't want to carry an extra weapon. I had my rifle all the way through the battle, and they knew that if I became a casualty, they'd strip me.

I want to emphasize how we Marines coordinated things, how we exposed ourselves trying to find out where the fire was coming from those apertures, those pills boxes, those bunkers and caves. We had to suppress their fire with our fire to pin them down and get our demo man up there and throw a satchel charge and follow up with a flamethrower. Then we'd come up with our hand grenades.

I was hit with either artillery or mortar shell. They got me in the legs. My right leg was paining me more than my left, and I got a little piece of shrapnel in my stomach. I dressed myself right away, cut my pants leg with a K-bar, put sulfa powder on it. The corpsman gave me a morphine shot and he put a big M on my forehead. When he put that M on my forehead, it meant evacuation. I wiped that thing off because I was at the Quarry at that time and I could see the beach and the LCVPs and LVTs going back to the ships with the wounded getting blown out of the water. I thought, man, I'm not going to get on one of those boats and get blown out of the water.

If I'm going to die, I don't want to die that way. I'll die here where at least I can do something. Fortunately, we didn't move that much, otherwise if we had to do a lot of running, I couldn't lead my company any more. When you stay in the same foxhole for six days, you are not doing much moving. I was company commander and I had to lead but that morphine gave me a lot of good adrenaline. I did things that I thought later when I got off that morphine, man, I'm still around. I threw more hand grenades than I fired my rifle. I mean that's how hectic it was.

We were under intense artillery fire. We were moving ahead and I was still the company commander at that time. We got hit and naturally you jump for the biggest shell hole to get some cover. We were there I don't know how long.

"I'm getting the hell out of here," Cusimano says.

"Where in the hell are you going to go, it's landing all over," I said. "If you get out of this hole you're going to get killed, stay where you're at."

As soon as I said that BOOM! A mortar shell hit at the top of the parapet, six of us were in that hole and every one of them, including my future brother-in-law became a casualty except me. I don't know how long I was out, hours, minutes. I heard ringing and I heard angels singing, I thought I was dead but I opened my eyes and I'm alive. As soon as I opened my eyes I see this Marine right in front of me, DeNunzio. He's got a big gash on the back of his head, and just on instinct I ripped open his first aid packet and grabbed the sulfa powder, put it on the wound and bandaged him. We knew elementary first aid, stop the bleeding, protect the wound, and prevent shock---that much we knew. After the blast, I couldn't hear anything. I picked up old DeNunzio, got him back a couple of hundred yards and that's when corpsmen picked him up with stretchers and evacuated him. I figured DeNunzio was dead, died aboard ship. Didn't hear a thing about him. About 40 years later, I see him at the Baltimore reunion.

"Thank God you made Iwo," he said.

"Thank God you made it out!" I said, and twisted him around to look at the back of his head. "That's a pretty nice scar." He was bald-like, you know.

"Mike, if it wasn't for you I wouldn't be here."

"If it wasn't for those by damn Marines on Iwo Jima, I wouldn't be here!" When I was wounded and lost my hearing, I thought to myself, if

I lost a leg or an arm or even my eyesight I would still be coming out ahead on Iwo Jima. That's my feeling, no big deal. Hearing? What the heck, I gave arm and hand signals to my Marines, semaphore. After a few days or weeks pop! my hearing came back, thank God, and today I'm a little hard of hearing, double high frequency, no big deal. I can't hear women talk too well. When we go to reunions, we talk and fight the war over again. We remember things that happened 60 years ago, naturally you would, and almost word by word what we said in those days 60 years ago. The wives are there listening to this.

"You can remember," my wife said, "and they can remember what happened 60 years ago, but you can't remember what I said 60 minutes ago!"

Sgt.Oksendahl was one of the old timers and was one of the section leaders when I took over the platoon there. He was at the battle of Midway. Midway was tough. We were in the same foxhole after weeks on Iwo and he said, "All this stuff, all this mortar, I was at Midway with those 16 inch shells, 12 inch shells, planes bombing and it's no comparison to what we are having on Iwo. It's worse here than it was at Midway. This is really getting to me."

"We are not all going to die," I told him. "Some of us are going to make it."

He called me combat crazy. Even in the rest camp, they called me combat crazy

"I'm combat orientated, not combat crazy," I said.

I don't like being called that. Being a leader, you don't love it but you have to show leadership. Here we were in this foxhole and getting hit.

"This is not for me," he said.

He dug himself a hole straight down where he could stand and shoot his rifle. About six or seven hours after being pinned down, here comes a mortar shell, right smack on top of his head, right in that hole. His remains you could pick up with a shovel.

It seems like every Marine on that island was in the Amphitheater area, especially the 4th Marine Division. The whole northern part of the island looked like a minor earthquake. I'd never seen terrain like that. It looked like a lunar landscape, a mini Grand Canyon, crevices, ridges, what have you. Sometimes I couldn't distinguish between Hill 362 and 382 because it's only 20 feet difference. The heck of the part of it was it did give us some places where we could take cover and get behind those sand stones.

The Amphitheater was more of open ground and to get across that was intense. The Japs had every square yard covered. I know of one situation where we were being hit with artillery and mortar fire. We hugged up against the crevices to be less of a target. When I hugged up, BOOM! Something hit me in the back like a horse had kicked me or someone hit me with a baseball bat. Actually, it was either a mortar shell or an artillery fragment that hit me dead center in my pack and it tore up my pack and my C-rations and my binocular case. I'll tell you what, if I didn't have that pack on, and I could have moved a little better without it, I would have been a goner. I only used those binoculars once. I think I was in the Quarry area when the flag went up on Mt. Suribachi. I could sense something because we weren't getting any fire from the rear, it was kind of quiet. Maybe the 5th Marines secured that thing. At least they are fighting hand to hand over there to get a toehold. We got a rumor that the flag had been raised. I got the binoculars out of my pack and looked to see if it was our flag. I was looking for several seconds and bing, bing, bing, one round caught the side of my cartridge belt. My exhilaration wasn't at seeing the flag, my exhilaration was that these sons of bitches are poor shots. I only used those binoculars once, never again, but I kept them as a souvenir.

I brushed my teeth once, and I shaved twice. I dry shaved once because I wasn't going to use my water to shave and anyway you don't have time to shave. The second time I shaved was when we were secured. I didn't change my underwear, the bottoms; no way do you take your trousers off. I changed my skivvy shirt once because all I had was a change of underwear and a pair of socks so it wouldn't take too much room in the pack. I didn't take baths for weeks on Saipan. But this time, 36 days, I managed to take my shoes off once, got rid of those socks and put the other ones on and that was the extent of it.

But brushing my teeth? I used that toothbrush to clean my weapon. Man, you clean that weapon. Of course, with that volcanic ash and dust, you want to keep that clean. The M-1 rifle was pretty good. It's not as delicate as the M-16s we had in Viet Nam. We had a lot of malfunctions with the M-16s and they blamed it wasn't being cleaned properly. But we found out otherwise; it was the weapon itself. The M-1 was pretty reliable. After that one time when it jammed on me, that weapon got cleaned before me. Any time you had a lull, which was very sparse, the first thing you do is clean the weapon. I used that good ol' toothbrush and the paintbrush that I had in my kit there, a rag and a little can of oil.

Afraid? I would say, afraid of what? What are you going to be afraid of, for crying out loud? I felt pretty secure because these Marines were just so tremendous in their attitude and everything like that. No matter what I told them to do, they did. How could I be afraid when they didn't seem like they're afraid even though they may be? You hear a lot about fear in combat, heck, my fear would be if I was hopeless or out there alone and didn't have a chance because there were no Marines around, maybe I'd have some fear. But here are my Marines and they're so get up and go. Adrenaline is going and when it shoots in, fear leaves you. I'll put it this way, we all wanted to live, but we weren't afraid to die. We knew we fought on Japanese homeland, the last bastion before the big one in Japan. We knew that our families, my brother and sister, and our country are pretty well safe and that is what we are here for. That's the way I felt.

We were still eating C-rations even though the island was secure. I didn't have my real first hot meal until I got aboard ship. We lost a lot of weight, our stomachs shrunk, and we were breaking out with little infections because of the embedded ash, but that was nothing. There is always humor in battle. Coming up that cargo net was really tough because we were so weak. Sailors helped the Marines the last few feet grabbing them by the arm to get them over the railing. A sailor got me by the arms and I said, "Get away from me swabbie, I made it this far, I will do it on my own. I want to do it on my own, by dammit, we're Marines."

It was kind of sad to me because there were so few of us left out of the company. Where's Cusimano, where's DeNunzio? Where's Marston, where's Taylor, where's Buzzard, where's Miller? They're not here. It's sad, it's quiet. I didn't even want to take a bath. I didn't even take my clothes off. They assigned me my bunk rack and that was what I wanted to hit. I don't know how long I slept, I didn't care what time it was. I didn't know what day it was. That was immaterial. I was dead. Then I took my bath. I don't know when it was that we last had fresh water for baths, not salt-water baths, not salt-water soap, but fresh water and soap. The Navy was good to us for a change. I don't know how many times I washed my head. I went back in the rack again and slept some more. The trip took weeks to get back to Maui. Aboard ship the first few days they let us go, let us relax and rest up. After that, it was normal routine, rifle inspections, clean up, schooling, physical exercise, everything like that. The best you can do aboard ship. Of course, the chow lines were so long that by the time I ate breakfast, I'd go back in line for lunch. That's why I got a lot of reading done. I could read a whole novel by the time I waited for lunch! The fact is we were stacked four to five decks below the main deck of the ship. The bunks were about a foot apart and about five or six stacked high, and naturally, when you turned in your sleep you would hit the guy on top of you. My pack was my pillow and my life jacket was my pillow. But it was so hot down there, so sticky, muggy, no air conditioning. All those troops down there made it even hotter. When making a head call, you had to go up two sets of ladders because we didn't have a head on our deck. Waking up at 3 or 4 in the morning to make a head call, having to climb two sets of ladders and back down again, oh boy, that was fun!

Back on Maui, they let us rest for a while until we got our replacements and we got re-supplied and all us old timers were training our replacements. Then it was always training and training for the big one, Japanese homeland. Two A-bombs later and the rest is history.

I would like to give a lot of credit to the 240 Marines of C Company, 1st Battalion, 24th Marines, of the 4th Division who landed on Iwo Jima on D-Day. Only 31 of us survived. Half of us were the walking wounded so the other half was pretty lucky. They had some scratches, every one had nicks. I still had pieces of shrapnel in the back of my head. As far as I was concerned, every one of those who survived in today's standards would have received at least a Silver Star. All they got was a Purple Heart. None of them got any kind of medal for valor or heroism but to me they are all heroes. We never looked at it that way because there were so many unselfish acts of bravery. The ones who are real heroes are the ones who never came back.

People ask me, "How many medals did you get on Iwo Jima?"

I say, "I got five—two arms, two legs, and one head." Those were my medals.

I fought in three wars. I was in my late 60's when Desert Shield was building up. I wrote letters, made calls to Headquarters Marine Corps, saying I wanted to go on active duty. I got a lot of combat experience. No response.

I finally got a call from Col. Jan Huly, he's a Lt. General now and he said, "We read your record, Mike, you got a beautiful combat record, but we looked at your date of birth and we thought we should give the youngsters a chance."

"Look, I can save lives," I said. "I got one more good war left in me, get me in there!" A week later, I got a letter from HQMC and I smiled to my wife and said, "This is it, I got orders." Unfortunately, it was a beautiful letter of regrets.

* * *

PFC Peter Santoro
G Company, 2nd Battalion, 24th Marines, 4th Division

Pete Santoro, wartime photo.

I was born in Norwood, Massachusetts, twenty miles south of Boston, on January 22, 1917. I'm the youngest of 10 children, five boys and five girls, and they all lived to be over 80.

I served three years in the Army National Guard, then received an honorable discharge in 1940. Then the war broke out and since you are in the reserves for 10 years, I thought I would get papers to report in the Army.

"Now you got to go in the Army. It's war," my father said.

But I enlisted in the Marines. You know why? My father and mother came from Italy. I'm Italian, full blooded. During WWII, my mother and father had relatives fighting in Mussolini's army who were fighting against us through Hitler. I had relatives in Salerno, Anzio.

"Go ahead, go kill your cousins," my dad said.

I couldn't do that, so I went to the Marine Corps recruiting office in Boston.

"No, you got to go into the Army, lad," a colonel said.

"I know I have to but I don't want to," I said.

"Why?"

"I don't want to be shooting my own cousins. I have relatives fighting in Mussolini's army and I'll be up against one of them, you know."

"Oh I understand," he says, "so join the Marines."

I joined in November '42 got out in '45. I was 26 years old in boot camp. I was PFC on Iwo and throughout the whole war. Two years overseas, one year in the states. That was it.

I talked to some fellas from one of my Army outfits from New England who went to Salerno and Anzio, and they talked about all the Italian girls they met. I said I hadn't seen a white woman for two years. I was on Roi-Namur, Saipan, Tinian, and Iwo Jima as a rifleman. I got my PFC stripe after the Marshall Islands. I got my first stripe, a hash mark, before I got my PFC stripe. I got hash marks for 4 years of service. I did three years in the Army National Guard and one in the Marines.

Mike Mervosh and I were on the boxing team. I was the trainer. In 1938, I was the New England States Heavyweight boxing champion. The first thing they told me in boot camp, "Don't hit nobody!"

Then during the war in the Pacific, back on Maui, we had a boxing team. I brought Mike in, he was with another battalion so that's how we got together and we've been together ever since. He was the middleweight champion of the Division.

What did I expect on Iwo? I expected to get shot! It was a nightmare. You wouldn't see anything, but the Japs would shoot at you. The bullets came at you, one round then another round.

When we went in, the boat next to me got a direct hit from a mortar shell or something; bodies flying all over the place. The Japs let the first wave in, then they started shooting us. I was in the second wave. With the second wave, they were shooting us before we came in. Our boat got in all right, but they didn't welcome us too well.

We were supposed to take the airfield the first day up there. It took us all day to get up there much less take it. The next day we secured it. Meanwhile we got hit left and right. They said Iwo would be a piece of cake. We really didn't think it was a piece of cake but just another operation. It didn't turn out that way.

We landed and the Japanese zeroed in on us. I was in G Company, but the Japanese zeroed in on F Company. F Company was getting hit left and right. The Japanese knew where they were but they didn't know where G Company was. We needed a few men to knock out the Jap position on a hill, so I was one of them. I'm not going to go in a group, though, because the Japs would wipe us all out as we went over this hill. So I went around and met them on the other side of this hill. When I looked down from the side of the hill, there were two Japs coming out. I was over the entrance to the tunnel and I didn't know it. Two Japs and me with a rifle. Of course I had to shoot them in the back; I didn't know how to say "turn around" in Japanese. At that close, you didn't even have to aim, but I hit them.

I was waiting for more to come out, but I shot those two and I guess any more were smarter than that. I know one ran back in again. Then the captain comes around the hill. He didn't see me up there and he shoots them again.

"They're already dead, I got them," I said.

He throws a hand grenade inside, BOOM! "OK, let's move on, move up."

He got the Medal of Honor for shooting two Japs I already shot. He's a good man, though, a good leader.

Then a Jap sniper got me. I got shot in the back, the bullet hit a belt with ammunition and went through a clip and that's what saved me. It got me near the spine and I couldn't move my legs. I was carried off to the hospital ship but I didn't stay on the ship for long. They needed men so I went back in.

I was waiting at a first aid station and talking to the corpsman who said there's a guy down there from your area named Murphy. He's a beach master. I knew him. I went to school with him. He's a lieutenant. So I went over to Murphy. We're talking and we saw the ground crew from the P-51 Mustangs that were going to come in. Of course, the ground crew came in first to put up the tents, cooking facilities for the pilots, stuff like that. They were putting up sand bags here.

"What's with the sand bags?" I ask.

There was a sniper and he was getting one guy every night, about 5 o'clock, something like that, one shot, one guy got dead. It would be one of the guys from the ground crew for the airfield, or a Marine.

So I says to him, "The Jap can't be here where we are and he can't be running across the field to shoot and go back or he'd be seen, so he's got to be hiding between those big rocks. The lights between the rocks."

The bombing had blown up all the lights on the airfield into a heap of pipes and poles. I walked up the hill in the sand, they called it sand, it was ash, volcanic ash, not sand. "Go over there and gimme a rifle; I'm going to get that sonofabitch."

So I test fired the rifle to make sure it was good. A little Japanese guy between those big rocks has gotta look both ways across the airfield, so I walked up to the end and I sat there at the edge of the airfield where I looked just one way down the airfield and I could see the whole thing. I was sitting between two big stones with Mt. Suribachi to my right. I stayed there for just about an hour, an hour and a half, maybe two. It got dusk so I waited a little longer. Sure as hell, I saw something move. A head would come up, no helmet, just twigs. I think, yeah, that's it.

He was coming out of a big barrel, a fifty-gallon barrel, it's covered with twigs. I was sitting down and had my rifle aimed and half his head came up but I want to waituntil his whole head comes up. Then the whole head comes up, and I blew half his face off, BOOM! It was a 30 aught six, one shot, BOOM! I went over there to look in and he was dead. Guys came running up.

"I got him, I got him!" I yelled.

They knew a Marine was looking for him and then they'd yell back, "The Marine got him!"

Some guys came out and wanted souvenirs of the rifle and stuff like that. I decided to go back to my men.

"What are you doing back here? You were wounded," my captain asks me.

"Yeah, I went back to the first aid station." I told him about how I shot the Jap. "I want to shoot some more!"

He took a look at the bandages on my back and said, "You can't fight like this." The bullet was still in me. Meanwhile I shot another Jap between some other rocks.

Medal of Honor recipient Joseph J. McCarthy from Chicago, our company commander, led us until we both got wounded. Anyway, he put me in charge of the ammunition dump because of my back and I had this young fella, Larry Beaudrow, with me. At the base camp on Maui before we went to Iwo, he was on our baseball team. He played in high school and signed a contract to play for the Boston Braves. Oh, he was handsome and he played good baseball. I told him we had a baseball team and he said, "Yeah I know."

I told Ace about the guy and he asks, "What does he play?"

"Shortstop," I says.

"Jeez, I could use a good shortstop," Ace says.

A couple of games went by, a couple of weeks, and I asked Ace, "Hey, how's my boy doing?"

"That kid is good, not one ball gets by him, and can he hit! No wonder the Braves have him signed up."

Beaudrow was killed when the Japs blew up the ammunition dump. He got shrapnel that cut half his face. I got a concussion out of it and was spitting blood. I couldn't hear for hours. That was it; off I go again. I walked this time to the first aid station on the beach. I knew where it was. They told us they would make a trip to Guam, unload, and come back. I went back on the ship.

"Hey, you were on here before," the guy says. "You're not going to get off this time." I was evacuated on the tenth, twelfth day or so on Iwo. There were 347 Marines in my unit but at the end of the fighting, there were only 35 left.

On Guam they had Quonset hut hospitals there for the wounded from the battle. That's where they took the bullet out of my back. They took X-rays, saw where it was, laid me on a table, put in a needle of Lidocaine then they start cutting. Cut, cut, clonk, clonk sounding as the Doc put the pieces in a can.

A corpsman standing by asks me, "Can you feel that?"

I looked at him, "I better not!"

The Doc had a big round can, like a peanut can, full of shot he took out of Marines. He was going to bring it back to his office when he went back to his practice.

I went back to Honolulu and stayed in the hospital. From there I went back aboard another ship, a cruise ship that was a converted hospital ship. We sailed from Honolulu to Treasure Island, San Francisco, to San Diego. Then they put us in hospital cars behind a train. Each car had a male nurse. A car would be let off in Houston, then the next car was let off in New Orleans, then the next car up in New York. The last car stopped in Boston. I was on the last car.

I had no girlfriend when I got back. I met my girlfriend, Marie, in a skating rink. She was beautiful. We were married nearly fifty years when she died of cancer. We had five children, one girl and four boys, six grandchildren and five great grandchildren.

* * *

Pvt. Domenick P. Tutalo
C Company, 1st Battalion, 24th Marines, 4th Division

Domenick Tutalo, 1943

I was a Selective Service volunteer and I requested the Marines. I was 18 when I joined. I didn't graduate high school. One minute my parents were undecided about me joining; the next they went along with it. A bunch of my family was in the Marines. That's what made me actually join.

When I first got out of boot camp, they put me in the Philadelphia Navy Yard. I didn't want to stay there because everyone was going into combat. At that time, everybody wanted to get into battle. I wanted to get into the battle, too. Crazy at that time.

So I got transferred and I came to New River, North Carolina, and I was put into the 3rd Provisional Marine Detachment on Maui and we set up the camp for the 4th Division.

When we went to Maui, we went straight into working at the camps, just taking care of the camps. One of my cousins took care of the generator for the lights of the camp and the other one was with the 4th so that's why I wanted to be in the 4th. Actually three of my cousins were in the 4th. C Company was looking for machine gunners so I requested that and they put me in it. I got to know the fellas in there and Sgt. Harry Koff was looking for men for demolition and flamethrowers so I got out of machine guns and got into that.

I couldn't tell you why I chose to become a demolition man and flamethrower. The training was very rough. You continuously had to work with explosives and the flamethrower together. They'd train us on explosives, blowing up different things. Whatever you were called to do, you would do. You had to be equally trained in both.

The guy that was head of the demolition unit was my size, about 5'5". I don't know exactly, but I guess the equipment weighed about 60-70 pounds. I weighed 126, but those days I was a lot stronger than I am now. I was 19 then. At that time, it wasn't that heavy. You're carrying a tank of napalm but actually, at that time, you don't think it's dangerous. Your mind doesn't think about that.

Iwo was my only battle. I had just turned 20 a week or so before. I couldn't tell you what wave I was in, but it was one of the first ones. We were on the right flank and went towards the Boat Basin, Quarry and the Cliffs. That was very rough. There were a lot of snipers and a lot of pillboxes on the way up. You really couldn't see them. Some you could see, some you couldn't. When somebody got pinned down by a cave or something, the demolitions went for the cave. It was mainly cave work, satchel charges that you had to try to get into the cave.

You never know what to expect. It was supposed to be just a three or four-day operation. Just go in and get out. But it didn't work out like that. Actually we were in training for that one battle for eight months, I would say, on Hawaii. The training helped but you never know. The Lord has to be with you because no matter how good you are, when it's your time, it's your time. It wasn't my time. I was never injured. Why? I don't know. I was there the whole time.

There were a lot of casualties in my unit, every day, all day long, all night long. I remember one time there was about 12 guys in the squad and everybody got killed but me and the sergeant. The platoon leader got shot through the head. The bullet went through his helmet. That's why I said sometimes a lot of things went blank. It's hard to talk about battles.

We couldn't see the flag-raising from where we were. We heard it was up but I couldn't see it. If you had binoculars, you might have been able to. You slept whenever you could. Sometimes you stayed awake and sometimes somebody watched for you. You got shuteye any time you could. I can't explain it, but it wasn't like sleeping. You are always on alert, you are always moving. All we had was K-rations. We did run out of food and they tried to re-supply us whenever they could.

One of my cousins was on Iwo. I didn't see him on Iwo because he was with the 14th Regiment. My other cousin got killed on Roi-Namur and he got the Navy Cross, James Zarrillo. I heard about it right away.

By Dammit, We're Marines!

Happiness was what I felt when I left Iwo Jima. We had to wait for the first ships that came in. I don't remember it that great, but there's one thing that always stuck in my mind. Our commander in charge made sure we shaved, washed up and shaved. He insisted we all get a clean shave. That stuck in my mind for some reason. I guess it was for the cleanliness, you couldn't wash or nothing while you were there, but if you have a heavy beard, it grew. But he didn't want any beards or nothing like that. I made it up the cargo nets; no swabbie helped me.

We left Iwo and went right to Maui. I was promoted from private to PFC, and got $4 more a month. We were supposed to go right from Iwo Jima straight to Okinawa, but they sent us back to Maui because we were shot up too much. We just had to go back there and get replacements and get reorganized.

I heard about the war being over when we were on Maui. We were happy. We didn't have a celebration. They might have given us a couple of cans of beer but there was no town where we could have gone to celebrate. The war was over and they told us if we had 80 points, we could go home. So everyone who had 80 points were the first ones to leave the island. I had about 90, so I was all right. You got points for how many months, years, you were in the service, and you got points for battle. We had to go to San Diego first then they gave us a 30-day pass to go home, a furlough, and from there I had to report to Quantico, Virginia, to be discharged. They gave you a full medical and stuff like that, and then they gave you a discharge.

I was discharged in 1945. I adjusted pretty well when I got home. I had to go to work, that was the main thing. I just had to get a job. I married a couple of years later and we will be married 59 years. We have three children, 11 grandchildren.

* * *

Family

Having grown up in different parts of the country, cousins Angelo and Frank Dugo barely knew each other. A random meeting aboard ship brought the two together for a short time.

Staff Sgt. Angelo M. Dugo
Combat Photographer, 9th Marines, 3rd Marine Division

Angelo, left, with cousin Frank aboard ship to New Zealand 1943

I was interested in photography so I came to Los Angeles, California, and went to visit a photographer and told him I needed a job. I didn't care if he paid me or not, I wanted to learn. I had a Speed Graphic camera. That's the big camera the old photographers used to use; the best camera ever made.

Then the war broke out. I told the boss that I liked this job, it's what I always wanted, but I am trying to shoot universal newsreels. I'd love to shoot newsreels.

"Where are you going now?" he asked.

"There's a war going on," I said. "I'm going home and join up."

"Don't do that, you're going to get killed."

"You can't live forever. Those Japs pulled it, we're going to finish it."

By Dammit, We're Marines!

I liked deep sea diving so I looked at the Navy first, but I didn't like their uniforms so I went next door and the Marine said, "Ah good, here's a good man. We'll take him right now!"

So I lost a good job. It was February of '42, I was 24 years old.

I never did shoot newsreels. In fact, I didn't see a lot of my pictures until I saw some of the archives. I'd put finished rolls back in their cans and they'd be sent to Hawaii to be developed and censored. There's a lot of stuff that shouldn't be seen so they would censor first. If they thought the people could stand it, they would release them. My mother saved a lot of pictures that were photographed on Bougainville and when I got home she showed me. It said there "Photographed by Angelo Dugo."

I met my cousin Frank aboard ship when we were going to New Zealand. Frank was a good boy. We were just standing at a table having coffee, the two of us, and he said, "Man I hope this battle is over and we can get going home or do something. I'm getting tired."

"Just relax," I said. "If it's going to last five years, it's going to last five years. It all depends on the big shots and what they want."

We're standing there drinking coffee and a report came over the speaker, "Dugo, report to the quarterdeck."

So both of us automatically put down our coffee and started to walk out and we bumped at the end of the table. I asked him where he was going.

"Quarterdeck," he said.

"That's where I'm going," I said, "what's your name?"

"Frank, Frank Dugo."

"I'm Angelo Dugo, where are you from?"

"Chicago."

"What's your father's name?"

"Carmelo."

"Carmelo, that's my godfather's name!" I said. "Let's go and see what the captain wants." So we started up the steps and got up there.

"Dugo, go get your camera," the captain said. "I got the Admiral and I want you to take a picture of him."

So Frank went one way and I went another way, and I went back up to take a picture. When I came back down, I looked for Frank again and went for coffee. I wanted to finish our talk. So that's when I met Frank. My father and Frank's father were brothers. I'll tell you one thing, war is hell.

Frank Dugo, second from right, on the Numa-Numa trail,
Bougainville. Official USMC photo by Angelo M. Dugo.

We spent a lot of time together on Bougainville. There's a shot I
took of Frank walking in the mud. Frank was the best man the Marines
ever had to shoot a mortar. He could put a mortar anywhere. You give
him the directions, so far north so far east and he's working the dials.
The fella's going to drop the shell in the pipe and when that shell left
that tube, it's going to flip right where Frank wants it. He never missed.
I think if the kid would have lived he would have got a Medal of Honor
because he was that good. I had some letters from him when I was in
the hospital. I had maybe six letters from Frank telling me how he was
doing and how he was getting along. Frank wrote me these long letters.
Frank never talked about his family. A good-hearted kid, everybody
liked him.

On Guadalcanal, we had a hospital where we used to go for a rest
and to take care of ourselves. The Marines turned the hospital over to
the Army and the Army was supposed to put guards all around because
we had patients, doctors and nurses in there. Well they didn't put the
guards up. The Japs came in one night, went in the hospital, bayoneted
nurses and killed the troops who were wounded; and killed all the
doctors. The general had me go in to photograph all of it.

He showed everybody and said, "No more prisoners. We are not
going to take anybody alive."

We had one mean general. We put up a big sign that said "Kill The Bastards."

"Dugo, you go get a picture of it before we tear it down," he said.

"No let's leave it, let's show 'em what the Army did; that's the Army's fault, leave it up."

So we left it and when the Seabees moved in they moved the sign and put it up on two coconut trees, you had to walk or drive through it.

"KILL THE BASTARDS! Down this road marched one of the regiments of the United States Army, knights serving the queen of battles. Twenty of their wounded in litters were bayoneted, shot or clubbed by the yellowbellies. KILL THE BASTARDS!"
Photo by Angelo M. Dugo.

On Bougainville it rained day in and day out. We were there 72-73 days in battle. Rained all the time. It was raining when we left. That was the most miserable island in the whole chain. It was the biggest island and it was long so the Seabees put up a landing strip. They had to pull up maybe 40 acres of coconut trees that belonged to Lever Brothers Soap Company who owned all the coconuts out there. Then the U.S. government had to pay $15 apiece for every tree that was damaged and the Army counted them all.

Our clothes would rot on us. Once in a while, I took one of my shirts, washed it, hung it up and when it was just getting dry, it rained. I left it out all night and in the morning it was still damp. I thought dammit, I wish it would dry. When I went to pick it up, it fell apart. It just rotted. But one thing, when the sun did come out it was about 120 degrees, but it never felt like that.

I did everything on Bougainville. When it rained, I was a scout and observer and would go on patrols. I always volunteered for it because I didn't want to stand around. I photographed 90% of Bougainville. I didn't do much firing. I didn't carry a rifle when I was on duty with them. I had a pistol, but I had two hands with two cameras. I had three cameras one time and then you're really not able to shoot. If a Jap comes up to you, you're dead. I was lucky.

I did a lot of guard duty. At night we have a perimeter and our officers are in the middle. You don't talk at night and you don't shoot at night. You use your bayonet or knife if a Jap comes in. You don't answer them or anything. They would start up at night

They'd say, "You die Maline, you die Maline." They can't pronounce their 'r's so they said Maline. The colonel gave advice, "You don't answer them. Remember that or you'll put the whole company in trouble."

So nobody answered them. We wanted to talk like hell but we didn't. They never breached the perimeter. If you answered you'd have a banzai attack and that's dangerous.

They'd start mortars coming in which killed lots of good people. I was on an outer perimeter when a bomb hit a tree maybe 250-300 feet tall. Our artillery coming over hit that tree and it came right down, raised me up, dropped me and the only shrapnel I had was stuck in my hand. Hurt like hell. That happened at 2 o'clock in the morning and I laid there in blood and wet, raining like hell, and I thought I'd probably die in the morning. I was a fatalist, I believe. They couldn't move me at night because they'd get shot so they took me out in the morning. I had a combat photographer friend, Pete Pavone, a hell of a good buddy from New York. He took me in and laid me in the hospital bed. And this damn doctor thought I had a bad case of malaria.

Old Pete says, "Doc why don't you look at him?"

So he told the corpsman to take an x-ray of my back. Never did get the x-ray taken. All you have to do is feel my back and you can feel the bones crushing in there, they don't hurt but the corpsman said that's your nerve center, all your nerves are back there. That night it was starting to get dark and I told Pete to go up to my hole up there and get me some clothes. I put them on and left the hospital. About 10 days later we left Bougainville and I got to Guadalcanal to see a doctor. He asked, "Who released you?"

I said nobody ever released me. I just released myself. I'm still waiting for a back x-ray. I told him I was blown up and laid up in the field all night from 2 o'clock on and in the morning they took me to a doctor who told me I had malaria.

He was shaking his head and so who comes in? That same doctor and he says to me, "What are you doing here? You were on your way home."

I said that I wouldn't leave my buddies; we've been together for four years. I wouldn't leave them. No way. I never did get my shoulder fixed. My mother and father never knew what happened to me. I wouldn't tell them.

I didn't get to Iwo Jima. I was on a hospital ship coming back to the United States. I was bleeding inside and they were going to try to find out what happened. Still didn't find anything. I was in the hospital in Oakland when I heard Frank died.

There's a fellow at the Smithsonian who called me recently asking me if I had some pictures of the Navajo Code Talkers. I told him I got one that's outstanding. He said they're making a display for the Code Talkers that's going state to state and wanted to buy some of my pictures.

"These boys, I ate with them," I said, "I slept with them and you want me to sell the pictures to you? I'll donate them, how's that?" If you would have seen them work out there, they are the best damn Marines I'd ever seen. The Code Talkers went up in the jungle, and I went with them a couple of times, stayed with them, guarded them. They'd have their radios and were out there decoding. The Japs couldn't break the code. That was the best thing we ever had.

I photographed a lot of the Code Talkers. I always carried my Speed Graphic. I brought that thing along like a lunch pail. The photograph I sent to the Smithsonian was of four Indian brothers. We were in this New Zealand building that had a stage and they were going to perform a dance. The guy from the Smithsonian called me again and said to send him three more. I asked him what in the hell was he doing with them. He said they were making a bronze display of that photograph and needed pictures from all angles. The Code Talkers were damn good Marines.

I have a bracelet that one of the Code Talkers made for me. He took a piece of aluminum from a wrecked Jap plane and cut it to fit my wrist. He didn't have any tools; all he used was a nail and a rock. He sat there and punched in '3rd Marine Division, USMC Staff Sgt Angelo Dugo.' It took him a couple of days to do it.

I was discharged in 1946. I came home and was a policeman for 30 years. When I got about 70 years old I started talking about the war and then I started working on my negatives. And it brought back memories and all that.

The other day I got a book from the archives with my pictures. My photos all around the Code Talkers were in there. I was wondering if they were going to use them. A lot of the photos are coming out from the archives. I sure would like to see my films. I had a 16 mm Bell and Howe with a little telephoto on it, a regular lens and a wide angle. I used mostly telephoto because it brings it up closer. I have that camera at home. And I got the 35 mm, still working good.

Navajo Dance, New Zealand.
Photo by Angelo M. Dugo

Cpl. Frank P. Dugo

A Company, 1st Battalion, 21st Marines, 3rd Marine Division

The chance meeting aboard the ship to New Zealand developed into a close friendship between the cousins. Often the subject of Angelo's wartime photos, Frank's boyish smile hid the physical and emotional toll the years of combat had taken.

Like other young Marines, Frank wrote his parents not to worry about him...he was lucky...he'd be coming home. These are the letters he wrote to his family.

Frank Dugo on Bougainville, November 1943.
Photo by Angelo M. Dugo

Guam, undated

To folks

Knowing you're worried to death, I want to relieve you. Had quite a lot of close calls but I am still OK. I think I can say we're in a rugged campaign. We're in Guam and I hope to get home after this, heaven knows I rate and need it. Say hello to all and to Marie especially. Have had only a couple of letters in weeks and one was from New Zealand. They received your package and the pipe must have been swell for that's all I heard. They were well pleased and so was I. England will be home soon. He wasn't as lucky as your son or is it vice versa. The climate here is OK & we are regaining one of our ex-Islands. Faith in your son for he will come out ok & soon.

All my love to all, Frank

August 3, 1944. Guam

To Folks.

Have your V mail of July seventeenth. Well if the Japs take many more beatings like on Guam this war will soon be over. Had a lot of close calls and I do mean close—got two Japs with my pistol, one blew himself up with a grenade when I had him cornered—messy. We got hundreds with our mortar and I can't see how I'm still here but it's always the guy next to me and I hope it stays so. I'm in fine health but I've never been so pressed and tired in all my life—five days and nights with about two hours sleep. I don't think England was hurt so bad. Mike Whalen was only hit lightly. I also will wear a purple heart but only for very slight shrapnel cuts & a couple of burns from the mortar.

All my love, Frank.

By Dammit, We're Marines!

August 12, 1944, Guam

Good morning.

For the second time yours truly slept dry. Had a dumb asshole shoot a pistol thru his hand right next to me. Thanks be, the dope shot himself and not one of us. There's not much happening but I'd like it a lot safer. Some of the Chamorros—Guam natives—are pretty nice. They're also pretty pleasant. Did I tell you we ran into some Jap beer, wine, sake, and real whisky? Also canned candy, salmon, octopus (not so bad) shrimp, etc, etc. For days we ate more, should say only Jap food. The beer is good and the whisky was the best I've had in two years. We've got a lot buried only it's twenty miles away and we're not free to travel yet. We'll get it though.

Adios to all. Love, Frank.

August 14, 1944 Guam

Well Folks,

I kind of have the time and may as well write a long one. My mail has only been fair, we expect to get our second-class mail soon and I hope so. I'm in good health although I know I'm ready to go home pronto. It's been three years of Marine Corps, and I'm fed up. I've seen more normal & sensible things done by three year olds.

The weather is pleasant on Guam but it rains at least one inch per twenty-four hours and the flies, ants and wood ticks here are in the billions. The natives are better than a lot of Americans in looks but they're nothing definite, some mix out of Jap, Chinese, Korean, native, Spanish, German and American. So far only a few have acted as scouts and other than that they've done nothing. I don't think there's one house or abode fit to live in without repairs. Talk about repairs, for twenty some days, we've been getting soaked and they wouldn't replace my leaky poncho or give La Porte one so we got about seven square feet of tin off a shack and put it over our hole, looks like we'll stay here for a few days then move into a permanent camp and put tents up. There will be stray Japs waltzing around here three months from now but all in all it's pretty safe. Enclosed are three pictures, one is Mt. Fuji and the other shows some nice cherry blossoms. # three must be a Geisha gal, eh? There's been a lot of nice things picked up here. I saw one of the prettiest rings. Even American money on those yellow So and So's.

Now here's what I think will pass the censor. Our platoon was in an amphibious tractor that pooped out about two hundred and fifty yards off the beach. Well that was sweet; we waded in thru artillery fire and got to a hot shore. We had about five hundred yards of beach to traverse & the artillery got the man before and behind me. We then waded up a river just full of wounded and dead. That's where England got hit in the neck & nearly drowned; it was a man from our platoon who pulled him out. He's back and he's perfectly ok. Well, that evening we dug in next to some tanks in a clearing so if needed we could fire our mortars. There's three of us dozing, couldn't sleep because the Jap artillery was trying to hit the tanks near us. Well as we'd never expected, three Japs somehow survived on the beach & being it was dark they ran by our hole. the middle one returns and pulls out a pistol.'Til he returned, I'd not moved, never thinking it was Japs, well I started to draw my pistol and he fired. He hit David Hallett low in the chest (not bad) and then ran. That one shot wasn't three inches from me & they were in the dark before I could fire. About this time Hallett woke up. "What's up?"

Well he tried to sit up and he then knew he was hurt. He was a man about it for he had to stay quiet and bear his pain all night. We called the corpsman but they wouldn't get out of their holes & I don't blame them for the artillery was all around us. Finally we got one of the tank men awake and they thought we were Japs so for one half hour we had to answer questions before they'd let one of us approach. Well they had some morphine and then, and only then, could we make Hallett painlessly comfortable. It was a shaky night with Dave thinking he was dying & me thinking he should already be dead trying to enlighten him & make him think he was just lightly wounded. Well that's the first day & night & was tame compared to most of the following days of which I hope soon to tell you about—more in this letter might scare you. Sometimes you wonder how your luck, good judgment and quick wit keeps you alive.

Well I'd better stop on this page or this will be the Guam Gazette. I hope you've a lot of letters on the way & that Marie gets a nice clean easy job. Say hello to my two sisters and give my best of regards to the old man. I've not heard from any of the boys. Arvid may be on Saipan if he's not gone home. I'll write whenever I get the facilities and now you can send the Parker fifty one pen out & maybe it'd be a good idea to send some ink for it and some light paper and envelopes similar to this. Adios for now & hope this finds you all in tiptop health and shape. I don't want you to go & worry too much for I'm determined as bloody hell to get home soon. You can bet your poke on that.

Love, your son, Frank.

February 17, 1945 [D-day minus 2 Iwo Jima]

Hi folks,

I'm big and easy writing you a V mail & also this letter... I'm not building up your hopes for nil because I will be home soon now. You may tell Gram to pray for her grandson's charm to remain as it has. I am feeling fine although my bowels still act up on long hikes or strenuous dooties! I had three seasick men in my squad and the sea is calm. PC Knerr wrote me & he'd seen Hallett, the boy who got shot in the lung on our last stinker. Well he lost his left lung and is to get a medical discharge. We are promised cooler weather which is natural. Heard on the radio that Tokyo is getting its due. Well that is the first of it and from here on up old Tojo and his slimy sons are going to get scrap metal a la carte.... The medals you saw in the pic are two dog tags, a St. Christopher medal, and my New Zealand green stone heart which is my good luck charm & that is no bunk. There's not much to say. This letter will be held til security deems its release so it will be a while before you folks get it. So it's still cold in Chicago, eh?

The Marine Corps got big hearted and gave all the squad leaders etc, a new Elgin wristwatch, fine time pieces, waterproof, etc. They only cost fourteen seventy-five if the individual loses them. I'm traveling light this time and I do mean light. The lighter you travel the faster you can duck and I'm an eggbeater in the right place...... Enough for now so with all my love and regards to all of you, I'll say adios for now.

Love, your son, Frank.

February 27, 1945 Iwo Jima

Hi again,

This is all of fifteen minutes later than the other. Wish I had a couple of the letters that are someplace waiting for me....We won't get mail here and I hope we are shortly back aboard ships for we need some cleaning up and chowing up. It is plenty hot here for it's a small place. Well the evening is setting in so good night, eh? Will write each time I get to relieve your tension. The boots are ok. Glad they came when they did. The size is trivial here. Adios for now and I hope you got my letter from aboard ship.

Love, your son, Frank.

———————

February 28, 1945 Iwo Jima

To folks,

This will readily explain why I've not been writing. I'll soon be able to write and I'll do so. All is fine as can be expected. The Japs have a bit different tactics, eh? Don't worry for I'm still dinkum. When this shindig is cooled down I think I'll drop by Chi. way. I'm sure you know I'm on Iwo Jima and it's a bit crowded. Now if the Nips would amscray! I shan't tell you not to worry but I will say, don't get gray hair. I'm getting mighty tired of this old game & I'm using care, caution & foxholes. Give my regards and health to Sis, Gram, Pa & all.

Adios for now,

Love, Frank.

———————

By Dammit, We're Marines!

The letters from Iwo Jima were the last he wrote and were received by his family after his death on March 2, 1945. He died from a bullet wound to the neck. For his actions on March 1, Frank received the Bronze Star posthumously. The award reads in part:

"Quick to act when an enemy counterattack overran his squad's position, Corporal Dugo carried four wounded men to safety through intense hostile small-arms and general fire and although fatally wounded in this action, staunchly refused evacuation until reorganization was completed and the position recovered from the Japanese. His steadfast loyalty to his comrades in the face of extreme peril and his fearless disregard for his own personal safety reflect the highest credit upon Corporal Dugo and the United States Naval Service. He gallantly gave his life in the service of his country."

Frank was evacuated off Iwo Jima but died aboard the hospital ship and buried at sea. He was 24 years old. The man he carried to safety survived. Frank's sister, Teresa Dugo Akers, still remembers the day the Marine knocked on their door and handed their mother the telegram informing her that her only son had been killed in action. She was overcome with tears.

Continuing the tradition started during World War I, mothers of those serving in the military placed a Blue Star Flag in their window. The Blue Star Flag became a symbol of love, sacrifice, and pride in the commitment of America's youth. Each flag reminded Americans of what they should do for the war effort to insure that a mother would see her son's safe return. The flag hung in the Dugo's front window, and, like thousands of other families, the blue star was replaced with a gold star when told of their son's death. After the war, the street the family lived on in Chicago was dedicated to Frank and a plaque placed above the street lamp.

* * *

Machine Gunners

Cpl. Edward L. Justice
Machine Gun Squad Leader F Company, 2nd Battalion,
27th Marines, 5th Division

What the Marines did in Belleau Wood in WWI still had people talking and that made me want to go in the Marines. A fella used to come down to see his mother about two doors down from my house in Montgomery, Alabama, and would stop to talk to us boys on the street. That was Holland M. Smith, who was later in charge of the operation on Iwo.

The Army made a movie about a parachute battalion, which I saw and I just got hooked. I tried to join that but my dad had been in WWI so he wasn't anxious for me to go to war. I was 20 at the time and of course the war had started and I was anxious to go. I kept after my dad about it and one day I went down and signed up for the Marines. When I was going through boot camp in San Diego, I read a bulletin that the Marines had paratroopers. I went up to see my drill instructor and he put me in. I went to Camp Gillespie right out of boot camp and I started parachute training.

At that time the paratroopers only had one battalion and they were hitting Tulagi, Gavutu and Guadalcanal as I recall. When they finished there they sent them to New Caledonia and that's when I joined them as a replacement. I was with the paratroopers out in the Solomons and I did some behind-the-lines operations with Dave Severance* on Bougainville. They were forming the regiments so they took all the machine gunners, which I was in at the time, and sent them to Weapons Company. We went back up to Guadalcanal, that was all secured, but went out on patrols I think just to refresh us new guys. We found out they were breaking up the paratroopers to form the 5th Division and they sent us back to Hilton, Hawaii. We couldn't see why they just didn't form it over there and save that boat trip back and forth.

We didn't know where we were going next until after we left Hawaii. We set sail, ended up in Saipan, and transferred over to LSTs. While we were going to Iwo, they explained to us about the island. We had seen photos and studied the island. When we hit that place it was like we had been there before. It gave you a weird feeling. You knew you hadn't been there, but everything looked so familiar.

By Dammit, We're Marines!

We were on the deck at daylight and we could look over and see the island. They found some drums out in the water and didn't know what purpose they were there for. We didn't know if the Japanese would blow them up to spread burning oil so we had to have fire retardant sprayed on all our clothes. We had burn salve on our faces. You could tell the guys that hit with the first, second or third wave because we still had that grease on our face and we looked funny. Of course it didn't help any in that sand because that sand would stick.

We got our gear and went down to where the Amtracs were. They'd crank those things up but didn't have the vents open to get the carbon dioxide out. Talk about getting sick! Guys started throwing up and with the roar of those engines nobody could hear anybody screaming all down in there. I guess somebody got the word and they started moving out but the boys were sick. Some passed out. We finally got out in the open, which was good. We were so loaded with ammunition and stuff that we were beginning to take on water so we had to throw some of our ammunition over the side to raise up a little bit. The battleships, destroyers were parallel to the island and were firing their guns one after another. We had to go around one of them to get back in the line. We'd get back underneath them and those guys would fire the guns. After they'd get through, they blew everything out of the barrel so we got all that sulfur smoke. We told the guy running our boat to speed this thing up.

We went in on the first wave and didn't encounter anything. We weren't where any drums were but it turned out they didn't have anything in them. We hit and rolled up on the beach. With some of the bigger Amtracs, the back end fell and you just ran off. Ours, we had to throw the stuff over and then jump over the side. One of the riflemen riding behind either tripped or fell, but this tank came upon him, right dab over him, smacked him down in the sand face first with his pack on. That tank rode on its belly anyway in that sand. When it went over him, we thought well he's our first dead. But he gets up and takes off just like nothing had happened. I'm sure his heart was in his throat and the adrenaline running and all.

I carried about 200 lbs as most all of us did. It wasn't our packs so much as it was our ammunition. Being I was the squad leader I thought I should take all the spare parts. The bolt of the 30-caliber machine gun itself weighed a lot and I was struggling with it. I also had four cans of ammunition which have 250 rounds in each one. You have a strap that comes across your neck and hooks on to them so you're not carrying it in your hands per se but you do have them to help out. When you go to fall you pitch them out so you can fall in the middle. All of the BARs and M-1s were choking up with sand because they're gas operated. The machine gun was spring operated so that was about the only thing that was operating at the time. We kept moving and we were told to get off that beach and get going because other waves were coming in behind us.

We were to go across, pivot and go up the island to the airport. The 28th went across, turned left and went up Suribachi. We were moving fast and we ran into little bunkers, hideouts, that the Japanese had made in camouflage so they could raise up, shoot and drop back down. We were able to get to those, but once in a while we got by one and it picked up on the next group coming in. I think we were across the island in about an hour. Now we wondered what to do. While we were sitting there and waiting, the Japanese started firing down from Suribachi. We were told to move out. We started on up the island. I think by noon we were where we were supposed to be by 3 or 3:30 so we stopped and were told to dig in, set up and wait and see.

When they told us to move forward, we started up and tried to take advantage of some of these trenches the Japanese had dug. We couldn't bend over to fit like they could so we had to crawl. I'm in front of the group crawling along the trench and as I look back, I'd come upon where one of them had just gone to the bathroom and it covered my hand and knee. I could have died. There's a shortage of water, so I can't use my canteen because I don't know when I'm going to get it filled up. I used sand to get it all off. Of course, the guys are laughing at me. People want to know what you remember about Iwo, well, that is something you don't forget. The guys shared some water with me so I could wash up a little bit.

It was about the fourth day and somebody made the comment, "Looks like we got a flag up on the mountain." We didn't know our troops were up there or not. I remember seeing the flag but I don't think we could make it out because we were that far up the island. Once in a while, we'd look back to watch the planes bombing and strafing the mountain. Other than that we were just busy looking the other way. We watched our right, left, and in front of us and figured that was somebody else's problem.

Moving from one spot and coming over to another one, we had been hit pretty heavy. There had been a hole dug out and it was about waist deep. Some of the men had been hit in there and been blown up. One guy was on his knees like he was looking over the side, and his head was cut off right at the shoulders. He was still in position and of course that was unnerving, a bad thing to see. We saw both dead Japanese and Marines because they just left them laying there because of the shelling. Seeing that affects different guys different ways. This wasn't my first battle. You don't want to see anybody dead. You hate to see anyone dead. But then again if you don't kill him, he'll be killing you.

We got up past the airfield and I hadn't lost any in my squad. I don't think in the whole section we had lost any. I was the first one to get hit in my squad and of course the second was this friend who came out with the corpsman to get me.

It was on the morning of the seventh day and we pulled in to relieve some other group who had pulled back up to higher ground. During this period we were looking down and this guy stood up and started waving. Everybody was ready to shoot until they found out he was one of our guys. Somehow he had been left down there and he had been hit. He was with E Company, so we went down and brought him back up. Then a runner came by and dropped these big red panels that we'd put out as spotters for the planes so they'd know where the lines are. We were supposed to get them out even with the lines or 50 yards ahead if we can. I grabbed them because I asked the guys to do so much and they had been pretty busy. I went out about 50 yards and placed the panels down and put sand on each corner so the wind wouldn't blow them. I just finished the last one and was ready to rise up when an artillery piece that had been shooting at us the night before honed in on me. It knocked me flat, but I was on my knees anyway. I didn't feel like I was hit. I looked and there were some trenches farther down and some shell holes right in front of me. I debated getting in one of those. I thought they were just firing for range now before they would lay down a barrage and I could sprint back up the hill and be there before they did that.

But they had their sights on me. I rose up on my knee and the next hit sent me flying through the air. I went to check and I could feel that something was wrong with my leg. I looked and it had already been blown off. They kept shooting but by that time I was on the ground. They would get the range then lay a barrage across, click up and then come back. I must have been in the right spot because I was in between those clicks and the shell would go over me or below me. Finally they quit so I went to crawling back up dragging that leg with me. I don't know how far I crawled but then they would shoot some more. By now I'm losing blood and my helmet feels like it weighs a ton so I tossed it off. Of course, by that time it seemed like an eternity. I kept inching my way on up and one of the guys in my squad came out and saw what had happened. Another guy comes out with the corpsman who real quick puts a tourniquet on and then they grab me under the arms and drag me up. A couple of guys get out of the foxhole and they drop me in. The Japanese fire again and hit the guy standing there who helped bring me up and hit the corpsman. I was anxious for him to give me a shot of morphine.

"Give me something and I will help patch you up," I said.

He pulled out his kit. I helped patch him up and he gave me a shot of morphine. I don't know how long it was until the stretcher bearers came. It happened to be a guy who had come over as a replacement when we were in Hawaii so he knew me. I'm sitting down in this hole, now covered up with sand from the artillery explosion while they tried to figure out how to get me out. I said to grab me under the arms and pull and they did. When they saw that leg, they dropped me. But they got me on the stretcher and ran back with me.

We got to the aid station--just another hole in the ground and Dr. Tom Brown took care of me. They had us all laid out there. Back then penicillin had just come out but we carried a little kit that had a sulfa tablet about the size of a silver dollar. They shoved that in your mouth but won't give you any water. In the meantime, they asked me questions, they're filling out forms, and I'm trying to mumble it out while passing out over and over again. The guys had put my leg on the stretcher so I didn't have to hold it. I guess my pant leg was what was holding it together. The corpsman came over and he was going to take the leg off, remove it, and I put up this squawk.

He goes to Dr. Brown who says "Look, get a piece of gauze or tape or something and wrap it around his other leg; they will take it away when he gets out to the ship. Don't argue with him. Let it go."

They put me on an amtrac and had us stacked on like cord wood. We got down to the beach and they transferred us over to a landing craft and stacked us on the same way. I'm still passing out and coming to. They got us out to the ship and had us all out there on the deck with the corpsmen taking care of us until they can get us in the operating room. I don't know how long I was there. Finally, I got into the operating room and these guys are cutting my clothes off. I still had a little .32 silver revolver my daddy gave me and had worn in my clothes as a side arm. Of course, when they saw that they panicked. They are supposed to take away any guns before they give any shots because it makes you incoherent but nobody knew I had it.

"We've got to have that," they said.

I reached for it and said, "The first guy who tries to take this I'm going to fill him full."

We talked to a lot of guys who had gone into the hospital and they never got their wallets or anything back they had on them, or if they did, they were empty. The doctor was called in.

"I'll never see it again." I told him. My wallet and stuff, I didn't care about that.

"Look, we are gentlemen and officers. I promise you when you leave this ship you will have the gun," the doctor said. "You might as well give it to us because you are going to go out when we operate on you."

There's nothing I could do. I asked the doctor if he could save the leg because I had read that they started experimenting with attaching limbs back on. That's one reason going through my head to put the gun down.

"We'll do what we can."

The whole middle section of my leg was gone. I have a civil mind, what will be, will be. If they can, they can. If they can't, then I'm not going to get too upset over it. I came out of the operation and looked down and saw the bandages and thought OK, that's the way it is, there's nothing to do. I had just turned 23. I set my mind then that I wasn't going to let it bother me. Every day, one of those sailors came up and wanted to buy that pistol. I told them all no and I thought I'd never see that pistol again.

We went back to Saipan and they pulled up to the dock, but those docks are right down on the water and the ships are up high. They pull the injured off on a boom and swing over and lower them. When they swung me over, one of the ends holding the stretcher came loose. I'm dangling there and they don't know what to do. They're afraid if they swing me back I'm going to slide off. I can't hold on to anything because I'm weak. I went from almost 200 lbs to under 100 lbs and there is no way I can hold on. They finally made a decision, which I overheard, just to start lowering me down. They had guys underneath there so in case it came down too fast they would grab it before it hit the ground. They did it steady and the guys caught it.

Here's a funny one for you. I'm leaving the Navy's care and the Army is taking over. The Navy guys had taken my pajamas and then at the last minute they turn and jerk the blanket off. I'm laying there with no clothes on so the Army had to come and put a blanket on me. I don't know if it happened in all cases but I talked to other guys and they went through something like that, not quite exposed out there like I was, but similar. They got ready to put me in the ambulance to take me up to the hospital when these two doctors came up and checked to see how I was doing because they saw what happened with the blanket. They had this little ditty bag and slipped it on the stretcher.

"Here's your gun. Don't pull it out at all or let anyone know you have it because they will take it away," he said.

Sure enough when I got to Saipan and got in the Army hospital, they came around to make sure there were no guns. If you do have one you're supposed to turn it over to ordinance. So I never said anything. Brought it back through Pearl Harbor, San Diego and into Philadelphia. I carried it all the way and nobody knew I had it. One of my sons has it now.

I went to the Navy hospital in Philadelphia for amputees. This is a huge hospital; they not only had the Marines and the Navy but they had some Army in there, too. I was with a group and we all had the same problem. Anybody you're talking to there has got a limb off, so that helps you. When I was in the hospital, I met my future wife, a Navy nurse. She was an officer and I was an enlisted man. I had a brother, a Navy pilot, who gave me some of his greens to go out in. I put those on with no stripes so no one knew my rank. The guys didn't know, but the nurses did. When we got married, the guys in the ward didn't have any gifts for us so they stole the stainless steel ware, sheets, pillowcases, blankets, all with USN on it and gave them to us.

I told my wife, "We can't take that, they'll lock us up, and we'll never get out."

"Well, we can't give it back," she said.

My wife and I had four boys and I was busy raising them. If you don't keep boys busy, they get in trouble. So between Scouts (the two older ones turned out to be Eagle Scouts) and Little League (I was a Little League manager for 20-25 years between the oldest and the youngest) and the YMCA sports, I was going like mad. This includes summers going to the High Sierras. With crutches, I can hike10-15 miles on the switchback with a 40 lb pack. We'd camp out for 10 days to 2 weeks. I spent a lot of time with my boys. It was difficult when my son enlisted in the Marines and went to Viet Nam. I didn't like the thought of him being shot at but I knew he knew how to take care of himself.

I came out of this good. I didn't have post traumatic stress syndrome. I don't know if it was my upbringing. I was brought up in the church and I believed in the Lord and believed He was on my side. I think that played a big part.

*Dave Severance was company commander of Easy Company that raised the flag on Iwo Jima.

* * *

Cpl. Dixon Porter
Machine Gunner, A Company,
21st Marines, 3rd Division

In 1943 when I was 15, it seemed to me that the war might be winding down, and I was scared to death that it would be over before I could kill someone. I had seen all those movies, *Back to Bataan, Guadalcanal Diary,* and those guys had so much fun killing people; I knew I just couldn't pass that up. Also, I'm part Chinese and I was a real racist. I wanted desperately to get in there and kill somebody, especially Japanese. I knew that if I got into the Marines my chances would be increased because Marines all went to the South Pacific.

I ran away from home, came to San Diego, and applied for Social Security under a false name, Dixon Porter. I was afraid my mother might have put out an all points bulletin so I changed my name and lied about my age. That was all the identification I had. I went to the draft board and started complaining about having to get drafted and go into the service. I complained so long and so loud they didn't even look at my ID. They passed me through the physical.

"Do you have a branch of service?" they asked me.

"Yes, the Marines," I said.

They didn't quite tie that together with a guy who didn't want to get drafted but I was hoping they wouldn't. I joined the Marines when I was 15 and went through boot camp and the advanced infantry at Camp Pendleton and shipped out to Guadalcanal.

I was assigned to the 21st Marines as a machine gunner. I wasn't on Guadalcanal more than a week or so when they called us down to the troop ships to invade Guam. I invaded Guam with the rest of my friends, and I made an epiphany. Killing people might be fun but it never occurred to me that they would be trying to kill me at the same time. The first time I heard shots go past my ear I began to wonder about my decision. Guam was not a tremendously intense operation, but it was tough. Our platoon of about 48 guys had two dozen casualties, three or four killed maybe 20 wounded.

We settled there on Guam and trained for whatever was coming next which happened to be Iwo Jima. We were told it was going to be tough, like Tarawa. It won't be a cakewalk like Guam. To me, Guam was not a cakewalk but I realized later on how right that description was. We were the reserve Division. We landed on Iwo on the third day and we went straight up the beach, no casualties, to about the middle of the island and turned north. We took the center where all the fun was.

The first day we had a dozen or so casualties and we could see it was going to be a nasty bit. The next day our company of roughly about 250 men and officers had about 100 casualties. About half the company was wiped out in a space of maybe three or four hours. Halfway through the next day we got replacements.

The word went around that they're raising the flag on Suribachi. I was very busy doing something so by the time I got around to looking, it was already up. It was a major event to everybody on that island. It really meant something because we knew how tough it had been getting up there. In the time that I was with the machine gun platoon, I developed really close relationships with some of the guys—Aloysia Joseph Piffkowski; our platoon sergeant, Alexander P. Dupnock; and my platoon leader Lt. Duncan R. Scott, the best man I have ever known. An ammo carrier in back of the second squad of a machine gun platoon doesn't normally establish a close relationship with the officers but he and I seemed to hit it off. He was from Illinois and I had been born in Illinois. The lieutenant was a bright guy, maybe 22 or 23, who had just graduated from college when he joined the Marines. There wasn't a man in our platoon who didn't like him as a fond uncle. He was without question a father figure for me and I loved him to pieces. When he got killed, it was probably the worst night of my life. I will never be able to get it out of my mind. I named my youngest son, Scott, after him. He was killed during one of the comparatively few banzai attacks that we had on Iwo. There were grenades flying in all directions and he had jumped down in the hole in front of me and was trying to direct fire at what he could hear. He couldn't see anything, as it was pitch black. A grenade landed right behind him.

I hollered, "Grenade" and ducked as it went off.

He didn't duck and it shredded his back…just shredded it…and he fell back into my hole and into my lap. About that time, the banzai attack petered out, and I sat there for about three hours trying to will him not to die. It was obvious the wound was mortal. I couldn't believe that Scotty could be killed. It just didn't compute. I knew by this time that I could be killed, but somehow he was not the kind of person who was supposed to die. When he did, I sat there and cried for about 4 or 5 hours, well beyond sunrise. I had been on Iwo about three weeks when this happened.

Some of the worst things are the clearest. Piffkowski got hit with a mortar shell that hit him on the back of his thigh. There was a crater that went from his knee up to his butt that looked like a watermelon that someone had scooped out. It was the most horrifying thing I have ever seen. He was laying there on his belly chatting with somebody else who was wounded and I talked to him briefly.

"You know you'll make it," I said.

"Yeah, I know," he says.

Well he didn't last 2 or 3 days. I remember Philpott got shot the same night Scotty died. His body lay there for 3 or 4 days, and the last day I went by they had covered him with a poncho. The breeze was blowing the poncho off, and his face was like a black basketball. He was totally unrecognizable except that he had Philpott on his uniform. Finally we had no officers and had no senior noncoms. I was in charge for a couple of hours until I got hit. All these men were knocked off one by one. Some of them had what was called combat fatigue. A lot of people didn't understand that. I did because I came very close to going over the edge myself.

I carried a shotgun which I had traded with a POW guard. I don't know what I gave him for it but it was a great weapon, a 12-gauge pump shotgun that fired eight rounds, and I used that at night. I also had a pistol and a bunch of grenades. I loved grenades—they keep people away from you. I got the nickname of Pineapple because I would scrounge a case of grenades, that's 24 of them, every night that I could and by morning I didn't have any more left. The rule was you didn't get out of your hole because anything moving outside of a foxhole is the enemy and you can rightfully kill him. So every time I heard a sound I'd toss a grenade.

I can't say that I enjoyed combat but I understood how it felt. In combat you're alive; you are so alive that it's scary. All your senses are heightened….you see and feel and hear things more clearly. You can feel the itches of the bugs biting you more clearly. There is nothing quite like the end of a battle when it's over.

They would re-supply us every few days and would give us four or five K-rations maybe three sets of C-rations and a handful of D-rations. K-rations came in a box about the size and shape of a Kraft macaroni and cheese box and inside there was three or four round hard tack crackers, a can of deviled ham or chicken or any number of different rations. It would have three cigarettes in a little package, five matches I think it was, a couple of pieces of hard candy and usually an envelope of some kind of instant drink. The lemonade was terrible, coffee wasn't a whole lot better and the tea wasn't too bad. C-rations came in two cans the size of Campbell's soup cans. There was meat and vegetables stew, meat and vegetables hash. The meat and vegetables stew was terrible; there was gristle especially if it came from Australia because it was always mutton. A D-ration was a chocolate bar that was the equivalent of a meal. We all liked D-rations but it was sort of like Styrofoam ground up and soaked in chocolate and allowed to harden. It wasn't great chocolate, but it wasn't bad. The best of all were the 10-in-1 rations, which meant 10 meals for one man or one meal for 10 men. There were several variations and numbers 3, 5, and 8 or 9 were the ones that contained canned bacon and it was the best bacon I have ever tasted in my life. It also had canned scrambled eggs, which were bad, but you got to where it didn't matter. You didn't eat much in combat, anyway.

When I got command of the machine gun platoon, we were very short of ammunition, so I would get a safety pin and put it under my lapel with just the pin showing. That's the way officers wore their insignias; they didn't want to wear them out because then they would be targeted as an officer by the Japanese. With a safety pin under there, other Marines would assume you were an officer. I would take two or three guys with me and we got all the ammunition we could carry ....didn't even have to sign for it...they are short on paperwork in combat. We'd do the same thing with rations. We'd always try to get 10-in-1's and we would go through and get the ones with the bacon in it. There were lighter moments in combat but most of the time it was being plain scared.

I don't know if it was common, but in our unit we always referred to the foxholes we dug as ashholes. "Did you dig your ashhole yet?"

You stayed in your hole, you didn't move around much, and if you did, you talked your way out. You knew who was on each side so they wouldn't throw a grenade at you. If anything came around, a wood rat or a Jap, and he wasn't speaking English, I'd throw a couple of grenades. I'm convinced that that's one of the reasons I survived. Every once in a while you'd get some sleep. We would go through the whole night sometimes with practically no sleep because the Japanese would holler obscenities in English. Some of them were funny.

"Babe Ruth eats shit." They just knew that would enrage us so we would holler back "Hirohito eats shit."

The biggest disgrace for the Japanese was to be taken alive, and we didn't want them to be disgraced so we killed as many of them as we could. I can remember shooting a Jap trying to surrender. It sounds horrible, it was a violation of the international law but we were encouraged to do it because if you didn't they might have a grenade under their arms and when they were among you they'd drop it and take out four or five people. Sometimes they would have a machine gun strapped to their back with a couple of them coming in with their hands up, then one would get down on all fours and another one would start firing. That happened two or three times to people that I knew. So we didn't take prisoners, and they didn't want to surrender anyhow. They were more than willing to die for their emperor, and we were more than willing to help them.

I wanted to get a rifle, and I saw a rifle next to a guy who had been killed. When I went to get it, a mortar round landed about 150 yards away from me. It was a small mortar that we called a knee mortar, and it threw a grenade a little smaller than an American grenade. I didn't pay much attention and almost immediately another mortar landed about 50 yards closer in a direct line to me, and I thought, that guy is after me. I saw a hole and I hopped over a body and stepped into the hole. Normally in a situation like that I would have dived into the hole, but I stepped into it and I don't know why, but as I stepped into it the next mortar round landed and sprayed me with little pieces of Japanese scrap iron. I fell backwards over the body I just hopped over and I knew I had been hit. It couldn't be fatal because I could still think…my mind was about as confused as it could get, but I was alive. I couldn't see anything because I was bent over this body and almost immediately a corpsman was there.

"How bad is it?" I asked. "I can't see much down there below my belt but I see a lot of blood."

"You're not bad. You got a few chunks in you," he said. "You are going to be OK."

I had turned 16 and had all the thoughts and urges of a 16 year old, but he patched me up, called for a litter and gave me a morphine shot. They put a cardboard tag on me and wrote down what treatment they had given. The morphine came in little styrettes about an inch long and they were like tiny toothpaste tubes with a hypodermic needle on them. They pulled the cover off the hypodermic needle and squeezed the morphine which is a pretty healthy dose. Then he got inside his sack and he got a bottle of Lee John Brandy, about 2 ounces.

"Suck on this, it will help," he said.

Well I downed it in nothing flat.

He got a stretcher and four litter bearers and said, "Aid station" and they took me back.

We were almost at the aid station when we received a couple of shots. One shot landed between my knees and the next one gouged a great big chunk out of my leg just above the knee. Then a shot got one of the stretcher-bearers. Some of those Japanese were unbelievably good shots. They got him right between the eyes. They picked me up and ran. The Japanese high explosives used picric acid, and when it explodes, it sends this puff of greenish-yellow smoke and coats whatever is near. My face was covered with the chartreuse powder. I guess I looked pretty bad because my nose was bleeding, too.

They loaded me and the other wounded into one of the LCVs that took us out to the ship, a beautiful white hospital ship. At that moment I realized that as far as I was concerned the war was over, it's all done. I am going to get to go home and whatever is torn up is going to heal I just knew it. It was the greatest feeling I have ever had. I have never experienced anything quite like that five or ten minutes of absolute ecstasy. The war is over. I am going home. I am going to see Sally again, and I'm sure I can explain the whole thing to my mom. It was a beautiful sunny day, brilliant sunshine, just gorgeous. It was the most beautiful day in my life because the war was over, but all of a sudden it wasn't....

Just then a destroyer pulled up alongside us and opened up a 5 inch 38 which is the loudest piece of artillery in the world. It is so loud and there was a pow-pow-pow. The war was suddenly back on and I flipped out. I just remember this terrible feeling of panic that the war isn't over.

They put me in the base hospital in Guam and I was there for a few days. I wasn't nearly as badly hurt as most of the other people in the ward. It was not a pleasant place but had some of the sweetest, prettiest nurses I have ever seen. I was in and out of surgery five or six times. One piece of shrapnel had gotten inside of my foot and scrambled some bones up, broke several of them and powdered some of them. I don't know how the doctor did it but he put my foot together again.

I came home, went to college on the G. I. Bill and became a teacher. I am inordinately proud of having served in the Marine Corps and having served on Iwo Jima. It is probably the single most important thing I have done in my life, historically speaking. I, like so many Marines, say there is no such thing as an ex-Marine. There are former Marines and Marines no longer on active duty but they are all Marines. Nearly everything that has been said about them is true. They are arrogant because they are convinced that they are the world's greatest warriors, mainly because they are!

About 20 years ago when my youngest boy graduated from high school we took him to Hawaii for about a month. I took him to the Punch Bowl and I found the graves of Philpott and four or five of the guys that I remembered. I cried. I knew I was standing on Philpott's grave, and I just couldn't hold the tears back.

* * *

Infantry

"When 'round the bend and up the road a pretty sight to see,
Came those grinnin', dusty, fightin' men—Marine Corps Infantry!"
— Leatherneck Magazine

Cpl. John Armendariz
1st Platoon, A Company,
1st Battalion, 28th Marines, 5th Division

Seventeen-year-old John Armendariz

One of my best friends decided to join the Marines, and he asked me to go down to the recruiting depot with him. I was 17. Before you know it, I signed papers and was told that they would let me graduate high school, but they beat me home with a telegram saying to report for duty. Fortunately I had enough credits so I was able to receive a diploma. About April or May in '43, I went down to MCRD San Diego for training and did fairly well because of the math, physics and chemistry I had been taking in high school. I had been in the ROTC so I knew my right foot from my left. In those days they were issuing out

PFC stripes on graduation from boot camp to 5% of the class, and I was honored to receive one. In fact, they made me guidon bearer for a while.

On graduating from boot camp I was still 17 and they sent me up to Bremerton, Washington. They have a lot of naval stations around Puget Sound and needed guard detachments, prisoner chasers. They sent people from there up to Alaska. I was really dreading that. They sent me to Whitby Island Naval Air Station and I was there long enough to turn 18.

"I see where you would like to be assigned," the captain said. "You would like to go into the Paramarines."

"Yes sir," I said.

They sent me to Camp Elliott in the northern San Diego area. When I got there, they told me the Paramarines were full but the regular infantry division or the Raiders were open. I said I'd try the Raiders because I heard they were pretty good. I was certainly glad I chose the Raiders because their training is extensive. They taught us how to fire any kind of a weapon from mortar to bazookas to flamethrowers because they wanted us to work behind the lines as the Raiders did most of the time on Guadalcanal, Bougainville and other places. When I finally graduated from the Raider camp, they shipped us out but turned back to Camp Pendleton because they were forming the 5th Marine Division and said we were going to be part of it. I fit right in because most of their training had been retailored to the Raider type of training. They shipped us out to Hawaii in October, and we ended up at Parker Ranch for combat training. There was a big mountain and we attacked it everyday. We stayed there until Christmas time then boarded transport ships, and off we sailed into combat. Our particular transport stopped at Saipan and unloaded some of us. We got into LSTs and from there we went over towards Iwo. I didn't think we were going to make it to Iwo because we hit a typhoon on the way over there. The LST is not a very strong ship. We could actually see the plates buckle on the deck. We were just about to Iwo when they broke out the maps and instructions. I didn't pay that much attention to how bad it really was, that people really died, because you're not cognizant of how horrible battle is.

We landed with the second wave. The second wave was three minutes behind the first wave which was not very much time. If you ever see pictures of the landing, you will see guys with faces and hands painted white like ghosts, that's us. The underwater demolition teams found that the Japanese had buried a lot of gasoline tanks that would ignite when the landing forces made it there so we had to fireproof our faces and hands to go through it. We landed on Amtracs. Everything looked hunky dory and we could see the shells from the bombing. My first impression was that it's just like the movies. I was still not at the point of fear creeping into me. I was the runner and radio man for Lt. Norm Brueggerman from Youngstown, Ohio. The lieutenant just cleared the front of the landing craft when he was literally cut in two by machine guns. We grabbed him and pulled him into the nearest hole we could find but he didn't last longer than 15 minutes. I took some of his private stuff off him, his pistol, the map he had, and tried to keep on going. You had to keep moving because the first wave was there already and was heading for the other side so we had to be right behind them to reinforce them. We could see the Japanese firing machine guns at us from the sides of Mt. Suribachi. We were able to move on ahead practically all the way across the island when we stopped. Pretty much, I was on my own until I found the captain and became his runner and radioman for a while.

We were extreme left on the island, Green Beach they called it. Most of the beaches had two sections, Red Beach 1 and 2, Blue 1 and 2, but Green only had one. They wanted to concentrate all our efforts on Mt. Suribachi. People asked me if it was a terrific battle. I really think it was. Let me give you one statistic. Our A Company landed at 9:03 with 250 officers and men. By 2:00 o'clock that afternoon, we were down to 75.

We fought the battle of Mt. Suribachi which took us about 3 or 4 days, but we never did go up. Our job was to go around the back side. It was extremely dangerous because the Japanese had mined quite a few of the big black volcanic rocks. I saw some of my buddies blown up including a very good friend of mine, Sgt. Barnes, a former Raider. The guy in front of him stepped on one of the mines and the both of them got killed.

We saw a lot of commotion when the flag went up. We really couldn't see that much of it, but we heard the ships blowing their horns. By that time we were able to regroup and come back around to the front. We had security, we thought pretty much, so they gave us a couple of days rest. By this time the rest of the 4th Division and the two regiments of the 3rd had landed. We were given a chance to take a bath by going into the ocean. They posted guys around us and gave us fresh undershirts and all that. It was refreshing. The following day we moved up and relieved one of the units over on the extreme left flank. From then on it was fighting every day, and we'd advance a little bit. We just kept on going through ridges, little hills, little valleys, and then my original captain, Captain Wilkins was killed on the eighth day, I believe. It was the same day Tony Stein was also killed.

Tony Stein was one of the guys in our company who received the Medal of Honor. He was a tough guy. He was a real stocky guy from Dayton, Ohio, and a former Paramarine. He had a big leopard tattooed on his shoulder. One time we went to Hilo on a work party and were unloading a cargo ship because they used us for that, too. He saw that we were unloading aircraft machine guns.

"I think I'll take one," he said.

Because he was a former machinist, he said he could turn that into one of our weapons. He took it back to the camp with us and put a handle and a butt stock on it. He modified it somewhat and he turned it into a weapon he could use. The bad part about it was that it used to shoot 1100 rounds a minute so he went through an ammo belt "harrumph," that fast. He kept the enemy down, no doubt about that but oh God, he would have to run back to the beach to get more belts of ammo. He wanted someone to go with him back to the beach but nobody wanted to run back with him. He took off his shoes so he could run faster, it was mostly sand around that area, and he ran down to the beach. He would do that a number of times and each time he did that he would get one of the guys who was wounded but still walking and drag him along down with him and leave them on the beach. He did this about 10 times that I know of. For that reason he received the Medal of Honor, not because of the Stinger. His Stinger was deadly though. He was killed the same day Captain Wilkins was killed. From then on we went through a few captains and some lieutenants who took command of the company. Some were very good; some were not so good. Captain Tucker was good I thought; he was an elderly man, probably in his 30's, a replacement. After you have been in combat for a little while, you tend to be somewhat critical of anybody who goofs up because that is what the Marine Corps hammers into you. You work as a unit, there is no individualism, and you defend each other. That's the basic premise of Marine Corps training. I think it saves a lot of lives and it gets the job accomplished.

The other fellow who received the Medal of Honor was our company armor; his name was Sgt. William Harrell. One night when we started to stop on a ridge, the captain said, "John why don't you get in with Harrell and Carter."

I went up there to them because it was getting kind of crowded down where we were. I tried to dig in but couldn't because it was hard rock. You couldn't make a good defensive position out of hard rock.

So I said, "I'm going back down because there is nothing up here that can really protect you," so they let me go.

By Dammit, We're Marines!

About 5 o'clock in the morning, I heard a lot of firing taking place, a lot of shooting, and here comes Carter. He comes running and bleeding like a fountain. I guess he had a bayonet run through his arm that sliced it open.

"I need a weapon. I need a weapon!" he yelled.

I gave him mine. "What's wrong?"

"We're being attacked from the other side by a whole lot of Japanese!"

By that time, he started running back but I don't know where he went. Then I heard Harrell cry from up there, "Help me, somebody help me."

I grabbed the radioman's or telephone man's carbine and I ran up there. I got up to the hole and sure enough, he was a bloody mess. He had both hands missing, one from a saber cut, one from a grenade. Evidently a Japanese officer wounded him with his saber but Harrell had the strength enough to pull him down, and with his good hand, grabbed the grenade that the officer had dropped and shoved it under him. It exploded but wiped out Harrell's other hand. Both legs were broken, and I said to him, "It's me, Johnny, I'm here." He knew me as Johnny.

I started pulling him out. I got him about 2/3 out of the hole and I was going to drag him down the slope but I see this Japanese helmet coming up at the edge of the hole about two feet away. I pointed my carbine at him and I waited until I saw his face and then pulled the trigger because I was sure he had a hand grenade or something. I pulled the trigger and his head snapped back. That was the closest I ever came to an enemy Japanese. I can still visualize the man's face. I really can. Some things just stay with you the rest of your life.

I was exceptionally well trained. When the captain released me as his runner, I said I wanted to go up to the front. Up at the front, they told me, "Hey we got a pillbox over there but nobody can fire this bazooka."

I said that I could fire it and did. I showed them how to load it, and I aimed and got it right through the aperture. That just comes from training. By that time, the company was made up of mostly replacements. A lot of them were not knowledgeable about any real combat. Maybe how to pull a trigger but that was the extent.

I still had Lt. Brueggerman's map of the island and wherever I saw somebody wounded or killed I would jot down where it was. Somehow or another somebody else wanted that map more than I did and absconded with it. I did pull one problem when Captain Wilkins was killed. I was his radio man and the first sergeant asked me to take care of the captain's personal stuff; take his rings off, because we left his body there with just his dog tags on. I got his pack which was a small, light pack that had a lot of personal things in it including a little notebook that he used to write in. I still carried my pack, also. One day we were told we were being relieved for a couple of days and they pulled us back from the line. On the way back we stopped at a place that was very hot, volcanic, you could actually see the steam coming up. You couldn't sit down or you would get burned so I sat on his pack to cushion and insulate me from the heat. When it was time to go, I got up but forgot the pack. We went all the way back to the rest area.

"John, where's the pack?" the first sergeant asked.

"I left it back there."

"Get your piece and go back and get it."

I tried to go back. I really tried my best to go back there, but it was very difficult. I was all by myself and was afraid that some of our guys would shoot me as well as some of the Japanese coming out of the caves. What I did, I think, was goof up a lot of guys because every time the captain would see something that some individual did, or hear about something some individual did, he would pull out his book and he'd write it in there. I am sure there were notes in there that would have meant awards or citations of some sort, even though it was futile because most of the men ended up being killed or badly wounded. As I say, I was the one who snafued that by losing the pack. It was never turned in.

Every time the captain, whoever was captain, wanted something knocked out like a pillbox, he'd call for a tank. I'd go back to the tank and show them what they wanted knocked out. I did that about four times. The first time they told me just to hang on to the phone in the back.

"If you want me to tell you where those spots are, I'm going to have to get in," I said. "There is no way I'm going to walk behind you." I would have been deader than a doornail inside of five minutes.

Sure enough, they let one of the gunners out and I climbed into the turret and sat in his seat and off we went. We would knock out the pillboxes the captain wanted knocked out, and we could actually hear the bullets zinging off the tank as we approached because there were a lot of snipers that stayed behind. They would let us push through and then get us from the back end. That went on for a few days, but it was the 15th of March and I was still alive. I went back this one time, got the job done and they let me off the tank. I was just going past the tank when he fired his 75 and for a while I couldn't hear anything, but I felt something just slam into my elbow and my rifle stock shattered. I'd been hit.

By that time, the tank was gone. I was able to make it back to the lines because my only wound was a shattered elbow and I could still run. By this time on Iwo Jima they had set up hospital tents, and the doctors operated on my elbow. They were able to use the airports by then so I got flown to Guam for further work. I stayed about four days then they put me on a ship to Hawaii and I went to Hawaii Naval Hospital where they did some more work.

They dismissed me from the hospital and sent me back to Camp Elliott where I was a guard. At that time they were just using Camp Elliott as a dumping station, just dumping material from overseas. Some of the guys were taking advantage of it and mustering off with some of the equipment. What they would use it for, I wouldn't know.

I was on leave at home in Los Angeles on Whittier Boulevard and had just gotten off the R car coming from downtown when I heard everybody yelling, screaming, "The war is over!"

I went past this tortilleria, a real fancy place, and the owner came out and said, "Hey Marine, come here, I'm going to take you home with me right now and we are going to celebrate!"

By that time, I was just a few blocks away from my house but he took me to his home and started calling friends up. I don't know where they got all the booze, beer and stuff like that but, God Almighty, it was a wild time after that.

I was discharged in February 1946. My brother Frank had been in the Navy during the war. My brother Victor was drafted and went to officer candidate school with the Army. He was a 1st Lieutenant with the 96th Infantry, 381st Regiment, and was acting company commander when he was killed on Okinawa. Alex, the youngest one joined the Army but the war was over by then.

* * *

Sgt. Maj. Joseph P. Kratcoski, USMC (Ret.)
Sergeant, 2nd Platoon, A Company, 1st Battalion,
25th Marines, 4th Division

Joseph P. Kratcoski, wartime photo

I joined the Marine Corps in 1941 before the war when I was 17 years old because I wanted to get out of Pennsylvania and the coal mines. I was one of seven children of a coal miner. I quit high school in the 11th grade. It was the Depression and all. I had an uncle in the Spanish-American War and an uncle in WW I so I just thought, well, I would join the service because I always heard about their adventures. I figured that was a good way to get out of the coal mines. The Army, I don't think took people in unless they were 18, and it just happened that I got into the Marine Corps.

I was in Iceland with the 6th Marines when the war started. The English had troops there to defend Iceland. The English were getting their butt kicked in Europe so they pulled those troops off and put us up there to defend Iceland. That was in June '41. I came up as a replacement in Iceland and at that time the Ruben James had just sunk off Newfoundland.*

The Icelandic Marines, they more or less formed the Marine Corps for all the invasions. When we came back February '42, we went to Camp Elliott in San Diego and formed the 9th Marines, which is part of the 3rd Division. Then the 9th Marines split up and formed the 23rd Marines, that's the 4th Division. Then the 23rd split up and made the 25th Marines so that's basically how the Icelandic Marines formed most of the Marine Corps. Nobody will say that, Marines don't say that; but that's what actually happened.

While we were at Camp Elliott, we hiked to Del Mar and slept in the horses' stalls there. This was probably March or April and they would take us out swimming. We were there about two weeks.

We left San Diego and landed on the Marshall Islands. The Marshall Islands was the first territory we took from the Japanese. Roi-Namur was my first battle so I had nothing to compare. Well, actually the first battle was easier than we all expected; our company took an island and there was nobody on it. After that, we probably hit about 30 islands and you would never know if anybody was going to be on it or not. Most of them were just empty. We stayed on Roi-Namur for 30 days and there were a lot of dead Japs there. I mean the island stunk. All we got was three cans of beans a day for 30 days. You'd get no chow. The Seabees then came in and built an airfield or something like that.

Saipan was bloody. We killed a lot of Japanese, and in fact, I was almost killed quite a few times. The first Jap I really killed was playing dead. He was sniping at us and the company wanted him so I went up there. He was lying there playing dead so I just hit him with my rifle butt and he moved so that's the first one I killed. The other ones we'd go up and throw a grenade in a bunker. In one bunker, a Jap handed a baby out. I bent down and reached for the baby and the Jap came at me with his sword towards my head. I was lucky. I saw that silver coming at me and I moved back.

Saipan was rough, and I stayed on Saipan the whole time until it was secured. I did the whole tour on Roi-Namur, too. The longer you stay in combat the longer you get used to being hot, having no chow and all that, and killing people. Saipan, to me, was probably rougher than Iwo because I was only on Iwo one day. As far as the landing goes, there was a difference, because Iwo was really the bloodiest of them all. But they were all tough.

I think we started out for Iwo in January some time. We went from Maui to Pearl Harbor and then we went to Eniwetok and then a mock landing on Tinian and then we went to Iwo. We were on board ship for 45 days on LSTs. The LST wasn't meant to carry troops so they just put us on there and said to make yourself a bunk. They had no bunks. We slept wherever we found a place to sleep. It'd be raining and we'd be on the top deck. We had maybe 200 men, a company, on board. They also had LVTs, the landing craft that carries the Marines in and takes them to shore, but the LVTs had bunks for the sailors.

We didn't expect anything special really on Iwo. I expected what we had on the other beaches would be about the same where the enemy was firing at us. We more or less expected a tough battle, but being a sergeant down the lower ranks, you don't know what's going on; you just do what they tell you and from there you try to do your best.

The first time I really thought about Iwo Jima was the morning we woke up on the ship. We got up about 4 o'clock in the morning and you could see Mt. Suribachi in the foreground. Iwo looked like a big pork chop with a hill but it didn't bother me one way or the other because I knew the next thing we would be doing was getting into landing craft and that we would be going to hit the beach.

However, when we hit the beach there we didn't get any fire or anything until we went up about maybe 10 to 20 yards. We had a new captain in there, and we had a lot of extra reserves. I guess they figured it was going to be pretty rough because they had extra people there to fill all the positions. The captain got up and said, "I wish all landings would be like this in the Marine Corps."

Ten minutes later, he's dead so there was a period of maybe about 10 minutes before they started shooting at us.

"OK, I got this far," I said.

We were one of the first 1300 who came ashore in the first wave. Then Japs started dropping mortars on us. Well there was a little hill in from the beach and there was a machine gun pillbox up there. They didn't fire at us so I told my lieutenant that I would go up and investigate what's in there. I got up ten feet from the pillbox and a grenade came out at me and I got hit in the hip. That's how I got the Purple Heart. The grenade fell; I saw it and said, "Ah shit, this is it!" It came maybe 5-10 feet from me. I thought well, it's been a good life, this is it, yesterday I was, and today I'm not. All of a sudden, something hit me and I could feel like a stone hitting in my ankle and I looked down and saw blood coming out of my dungarees. We'd carry four hand grenades with us, so I threw one grenade and that didn't do anything. The Japs threw about 10-15 grenades back at me. They didn't do any damage to us. I was lucky.

They weren't duds, the sand just absorbed the impact, must have, they were right in front of me and I felt with each one of them I was a goner. I threw my other three hand grenades and that didn't do any good. The lieutenant who was a replacement, a platoon leader or something, got out a grenade. Normally you have to count 1-2-3-4 and then throw it, but he threw it too quick and the Japs threw it back at us and it landed right in front of me. I was able to pick it up and throw it back, and then I got a little mad.

"Well, I got to do something or not do something," I said.

By Dammit, We're Marines!

I put my rifle grenade on my rifle and charged up to the bunker from the side. I fired it and blew up the people that were in there, I guess, because no one fired after that.

In the meantime, the corpsman bandaged me up and gave me a shot of morphine, I guess. After that, I kept leading my squad to the airfield. I don't know if my wound was bothering me. I thought, you don't lay on the beach, you move inland if you don't want to get killed. If you lay on the beach they are going to kill you; if you move inland they have a chance to kill you.

With the platoon on my right and on the left, we started moving inland to our objective there...the airfield. This time I never saw so much fire in all my life. It was going over my head, you could hear bullets whistling past, all kind of bullets, mortars and everything else were dropping on us. I guess everybody was firing, maybe the Navy was firing; we could hear it and see black smoke. I guess we got 5 or 10 yards and a mortar dropped in along side me and hit me in my right knee but not too badly. I never got a Purple Heart for it. The next thing I remember was a guy I called Elmer Fudd. I can't recall his real name, but somehow or another we got in the same hole, which was an artillery hole. I had always been told that artillery never lands in the same place twice. I guess his BAR man got killed or something because he had his BAR and says, "Hey, 'Ski should I take this weapon or not?"

I looked at it. "Well, it's full of sand anyway so just leave it there."

That's the last thing I remember practically of anybody in my outfit at that time. Being in the front, I don't know who got wounded in behind me or anything. I got to the airfield, the objective we had, at about 3 o'clock in the afternoon. My leg was giving out, and I couldn't go any further. I started crawling back and people would advance and grab my rifle and pull me a little ways and then pull me a little ways furtheruntil I got back to the beach. When I got on the beach, it was still as bad as it was up front. I think they gave me another shot of morphine, I don't know. The only thing I remember was being loaded up and mortars and everything dropping to the ground and around the boat.

I'm telling the coxswain, "Get this damn boat out of here before we all get killed."

That's all I remember. That's it for my tour on Iwo Jima. That was February 19th, my 21st birthday.

When we got back to the hospital ship, it wasn't really a hospital ship, but they had the 3rd Marine Division on it. They hauled me up and a Navy chief was going to take care of me.

A Marine said, "Get out of here, we'll take care of our own Marines."

The next thing I remember aboard the ship is that I was able to walk and was topside. The more serious wounded stayed and the rest got transferred to another LST. I remember walking topside and the Japanese suicide bombers were bombing us by air and I looked up there. You could hear the machine guns against the ship. Just prior to that, they raised the flag on Iwo Jima. I saw that, but I hadn't had too much feeling myself.

I said, "Well, we got to the top of Mt. Suribachi."

That's all I thought. I never knew it was going to be the big deal like it actually turned out to be.

Being a first casualty I guess I got good treatment and as other people started coming on, they paid less attention to you. Actually, when I got on the LST we were supposed to go to a hospital in Saipan but we ended up in a hospital in Guam. When we got to the hospital in Guam, it was at night and we went to the mess hall. There were nurses, Navy nurses, and that was the first time we had seen a woman in quite a while.

I made the rank of Sgt. Major in December of 1955 and retired in 1971, after 30 years. I was in Korea in '52 and did two tours in Viet Nam. Korea was probably a lot rougher than Viet Nam. As far as man-to-man combat fighting, Iwo was rougher than Korea.

* * *

Kratcoski was awarded the Bronze Star Medal for his actions on Iwo Jima. The citation reads in part,

"Landing with the initial assault waves on D-Day against terrific enemy resistance, Sergeant Kratcoski hit the beach with the second platoon and, when devastating fire from a hostile pillbox pinned down the forward elements, crawled toward the emplacement after his supply of hand grenades was exhausted. Although suffering from painful shrapnel wounds, he fixed an anti-tank grenade to his M-1 rifle, charged to the top of the ten-foot terrace and fired point-blank into the entrenchment, neutralizing the enemy's fire and enabling his unit to advance further inland. Still refusing evacuation until the beach had been secured and the first three platoons had reached the objective airstrip, Sergeant Kratcoski, by his daring and prompt action, dauntless perseverance and concern for his comrades, at great personal risk, had contributed to the saving of many lives and to the securing of the airstrip commanding the 'Blue Beach' landing area. His cool courage throughout was in keeping with the highest traditions of the United States Naval Service.

For his service in Korea, another citation reads, in part "...Master Sergeant Kratcoski and his company's patrols had been ambushed and surrounded by the enemy, he expressed complete disregard for his personal safety and left the command post in order to carry information to the mortar section....He was instrumental in the ambushed patrol's withdrawal....." For this he was awarded a Gold Star in lieu of his second Bronze Star Medal. In Viet Nam he was awarded the Navy Commendation Medal.

*The Ruben James was torpedoed by a German submarine on October 31, 1941 and was the first U.S. Navy ship to be sunk by hostile action in World War II.

* * *

Covered by riflemen, a flamethrower torches an enemy cave.
Official USMC photo/Silverthorn collection.

PFC Marold L. Miller
I Company, 3rd Battalion, 25th Marines,
4th Division

Marold Miller, left, with friend Paul Lynch

I went down and joined the Navy in 1944 with another buddy of mine. We got in and the Navy recruiters asked for volunteers for the Marines. I thought, what the hell? So I volunteered and my buddy volunteered but neither one of us knew that we did because we had been separated until we got outside the door.

"I'm a Marine," I said.

"So am I," he said.

I might have talked to my family about joining, I just don't remember. I had graduated from high school and was married at 17 to my high school sweetheart. I imagine we were married for about two years when I joined up. We had a son before I went to war.

I trained in San Diego, Camp Pendleton, infantry training and all the rest that goes with it. I ate up the training just like sugar. I'd do all the training I could get, I really did and it paid off. Some guys just throw it away and not do this and not do that. I trained, I really did. Whatever you could do by yourself, I ate all that up. I felt invincible and that I could take care of myself and I did, too. Some guys messed up, but I didn't. I took all the training they'd give me. I wouldn't have been here if I hadn't.

I spent a year over in Maui and from Maui, we went to Iwo Jima. They lied to us. They said we'd be off Iwo in three days. That's nothing, do the job and take off. I was there for 28 days. I got hit on D-Day and went back on D plus 5.

We had a map that we trained with to know where we would be going on the island. Blue Beach 1, that's all I can remember. It was all black sand. As a matter of fact a guy sent me a jar, he'd been over there, and he sent me back some sand. I didn't bring any home, only what I brought in my clothes.

We were heading for Blue Beach 1. I never will forget it. The sergeant on the Higgins boat said to shoot.

"Shit, there's nobody out there," I said. "There's nothing to shoot at."

We kept going and they dumped us off on the beach. I was loaded down with two bandoliers, a bazooka round, an M-1 and everything else. I got to the beach with the ammunition with me. I just dropped to my knees and unloaded it. Then we headed off, there was nothing going on, no shooting, nobody shooting or nothing. I don't know how far I was, but just about to the other shore and the Japs unloaded. They were all underground, buried. They let the first three waves in and annihilated the rest. It was terrible. I didn't know what to expect. I had never been in war before. The guy right beside me got killed. This other guy was his best buddy and he come up there and kept reaching around on him like he was looking for a .45 or something in his jacket. The corpsman didn't know what he was going for so he couldn't trust him. I got on behind him and collared him and pulled him back. It must have been 09:30.

I kept going and there was a kid up behind a rock. 'Chick' Harrison, I never will forget him. He just took off and was just a sitting duck there. He thought he was covered behind a rock.

I picked him up by the collar and yelled, "Come on, Chick!"

They called him Chick because he was so damn young. He was younger than I was and I was only 19. He must have been 16 or 17. After I came home from service, he went though my town. He was from California, but he went through Iowa by train, he wrote me a letter later and told me, "I went through Vincent."

I wrote, "Why didn't you stop I'd have taken you wherever you needed to go, ya know." That's the last time I heard from him, I don't know what happened to him.

After I got Chick to safety, I went a little further, and the Japs dropped a bomb on two of us. John Kelly was with me in the foxhole and died beside me. I was just lucky I guess. I got hit in my foot; where else I don't know. After I got hit and Kelly got killed, here comes this corpsman and a buddy of mine who took me to the beach to go back to the ship. Shells kept dropping around us.

I said, "Let's rest a minute." And we did.

We went on again, and here comes another shell, just like that. It didn't hurt me. I got aboard a Higgins boat that took me back to the ship. They patched up my foot. It wasn't that bad. At the time, I thought I took it off, but it wasn't that bad. I spent 2 or 3 days on the ship and they sent me back in.

Everybody else had said that when they got them off the island they weren't going to send them back. The captain of this ship, that didn't bother him a bit.

"You're ready to go," he said and sent me back D plus 5 and I rejoined the group.

But every other ship around the area wouldn't send them back in. If you got off, you stayed off. I just talked to this buddy the other day who took me off the island. He never got a scratch. He just walked around like there wasn't nothing going on.

We'd go to sleep at night, but I couldn't. The Japs would come up at night. I didn't sleep very many nights, I know that. I might have dozed off in the daytime. I must have took cat naps, had to because I couldn't have made it without them. After I got out of the Marines, I'd take cat naps. I can remember when I got back home, I was on the farm, I was raised on a farm and I'd be out cultivating; I'd get tired because I partied all night. I'd stop wherever I was, lie underneath the tractor and about five minutes was all I needed and I'd be ready to go.

One time on Iwo I had my hands behind my back some way as I slept. When I woke up I thought I had lost my arms but they were just asleep. I cried out, "I don't have any arms!" I scared the other guys. They thought I was cracking up but they just went back to sleep. I never will forget that. I thought we'd gotten bombed and I'd lost my arms, I didn't know where I was at, and my arms didn't have any feeling in them. I thought, oh no, but they came around.

It wasn't difficult being in the infantry; I enjoyed it. I trained well. How good a shot I was, I don't remember. I was in a demolition squad. I just blew up every hole I went by. I dropped a charge in every hole. I wasn't sitting there waiting for them to kill me, that's for sure. I only saw Japs who weren't living.

Then I got dysentery. It was so filthy over there it's a wonder everybody didn't get sick. I never had it before. I know it's the filth, I know that. This time I just walked off the beach. I was there 27 days when I got the dysentery. That's what I thought it was, but they said, "You got mental fatigue."

Whatever the hell that is. I didn't know, but didn't argue with them. "I'm all right," I said.

"You're going with me," the corpsman said. I couldn't argue with him. I was back aboard ship, and it was over for me.

I lost a lot of buddies over there. For nothing, I thought. But I guess the landing strips saved a lot of B-29 pilots. Lose some to save some. I just can't stand the Japanese to this day. I wouldn't trust them. They'd stick a knife in your back in a minute. Then we gave the island back to them. That hurt me. All those guys fought for it with their lives. I can see Iwo Jima right now but I don't want to go back.

It was about three weeks after D-Day that I left the island. I went back to Guam. I was aboard ship going to Japan for the invasion when I heard the war was over. That's where we were headed. It was paradise when we heard that the war was over. I was discharged from San Diego Naval station in 1946.

I went back to Iowa. I had been away from my family for over two years. My wife and I wrote to each other. We were married for 57 years before she passed on 10 years ago. I have three sons, seven grandchildren and 13 great grandchildren.

I'm still a Marine. I did all the training I could, that's probably why I am here today. I really went after it. I still have a death hole in me that if anybody wants to get after me, it will be all over for him. Thankfully, I've never had to use it.

* * *

Cpl. Bob "Mo" Mueller
D Company, 2nd Battalion,
28th Regiment, 5th Division

Bob Mueller, wartime photo

I graduated high school in June and joined the Marine Corps on September 15, 1942, at the age of 18. I joined the Marines because I thought it would be a good opportunity to get into combat, and I admired the Marine Corps. I knew they were a good, strong fighting outfit. Marines were more of a forward force.

They sent me to the Marine Corps Recruit Depot in San Diego for six weeks of boot training. What a shock treatment for a boy from Nebraska! I had only been there a week and almost got kicked out. There was a drive-in movie theater next to where we were camped. About four of us got the bright idea to go to the movies. The D.I. did bed check and we weren't in our sacks, so when we came back, he was waiting for us.

He lined us up and swore at us and said a few dirty things and then he said, "Get your sea bags packed; I'm going to kick you out of the Marine Corps!"

By Dammit, We're Marines!

We packed our big sea bags with our gear and he took us out to the grinder as it's called, where they do all the parading. He marched us around for about three hours with our sea bags over our shoulders.

He was yelling and threatening us and then he told us, "You'll go home and be a disgrace to your family, you SOB *%#*heads!" He marched us around and finally said, "I don't know, maybe I'll let you guys stay and see if I can make something out of you."

He didn't kick us out and he didn't send us home in disgrace like he had said. I couldn't begin to remember what the movie was that caused this trouble.

After boot camp, I volunteered for Marine Paratroopers who trained at Camp Gillespie in Santee, California. I joined the Paramarines because of the excitement and adventure of it and also the fact that you got $50 a month extra in pay. I thought basic training was tough, but it couldn't compare to the six-week training that we endured in the Paramarines. Morning started at 5 a.m. with a 5-mile run that was followed by 30 minutes of calisthenics, and the remainder of the day was spent with extensive training regarding parachute jumping. Check out at Paramarine School was the toughest day of my life. We had to run six miles, do God knows how many pushups, knee bends and all that stuff. It was an extremely difficult calisthenics checkout along with doing our jumps. The check out day was tough, but that was the day you got presented with your parachute wings.

I was 18 years old, bashful, wouldn't even talk to a woman, never smoked, never drank. Six months in the Marines and I'm smoking, drinking and chasing women. I met Ira Hayes at parachute school. We became inseparable after we got into a big argument aboard ship in early 1943. We were on our way to New Caledonia when he pulled a knife on me and cut me on the hand. I grabbed him around the throat and choked him until some guy separated us. God only knows what the argument was about.

I used to be sitting and playing cards, cribbage, poker or whatever and Ira would walk around asking guys, "Where's Mo?" Then he'd come in and sit down beside me and watch me play cards. We were very good friends. When we got separated after they broke up the paratroops, we weren't as close but we were still really good friends. He just kind of kept to himself at the time. He had his group of friends and that's who he hung out with.

In Noumea, New Caledonia, we made two disastrous jumps. We had people hanging in trees and bushes. It was then they decided that jumping in the jungles of the South Pacific wasn't feasible. We were to be used as infantrymen. We were sent to Guadalcanal on March 3, 1943, where we were introduced to real combat with the Japanese. We stayed there until October 14, then we were sent to Vella Lavella and fought the enemy until December 3. We went to Bougainville, another of the Solomon Islands chain on December 4, and left there on January 15, 1944, and headed back to the United States. Upon arrival, we were given a 30-day leave. We were sent to Camp Pendleton and were advised that the Marine Raiders and Paratroopers were being disbanded and we would join forces as the newly formed 5th Marine Division. Many other Marines, who had not been in combat, also were assigned to the 5th Division.

After four to five months, we were shipped to the big island of Hawaii. Our camp was on Parker Ranch near Mauna Loa Mountain. We trained daily assaulting the beach and heading inland toward the mountain. Little did we know we were being trained for the invasion of Iwo Jima.

I remember they gave us steak and eggs before we left to go ashore on Iwo. That was our breakfast, steak and eggs. The so-called Marine Corps steak is about 1/8 inch thick and is like shoe leather, probably serve the same stuff today. It tasted good then. We were hungry, and the Navy fed us good when we were on board ship.

I was in the second wave to hit the beach on Iwo and we landed on Green Beach. We were to deploy facing Mt. Suribachi. The 28th Marine Regiment was the point. We were to head for the base of the mountain, while the rest of the regiment was to get to the western side of the island. This maneuver would cut off the narrowest part of the island and isolate it.

When we arrived on the beach, we were met by an eight to ten foot terrace. Once past this, there was a second terrace about four feet. The going was slow due to the ankle-deep volcanic ash. I was lying on the beach and a mortar shell exploded between my legs. It raised me off the deck and exploded, but because of where it landed, the explosion caused the shrapnel to go up and out over my legs. It hit a good friend of mine in the neck. He was bleeding quite a bit so they got him to the aid station on the beach and he was evacuated. His total time on the island was probably about 15 minutes.

We were very disorganized when we first landed and it took us about 45 minutes before our D Company troops were all together in the same area heading toward the mountain. The Japs had the advantage over us because they held the high ground, and there was very little cover because of all the shelling and bombing. It took us three days to get into position at the base of the mountain. Casualties were running very high. After establishing our positions at the base of the mountain, we kept pressure on the enemy on all locations in the cliffs. We had eight tanks available to us, and they were all in strategic positions. They were unable to place them in action because they were out of fuel and ammunition and none was immediately available. They were blasted by heavy mortar barrage and knocked out of service.

On February 23rd at 9 a.m. our Commanding Officer ordered a four-man patrol from D and F Companies and a 40-man patrol from E Company to reconnoiter suitable routes and probe for enemy resistance. D Company went up on the eastern side, E Company up the front side and F Company up the western side. Our D Company patrol was led by Sgt. J. D. Mulligan, myself, Cpl. Wieland and PFC F. Ferentz. Mulligan weighed close to 300 lbs He was tall and had played professional football. Due to his weight, every step he took caused the black sand to fall back on to the rest of us. After about 20 yards, he turned back and the remaining three of us continued up to the top of the crater. It was really slow going because of the loose volcanic ash. Slipping back, going up and slipping back again. Keep your eyes open and see where you're going.

Upon reaching the top of the mountain, we joined E and F Companies. E Company brought a small flag, 54 x 28 inches, and they found some 1½ inch iron pipe, secured the flag to it and hoisted it up around 10:30 a.m. The troops below shouted and the ships at sea blew their horns. I don't understand how anyone can say they didn't know the flag was raised. All the ships sounded their horns. I saw them raise the first and the second flags, from about ten feet away. It was a very, very exciting moment, very thrilling seeing the stars and stripes flying over the piece of land the Japanese owned. We had taken it this far and the feeling was almost indescribable.

We were sort of milling around up there, checking things out to make sure no one was going to take any shots at us. From the top of Mt. Suribachi, you could see towards the north end of the island and how torn up the island was. Everything was practically flattened or leveled. There was some scrub brush left and pieces of trees, very bleak, lots of shell holes. I don't think we were paying too much attention to that though; we were more concerned about what was going on where we were. We wanted to get the hell out of there and get back down to our outfit. You could see all the carnage along the shoreline, the landing craft that were sunken, and all the debris. We had a pretty good view of it. We were probably up there 45 minutes to an hour. On the way down, it was a piece of cake. We walked off the face of the mountain. By then we pretty much had a line across the island. I'm sure there were a lot of

Japs still hidden but it wasn't bad going down. Going down was easier than going up.

After securing the mountain, we were engaged in combat with the enemy who were bypassed as we moved forward. The Japs always waited for us to come to them. They never tried any counterattacks. They were also very brutal. They would get a dead Marine, pull him into a cave, bayonet his body and dismember his private parts. Then they'd throw his body out to show us what dirty SOBs they were. You forget every piece of humanity you have in your soul. You hate them. More than once, it happened. Our retaliation was the use of flamethrowers and dynamite. We had a lot of flamethrowers with us.

We went into a big, huge cave at one time to count the dead. Inside of it were benches built along the sides of the walls cut out of the terrain. There were 20 or so Japs sitting there all bloated and smelled like you know what. The stench, bloated bodies, I'll never forget that. We figured they were killed by a concussion from the bombing because there wasn't a mark on them.

After that I said, "Forget this crap, I'm not doing it, let someone else go."

They didn't request that we go into too many caves, but they wanted to do a body check to see what had happened to some of them or something like that. You didn't know what you were going into. After you got used to being on the island, you knew they had so many caves and pillboxes. You weren't about to stick your head into anything. Blow it shut first or shoot a flamethrower in it.

Eventually, we were positioned on the western portion of the island and headed north toward the end of Iwo Jima. The terrain was rugged, deep valleys and gorges and many boulders. The Japanese had the toughest defense set up on the center portion and further toward the northern end of the island. In attacking these positions, no Japs were to be seen, all being in caves or crevices in the rocks. Attacking troops were subjected to being fired on from flanks and rear more than from their front. The 26th Marines reached the northernmost part of the island on March 15 and doubled back to join the 28th to close in on the remaining enemies. Combined, these two regiments bottled up the enemy in a deep ravine and held their position during a severe fire fight with the enemy. For once, we held the high ground.

On March 25, 1945, we were relieved by the Army and brought back to the 5th Division Command Center. That night, the Japanese who were bypassed decided to have a final reorganization of the remaining troops. Our perimeter defense was to set up trip flares behind our location. As they tripped the flares, which illuminated them as they came over a little rise, they were easy targets. I spent 36 days on the island and I got wounded on the 35th night when they had the banzai attack. I got hit in the leg and the butt with shrapnel, nothing serious, nothing life threatening or crippling or anything like that.

When we were leaving, there were 16 of us left out of our company of 250. The 5th Marine Division cemetery was at the base of the mountain so we stopped and had a service. We went into the cemetery looking for graves of our deceased comrades. It was very, very emotional to see all those rows of white crosses. I get the shivers thinking of it right now. I found some of my buddies' graves. That was part of our leaving. It was the same old crap when we got back on the ship after the battle…sleeping down in the hold with 100 other guys, all the body odor and stench. We had salt-water showers with salt-water soap. Try to get clean! You felt like you had soap all over you. It didn't rinse off real good. We went back to Hawaii after Iwo. I forget how long it takes, maybe two weeks. It's a pretty good distance. Then we'd start training to go into Japan. We knew there was another invasion. We were making beachheads, doing landings, and all this stuff in preparation for the invasion of Japan. We got more replacements.

I wouldn't have developed my personality the way that I have and been able to go on and do the things I have done in life had I not had the training the Marine Corps gave me. Total training, mental, physical, the whole shot. You know when you go into the Marine Corps they break you down to nothing and build you back up. You are like the slime of the earth when you go into boot camp. After boot camp, you develop into a different individual. You have a different outlook on things. Discipline was tough. Very tough, very difficult, but it developed my personality, period. If I stayed at home, I probably would not have gone to college. I would have ended up working at some shop or the stockyards because I was from Omaha. As it was, I went to work for the gas company when I got home and went to night school at the University of Nebraska at Omaha. The Marine Corps deserves all the credit in the world for the way I turned out, and I mean that in a good way. They made a successful man out of me. It took me a long time to adjust to civilian life. I still have a very bad temper. Never did completely get over the war, but my Marine Corps training helped me adjust when I got out. The bad dreams are over, but the memories are still there.

I married at 25 and we had three daughters, three years apart. My wife died when the girls were young. I had gone through the Depression, gone to war, and lost a wife. There's not much you can tell me about life.

I belong to an Iwo Jima veterans' reunion group and we have our reunions every February. Camp Pendleton tour is one day and Marine Recruit Depot tour is the next day.

While at the rifle range, the Marines let us shoot the M-16. The kid was telling me, "Get down, you gotta get down in this kind of position." I was sitting on my butt, but they wanted you to cross your legs in certain ways so you don't rock and you are more stable. Do this, do that.

"Listen," I said, "I'm not 18 years old, I can't get down like that any more and my old knees hurt and a few other things hurt. I'll do it my way; you'll never get me up if I get in that position!"

There were 12 of us in the group who shot the M-16s. The lieutenant said, "Do you know what you did?"

He gave me a pair of binoculars and I looked and saw where I hit the target. I had 10 shots and I got 6 or 8 in the bull's eye or right around it. "You're a very good rifleman, probably equal to some of those young kids."

This old man sat there and did it his own way!

* * *

Pvt. Walter Oelerich
K Company, 3rd Battalion, 24th Marines,
4th Division

Walter Oelerich, August 1944

I enlisted at 17 and got called the day after my 18th birthday in June 1944. I pestered my mother enough where I convinced her I could leave school to join the Marines because I was going to get drafted the next year anyway. We had a crowd of about 10-12 guys that hung out on the corners in Brooklyn, and four had gone into the Marines. I figured they're in there so let me go, too.

I went to Parris Island where they just break you down and build you up. Then I was sent to Camp Lejeune for infantry training at the end of August. They sent us by train in October to Camp Pendleton and kept us there for a week or two. November 10, which is the Marine Corps birthday, is the date we shipped out of San Diego to Oahu, Hawaii. They put us in big replacement depots and then they took my draft and sent us over to Maui to the 4th Division camp. The first day on Maui, I knew I would be going into combat. The 4th had just finished the Marianas and were already in training for the next one wherever it was going to be.

We shipped out in the middle of January and went to the Marshall Islands. From there we went to Saipan as a stopping point and they held us there I guess until four or five days before the Iwo Jima invasion. About the second or third day out from Hawaii, they told us where we were going. It's not like today with cell phones, computers and all. In those days when you left port there was no way in the world that you could get in touch with anybody. At first, everyone was guessing where we were going. The heavy bet was Formosa, called Taiwan today, because they figured it was more logical. No explanation why we were taking Iwo. Iwo was my first and only combat.

There were roughly 1,500 troops aboard the transports and there was no privacy. During the day, it was mostly calisthenics and a lot of brain work. They'd sit you down and try to explain different things about what to do when you land, where to go, who to follow. They had these big rubber relief maps maybe three by four feet. They showed where we would be landing, whether we would go right, left or straight ahead, and what our job was going to be. At first they told us about 12,000 Japanese troops were expected to be on the island, but somewhere along the trip they upgraded it to about 21,000. They hit it right on the head. Other than that, it was cleaning your equipment. I remember the machine gunners would go to the back of the ship and fire into the ocean testing their equipment.

I don't know if it was because I was 18, but I don't remember anyone who was scared while en route. On the way there you don't think about it, but on the last night they start issuing ammunition and tell you what to put in your packs and how to square it away. The last night you start getting a little anxious because it comes down to the real thing.

On Saipan about four or five nights before, they came around and said if we have any letters to write, now is the time to do it because this is the last mail drop. That's when it starts hitting home.

You are in awe because in the convoy, anywhere you looked there was always a string of ships ahead of you, behind you, and a quarter mile or so off your starboard and port sides. It was impressive so you were, I guess, in a way feeling sorry for the other guy because of all the stuff coming his way. On board ship we were in reserve but we could see them landing on the island. We were about a couple miles out, but our eyes were good in those days. We could pick out little specks like the tanks and things going on shore. It was like being in the theater. We saw ships firing, and planes bombing, but we were safe on the ships and no one was bothering us. About two in the afternoon, they told us to get our gear, we were going ashore. We got in the boats and started into the beach. We were out a couple of miles and still not that worried. As you get closer, they tell you to get lower because now you're in Japanese range of even the small arms. The coxswain of our boat did a grand job. He ran the boat right up on the beach so we weren't going to get our feet wet. Unfortunately, the ramp didn't go down and we were hung up at the landing beach waiting for it to go down so we could get the hell off the boat because there was a lot of stuff starting to fly around. We were all ready to go over the side. We weren't going to stay in the boat. The sailor in the back had a lot of guts. He walked along the side of the boat on what they call the gunnels, a little 8 inch walkway and went up and hit the ramp a couple of times wherever and it went down.

Once we got on shore, we just moved straight ahead. There were a lot of Marines ahead of us so it wasn't like we were in the front. But all the firing is coming in. It comes right down to the water. We just kept moving in until we got to a point, I guess a couple of hundred feet below the airfield, and they told us to dig in. I still wasn't really scared, I guess I was a little dense, but I wasn't scared. I was more or less trying to keep my eye on my corporal and the guys around me to make sure I didn't get separated. I really didn't have time to be scared. Your anxiety is before you do something, but once you get involved, the anxiety goes because you have too much to do. We dug in and we stayed there a couple of days. A lot of stuff was hitting the beach but we didn't move out until they needed us. We didn't have any casualties getting off the boat but during the night we had a few from shrapnel from the artillery bursts. I was never injured and I was on Iwo until March 18.

I remember it was raining the second day. There was some wrecked Japanese aircraft up right along the edge of the airfield.

I remember the sergeant came along and said, "You, you, you, and you, we got snipers in the planes. Let's go."

We had our ponchos on and stayed relatively dry. We took off our ponchos, threw on our equipment, grabbed our rifles and jumped out of the holes and went.

"Hold up," he says, "they got them. You all can go back in your holes."

We're soaking wet now and we had to throw our ponchos back on. It was the most miserable night in my life to that point. I froze. I shivered all night. I even told the guy in the hole with me that I'm not scared, I'm just freezing.

Then we moved up to what they called the Amphitheater or the Meat Grinder. That's where the Japs main defense was. I think the scariest time up to then had been that first night on the line. On the beach you're not too bad, there's a lot of firing going on but there are

500 Marines ahead of you that are moving out so they are like a buffer between you and the Japanese. But when we moved and got into the Amphitheater, we were the ones in the front. I remember the first night in the hole, my head was on a swivel. I didn't know where to look. Flares were going off and you could actually hear the Japanese yelling at you. I'd seen this in the movies; I thought it was Hollywood, but this is ridiculous. We could hear them. They weren't close. They were up in this cliff looking down on us. They were actually yelling down, "Marines, you're going to die."

That sort of started unnerving me a little, but we got through the first night OK, at least I did, some of the fellas didn't. I could hear a lot of commotion in the back of us and I thought that's not supposed to be. There were Japanese behind us somewhere and a lot of shooting going on but I never found out who was doing the shooting. I just kept my head straight ahead looking out to my front. You didn't want to lose track of that. Whatever was happening in back of me they'll either come and get us or some of our guys will get them. That was a scary night.

I didn't even know about the flag-raising. We were moving in the opposite direction. Suribachi was to the south and we were moving north. The first I knew about the flag was when we were in Hawaii, back from Iwo. We had just got off the ship and we were on this island in Pearl Harbor, it was a Navy recreational island. Jackie Cooper was there playing the drums, that's how I remember it. They would give you a Coke, give you stuff to eat and drink. We were standing in line for something and this guy had a Leatherneck Magazine. A bunch of us were looking at it and we looked at the cover. We saw a picture of the flag-raising.

"Geez that's a hell of a picture, what is that?" we asked.

"That's the raising of the flag on Iwo," he said.

We never even heard of it. We looked at the pictures and said that's one hell of a picture and that was the end of it. The only time I saw the flag was when they brought us back about a week or two after it was raised to pick up some replacements; they gave us a night's rest on the beach. I saw the flag waving, but to me it just meant that there were no Japanese up there. There was still so much ahead, the flag-raising didn't signify the end of the battle other than we got the high ground up there.

I guess we did get sleep because there is no way you can go 28 days without rest. In the hole it was two hours on and two hours off with your partner or whoever is in the hole with you. Sometimes you would all of a sudden wake up quick out of your sleep and you'd feel that you were falling asleep on your watch. But you would take a look and see that no I'm supposed to be sleeping. You got enough sleep to survive but there was no such thing as a sound sleep. The food was rations. You never ate unless you had a chance. I got a fondness for the sugar cubes in the rations. Like a pack rat I would save them and keep putting them in my gas mask bag that I used as my luggage. I threw everything in that, rations, sugar cubes, cigarettes. I remember any time we'd be moving up and if I had a chance, I'd pop one of them in my mouth. I guess it was my energy pill or something. As far as washing, I actually didn't wash once on Iwo, didn't change my socks, didn't change my underwear, and didn't change a bloody thing. Never even dabbed my eyes. Never washed my mouth. Never shaved. We used to see artillery guys or Headquarters people back on the beach and they're taking showers and have their helmet full of water. I didn't use one ounce of water for any hygienic purposes. But we all smelled the same, so no problem. To us we looked fine. If I looked at the other guy and he had a beard and didn't smell too good, well I couldn't smell him anyway. No matter how bad he looked, I figured we all must look the same.

We went to Tachiiwa Point. That part of the island was the area for our operations. I think somewhere around March 16 they declared it secured. They brought us back and we spent one night on the beach. We got a good night's sleep that night, the first good night's sleep we had. We didn't wash. The next day we boarded some LSTs that took us out to some transport. We had to climb up the nets to get on the ship. One thing I'll never forget as we climbed over the rail at the top of the ship, the sailors would take our gear, help us up. They'd carry our gear and take us below to our bunk where we could sleep. The Navy took excellent care of us. The next day I took a salt water shower, shaved and brushed my teeth. My gums bled.

I lost many friends. I lost two very close buddies. One was Joseph P. Naulty who went through boot camp with me. The other was Elmer A. Myers.

Naulty was killed by a sniper in the Amphitheater. Myers was killed by gunfire maybe March 12 near the end of the operation. Naulty was about 18 or 19; Myers I think was a little older, maybe 20. He was married and had a child. They were young no matter how you look at it.

After Iwo, they sent the whole Division back to its original camp on Maui. We were training for the invasion of Japan when we heard the war was over. We lived in tents and some guy came down the company street and he says they just dropped the bomb and wiped out some Japanese city. We told him he was full of something. Somehow or another someone got hold of a paper and sure enough, they had big headlines, "ATOMIC BOMB." We didn't even know what the hell they were talking about. The company officer sent cases of beer around for us to split up so we would have a couple of cans each. We just sat around drinking and laughing. Unbelievable. I don't think any of us would have come through the invasion of Japan, that's for sure.

We were happy with doing what we did and getting back. We weren't too happy with what it cost us. After a while they began to say that the bombers were landing on Iwo and explained how the B-29s could get to Japan without interference. That's probably why we were able to drop the bomb. That made us feel good. Everyone did a good job. I guess one couldn't do it without the other except some had dirtier jobs than others.

I never had a doubt that we would take the island. If I had a doubt, I think I would have been scared out of my wits. It's not like you could keep dropping back like in Europe where you could drop back 20 miles. You land on an island and you are either going to be killed or you are going to be driven off, one or another. I never had any doubts; we just had too much going for us.

A lot of fellas dropped out of high school in those days. You never went to college unless you were wealthy or highly motivated. It all came together for me in 1950. I got married and I took civil service exams and joined the Transit Police in New York City. I was there for 31 years. I landed a good job and a good woman. We have four children and three grandchildren. Oh yes, I finally received my high school diploma.

* * *

Cpl. William Swanson
2nd Platoon, C Company, 9th Marines,
3rd Division

Bill Swanson, June 1945.

I reported for duty on September 17, 1942. I chose the Marines for several reasons. I used to visit my great uncle who worked for the Edison Company at Shaver Dam. Around 1940, the state was concerned about the safety of these dams so they picked up a group of state guards who more or less guarded the dam. One was a former Marine who had served in China and got out around 1938-39. Over a period of time I got to talking to him and he told about the good old days in China and the camaraderie of the Corps. As soon as I turned 18, I joined the Marine Corps. After boot camp, I reported to Camp Pendleton and was put in 2nd Platoon, C Company, 9th Marines. I stayed in that unit for the whole war.

We left San Diego and spent a few months in New Zealand. We had a lot of hard training. We had no idea what would be happening later on, of course. We were busy but we had a lot of liberty. We didn't have any over night liberty but we had until 2 a.m. in the morning when we'd have to be back. We were in a little place called Papakura about 20 miles south of Auckland in an old New Zealand Army base. There was a little train that ran up to Auckland, so we would get up there maybe once a month. We would get into the little town of Papakura maybe twice a week for liberty---basically going to the movies or getting a good meal. The place was about 3 or 4 miles from camp so we just walked into town and walked back. We were there about four months. We literally cleaned the town out when we shipped out, there wasn't a bakery good left.

My first combat was on Bougainville. It was pretty miserable. It was something like Guadalcanal---a jungle---muddy, everything bad you could think of was there. Jungle rot, tropical ulcers, malaria, mosquitoes, flies, and bugs. I was on the front line just about all the time. You didn't have much in the way of protection against these elements. And, of course, there was a lot of rain along with it. It was so different from Iwo that it was like fighting two different wars.

I think we were prepared for combat in the sense that we were trained to do what we had to do. Very few people would be prepared for what you deal with under combat conditions; however, you soon learn to get acquainted with fear and misery. No matter how much you talk to people, you can't foresee or have any idea how it affects you when it comes down to the basic primordial element of being in combat. You can't prepare for it really except to be trained and well motivated to do what you don't want to do. Quite often you wished to heck you were somewhere else.

I was basically a rifleman although I started out as an assistant BAR man. I got to carry not only my own cartridge belt and gear but I also carried a vest with twelve 20-round magazines for the BAR which added quite a little bit to my load. I had to be available to take over the BAR if something happened to the BAR man. The BAR man was my foxhole buddy so it worked out pretty well from that standpoint. Our scheduled landing on Guam was shortly after the Saipan landing in the middle of June. We were floating reserve for the Saipan landing so we laid off shore there for a few days while that battle was going on. About this time, the Japanese fleet came out for a rather major naval battle and it took all of our naval facilities in the area to take care of that. With that in mind, they sent us back into the Marshall Islands to Eniwetok where we stayed for several weeks while all this was being cleared up. We were aboard ship for almost two months which was a long time on a troop transport. They are certainly not comfortable particularly for that long period of time. They even had to be re-supplied a couple of times while we were on board because they didn't carry the supplies for 1500 troops to stay very long. They were not meant for that.

During that time, they were concerned about us getting out of shape for that long without very much activity. We did all kinds of running around aboard ship but then they would send us off to some of the little atolls to get some exercise. The Marshall Islands had been secured but fought over a few months before. I remember one trip in particular. When we got on this one atoll, huge black blow flies were everywhere. The Navy always fixed sandwiches for us, peanut butter and jelly or something like that. It was a race to eat a sandwich and get the food to your mouth before the flies got it. Coming back, I remember we got on board our landing craft and the gunnels on the landing craft and our helmets were literally covered like black paint with all these flies. I think they considered us a heaven sent way to get off that atoll. Once we got underway, the wind blew everything off. But that was a miserable kind of a place to be even for a short time. Finally we were cleared to make the landing on Guam on July 21.

Guam was a different kind of battle from Bougainville although it had some of the same elements. There was some jungle area, not the kind of jungle as there was in the Solomon Islands which was about as much of a jungle you could find anyway, but there was a lot of cave warfare. After the campaign was over, we patrolled for several months in the different areas where we thought the Japanese might be, and to clean up and train for the next campaign. They were in rather a hurry for some reason to get it done by my 20th birthday, which was August 10. After we left New Zealand, it was about two years before we had liberty. We had our R and R on Guadalcanal after Bougainville and we stayed on Guam for our R and R.

We were usually told where we were going once we got aboard ship, but Iwo Jima still didn't mean anything to us. About half the Marine Corps was involved in Iwo. I don't know the thinking of the powers that be, but with everything that was thrown in there, if it was going to be a piece of cake they wouldn't need three Marine Divisions.

On February 23 the flag went up while we were aboard the ship laying offshore. Everybody was happy thinking maybe this thing is going to be over and we won't even have to go in. Before the end of the day we were told we would land the next day, February 24th. We came in on what they called a tank lighter, LCM, which carries a Sherman tank. It carried about half of our company. I remember the beach was just a hellacious mess of broken equipment, landing craft all over the place like a tornado had hit. There was still some sporadic shelling on the beach but most of it was going up to where the infantry was in the attack. They moved us into an area around Airfield No. 1 for the night. It's funny; we had been in the tropics for nearly two years and never felt cold. We got up to Iwo and that night I remember shivering and wondering if it was from fear or cold. It was cold enough to make a difference to us. We couldn't really dig in because of the type of ash; it was like digging into dry oats. We spent the night there. The next morning we sat around shooting the breeze and eating a cold can of hash while getting ready to move out. Some guy mentioned that things were getting kind of tough back in the States with shortages.

"The rumor is that all the good stuff is going to the troops overseas," he says. We looked at each other and tried to figure out what the good stuff tasted like. We hadn't had any good stuff in a long, long time.

About that time the sergeant hollered over to knock off the crap and get our gear that we were moving out. We moved up to just below Airfield No. 2. There was about a 10 foot abutment there and as we moved up, we were picking up a little artillery. We laid-to there in a position we were told and waited for our next move. We relieved the 21st who had taken most of Airfield No. 2. They had taken a lot of casualties the day before. We relieved them and continued the advance. We had fixed bayonets and were ready as mentally and emotionally as we could be for whatever was going to happen. By this time, we had been through one or two campaigns. There's a way you get men to do the things that were very difficult to do, and I think it came down to a very basic thing: camaraderie. The guy next to you knows you are going to be there and you know damn well he's going to be there, and it really isn't much beyond that. You don't want to let the other guys down, and you don't want to be the first man to let the Marine Corps down. The rest of it, mom, apple pie, country, had been lost a long time ago. Our world was just us. It's kind of hard to think you could really separate yourself from the rest of the world that way but you can, particularly for those of us who had been out there a couple of years. The other world is out there, but it's not your world anymore. You wish to hell you were there, but you just look differently at things.

We were waiting for the word to move out. All of a sudden there was the raised hand up ahead from the platoon leader and sergeants all yelled, "Let's go."

We all ran up this abutment onto the airfield, which was really a jumbled mass of bombs and shell craters, slit trenches, small pill boxes and everything you could think of. We had been getting some sporadic fire while we waited, but once we got onto the airfield itself we were basically out in the open and it really began raining artillery mortars. This was a concerted core attack. The 5th Division was going to be moving out on the left, the 4th on the right and the 9th Regiment in the center. Over on the right there was some high ground, and I remember somebody said they had depressed anti-tank and anti-aircraft guns up there which fired down on the airfield, plus mortar and artillery of different types and machine guns from up ahead. You really couldn't see. You were so intent on running along and surviving the thing that you focus on just what was happening to you and what the next step was going to bring. It's kind of a blur to me now to pick out where I was or how we went though small battles along there. Finally we wound up toward the end of the airfield where there was another abutment and the regiment halted to reorganize. We'd already had some casualties. We were told to take what cover there was and there wasn't much in the way of cover. I remember I was just laying down about ten yards from this abutment. A squad leader and some of the other guys were lying on the abutment itself.

I remember looking over to my left where there was a pretty big shell hole, and I was thinking seriously about running over and jumping in there. Some other guys did just before I did and they hadn't been in there more than a few seconds when a shell landed in it and blew them up. Not too long after that, the guy on my right was killed. We were trying to get a machine gun up on the parapet and get some kind of covering fire going up there. The first guys got up there, got hit, and slid back down. Some other guys went up and tried to fire the machine gun without looking. Then I got hit, and it felt like I got hit in the hand with a hammer to describe how a piece of shrapnel coming through felt. I moved up to the abutment and a corpsman came over and dressed it. It was my right hand. He wrapped it up and tagged me to go back to the aid station. I left from there. A couple of guys I knew quite well were there right near me. In prior times when somebody left, our parting words were always, "I'll see you in Frisco." That was always a great place to be. Of course, not too many of those guys ever made it back to Frisco. We hated to be there yet we also hated to leave our buddies. This was the first time in two and a half years that I wasn't going where C Company was going. I was leaving something that I knew and yes, it was my family. It was the world that I knew. Some of my very good friends were killed later on Iwo.

The Japs still had enough artillery and were throwing it at anybody who was going back or wandering around on the airfield. Several guys were carrying a man on a stretcher so I decided to go back with them for company. We headed back but kept hitting the deck when artillery blasts came close enough. Somewhere along the line, I ended up by myself. It was kind of an eerie feeling in a way. The reserves hadn't been moving up as yet. They were probably back there, waiting to move up. I was still running into artillery blasts, and one shell blasted 20-30 yards down to my left. Just as I went down, another one hit closer. I remember looking over at it and could see the V-shaped blast of the thing. I'd never seen that before. I hit the deck and then ran to a shell hole. There was a reserve guy in the shell hole so we started shooting the breeze. He was watching me move up, and he says he couldn't believe I was still in one piece. You've got to have a little luck. I got back to where we started, and I remember just jumping off the abutment and sliding down there just to get away from the artillery fire from up above. I moved on from there all by myself; I never did find the battalion aid station, but found the regimental aid station and they tagged me for evacuation.

I wound up back on the beach and got taken out to a troop transport. A lot of the guys on the troop transports were like me, the walking wounded. If you were able to be repaired enough to go back in, you'd be sent back in. Because I was hit in my right hand and I came up with a high fever, they moved me over to another ship that was going to a hospital on Saipan. I wasn't in the hospital very long, my wound wasn't very serious. There were a lot of casualties coming in from Iwo and the powers that be knew Okinawa was next with more casualties. A number of patients at this army hospital were put aboard ship like I was and sent to the naval hospital in Hawaii to make room. By the time I got to Hawaii and the paper work got caught up, I was discharged from the hospital and went to the transient center which is a place where people stay until they are assigned some more permanent location. I was there for several weeks, I guess. I had no money. We never thought about taking money with us. The chow wasn't very good, and I really wanted to get over to the PX. I think my folks sent me $5 one time and eventually my pay caught up with me. There was a certain point where we were all directed to a bulletin board to see what we were supposed to do. I was to report for interrogation. It's finally my turn and this guy asked me how long I had been out there. I said 27 months, three campaigns, and I'd been wounded once.

He looked at me for a second and said, "Mac, you're going home."

It was over but not quite over. The word is that I will be in a rifle company for the invasion of Japan. But that is tomorrow. Today is now and I am going home.

The atomic bomb changed everything. For the Japanese in the target cities, it was a horror beyond imagination—as is war in general for those who must root around in the thing. For us, however, and for a great many Japanese, the atom bomb simply meant life and from a purely personal point of view, I doubt this small story could have been written without it.

You had to have a bit of luck to survive—not only from battle casualties but from various illnesses as well. It was malaria, tropical ulcers and the like in the Solomon Islands along with dengue fever and yellow jaundice on Guam. On Bougainville, a good friend got a very serious type of fever called cerebral malaria, a type that attacks the brain. He was one of the first to actually be flown out because his situation was so serious.

We used to try and figure the thing out—fate, luck or whatever—but there just wasn't any easy answer. When the incoming was coming in, we tried to figure where the next one might hit. We all prayed—not here please, not here—but not all were saved. Was it all part of a plan? Were the good guys to be saved and the bad guys taken out? We never could get a handle on it, but we used to speculate on the various possibilities. Then there were the odds, the damn odds. Were they worse the longer we were out there or maybe it didn't matter at all. We looked for some kind of magic formula but never found it.

I came home after a diversion to the Marine Base, San Diego, for a couple weeks of re-training. The thought was that just coming off the front lines we might not be fit to join the civilian population. I never had that feeling myself and I don't know if there was anything to it but the powers that be decided that we should be 're-civilized.' So my long looked-forward-to trip home had to be delayed.

We had three or four years taken out of our lives but we were the lucky ones and we were ready to find a nice girl and get on with our lives. I did find a nice girl and have had a great life.

* * *

Tankers

Sgt. Joe Garza, Jr.
D Company, 3rd Tank Battalion, 3rd Tank Scout Company
3rd Tank Ordnance, 3rd Division

Joe Garza, wartime photo

I joined the Marines because I was a good American. I was 17 years old and in a Boy Scout troop and about ready to get out. The disbelief on December 7, 1941, soon turned to patriotic fever. That week, I was out recruiting all my friends into the Marine Corps. My dad said that I was younger than I should be to join and that he would have to sign for me. Since my country needed me, he would sign, but wanted me to wait until after Christmas. On January 16, 1942, I went to the recruiter. I called my buddies in my Scout troop. We had a very active backpacking troop and I got four of them to go with me. Two of them went with me into the Marines. One went to the Paratroopers and one went to the Coast Guard. I recruited for all branches.

Joining the Marines was the best thing I ever did. They guided me through life to this very day. Whatever we do, we do with that gung-ho attitude that keeps us going. I don't care what crisis you have, you can always get through it because you can always go back to the good Lord, the good country and the Corps. Can't beat that.

"Forget Pearl Harbor. Remember Wake Island, that's where the Marines were fighting against all odds," D.I. Corporal Dill bellowed out at us civilians in the San Diego Recruit Depot Quonset hut, "before we get done with you people, you'll be Marines!"

A short tour of duty with D Company, 2nd Tank Battalion, 2nd Marine Division followed boot camp. We learned to drive the Army discard tanks, Norman Harrington scout tanks, M2A4 Liberty radial engine and Gueberson diesels that we started with shotgun shells. In late summer they selected some of us to form the nucleus of D Company, 3rd Tank Battalion in the 3rd Marine Division. Such was the beginning of 'tanks' that proved themselves worthy on Guam and Iwo Jima.

We went to Auckland, New Zealand, in January 1943 on the USS Bloemfontein. D Company would not survive long. The unit was deactivated soon after arrival in New Zealand, and the Marines were scattered throughout the 3rd. Seven of us found ourselves with the 3rd Tank Battalion Scouts and Snipers (Recon). We stayed in New Zealand for about four months. A lot of training, but also good liberty, was on the menu in New Zealand. We loved New Zealand and its people. I will always remember the grassy knolls of the area and the camaraderie.

We deployed to Guadalcanal in June 1943 for advance training which was good, even though there was no battle going on there. There were still some stragglers out there, so it gave everybody an opportunity to get a feel of the thing. Washing Machine Charley, the Mitsubishi on night harassment visits from Rabaul, kept us awake at the beginning. It soon became a nuisance to jump into the foxholes by our tents.

We had some of the fringes we left in the states...made our own apple jack which was particularly tasty with assorted bugs. We craved fried chicken. We'd heard of a native village some miles east, but we had to cross a crocodile infested river, or so it was reported. For trading, we took a couple of obsolete green pad protectors and my old lemon wood bow I'd brought from Auckland. Getting there was no problem. We traded all our goods and left with a big red rooster that had passed the Social Security benchmark. We stayed too long and had to cross the waist-high river in the twilight hours. Our side arms were ever ready as we crossed and saw many a pair of beady eyes shining on the water.

Someone yelled, "Whatever happens, save the rooster!"

We knew our priorities well. The river was some 30 feet wide and we set a record for that crossing. We fried 'old Red' the next night out in a jungle clearing and realized how really tough Guadalcanal roosters can get to be.

But then we were here for a war, and so in November we sailed over to Bougainville...a perimeter surrounded by slimy muck. I recall that Bougainville is only about 75 miles away from Guadalcanal and we took our first combat there. Absolute quiet except for nice and restful jungle noise...that was to be the 3rd Scout's opening game. We set up a 50 caliber machine gun on Cape Torokina, and were part of the firing power against the Nip planes that zoomed in from Rabaul to work over our transports. We were there to set up a perimeter for them to build an airfield for fighter squadrons like Pappy Boyington's.

The first and only dogfight we experienced there, or ever more, had Marine fighters, Navy fighters, New Zealand fighters and Nip Mitsubishis, Zeros and Zekes filling the sky. Our tracers sought out the Mitsubishis as they came in for close drop on the transports. It was a good feeling; we were finally getting back at them.

We moved up the Piva Trail to Hill 500 where we built our bunkers and waited for the Japs. The first night on the line was unforgettable. We'd set up our concertina wire with the usual empty C-ration cans filled with rocks for a first alert. We strained to see through that blackness of the Bougainville jungle nights. Our ears were set for the slightest step of a foot coming down on the dark jungle ground. After 15 minutes of tenseness, our reaction time was an automatic split second. A burst of firing to the right was followed by a demanding reserve of eyesight and hearing. You knew you were seeing movement by large masses of men, but you waited for a first alert. C-ration cans were our best sentinels. This was our greatest threat—the waiting and the uncertainty.

Christmas found us back on Guadalcanal, enjoying a great turkey dinner, cold storage of many years notwithstanding. We restocked and got replacements for the men we lost. The first campaign can make a difference. We looked at replacements joining us as Marines who were links in the chain of legacy. They, too, would soon be tested and we knew the Corps would prevail.

Training gave way to the usual guessing of where to next. Boarding the transport Fuller, we began the long journey to the Marianas as floating reserves for the 2nd and 4th Marine Divisions on Saipan. We weren't needed on Saipan. Our mission was to retake Guam which had been seized by the Japanese in December 1941. We were honored to be picked as one of the divisions to retake that American territory. The landing on Guam, a long walk across the exposed shallow reef, added another dimension to our history. Japs breached our lines, moved us up on the high ground perimeter to block off an approach. The first things that went into our foxholes were cases of crabmeat cans and bottles of Asahi beer. We guarded all this with our friends, the land crabs.

As we established a high ground tank farm, we spent some time on combat patrols looking for strays. We had finally moved to the high rent district. Our tank farm was on a high plateau surrounded by coconut trees and a banana plantation. It quickly reverted to training and fighting off the scourges of dengue fever and impetigo.

Most of us had been in the Pacific for more than 18 months with two campaigns behind us. We knew we needed at least one more for rotation, and we had no expectations of anything less so we were not disappointed. The next campaign was soon building as training intensified.

In early January, we sailed for Iwo Jima. We were going to be floating reserves in case the 4th and 5th Divisions got in trouble and then they would release us. Well, it didn't take but three days; it was obvious that there would be a lot more than two Divisions could do. So we landed. Boarding our transport in early February 1945 had, as I remembered, that same feeling of excitement. However, we felt this would be a different engagement. The weather turned cold, with a brisk wind...nothing we had experienced for a long time...and the seas got rough.

Our job was to try to retake the second airfield, unbelievably tough because you couldn't dig in, you couldn't dig a foxhole. We went in with tanks and the infantry walked beside us as we made our way up to Motoyama Airfield No. 1 terrace. As soon as we got in there, the Japs laid in a heavy mortar barrage. We had about ten casualties in that first encounter. The Japanese hated two things...the flamethrowers and the tanks. They would throw everything at you, and they did it with accuracy. We knew it was going to be a long stay.

Fortunately, we were experienced. It's not that you are not afraid but at least you kind of know what's coming. But think about the poor replacements we got. They were coming in just out of boot camp, maybe three months out of boot camp, no prior experience and they go into this hell hole of a battle. They were the ones who took it bad with shell shock all over the place. The rest is history.

We said goodbye to Iwo and all those we left behind shortly after the first of April. I traded a .45 sidearm that I carried through all the campaigns to an Army lieutenant for a fifth of bourbon. It was a good trade. I was going and he was staying. Following a quick return to Guam, we had a reunion, rationing the bourbon I had carefully packed.

I was discharged in October 1945. I used the G.I. Bill to earn my degree in engineering at the University of Southern California and then my Master's degree in Business Economics from Claremont Graduate School. The G.I. Bill of Rights is the greatest thing ever.

I later married Ila, the secretary at the adding machine company where I worked. She used to type my reports for school when I needed them. We were married 43 years and I buried her 6 years ago. My love for her was great. We were both lucky. We had a marvelous life together. I have two stepchildren, four grandchildren and 12 great grandchildren.

I first returned to Iwo Jima in 1985 at the 40th anniversary when we met a few of our former enemies. That took care of a lot of ghosts we might have had. It was awkward as hell meeting them. I'm sure for them as well as for us. Maybe more for them than us. We overpowered them. We had come back—not to conquer but to pay our respects. We returned Jap flags, swords and photos to the families.

* * *

Cpl. Lyle Radeleff
A Company, 3rd Tank Battalion, 3rd Division

Lyle Radeleff, 1943.

I enlisted in the Marines in June 1942 a few months before I graduated high school. The recruiting sergeant said he would start the paperwork but that I should finish high school and then we'd complete it. In the late '30's, I had a cousin who went out with a Marine when she was a young girl, and I remember him in his dress blues. It must have been that uniform that made me want to join the Marines.

I went to boot camp in San Diego. At that time they were shifting people around to get them to the Pacific. They'd send you from casual barracks at some place for two weeks then they'd shift you over to another place. I first started with the 2nd Marine Division and then they formed the 3rd Marine Division. I went from the 2nd Marine Scout Company to the 3rd Tank Company, Light Tanks. I remember when President Roosevelt came to dedicate Camp Pendleton in November of '42. At that time the Marines wore summer khaki and we lined up along the road. President Roosevelt drove by in his open car with his cigarette

153

holder. I grew up under Roosevelt so he was the only president I really knew.

From San Diego, we went to New Zealand for about six months. The 3rd Division actually formed overseas. From there we went to Guadalcanal a few months after it was secured. We went up to Bougainville for that campaign and then back to Guadalcanal where we went into medium tanks and trained in those. Then we went to Guam.

Each tank company in the battalion had one recovery vehicle. We were trouble-shooting modified tanks. The retriever tank was the hull of a standard tank and a stationary turret welded to it with a machine gun mount. We had cables that would go out at least 50 yards so we could pull a tank out if it got stuck in the mud. We had track blocks to replace any tracks, tow bars to pull tanks, and a couple of bogie wheels. We had a big A-frame structure on our tank so if we were in a bivouac area we could lift a turret off a tank for repairs. We would go in under fire to repair the tanks. It was all slow work. It wasn't like Europe where the tanks drove 20 miles an hour down the road. This was first gear work all the time.

Tanks are not a good vehicle for jungle warfare. We had light tanks on Bougainville but even they didn't work out. There was a lot of mud and swamps on Bougainville, very hilly where we were and it was unsuitable for tanks. We went back to Guadalcanal where we junked the light tanks and we got the 32-ton Sherman M4A2 tank. A light tank was about 13-14 tons; it had a 37mm gun and two machine guns. Medium tanks had a 75mm gun and a couple of machine guns.

Our next campaign was Guam. We were advancing to Apra Harbor and one of the tank drivers saw the nose of a bomb the Japanese planted on the road to blow up anything that drove over it. He thought he would go down the side of the road but he broke a track running over a mine. He called us to come help him and we could hear all the firing going on around him. We never really worried about the firing until it started moving toward us, then we did something about it. If the shelling was 50, 100, 200 yards away, we didn't pay any attention to it.

We took Guam and trained some more there. We left Apra Harbor for Iwo Jima on February 16. We were on LST 477 with our 24 tanks, 298 enlisted personnel and 16 officers. Headquarters Company was there with tanks, too, so there were about 35 tanks altogether on the LST. After a day out to sea, they brought out the maps and told us we were going to Iwo.

For half an hour in the morning when the sun is coming up and half an hour in the evening when the sun is going down, General

Quarters are always called. That's the favorite time for the submarines to operate because a ship is always lit up by the rising and setting of the sun. The escort vessels during the day would pick up some suspicious noises with the sonar, possible submarines, so GQ was called during the day, too.

On February 19, we were in the area of Iwo Jima when our LST developed steering trouble and dropped astern until control could be regained. There is not much we can do on an LST except stand around and talk and watch the waves, I guess. A few of us were back underneath a gun tub because we had run into rain squalls when we heard this explosion go off inside the bridge. Later, we learned that Lt.(jg) Reinhard was killed when the IFF, Identification Friend or Foe, detonator which he held in his hand exploded. The detonator blew up in his face and killed him and injured a seaman first class. Reinhard was buried at sea. It was the first time I had seen someone buried at sea. A couple of heavy artillery shells were sewn into a canvas bag for weight, and the body placed inside. The body was put on a stretcher and covered by the American flag. One end of the stretcher was put on the rail and as it was slowly lifted, the body slid off from underneath the flag into the water. They noted the location where this took place. The captain read a passage and the Marines from our battalion fired a gun salute.

Lt. Reinhard was killed in the morning and his funeral was about 2 o'clock in the afternoon. Around 5 o'clock, a kamikaze plane hit our position. We were only about 7 miles off Iwo Jima when we were hit. Our company received the first casualties of the battle; three Marines were killed and about half a dozen wounded. Quite a few sailors were killed and wounded, too.

I was with a tank commander and another fellow lining up to go to chow, which was served in the bridge area. We heard aircraft engines and I remember telling my friend, Camden, that the aircraft must be our air cover, but they were not. The cloud cover was an 800-foot ceiling and we could hear these planes flying around looking for an opening. Because of the cloud cover, the Japanese planes couldn't spot us quickly. The kamikaze aircraft were part of a 50 enemy plane group that staged a three-hour attack against U.S. ships off Iwo. The Bismark Sea (CVE) was sunk, the AKN Keokuk, the Saratoga (CV), and the Lunga Point (CVE) were damaged. When the Japanese plane struck, it was too shallow in its approach and horizontal to the water. If it had been clear skies, the plane would have been coming down at about a 45 degree angle and it would have gone right through the ship. At the angle the pilot flew, he hit the side of the ship.

It tore more of a long hole in the hull instead of breaking critical parts of the ship's structure. It hit on the starboard side and I was standing on the port side which I guess is about 40 feet away. Battle stations were called immediately and the fire started. Sailors tried to get the pumps going but they were disabled, so they brought out some little Briggs and Stratten pumps and threw a 2-inch hose over the side of the ship. I helped to pull hoses. Marines from our tank battalion fought side by side with the ship's company by manning guns, working as loaders, fighting fires, heaving hot ammunition over the side and helping care for the wounded.

There was a Japanese pilot who jumped out in a parachute when his plane was shot down. Watching the parachute astern on the starboard side slowly drop into the water, some crewmen standing next to a Marine remarked, "I bet if we gave a rifle to one of these Marines he would shoot the bastard before he hits the water."

A ship's officer issued orders that there would be no firing upon the Japanese pilot in the water. No attempt to pick him up was seen. Five Japanese aircraft had attacked the convoy and no aircraft survived.

When the plane hit there was a big explosion from the two bombs it carried. In about a minute, you could hear ready ammunition start to pop. Gun tubs have ready ammunition stuck around them so they can feed the gun real fast. In one gun tub, ready ammunition was starting to get warm so some guy started to pull that stuff out and throw it overboard. The plane took out one 40mm gun and two 20mm guns. The 20mm guns have a big ammunition box which is picked up and attached to the gun. They had to toss that over because of the heat. Ammunition is very critical to temperature and about twice a day sailors would take the temperature where they store the ammunition to make sure it is within a certain range. Ammunition could explode if it gets hot enough, and if you use it when it's hot, it doesn't have the pressure behind it.

It must have been several hours before it was all over and then they had to extract the bodies. Chow was forgotten. We ate K-rations instead. I knew the three Marines who were killed. I remember Axelroth had a big handlebar moustache, and he was a tank driver. A tank driver has his eyeballs above the hole when he drives but Axelroth's moustache was like a sweep. Every time he turned, it would dust the dirt off the rim. I think these guys were playing poker on top of the tanks down on the tank deck. When the explosion happened; they tried to get out of there but were trapped. Those killed were buried at sea in position 24 degrees 41'N and 141 degrees 19'E. The five wounded were removed earlier to PA 206.

By Dammit, We're Marines!

Later we had an air raid alert and guns started firing. Pinky Samsoe and I went out on deck and stood behind a 20mm gun that these two sailors were firing. It was quite a 4th of July celebration with ships standing off Iwo. I think there were hundreds of them. They would fire off their big guns, 3 inch and above, and you saw the shells explode in the air. They were sort of following radar tracking so everybody with 40mm guns, 20mm would fire in that direction. There may be a ship two miles away that's firing in our general direction and, naturally, whatever goes up has to come down. Samsoe and I heard an explosion right in back of us and I felt a sting in my right leg. A fragment from friendly fire was stuck in my leg. I went down to the corpsman and he put a band aid on it. He said I could get a Purple Heart for that, and I said I'd be ashamed. Samsoe and I decided to go below after that.

We knew what we were getting into on Iwo because we were listening to the radio transmissions of the reports from the tank companies that were ashore from the 4th and 5th Division. You could hear that they spotted pill boxes and that kind of thing. All the tank battalions had different radio frequencies so the 3rd Tank Battalion could not immediately contact the 4th or 5th Division because of the different frequencies. The radio operator has to dial around trying to find the right frequency. A good radioman could rig the radio to directly pick up the other division's frequency. Samsoe was our radio operator and he could do this. He told some officers about this on the LST, but they said it changes the radio, and it is no longer the original radio they got from the supply depot so he couldn't do it.

The ship's commanding officer was determined to beach and unload our cargo. Debris littered the shrapnel-riddled tank deck. The five-ton elevator was hanging sidewise into the opening so that it blocked the tank deck ramp. Two compartments forward were punctured through the bottom, and water jetted in faster than the pumps could remove it adding weight to the ship's bow down far below proper draft for beaching. Cargo shifted aft as the aft fuel and water tanks were filled to the limit. Men entered the bottom tanks forward and actually bailed out water to get the last gallon.

We went in on the 24th at Green Beach 1, which was at the base of Mt. Suribachi. I remember seeing the first flag. We could see the small flag and the next day we saw the larger flag. The Seabees tried to lay Marston mats down for the tanks, but the first few tanks did not go on the mats and one of them broke a track. We had to repair that. We then moved up to a bivouac area at Airfield No. 1 during the nighttime.

Normally what we did with the tanks when we are in the bivouac areas was to dig a pit about 18 inches deep just narrow enough for the tank to drive over. Then we'd put sand bags among the bogie wheels and we'd form our own little fortress you might say. It was difficult to sleep. There was always lots of noise from all the shelling.

Two days later, I was wounded on Airfield No. 1. The tanks made an operation against Airfield No. 2, half a mile away. They came back with one tank pulling another one. We were trying to repair that tank when we started to receive artillery from some Japanese positions that were not taken care of yet. We crawled underneath the tank into this pit where we thought we'd be safe. The shell followed us in. Everybody was killed or wounded except the guy who went up in the turret to eat some chow. That kid from Arkansas never received a scratch. I was evacuated and taken down to the beach to a big pit with canvas over it where the wounded were brought. We were classified and tags were put on us, then we were taken out to a floating barge. From there we went out to the various ships depending on what the ship could handle as far as type of wound. These corpsmen are angels. I went back to Saipan and was operated on and then went to Tinian. I was there for two weeks recovering and then they sent me back to Guam. I was there for a week and then sent home.

I went back to Iwo in 1997. It was my first time back. I couldn't recognize it with all the foliage. It was so well cultivated. Nature does a wonderful job recovering from battles. When I got off the plane, I did go down on bended knee. For some fellas, it was very emotional.

Bougainville was different from Guam and Guam was different from Iwo. From the three battles, you could see the expansion of the American military strength especially the growth of the ships. When we landed on Bougainville, the Japanese Navy and Air Force were quite strong and you saw lots of Japanese aircraft. They had a big naval battle one night off shore that was a sight to see. When we were in Guadalcanal, the Japanese would come in to bomb and anti-aircraft fire would go up. We saw a lot of Japanese aircraft around Bougainville, but by the time we got to Guam it was a different story. Our naval strength grew so much in that year and a half, it was just amazing. By the time we got to Iwo, I was just flabbergasted by all our ships that were there and how fast they could build this armada and still fight a war in Europe, too.

When I've visited Camp Pendleton, I've seen the tank recovery vehicle they have now and it is far more specialized. Each member of the crew is a specialist, you might say. One man is a specialist in hydraulics, another well trained in welding. In World War II, none of us knew what the hell we were doing, we learned on the job!

By Dammit, We're Marines!

My wife and I were married on November 16, 1945, about 6 or 8 months after I got back. You could say we met through the U.S. Post Office. When I was on Bougainville, my foxhole buddy gave me the address of a girl he knew. I wrote her and it turned into a love affair after two and a half years of correspondence. We've been married 62 years.

* * *

1st Lt. Edgar Steinau
B Company, 5th Tank Battalion, 5th Division

Edgar Steinau, wartime photo

We left Hawaii six weeks before D-Day. Our ship number was LSM-7. It carried six medium tanks lined up in a row one behind the other and chained to the ship's bulkhead. Living quarters were on either side of the open hold—it was a flat-bottomed ship and less than comfortable. I was half sick most of the time, and my only salvation was to stay topside. It was a long, hot, boring trip. One exception was an encounter with a heavy storm that pushed the bow of this small ship into the sky. This storm lasted two days and three nights.

I did enjoy the early evenings as the sun was setting. I watched the clouds changing colors from deep reds to rosy pinks and bursts of lavender. The ocean was a beautiful deep blue changing to turquoise and bright green. I sat near the bow and was able to look down at the fish jumping out of the water and creating a phosphorescent glow and sparkle. It was a delightful way to spend the end of each dull day aboard ship. Cramped quarters, the smell of diesel fuel, iron and steel all around me, salt-water showers, lousy food and a queasy feeling in the abdomen wasn't my idea of an exotic cruise in the Pacific.

160

By Dammit, We're Marines!

We finally arrived at Saipan which was to serve as a staging and rendezvous area. It was an inspiration to all of us as we watched the B29s take off from Saipan, circle the island and head north to bomb the cities of Japan. The planes formed a long thin line that stretched for miles. An eerie sight was to see our submarines slide silently and swiftly through the pass as they headed for their own rendezvous on the way to Iwo Jima.

The morning of D-Day was spectacular. My feeling was one of quiet anticipation and curiosity. The orders were meticulously prepared, final instructions given and repeated so many times, an idiot knew when and where he was to go on this day. So all of us idiots watched and waited. We watched the Marine infantrymen go down the rope ladders into their still smaller landing craft.

I watched seven waves of Marines and knew our turn was next. The eighth wave, of which I was a part, was the first wave of armored vehicles. Our tanks were welded with waterproof kits over the engines so that we could operate under water for a few yards if we landed in deep water off the shoreline. We headed toward the shore and hit the sand with a crunch. We quickly lowered the ramp and my tank was off first.

There was no time to think. Our training took over, 'accomplish the mission.' The first thing I saw were strings of white plastic tape to the right and left of our tanks. Marine demolition crews were marking a path for us through dangerous mine fields. They were on their hands and knees probing the sands with a bayonet blade and clearing any mines they found. This was not part of the training, not part of the plan. The idiots forgot to tell the other idiots that the Japanese knew how to lay minefields.

We were barely able to maneuver up the twisting and narrow confines of cleared minefield. Marines were advancing rapidly and on schedule across to the other side of the island. Our orders were to split Mt. Suribachi on the south and the airfields to the north. It looked easy, no resistance, no sweat. My first thought was that our commanding generals were mistaken as to enemy strength and fortifications. I grew less apprehensive as I saw our Marines directly in front of us advancing without encountering enemy fire. Suddenly there was a rapid burst of machine gun fire from my tank. The gunner seated directly below me had mistaken Marines for Japanese. The rifle fire stirred up dust and dirt and our vision was impaired. The short burst of fire ended as quickly as it started. As we reached the top of the hog back of the hill, I noticed movement of enemy soldiers to my right in a tall grassy field looking like western prairie dogs as they scurried about seeking shelter in their underground tunnels. I was no further than 50 yards away. We had accomplished our first day's mission as dusk settled in and were ordered to halt and prepare for our first night. The gunner was heartbroken, sickened by his error and asked me if any Marines were hit by the machine gun fire. I assured him no one was injured and tried to kid him out of his depression by saying he was a lousy gunner and never could hit anything. It was a very difficult time for this 19-year-old Texas boy Marine trained to be a tough guy.

What a night! Japanese mortar fire landed in a crowded small area filled with Marine infantry, support troops, ammunition, supplies and food. We were pinned down, going nowhere. The enemy couldn't miss. That was a terrifying night. The noise of the 90mm mortar fire exploding was like a loud bass thud followed quickly by a thunderous boom. I heard the cries of the wounded all night long. Of all things, a storm came up with heavy rain and strong winds. One of my tank commanders, a tough, steady and solid individual asked if we would be evacuated. In my true Marine training, my response was, "We are here to stay."

I knew we would prevail. Marines don't quit and would never accept defeat.

The next morning our orders were to advance north on the western side of the island. I would be the seventh in the line of tanks supporting an advance of infantry north bound. The lead tank went down a very narrow path with little cover of foliage. This tank commander and his platoon were right out in the open and were pinned down by enemy machine gun fire. There was a sudden explosion and huge black clouds of smoke seeped through the brush. The tanks in front of me were turning in all directions kicking up dust and retreating. I pulled my tanks back and waited. That evening, I found out that Japanese infantry assaulted the lead tank by climbing over it and planting a small magnetic bomb on the side of the tank. The crew was able to scramble out seconds before the 75mm shells exploded inside the tank. The explosion blew the 9-ton turret completely off the bottom of the tank.

For the next several days, we were forced to ride past this reminder of Japanese ferocity until the first defense line of the Japanese was broken and we had clear movement for several hundred yards. A coordinated attack was to begin at daybreak. The Marines were advancing steadily with our tanks leading the assault. Now the Japanese knew that our tanks signaled a major campaign and zeroed in on them. I made a tactical error by allowing one of my tanks to assist one of the others that had thrown a track. These two tanks were almost together and mine was a dozen or so yards away. The Japanese still controlled the high ground and easily spotted us as a favorable target. There was a sudden mortar burst about 50 yards behind us. We speeded up work to repair the disabled track. Another mortar landed 30 or 40 yards in front of us. We were bracketed by mortars and artillery.

It was my fault and I quickly ordered our tanks to move as fast as possible several hundred yards in front of our infantrymen. As we began our forward move, a barrage of mortars hit all around us. I do not know if there were any casualties but it was a frightful and sickening feeling. At least we were clear of the infantry and in open ground. Of course, we were a perfect target. I radioed the other tanks to use smoke grenades. The smoke concealed our exact positions as we moved forward and back, side to side in an attempt to avoid a direct hit. The infantry had been called back and to take cover. I finally was forced to order our tanks to fall back behind the infantry. What confusion, tension, strife, fear and a racing heart beat. As I turned my tank, a 90mm mortar hit the ground behind and under the tank. Shrapnel tore through the engine compartment and black smoke poured out. We were on fire! A tank full of 100-octane gasoline plus a full load of 75mm HE shells were in danger of going up. I told the crew to use the escape hatch in the under belly of the tank. Japanese infantry were excellent marksmen and their sights were set on hatch doors. We crawled out the bottom and got into the nearest crater. We dug ourselves into the sand, buried our faces and bodies and shook with fear. Marine training made us feel safe and protected inside a tank. Three inches of armor all around, speed of movement, 30 caliber machine guns, 75mm cannon, all served to create safety. Now we were out in the open and we were scared. We could see smoke rising from my tank but there was no explosion. The barrage finally slowed down, and I saw one of my tanks moving slowly down a path to a rear position. I waved them to stop, and my crew and I crawled on hands and knees to the escape hatch under the tank. The crew went in first and I was the last to enter. Ten men in a tank built for five gets crowded. We made our way back to safety, but I was not the same Marine or person after that experience.

There was plenty of action on the east side of the island. The 4th Division was taking a heavy beating there, and we were called upon to relieve some of the pressure by a diversion on the 4th's left flank. Again our tanks were in support of an infantry advance. My tank elected to try and traverse across the black, deep, and damp sand to get better footing along a path running north and south, parallel to the airstrip. We hit a land mine and were unable to be of any help that day to the rest of my tanks. Our infantry pushed on as we spent the rest of the day putting the track back together. That day, the 3rd Division tanks arrived as reinforcements. They promptly went to the front and came back with eight tanks lost in less than half a day's combat. The tank commanders came in with their hatches open, a cocky look, and pennants flying off the radio antennas. They came back with anti-tank holes in their sides and learned a hard lesson in a hurry.

After more costly battles, Airfield No.1 was in Marine control. We all saw why we were fighting to take the island when we heard the sputtering of one engine on one of our bombers coming back from a run to Tokyo. Seeing the American flag flying atop Mr. Suribachi and saving this plane gave us a lift.

One time I wanted to get a better view of the area of our next assault. There was a steep knoll I had to climb. As I reached the top, I found it had held a Japanese aerial gun emplacement. It must have taken a direct hit because the gun was a tangled mess of metal, and the bodies of several Japanese lay strewn about. Pieces of bodies were everywhere as I looked inside this cavernous anti-aircraft gun emplacement. There was no feeling of shock or revulsion. I merely used the vantage point to survey the territory of the next fight and left. I believe God placed in our bodies and minds a defense mechanism that made one able to completely disregard the witnessing of carnage from battle. It was gruesome.

There was a road that we traveled almost each morning now as the Marines took more ground. Protruding out of the ground along the roadside was a hand and arm sticking straight up. The infantry also used the road and each morning some Marine put a lit cigarette between its fingers. It made a bizarre bit of humor for us as we passed by on the way to the front line action. One of the most macabre sights that did leave a feeling of remorse happened alongside a pathway. I came across the mangled remains of a Marine that was literally a mound of twisted flesh. Sticking out from it was part of an arm with the hand jutting upward at an awkward angle. It was his left hand because I saw a gold wedding band on his finger. That left a mark on my mind and maybe even my soul.

Hill 362 was crucial to the Japanese.* If they lost control of this ridge line, the end was near. Marines made daily assaults and would take control of the high ground. Japanese would counter-attack at night and would retake control. The night battles were often hand-to-hand banzai attacks. Our tanks were no help at night. Japanese flares made an unholy light over the terrain.

There was to be another dawn attack after the Japanese counter attack during the night. We started our engines and started up the same roadway as before. We were to fire into any cave opening we saw with our 75mm HE shells. One shell after another was loaded, trigger pulled and fired into a cave. We loaded one shell and it fired without the gunner pulling the trigger. The barrel was so hot, it fired by itself. This was fun. The terrain near the hilly area of northern Iwo Jima was filled with caves. The Marine infantry had to go across this open area, exposed and vulnerable. There was a steep, sandy hill that had to be negotiated. At the base of this hill, the enemy had dug a tank trap. A tank trap is merely a short, sharp downhill drop and then a straight up slant. Tanks point down the sharp slope and cannot get any traction to lift its nose up the hill. That lower short slope hill had to be removed or leveled by bulldozers. Marines were taking heavy casualties by enemy small arms fire and fell back to regroup. There were no tank bulldozers available and we needed help fast. I saw a most courageous man with the good Lord watching over him. A Seabee with a small dozer used for construction work slowly chugged its way across the open ground 'midst heavy small arms fire. He methodically worked back and forth leveling the tank trap. He was almost nonchalant as machine gun fire racked his dozer. He completed the job and chugged slowly back to his bivouac area.

The best American young men were ordered to take the hill. They charged, ran into the open area, were fired upon and fell mortally wounded but more charged on. Our tanks were ready to move but the soft sand made traction slow and difficult. These young Marines continued. I saw one Marine reach the top of the hill only to be hit and visibly in pain. Two corpsmen behind a rocky cover saw him and rushed to his aid disregarding their own safety. They slid on the soft sand, struggled to the top and each grabbed one of the wounded man's legs and dragged him face down to the bottom of the hill. The corpsmen then picked him up and carried him to their jeep.

The small arms fire was hitting off our tanks like popcorn. Finally we arrived at the top of the hill. Bodies were strewn over the wide expanse of ground before us. Rocky ridges were in the distance hiding more enemy soldiers with small arms fire leveled at our Marines. As we moved forward, I saw a wounded Marine and went to his aid. We were going to pick him up through the escape hatch. To get him, we had to drive our tank over him between the tank treads. I could see him yelling, he couldn't move and he thought we were going to run over him. We were able to get over him quickly. We dropped the hatch and pulled him inside. Less than an hour later we were in an aid station and transferred the wounded Marine. To this day I do not know what happened to that brave, frightened young kid, but our entire crew felt good about our effort. The bravery of the American Marine infantryman will always live in my memory.

Our most effective weapon throughout the entire operation was our flamethrowing tanks. The battalion commander had five tanks installed with this equipment. Metal tubes ran through the barrel of the 75mm gun. Napalm stored inside the tank was forced through this tube and ignited as it left the barrel. When the jelly-like substance hit a surface, it spattered over a wide area and burned. We employed these tanks outside the cave entrances.

The Japanese were now fighting in desperation. We had moved to the northern part of the island, the widest part of this very small Pacific hell hole. My involvement and participation in this next skirmish was a horrible experience. I had nightmares and sweats for years after.

A pocket of resistance developed to the northeast and a Marine company was pinned down and suffering casualties. I was ordered to take my platoon of tanks to help. Battle is mass confusion, radio communication spotty, crackly and difficult. We made our way to the front but could not locate the unit we were ordered to support. We halted our tanks when we saw some other Marines and I asked an officer for directions.

As I went past a deep foxhole, I glanced down and saw two bodies at the bottom and said, "There are two good Japs," to a sergeant nearby.

"Sir, one is a Marine," he answered.

I looked again, and yes, with a knife in his back under the shoulder, was a young American Marine. Their uniforms were so dirty and blood-smeared that both looked the same. This was hand-to-hand fighting by a desperate enemy and part of the same counter offensive that forced the other Marine company to call for reinforcements and tank support. My platoon was it! I found the exact location and headed down rough terrain, jutting ravines with cave openings in the hills all around us. We slowly made our way to a small open area where we spotted some Marine infantry flattened and dug in against a rock strewn ridge no more than four or five feet high. There was small arms fire bouncing off our tanks. We pulled our three tanks up behind the same ridge. Our turrets rose above the top of this ridge and we could see hundreds of enemy soldiers, prone against the ground in shallow holes. The ground behind them dropped off sharply. We were face to face with a large enemy unit holding up our advance. I needed information and orders from the commanding officer of the Marine infantry units in the area. Before leaving the tank to hunt up the CO, I called our Battalion HQ requesting two flamethrowing tanks. I gave orders to my other tank commanders to keep the enemy troops pinned down until the flame-throwers arrived. We depressed our 30 caliber machine guns as low as possible and fired over the heads of the Japanese. They were very close but at least forced to hold their positions by our gunfire and presence of the 75mm cannon. The entire area covered only about half the size of a football field. I dropped our escape hatch and made my way along the ridge asking Marines where to find their commanding officer. I discovered that all the officers had been killed in heavy action the night before.

A gunnery sergeant was in charge. His headquarters were behind some rocks and brush. When I got there, I saw a burly, bearded rough and tough red head career Marine. Tears streamed down his face, he was shaking, legs quivering, completely out of control. A corporal and a PFC tried to console and quiet him. The corporal was in command! I asked the corporal to spot where our troops were and where he wanted HE shells or flame. He had me follow him forward and pointed out the heaviest concentration of enemy. He called for one of the Marine riflemen on the extreme right of the defense line to point his rifle in the direction of a heavy gun emplacement. As he raised up to do this, a burst of rifle fire hit him in the face and he fell mortally wounded. The corporal and I quickly made our way back to the area of the gunnery sergeant. He was still flat on his back, eyes bulging, rolling back and forth on the ground. I told the corporal we would be using the flame-throwers. I edged my way back to my tank, confused, and with a deep knot in my stomach. It was my first experience with the mental and emotional breakdown of a person. Strain, stress, fear, sleeplessness, responsibility, blood, and the sight and sounds of death were the causes of these breakdowns. There was plenty of it on that day.

Hours passed as we waited for the flamethrowers to find us. We were able to keep and hold the Japanese where they were. When the flamethrowers arrived, I positioned one on my right behind the same rocky ridge within 20 yards or so of my tank. More Marine reinforcements moved up behind this ridge and they were all around our tanks. I didn't like so many being so close. I remembered that tanks draw mortar fire. The other flamethrower was moved further away to my left and up a path that really cut off the last escape route of the enemy. They were trapped. Our radio communication with the flamethrowers was excellent. What a relief! They knew what to do without orders; the carnage began. Our tank machine gun fire pinned down the enemy and our flamethrowers sprayed the napalm jelly over the entire area. Many were shot as they got up to run toward the precipice behind them. One Japanese was sprayed with napalm from head to foot and he was on fire. He was only about 30 or so yards in front of me. He got up screaming and running toward my tank waving his rifle. As he came up over the ridge, a Marine infantryman quickly used his M-1 rifle and shot him. His body rolled down the hill burning at the base and on my side of the tank. I could lower my periscope to see him burning within a few feet of me. This was a bloody massacre of an enemy vowed to fight to the death.

The end of the campaign was near. Japanese were leaping off the northern cliffs in suicide pacts. There was a rumor the Japanese Commanding General had been killed. I wrote my first letter home. I didn't write any letters home earlier because I was sure if I did, my number would come up the following day.

We returned to our bivouac area and saw Army occupation troops landing to take over control of the island. We were told to get ready for loading aboard ship. Our mission accomplished! The same LSM-7 was to take us back to Hawaii. I had no casualties in my platoon and all three tanks returned to Hawaii damaged but ready to go on to the mainland of Japan. It was to be our next mission. I wasn't quite so ready. I knew my number was coming up.

One observation I must make that is evident in our society and business life of today. The front lines were marked by very young kids, each in a small foxhole with dead Japanese close by, their blank faces covered with a white cloth. Stench of death filled the air. These young men represented our defense. They were our protectors, our fighters. The bivouac areas to the rear were crowded with runners, messengers, radio people, maintenance people, supply people, drones and hordes of helpers. They were joking, eating, shaving, drinking cool water, actually taking a bath and enjoying hot food! Farther to the rear more and more of the same; the few doing the rough, hard work and the many enjoying the fruits of their courage and labors.

I can honestly say there was never a feeling of hatred toward the Japanese military. For my part, it was simply a matter of serving our country. Freedom and democracy are worth both the risk and the sacrifice.

*The battle for Hill 362 commenced on D+9.

* * *

By Dammit, We're Marines!

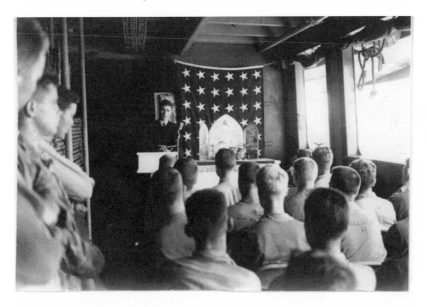

Chaplain Wolf conducting services for the 2nd Marine Division prior to Saipan campaign, June 1944, aboard the USS Frederick Funston.

Church services on Bougainville. Photograph by Angelo Dugo

Aboard ship, Marines plan for invasion of Iwo Jima.

Insect repellent and DDT are sprayed on clothing before the assault on Iwo Jima. Official USMC photo/Silverthorn collection.

The 4th Division lands on Iwo Jima.
Official USMC photo/Silverthorn collection.

With fire retardant protecting their faces,
demolition crews prod the ground to locate land mines.
Official USMC photo/Silverthorn collection.

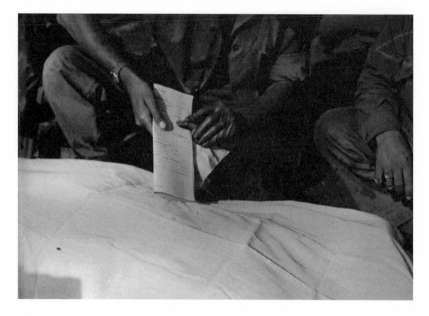

A Navy Pharmacist Mate puts the fingerprints of a Marine on the death certificate prior to burial (above).

Marines sprayed with disinfectant solution before burial on the beach on Iwo (below).

Official USMC photo/Silverthorn collection

Evacuation of the Marine casualties on Iwo Jima.
Official USMC photo/Silverthorn collection.

Marines open a special container used for the shipment of whole blood.
The contents can be kept for 21 days by this method.
Official USMC photo/Silverthorn collection.

Marines flock around the first B-29 bomber to land on the Iwo airfield.
Official USMC photo/Silverthorn collection.

Headquarters and Service

Master Sergeant Bill Behana, USMC (Ret.)
Pvt., HQ Service, H & S Company, 28th Marines, 5th Division

My good friend turned 18 before me and went into the Marine Corps. So when I turned 18 and the draft board called me, I went into the Marine Corps to follow him. He went to Parris Island but I went to San Diego so we never did see each other. You were either a Parris Island Marine or a Hollywood Marine. I was a Hollywood Marine. It was a big joke.

I went through boot camp and went to telephone school in San Diego. I was a wireman and a communicator and basically that's what I did all the way through the Marine Corps except that I did two tours on the drill field as a drill instructor in the 50's and 60's.

I went to boot camp, then went home on leave, came back and joined a replacement outfit at Pendleton. The war was going on and they needed men. I went overseas on a troop transport to Pearl Harbor, Hawaii. When we were aboard ship, everything was blacked out. You couldn't have any lights at all. You had to wander around, stumble over things if you went topside. People have no idea how guys lived; it was terrible. There was always a line to use the head, the showers, and there were no fresh water showers. I had never been aboard a ship like this as a kid in Pennsylvania. Nobody told me about salt water showers so I went down there to shower and put regular soap and salt water in my hair. I couldn't get the shampoo out so I had to get all my hair cut off. There is salt water soap, but I just didn't know that. There were two meals a day on that ship and you stood up when you ate because they didn't have the room on the mess deck. The sailors had their own mess; but in the Marine mess deck, we stood up to eat and got out so the next guy could get in and eat.

I was then assigned to the V Amphibious Corps Signal Battalion and was sent over to Maui with them. They were getting prepared to go to Iwo Jima. They were short of communicators in the V Amphibious Corps. Our Signal Battalion was a pool of people so I got transferred to H & S Company, 28th Marines on the big island where we trained before we got aboard ship. I was 45 days aboard ship going from Hawaii to Iwo because we would sail one direction then zigzag in another.

Life aboard ship was very, very bad. In an area about the size of a living room, there were about 100 people sleeping, stacked eight to ten high. The bunks were iron poles with canvas stretched on them and you're up there with all your gear. It wasn't very pleasant. In fact, I was glad to get off even if I had to go into Iwo! There was probably six to eight inches between you and the man above you. You couldn't sit up unless you were sitting on the top bunk. And if you got some heavy guy in the bunk on top of you, he sagged down on you. You were in there with your rifle, your pack, everything because there was no place to store your gear. It's not like they ride today on the ships, they have bunks with mattresses, lockers.

The Navy guys lived separately aboard the transports. They weren't living much better, but they had it better than we did. We didn't like the sailors getting better mess and bunk area. Sailors and Marines always fought. If you have ever been to a fleet landing you know the Marines and sailors are always fighting.

We got to Iwo, and we could hear the bombardment that started. My unit was going to land in the 14th wave, so we got up for chow and it was the first time I had any steak or milk in a year and a half. We had steak and eggs for breakfast. They call that a warrior's breakfast in the Marine Corps, steak and eggs. That tradition was picked up by the Marines in New Zealand and Australia because the Aussies had steak and eggs for breakfast. We were sitting around down there getting ready to go, waitinguntil they called our boat number to go topside. We went down in the boats in the nets. It was difficult. We wore combat packs. We didn't have field transport packs. The field transport packs have everything in it. The combat pack had just the stuff we need for a couple of days on the beach. They told us that in two or three days we would clean this island up. Of course they had no idea the Japanese were all underground.

When you climb down the net, you don't grab onto the horizontal piece of the net because the guy above you may step on your fingers. You have to grab on the vertical side all while the boat is pitching up and down. You try to gauge it so that you go on the down side so you are not on the up side, or else you're up too far and you can't reach the boat. We got into the boats, went out and started circling until it was our time to go out to the line of departure. It made you sick, too, because of all the diesel fumes and the waves.

We landed on the beach and I came busting out of the end of the boat. The first thing I saw was an amphibious tractor called a weasel and all I could see were eight dead Marines laying all over that. It was really bad. Aboard ship, they issued entrenching tools, but I said I wouldn't need one of those when I get on the ground. I didn't want to carry it. I got out of the end of the boat, and everybody was digging a hole. That volcanic ash was like walking in a sand pile. I didn't have anything to dig with and the Japs were hitting the beach with machine guns, mortars and artillery. It was really bad. There was all this stuff going off all around, so I popped off an ammunition can and I dug myself a hole with that. I got an entrenching tool from a dead Marine later on in the day. I didn't have it as bad as the grunts. They were the guys who were really taking a pounding. If you figure it out, every eighth man got killed there. Every second man got wounded.

There was supposed to be a wave land every five minutes. Nobody got on the beach for about two hours after we landed because the Japs pounded the hell out of us. The regiment set up a little CP on the beach and I operated a little switchboard there. They moved up, and I stayed in the rear with this piece of equipment to keep contact with the elements that moved into the middle of the island. I was there all night by myself on the beach. I could hear this clank clank clank....the Japs were cranking a gun out of a cave over on Suribachi. They cranked it out and fired an illumination shell into the bay towards all the ships that were out there. The ships must have cut their anchors because they all disappeared before the Japs could get a second round off. I spent the night there alone, if you can imagine. I was 18 years old and frightened to death. I didn't know who was around me or anything.

I was stuck there, but they said they would come and get me the next day. The next morning a tank pulled up behind me and got in a firefight with the Japs over on Mt. Suribachi who started shooting back. All these mortars and everything are landing around me since I was between the tank and the Japanese. The tank pulled away so the Japs quit shooting but then the Navy bombers came in and dropped bombs. A hundred-pounder dropped short and hit right next to my hole. It practically buried me. I thought, my God, if I ever get out of here I'll be lucky. Later, somebody crawled back to get me. As I crawled up out of this trench, the first thing I see is a dead Japanese who had been worked over with a flamethrower.

We moved in and started the fight for Suribachi. We'd run phone wire lines up to the battalions. We had three battalions facing Suribachi so we had to keep communications between the regimental CP to each battalion. The line went in, they'd blow it up and we'd have to go out and fix it. On the fourth day they put the flag up, and I could see it from where I was. It was nice to see because it told us we were winning part of the war anyway. It was a great moment. When they came out with the 7th War Loan and the monument, well I was pretty proud that it was my outfit. Once Suribachi was secured, we swung north and moved in on the left of the 27th Marines and started moving forward. It was day by day, yard by yard. Marines were just falling like flies. I was setting up one day working on the line up along side the road when they brought a whole bunch of replacements in who still had their barracks caps and stuff with them. The next morning they brought about half of them back as casualties.

You don't really get to see the whole picture because you are just in one little area. On Iwo, you didn't know where the forward line was because you would go forward but the Japs would be down in these holes and pop up behind your line. Stuff is dropping all around and you just hope it's not going to hit you. You don't want to see anybody hurt, but you hope it isn't you. That's a hell of a thing to say, but you want to see tomorrow. That's the way I felt. I had two friends who were killed. One was in the same regiment that I was and the other in the 27th Marines. That was terrible.

After we had been there for three or four weeks, the word came down that the Army was coming in to take over and they started pulling units out. I was on Iwo for 26 days. We had gotten to the end of the island and captured some Japanese prisoners, just a small fraction of the 22,000 who were on the island. I saw the 5th Marine Division cemetery on the way back to the beach.

We got ready to go and they transported us back to our units. I went back to Maui with the V Amphibious Corps Signal Battalion. We were on Maui for about two days before we were back out in the field training to get ready for the invasion of Japan. The V Amphibious Corps was scheduled to go to Kagoshima. I read articles where they figured there would be half a million casualties on the beaches if we invaded Japan.

While we were on Maui, V-J day came so we got pulled out and we went to Sasebo, Japan, as part of the occupation forces. When we went into the city, there wasn't anybody there. There wasn't a soul; everybody was gone. It didn't take the Japanese long, about two weeks, to have all the dance halls and beer halls opened up downtown. They wanted to make that money, you know. I harbored no ill feelings for them and they didn't harbor any for us. It's just the way it goes. They wanted our money, sugar, cigarettes. We couldn't keep sugar on the tables in the mess hall because when the guys found a bowl, they would put it in a sock and go to town and sell it. I didn't smoke and never have, but cigarettes that cost a dollar a carton, you could get $15 for them in town. I stayed there for 16 months and then came back. The ship I came back on went all the way through the Panama Canal. But this time I was smart. When I got aboard, I volunteered to go work in the officers' mess so I got better food. We hadn't seen any milk or fresh eggs for two years.

I stayed on in the Marines for 27 years, served in Korea, and did two tours of Viet Nam. I was in Viet Nam during Tet in '68. I retired in 1971 with the rank of Master Sergeant.

* * *

A Weasel loaded with medical supplies moves up to the Iwo front.
Official USMC photo/Silverthorn collection.

Gail Chatfield

PFC Nicholas L. White
HQ Company, 3rd Battalion, 21st Marines, 3rd Division

I joined the Marines in 1943 after graduating high school. I went from Camp Pendleton in July 1944 to Pearl Harbor to Eniwetok and to Guam where I joined L Company. It was August 16, 1944, the last official day of combat on Guam although we spent the next three months hunting the Japs in the jungle and caves on Guam.

I was a rifleman in a four-man fire team. When the First Sergeant learned that I could type and spell, he made me his clerk and runner. Then someone in battalion headquarters 'discovered' me and matched me with the need for a clerk and runner for Sergeant Major Vernon Davis in Battalion Headquarters Company. He was the highest rated enlisted man in the battalion. I was a private first class, his runner and clerk. The Sergeant Major was over six feet tall, about forty years old, slim, hawk-faced, with a black moustache. He was from Virginia. He was tough, stern but fair. He looked on me as a kid of nineteen...to him, I was 'Whitey.'

After training for several months, we loaded the attack transports. I hated to be aboard ship since we slept below deck in compartments with bunks stacked four and five deep. Worse was the fact that, when you entered combat waters, each compartment was sealed off in the event a torpedo or bomb would hit the ship. Sealed off, the compartment might fill with water, but the ship could stay afloat. Since I was the sergeant major's runner and clerk, I worked in the battalion office aboard ship. This small office was on the top deck, and I slept there on the steel deck rather than below deck in the compartments.

It was only after we were aboard that we learned our role and our destination...Iwo Jima. I got an assignment from the sergeant major to be the Burial and Graves Registration NCO for the battalion. I was to keep track of our casualties and the replacements if we received any.

On D-Day, we were several miles offshore and could see the bombardment preceding the 4th and 5th going in. From that point on, we did not know much about the invasion except what the colonel would relay to us on the intercom. At first things seemed to go well, but then reports started coming in about the terrible casualties that the 4th and 5th were suffering. That evening we were told to be ready to go in the next morning.

On D+1, we went over the side from our attack transports, down the cargo nets, into the landing craft – about 40 of us per craft. We circled for nearly six hours in choppy seas waiting to land. We then

180

returned to our transport. The weather had turned bad and waves and swells were 6 to 8 feet. Getting back up the cargo nets was very difficult. As the landing craft rose up along the transport, we would grab the cargo net and take two or three quick climbing steps to get out of the way. Some were not quick enough and suffered crushed legs between the landing craft and the side of the ship, and some fell into the ocean but were rescued.

We thought that the battle on Iwo had changed and that we were not needed. Then we learned that the reason we did not land was simply that there was no room for us on the beach. Wrecked and swamped landing craft clogged the beach area where we were to land and the 4th and 5th Division had not reached their D+1 objectives. We were then told to be ready to land the next day, D+2...21 February '45.

Going down a cargo net into a landing craft is a very emotional experience. You know that the Navy will get you as close as they can to the beach, but from there on you are on your own. To this day, I can still recall the apprehension of going down the cargo net knowing what was ahead. One of the junior officers would be first over the side and the rest of us would follow him down. No one faltered in our group.

On D+2, we again circled for several hours before heading in. The wreckage on the beach was unbelievable and the landing craft had to pick spots where the beach could be reached between the wrecked landing craft. The ramp dropped and we waded ashore in late afternoon. What I remember most about the war was wading ashore and looking up and down the beach and seeing hundreds of dead Marines wrapped in blankets or ponchos. I learned later that nearly all were from the 4th Marine Division.

The beach was chaos...dead, wounded Marines, and wrecked equipment. We gathered as a battalion along the east or beach side of Airfield No. 1 and dug in for the night. The 21st RCT was now ashore and attached to the 4th Marine Division. During that first night, Jap mortar and artillery shells fell among us on the beach. That night, several Jap planes flew over Iwo and the fleet. The anti-aircraft fire was so intense that shrapnel was falling like rain. Several of our Marines were wounded from this. On the horizon, we could see a naval and air battle taking place, and later we learned that the aircraft carrier Lexington had been hit that night. It had drizzled most of the day and thus ended 21 February '45...cold, wet and in a foxhole scraped in volcanic ash.

Being in HqCo, I learned that the 21st RCT was to relieve elements of the 4th Division on their left flank in the middle of the island between the 4th on our right and the 5th on our left. When we moved into the 4th Division's sector, two rifle companies passed through the

4th Division lines and led the assault with the third company in reserve. HqCo was usually moving just behind the assault companies. In the first few hours, word came back that Captain Rockmore of I Company had been killed and Captain Heinze of K Company severely wounded. One day on the line and two of four company commanders gone.

We moved toward Airfield No. 2 in the middle of the island. We had reached the east side of the airfield and were hundreds of yards ahead of the 4th on our right and the 5th on our left. We were catching fire on our front and on both sides. On the west side of the airfield was some high ground held by the Japs and from which they could direct fire down on us. It fell to the 3rd Battalion, 21st Marines to cross the airfield and take the high ground. I will never forget as K Company started across the airfield dodging from one shell crater to the next. Finally with Lt. Archambault in command, those who were left reached the other side. According to reports that I read later, including citations for medals, they assaulted the high ground, took it, were pushed back and then retook it in a bayonet fight just before dark. That night, the rest of the battalion including HqCo moved over the airfield and dug in on the reverse slope of the high ground.

As it dawned, there were dead Japs all around us as well as dead Marines from K Company. The Japs knew that we were there and we were pinned down for hours by mortars, artillery and small arms fire. Shells kept hitting the top of the ridge and showering us with sand and rocks. The concussions shook the ground and the din was constant. At this point I have always had a blank in my memory. I do not remember the next hours or even several days. I was told later that we moved out when the rifle companies cleared the way. As we moved up, I later learned that Major Folkes, our HqCo commanding officer had been wounded and his runner killed. Major Folkes lost his leg, amputated in the field, and it was buried with his runner.

Somehow, we got to what was called Motoyama Village...nothing left but a few stone shacks. I remember vaguely trying to dig a foxhole in sandstone until the sergeant major stopped me. I recall that we made Motoyama Village our battalion headquarters for a day or so as we regrouped for the next assault. I then learned that my best buddy, Pat Luckett, had been wounded and evacuated, but did return. We were both promoted to corporal in May 1945, while preparing for the invasion of Japan.

While driving north through the middle of the island, we lost my favorite officer Captain Steve (Stephenson) of L Company, my old company. He was reported killed in action. I think of him to this day as I used to take him his mail when I was in L Company. He would open it and show me pictures of his wife and children back in North Carolina. He was the kind of officer whom his men loved and respected. I still miss him and wonder how his wife and children took his death.

We went to Iwo with about 900 Marines in the 3rd Battalion, but after several weeks, we were down to 300. All four company commanders were killed or wounded; most platoon leaders killed or wounded, leaving sergeants and corporals leading platoons. All the time I was trying to keep track of the dead and wounded, who was evacuated or who was sent back to be buried. You have to understand one thing about the Marines in World War II. We never left our wounded or our dead on the battlefield. We either brought them back or, at first opportunity, would recover them even if we suffered more casualties doing so. After one day's fighting, another buddy, John Garrison of New Jersey, was with a squad from HqCo going over the battlefield to identify and bring back our dead. I was told that he was shot through the back of the neck and was evacuated alive. I never saw or heard of him again except that he had survived.

When I first joined L Company on Guam, Bobby White from Hillsboro, Ohio, was in my squad. His twin brother was in K Company. After the same fight that John Garrison had followed up on, Bobby was in a squad from L Company recovering dead and wounded. He found his twin brother's body. When I last saw him on Iwo, he could not speak as he was in such shock. He was immediately evacuated. I never saw him again until the winter of 1946 at a basketball game in Williamsburg. Bobby and I talked for a few minutes, but never mentioned Billy, his brother. Neither of us seemed to want to remember it or talk about it.

Captain Marshall, who took over I Company when Captain Rockmore was killed, was wounded in a bizarre way. A Jap bullet went into the front of his helmet and was deflected upward where it traveled up and over his head and exited out the back of his helmet. His plastic helmet liner was shattered, and he received a deep scalp wound on the top of his head. We all carried a first aid type packet, which included a battle dressing and sulfa powder. The dressing was a large, thick gauze pad with gauze strips about 24 inches long which could be tied together to hold the dressing in place. For several days, Captain Marshall wore this battle dressing with a big bow tied beneath his chin and a new helmet perched on top. He would not be evacuated. While it was funny, no one joked about it. When we returned to Guam, the men of I Company could kid him about it, but no one else. He brought the helmet with the holes back with him.

One tragic note among many was one of the Scout & Sniper Platoon Marines of HqCo. It was one of the most hazardous jobs in the battalion as they were always sent out ahead to scout the enemy positions. This PFC had fought with the 3rd Battalion on Bougainville, Guam, and now Iwo Jima. We were off the front line near the end of the campaign and had just received some fresh water. Most of us stripped to the waist to wash, in particular, our feet and socks. He was sitting on the edge of his foxhole about 20 feet from me washing his feet. Suddenly he slumped over, almost like in slow motion. When he didn't move, we went over to him and discovered that he had been hit in the temple by a stray bullet and killed almost instantly. After three bitter campaigns, he was killed washing his feet. When his body was evacuated, I can still remember his bare feet sticking out from beneath the poncho that covered his body.

Another tragic death occurred near the end of the campaign. We had received replacements and they were assigned to the three rifle companies. As we cornered the Japs on the north part of Iwo, they began to run out of food and water. At night, they would come out of the caves and underground bunkers and infiltrate our lines to find water, ammunition and so on. To alert us, we put trip flares across trails and paths leading into our area. A trip flare is like a little rocket with a parachute. When the wire running across the path is tripped, it explodes into the air for about 150 feet and then floats down on a little parachute with a flare beneath it. While setting one of the flares, this replacement leaned over to straighten it, but tripped the flare causing it to explode in his face. I had only recorded his name and assignment several days before and now he was dead. I always wondered what the lieutenant or captain wrote to his parents and family…we hardly knew him.

While the island was deemed secured, we continued fighting at least ten more days and suffered more killed and wounded. While news reports apparently said that the fighting was over, it was not. The outcome was not in doubt after the first five days, but the high cost in killed and wounded was not expected.

My job in accounting for all of the Marines in the 3rd Battalion continued to the day that we left Iwo. My recollection is now somewhat dimmed, but I believe that we accounted for all but three or four of the 600 killed and wounded in the 3rd Battalion before we left the island. The Army came in and we were relieved. We went from the north end of the island back to the center of the island and the beach area. The Seabees had set up fresh water showers for us by desalinizing the ocean water. For the first time in three or four weeks, we could shower, shave and get clean uniforms before we left the island.

By Dammit, We're Marines!

Before we left we were given the opportunity to visit the 3rd Marine Division Cemetery, which had been started on Iwo. Hundreds and hundreds of crosses and stars stuck in the sand in the area between Airfield No. 1 and Mt. Suribachi. The American flag flew over the highest point in the cemetery. To this day, I can still recall seeing our flag with Mt. Suribachi in the background. When I hear our national anthem, I always think about the flag over the cemetery on Iwo Jima. The two things I remember most are the first five minutes on the beach with hundreds of dead Marines and visiting the cemetery where Captain Steve and the other dead from the 3rd Battalion were buried.

By that time, the B-29 bombers were landing regularly on Iwo generally on their way back from bombing Japan. P-51 Mustang fighters were now based on Iwo to accompany the bombers to Japan. It is still hard to believe that we had to fight so hard and lost so many for this little island.

When we arrived back at Guam, it was just after dawn and hundreds of B-29's were returning from their raids on Japan. As many as 40 or 50 would be in the air over Guam preparing to land. The first thing that I did back on Guam was contact my brother, Jim, at the 5th Field Depot. It was a great and somewhat tearful reunion. He was able to get word back to Mom and Dad that I had made it back from Iwo Jima. Of course I wrote them, but my mail was censored and it took longer to get it on its way. But being an officer, Jim's mail was not censored. Our parents said they would be worried to death with both of us in the Marines, and we needed to set up a code of some kind so they knew where we were. We devised a code where the last letter in a sentence would be the first letter of our location. We spelled out 'Guam' so our parents knew we were safe and together on Guam.

We pondered why the 3rd Marines RCT was not committed when we had so many casualties. Later we learned that they were not committed in order that one regiment of the 3rd Division would be at full strength with experienced officers and men for the invasion of Japan. After Iwo Jima, the 9th RCT and 21st RCT would be more than half new officers and men with no combat experience. This was especially true for platoon leaders and company commanders.

Iwo Jima changed my life. There has always been a 'guilt feeling.' I survived unscathed except for some loss of memory for several days, while friends and other Marines were killed or wounded. What did I do 'wrong' to escape so luckily? I think that many of us who survived feel the same way.

I never made any close friends or buddies after that. My two best buddies were wounded and evacuated and I never saw them again. To this day, I have difficulty being close friends with other men. I never go on trips with the guys or go out with a gang of men. Fortunately I have my wonderful wife and all my children.

I have never wanted to get together with the survivors. I never sought out Pat Luckett or John Garrison or any of the others. I now feel somewhat guilty about this and in retrospect it probably is why I did not go back to the 50th Anniversary Commemoration in Washington on February 19, 1995.

Thanks to my son, Nick, and his wizardry with the computer, he located John Powers from HqCo. I contacted John by e-mail and he put me in touch with Pat Luckett. It was 57 years after we had parted. We all went to the 3rdMarDiv reunion in San Diego. We plan to stay in touch.

I always 'suck it up' and stand straighter when they play the National Anthem, and when I see the flag being presented I think of the 3rd Marine Division Cemetery on Iwo Jima. I cannot hear "Taps" without thinking of my dead Marines from the 3rd Battalion. I was no hero, just a Marine PFC doing a job. I survived not because I tried but because I was lucky. Surviving changed my life forever.

* * *

Pioneers and Shore Party

1st Lt. Robert B. Hansen
Pioneer Battalion attached to the 28th Marines, 5th Division

Newly commissioned 2nd Lt. Robert Hansen,
Quantico, Virginia

When Pearl Harbor was attacked, I was 20 years old and a student at UCLA. I tried to get into the Navy because I wanted to get into the Naval Air Force but I was rejected because of my eyes. I tried the line Navy, but I was rejected because of flat feet, so I thought well the heck with it, I'll just wait until I'm drafted.

While at UCLA, a Marine officer came to recruit officer candidates. I saw him walking across the campus and I thought boy, he does look smart! So I signed up with him and had my physical exam and my eyes were OK, feet were OK, everything was OK. I figured out later the reason I was rejected by the Navy was because they were using their Annapolis standards and only took the cream of the crop. I think they realized there weren't enough of those people around to fill those slots so they lessened their requirements. That was how I was able to get into officer training with the Marines.

After OCS I went to Norfolk, Virginia, to have specialist training as Transport Quartermaster which has to do with the loading of equipment on transports. There is just so much room and things have to be fitted in just right and in the proper sequence. The things that you want to come out first have to go in last.

We were at Camp Pendleton until we shipped out for Hawaii the later part of 1944. We trained there for a while then from there we went directly to Iwo. We studied maps of the island, which was simply identified as Target X. Then one day, on the front page of the Honolulu daily newspaper, there was an article about the Air Force bombing Iwo Jima, complete with a photo of the entire island which was the same configuration as Target X. After that, we also heard on the radio a broadcast by Tokyo Rose that we were going to Iwo. But she mistakenly told us that we would never get there.

The 5th Marine Division was involved in only one battle and that was Iwo Jima. Now we had people in the Division who had been in other operations and then were eventually transferred to the 5th Division, but for those of us who had not been in combat and joined the 5th, Iwo Jima was our one and only battle.

I didn't hit the beach until 2:30 in the afternoon. It was a very interesting experience going in on the landing craft. We weren't tense at all, it seemed like everything was just going like it had always gone in training. And then a couple of explosions occurred near the landing craft and everyone realized that by golly somebody is trying to kill us. In all of our training nobody had tried to kill us. Everything kind of tensed up. You could just feel it. We went on in and we could feel the boat hit the sand. The ramp went down and everybody went out. I was in the rear of the boat and the men left some of the gear there that they were supposed to take with them. I guess they forgot what they were supposed to do so one of the sergeants and I carried the gear out to the beach. When I got on the beach, everyone started to dig a foxhole. I got a hole dug and a wounded Marine with bloody bandages rolled over into my foxhole. I thought why are you getting into my foxhole? This is my foxhole. Then I thought what the hell, this guy is wounded, so I left him there and I went over and dug another hole. The beach was under very heavy bombardment that afternoon and we didn't do anything, we just stayed in our foxholes.

It wasn't until the next morning that we started to get organized. I had my runner with me and we could see the battleships out there firing their salvos. It was interesting to watch the guns fire. There would be a puff of smoke, like a smoke ring, come out of the barrel first and we could see the projectile come out then the big blast of smoke. Explosions were going off on the beach there and one of my sergeants, Sgt. Richeson, was running around the beach, organizing things, without a helmet on. He hated a helmet, thought it was very uncomfortable. I thought my God, that's what I'm supposed to be doing.

I got up and did the things I was to do to get organized to receive and unload the landing craft that came in. One nice thing happened to me on the beach after we had been there for several days.

Another one of my sergeants, Sgt. Williams, came up to me and he says, "Hansen, I knew you'd be all right." He was one who had been in combat before as a Raider.

As part of the shore party, we stayed on the beach and didn't go in. This was our assignment, this is what we trained for, and our job was to unload landing craft that came in with ammunition, gasoline, food, whatever, and to store it on the beach in shell holes where it would be protected. The front line troops would call for supplies and send people back to pick up the different items to take up to the front lines.

After the first day, we got things running pretty well. I was a platoon leader in the Pioneer Battalion. I had started with 6 or 7 junior 2nd lieutenants and about 100 men under my command. After the second day the platoon leader that I was serving with in the 3rd Platoon suffered from combat fatigue, I guess you would call it. He just became non-functional and couldn't perform his duties so his shore party platoon was assigned to me. At one time, I had a little over 200 men and 13 junior 2nd lieutenants at my command.

There were a lot of bodies on the beach when we got there. We really couldn't work very efficiently until we got all the bodies out of the way. We picked them up and put them in a row over in one area so we could move around. Some of the men had qualms about touching a dead person so I had to set an example; a platoon leader was supposed to do that. I helped the men pick up the bodies. I saw this one leg sticking out of the sand and I thought oh boy, that guy got buried. I gave it a tug and just the leg came out.

Early in the invasion, the second or third day, I noticed a wounded Marine at an aid station off toward Mt. Suribachi maybe 50 feet away. A rifle was stuck in the ground next to him with a plasma bottle attached to it giving him plasma. There was a hell of an explosion over that way and there that kid was with grey matter hanging out over his face. It had blown the front part of his head off.

How do you deal with this? You just do. And the smell, you can smell death and the cordite, the gun smoke. The dead were wrapped in muslin and formaldehyde sprayed on them as a preservative. For years, my wife used to do the home perm, and I could not stand the smell; it really got to me. The roar of a bus with a diesel engine was the same sound the landing craft would make.

We had so many landing craft and other things on the beach that it got to the point where there was the danger of not being able to get new landing craft to come in; there was no place for them to land. Cranes were used to get the junk out of the way. We also used demolitions to free up the beach so we could get landing craft in. It didn't take long to clear. I don't think we ever had a case where a craft coming in with supplies couldn't get in to the beach. We saw the situation developing and took measures to keep the beach clear. It wasn't very long after the invasion that they brought in the big LSTs, the huge landing craft. We were under bombardment for quite a few days after we landed. As the front line troops pushed the Japs up the island, we got less and less bombardment on the beach.

I was on the beach when the flag was raised. It gave everyone just a wonderful feeling to know that our guys had gotten on top of that mountain because the Japs were looking right down on us. It was a great morale booster. I didn't know they changed flags. I had no idea there was a first flag or a second flag until I read about it.

We were quite comfortable in our bivouac area. They brought in our cooks for the battalion and we had hot food and went down to the ocean and bathed, that was quite a treat. Then on the trail to the front lines, we would see stretcher-bearers coming down with the dead and the wounded; quite a few came back. On the beach, my unit didn't have too many casualties, but there were some. I remember one kid in particular I saw on a stretcher, bloody bandages, smoking a cigarette, and he just seemed so happy. I thought it must be bad up there, and just shortly after that, I found out that it was.

After a couple of weeks, they took our battalion off the beach and the Seabees took over. We moved to a bivouac area behind the front lines and were used as replacements for the infantry.

I recall when our captain, Capt. Ellis, called A Company all together to tell us that we were going to go up to the front lines and that I would be taking my platoon up. I got so nervous, I had to get up and walk around. I didn't want to have any of the men see me. It would be my first combat on the front line. It had been pretty bad up to that point but it was nothing like the front line.

When I took my platoon up to the front line, which was the Bloody Gorge area, we replaced a company. In a company, there are over 200 people. A guide took me up to this position where we were to replace the unit. This company was pretty well decimated. All they had left was one officer, a 1st lieutenant, and he had kind of a wild look in his eye. He had a runner and a mortar section, which means two mortars and their crews, and that was it. All the riflemen and all the other officers, the non-commissioned officers, the enlisted men, were gone. I took his runner to show me what area we were supposed to occupy, and he took us over to the left flank of the unit that we were to tie into. It was a dumb time to go in, but a lot of dumb things are done in the military. Maybe it couldn't be avoided, I don't know, but it was dusk and there was a rule that when it got dark on Iwo anything that moved got shot at. We were moving in there all kind of crouched down when a hand grenade came down right in our midst. I saw it land with the fuse burning so we all hit the ground. It turned out to be a dud so nobody was hurt from that. We got up and moved further along the route to get into position when a shot rang out and one of my squad leaders was hit. He was shot by one of the guys in the unit we were tying into. I yelled at him; I won't tell you the language I used.

"Tough, anything that moves gets shot at," he said.

"Well don't shoot any more until we get situated here," I said.

We tied in there, got into position and put the machine gun where we thought it would do the most good and stayed there that night.

The Japanese would fire from their hidden positions. You wouldn't know where they were until somebody got hit. The Japanese had a smokeless, flashless gun powder so when they fired, you couldn't see the muzzle blast or the smoke from it. They'd shoot us and we would have to figure out where it came from and figure out how to neutralize it. The fighting spirit of the troops was excellent. I think this is what makes Iwo Jima so unique. We had to move ahead standing up and the Japanese were in their concealed positions.

The Japanese were firing and inflicting casualties from a cave in front of us. We couldn't knock it out with our 30 caliber machine guns, so we brought our 50 caliber machine gun up and that didn't work. We couldn't neutralize this position so then we called up a flamethrowing tank. It was kind of interesting how that worked.

The next thing we knew, we got the word to attack which we did. We moved out, but you don't really move out, you go from one rock to another. PFC White was right behind me. When you blast a cave, you kill everybody right in that part of it but then some other Japs would come up and take over the position. PFC White was behind a rock behind me and we knew we were getting unfriendly fire from this position again. White, I guess he figured he had enough of that, got up from behind this rock and with his rifle he was going to take care of that Jap. He got shot right between the eyes; killed him dead. Of course he didn't do what we learned to do. You don't look up over a rock, you look around the side of a rock. You never provide that kind of target or silhouette to the enemy.

You get so you can cope, and it's amazing how the human mind and body can accommodate. We had plenty of food, plenty of water. We did have a little problem on the front line. The cartridges with the lead bullets ran low so they sent up armor piecing ammunition. It fits into a rifle all right but the rifle would not fire semi-automatically. We would have to use the bolt like an old bolt-action rifle. Every time we fired, we had to eject the spent cartridge so another one would go in.

I got injured on the last day, March 25, just a few days after my 24th birthday. Half of our unit went aboard ship on the 25th, and half was to go on the 26th. Unfortunately, I was in the second half. It was on that morning that about 200 Japanese, mostly officers and non-commissioned officers, came down from the caves where they had been up in the north end of the island and came right through our bivouac area. Unfortunately, we'd had orders to turn in our munitions — all of our ammunition for our rifles, machine guns, hand grenades, all that sort of thing. But that's fine, the island is secured, anything they wanted, just get us off this island. I was wounded in this attack by the Japanese but I think I must have been on the outer fringe of the attack. I did see some of the Japanese troops, but I think the main thrust was a little further north. These were Japs dressed in their uniforms. Some of them had American weapons taken from our dead on the battlefield. They came through our unit. We slowed them down anyway, and accounted for some casualties but they went right through our unit. The officer in C Company, Lt. Harry Martin, got his men together and formed a defense line. They had time to get to the ammunition, which had all been stored in one location so they could repulse the Japanese and they did. He received the Medal of Honor.

I crawled to the aide station during the attack. I couldn't walk. They looked at it and put some sulfa powder on the entrance and exit of the wound and a couple of band-aids and that was it. A little later in the morning we went aboard ship. I went to sickbay, and that's where I stayed until we got to Honolulu and then I went into the hospital there. I was on Iwo the whole darn time and didn't get wounded until the last day.

My soon-to-be wife and I were on a date in Long Beach at the Pike, an amusement park, when word came down that the Japanese surrendered. It was great news. I didn't talk about my war experiences when I came back. It wasn't until quite a number of years later. Here I was a young fellow who had just gotten married and started a family. I was going to law school, trying to get established, and there just wasn't time to talk about it.

By Dammit, We're Marines!

My wife, Arlene, and I have been back to Iwo Jima twice. The first time we went in 1985; it was the first time that any Marines had been there as an organized group. I could not believe it. There was growth, bushes, shrubbery. There were roads, even some wildflowers. I recall on one beach back then, on the far side, there was hardly a square foot where there weren't pieces of shrapnel. We met with the Japanese veterans, and the deceased veterans' widows. A band played the Marine Hymn. In fact, I made a friend there with one of the Japanese. He and I corresponded until he died a couple of years ago.

Both visits were helpful because I was able to think of Iwo Jima as being an ordinary island, and not the hellhole I remembered from 1945. You realize that the Japanese were people just like us. They had wives and children and they were fighting for their country and we were fighting for ours. There is no difference. No difference at all. They are not inherently bad.

* * *

Gunnery Sgt. Damaso Sutis, USMC (Ret.)
Pvt., Shore Party, Third Force Service Regiment,
5th Field Depot, 3rd Division

Damaso Sutis after boot camp MCRD,
San Diego, June 1944.

I enlisted at 17 ½ in March of 1944. I had bought my cap and gown and was ready to graduate in June of 1944. I got antsy so I went down and enlisted. I couldn't wait the two months. I was like the rest of the young guys my age, just chomping at the bit to go do your part. I was from the south side of Chicago. Our neighborhood was ethnically mixed. We had every nationality in our gang except blacks and Eskimo. I'm Filipino, French, Spanish and part Cherokee Indian.

In my day, anyone in uniform was looked up to as doing something really worthwhile. I looked up to the Marines. The Marines took all this restless energy I had, channeled it, focused it, and taught me a lot of things about responsibility and integrity. I think the regimentation from the moment I got there made me find out that I wasn't such a big bad dude as I thought. Everybody had something to contribute. The Marines gave me a sense of responsibility and purpose. I think the word responsibility is more important. At that time, the Marine Corps had done a magnificent job on Wake Island. There were just a few Marines and they stood there and fought against overwhelming odds. Of course they were finally captured and the island taken by the Japanese, but their bull-doggedness was something I thought was magnificent. In retrospect, I think some of that American Indian blood in me admired that kind of warrior spirit.

I went to boot camp in San Diego and Camp Pendleton for advanced infantry. I decided that I could be a good warrior but I talked to a sergeant and he said I should think about going to some school, machine shop maybe, and learn some kind of a trade because I had absolutely nothing. I let it be known while doing my infantry training that I wouldn't be adverse to going to school. Most of the young men I was surrounded with wanted to be grunts, infantrymen. I did too, but I thought what that sergeant said made some sense. I was sent to machine shop training, shoe and textile training, and I got a lot of skills. They selected replacements to go to the various divisions in the Pacific to reinforce the platoons so I got sent to the 3rd Division. That's how I got to Guam. I was with the 28th Replacement Draft. The battle was still on when we went in, and just as we got there, the battle ended. Some of our guys went right into the infantry with the 3rd Division. The rest of us if we had any schooling usually went to the service battalions of service regiments, in my case the 5th Field Depot.

The 5th Field Depot supplied ammunition and major maintenance shops for the trucks, the tanks and the artillery. In that group they had carpenters, electricians, people who would do water purification, electronics, engineers to put the roads and bridges in and all that sort of work. We're part of the people who do the staging and get the boxes and crates, all numbered with certain tactical markings, to the right place, the right outfit, at the right time. We are among the first to land and put up banners or some kind of a visual marking so that the coxswain on the attack ships knows where to drive what units. It also tells us where the ammunition is supposed to come in, where the tanks and the vehicles should come in, where the wounded go out. With each succeeding wave of infantry that comes in, there are people assigned to work with the shore party and on the beach because the beach is extremely important. When they can move inland, the beach expands so more supplies can come in. The shore party helps set up the first areas for the medical staff, hospitals and landing zones so they can get those who are badly wounded back to the hospital ships. You actually build a city right on the beach.

Of course all this time, the enemy doesn't want you on there so they are being very nasty about it. For a long time, even after the infantry moves off the beach and are being successful moving inland, you're still subject to a lot of mortar fire and artillery fire until the infantry knocks them out. You are always under machine gun fire. Several weeks down the line, you are subject to sniper fire. Many times you have to work ten and twelve hour shifts. If that goes into the night, you need lights to unload the LSTs and various cargo vessels. We set up lights and now it's like Las Vegas. "Ground-pounders" are the infantry, "cannon cockers" are artillery people. We were "beans, bandages and bullets." That's what Marines called Supply and Logistics.

On Guam, I was an engineer and I was in Service and Maintenance and we did everything. I got involved in the repair section. At that time I did canvas repair. That's the guys who repair and make tents, gun covers, jeep covers, and the tarps that go over the back of the six by six trucks. The covers get pretty well shot up during the campaigns. My company got tied up repairing shoes, a big thing in those days. The coral cut up shoes so badly. We didn't have combat boots at that time we just wore boondockers, which are work shoes, and leggings. Your footwear was pretty important. Of course, being a youngster I wanted to be in something more glorious.

A couple of senior sergeants who had been in the infantry said, "Hey, be thankful, what you're doing is so important because the guys can't walk across that coral barefoot. They need tents, they need shade, and they need the covers over the trucks and guns, so this is really important." He convinced me that what I was doing was important, unsung, but really important. For a long time, I still frothed at the teeth wanting to go into the glory end.

Loading the ships to go to Iwo took at least a month. Traveling there took a long time because there were a lot of Japanese submarine problems. There were about three thousand men aboard the ship and it was crowded and hot. There was a lot of training on the decks like cleaning weapons. Even though I was with the service regiment, our daily talk was always preparation of our rifles. Some of the guys were grenadiers and they had rifles set up for launching grenades. We were constantly trained as infantry while aboard ship even though we knew when we hit the beach, we had other functions. We carried weapons all the time.

I was 18 when we hit Iwo. The water was choppy going in and naturally a lot of guys were immediately seasick. Luckily, when our vessel went in they could drop the ramp and we walked in on some of the water, but we didn't have to walk in up to our necks as some did. I went in with the first units of the 3rd Division. As we were landing, the flag went up. Somebody said, "Look at that." It was really something.

By Dammit, We're Marines!

The beach was really packed; there was no place to go. You went in and you were only up 20-30 feet and you'd stop because there were other guys laying there all jammed in. Some of the areas as I recall already had some sites set up for ammunition and food coming in. We were prepared for a pretty long haul. We went in with full transport packs. I thought by carrying all that stuff that we would be there for a while and we were. Most of us in the shore party and on the beach detail were there until the end of the campaign.

We got on the beach in one spot and hunkered down. We dug ourselves in as best we could because the sand was so shifty. There was a lot of wreckage on the beach—trucks that had been blown up, landing craft that had been hit, and tanks that couldn't get too far. The lieutenant said we were going to move up so we moved up and dropped all our gear. An LST came in and dropped its ramp and we went aboard and started hauling off boxes. There were a lot of oxygen and acetylene tanks that came in and we had to have places for them. We had big holes dug for the ammunition and these tanks. One of those dumps got hit and what an explosion that was.

There was an awful lot of small arms fire and machine gun fire and some mortars for about a full week while I was there. After a while you got used to those things buzzing over your head. Out of the corner of your eye, you'd see a group all of a sudden drop to the ground and you automatically dropped. Your instincts got really sharpened. In my particular squad, we didn't have many casualties. Some units lost quite a lot. The island was so well laid out that there was really no safe place no matter what your job was. After a while, we could walk around quite freely when all the troops, particularly the 3rd Division, had gone up the middle and got to about the last third of the island. You would have thought we were on a vacation beach somewhere. There was still sniper fire, but we just had a lot of bravado, we survived this. We continued to unload equipment and a lot was being pulled off because it was unserviceable. Wounded were being put aboard LSTs and sent back out to the hospital ship. We helped put in Marston matting from the water's edge to wherever there was solid ground so the tanks, trucks, and jeeps could roll off the ramp right on to it. The Seabees came in with their bulldozers and immediately began repairing the first air strip as soon as the Marines had gotten it half way cleared. A week or two after the flag was up I got up to the first airstrip and walked around. The Seabees were still filling holes and about that time the first B-29 came in for a landing. It was pretty shot up and didn't have fuel to make it back. The landings were a continuous process and we realized how important the island was.

Until then we privates and PFCs had no idea and asked, "Why are we here? This is a lousy beach!"

I do remember that we helped stop several banzai attacks that came from the north. We were told we could expect some kind of attack so of course at night we set up our perimeter. The whole beach bristled with Marines waiting for them. As soon as somebody started firing up there, you knew they were coming. You could see the firing and the tracers and you'd watch it coming down to where you are.

Then somebody in a foxhole maybe 20 or 30 yards ahead of you shouts, "Here they come!"

You can't see anything in front of you but you knew you could fire two or three feet above the ground because most Marines were down in some kind of depression. Your eye picked up on anything moving and you fired at it. We had to do quite a bit of firing, but the Japanese never got through our particular area because everybody was alerted. It was pretty loud. I know I was scared to death. I hoped I could do what I was supposed to do. I didn't want to let my friends, the guys in my unit, down. That kept us all brave.

We had a guy in our squad who was just a basket case. The guy tried as best he could, but once he came out of the hole his hands started shaking, his rifle started to shake like he was making a malted milk shake. We told him to stay in the hole and keep it safe. It was great for him because he could think he was doing something important, and we needed a place to come back to when we weren't working where we felt secure.

The guys in my squad were pretty creative with our foxhole. We'd gather up these round cardboard tubes that large shells came in. We'd use them as walls. We'd make a big depression in the sand, line it with these tubes, and fill them full of sand. We even had floorboards… little round tubes, but they worked. When shells went off all around and the ground shook, our foxhole stayed up. Nothing slid in on us. Some guys' houses would collapse on them every time a shell would hit the ground. That sand was very mobile with the shells' vibration. We even had an entrance and had packing cases we used as steps to keep the sand in place.

There were sand crabs at night and you could hear this clickety, clickety sound. You would look over the edge of your hole and you'd see these sand crabs, hundreds of them, walking all over the place. If you crushed them they stunk, so you let them go wherever it is they wanted to go. They were sure a nuisance. By daylight, they were gone. I don't know where they went.

By Dammit, We're Marines!

I was on Iwo the whole time. Most of the shore parties stayed there for a long time. Crates had been brought in of ammunition, and bandages and boxes of food. Once the troops moved up in the very far north end then it was just a matter of time until the island was totally secured. We packed up as much as we could that was usable and started putting things up ready for debarkation.

We boarded ship and left for Guam. We got there in time for Easter. To be back aboard ship, you felt totally relaxed for the first time. Even though we weren't under all that bombardment towards the end, there were still occasional shots being fired and you stayed totally alert. When you got aboard ship, you were totally relaxed. I didn't care if I was in a little six foot cubicle with 12 guys. I finally showered. It was the first time in my life I had a salt water shower. I never did feel clean. We didn't get any replacement uniforms until we got back to Guam.

One thing has always been a bright spot in my mind. When we weren't unloading ships and helping realign or rebuild new dumps for food, ammo, we tried to get out to an LST that had their ramp down. We'd ask them if we could come aboard maybe to shower or get a hot cup of coffee. We tried to go aboard several of the Navy LSTs and of course, they were having none of that. They weren't having any scroungy Marines aboard their vessels. Some of these guys didn't know how close they came to not going home. Even though we weren't infantry, we were still Marines. Then a bunch of us went down to a LST and asked if could we come aboard and get a cup of coffee and use a clean head.

"You're certainly welcome, jarhead," the guy said.

It was a Coast Guard vessel. The Coast Guard guy talked to his chief and the chief came down. They broke out the galley and gave us fried eggs, bacon, and hot coffee. We were all sitting there in our skivvies while our other clothes were being washed. I'll never forget it. That's when I first realized how many Coast Guardsmen were involved in that operation. You hear almost nothing. They drove the LSTs and the LCIs, and they also were the coxswain of the smaller landing craft that took in troops to fight. They are experts at small boats. I since have found out that it was the Coast Guard that trained the majority of the Navy coxswains how to handle the small boats. There is a real soft spot in my heart for the Coast Guard ever since that day. So much so that I have been part of the Coast Guard Auxiliary for the last 10 years. We are all volunteers and I work at the sector in Los Angeles/Long Beach.

I stayed in the Marines until October 1967. I was in Korea and Viet Nam. I had gone to more schools and by that time, I was called a machine foremen, metal smith foreman and became an expert sheet metal man. I was learning trades all along. That sergeant's advice really paid off for me. You always feel you want to be a grunt but then again you can see as the years go by how the maintenance and services you've set up are valuable to the troops.

I liked the Marine Corps. I liked the camaraderie. I like the fact that I was a Marine. Luckily the way the Marines operate, all Marines are Marines and you are a rifleman first. No matter what you are trained in, you are still a Marine. The fighter plane mechanics, they don't run around with rifles and bayonets all the time but they're Marines and they can use them. They stay as Marines and can be used as infantry at any time. That's the one difference between the armed services. Even our jeep truck mechanics don't look at themselves as a mechanic. If you ask them what they are, they will tell you…They are Marines.

After I retired from the Marines and had my parade at Pendleton, I was driving through Orange County and I saw a sign that said 'welder wanted.' I was still in my dress canvas and I went in, applied, and got the job. I went on to get my Associate in Arts degree, my Bachelor's Degree, and I earned my Masters in Education. I left my civilian job and became a high school shop teacher for over 20 years.

* * *

Weapons

Pvt. Henry Koellein, Jr.
Flamethrower, I Company, 3rd Battalion,
25th Marines, 4th Division

Henry Koellein, right, and friend at the Washington Monument

I went in at 17. The Japanese attacked us in our sleep at Pearl Harbor, and I wanted to help the country get back on its feet and defeat our enemy. I joined the Marines because they were the toughest; they would give us the biggest challenge.

When I went down and enlisted, you had to stand in a very, very long line. Everyone wanted to enlist. It was war and it was a war we didn't start. I went down by myself; I just wanted to go and I went. I'd do it all over again. I took the examination and physical and then they gave me papers. I had to go home and get my father to sign them because I was under 18, and he had to give his consent. My father didn't want to sign them. I'm first generation American. My father and mother were refugees from Germany in the Kaiser's era.

"If you don't sign them," I said, "when I'm 18, I'm going to enlist anyhow; you can't stop me and I will never come home no more." So I blackmailed him into signing.

"Well if you're that damned determined, OK, I'll let you go." He wanted me to stay and he was right to a degree.

I took advanced combat training at Parris Island, Camp Lejeune. I was a rank ass private. Then I went across the country by train in July, in an un-air conditioned train, hotter than 40 hells, across Texas, Arizona, New Mexico and into California. We were young and tough then.

I was a flamethrower operator, commonly referred to as a 'cooker'. The flamethrower killed faster than other methods. A flamethrower carries two steel tanks with napalm and another little tank with oxygen and it weighs 63 pounds. When you release the tanks and get the pressure lined up, it comes through a hose and through a nozzle. There are steel matches on the end that you wind up like a clock and when you pull the trigger, those matches ignite. When the napalm comes through that flame, it ignites the napalm and we cook them. If you were shooting with the wind, maybe it would go 50 feet. If you were shooting into the wind, then you'd better be careful or it would blow back on you. In that case, we would go up on a flank and try to angle it in.

We were young and full of, excuse the expression, piss and vinegar. We didn't worry about being scared. We had a job to do and we just wanted to kill the enemy because if we didn't, they were going to kill us. It was kill or be killed.

I expected to go in there and kill them sons of bitches. I really never thought about how difficult it would be because we were regimented to do our job as Marines. I don't know any heroes; they were all just plain Marines. We were going to take that island away from the Japanese so the B-29's coming back from Japan to the Mariana Islands had a place to land.

We were ready. We were ready and very obedient and did what we were told to do. Iwo was my first battle and I landed in the absolute first wave. I was 18 when I got there. It was a nightmare. Men were getting killed all around us; some great people I was very close to were killed on the first day.

I jumped out with 63 lbs of flamethrower on my back, and when I landed in that ash I went down up to my knees. I struggled my ass up and went up that damn ridge and went up there to do my job.

After I got over being scared half to death, I started trying to kill the enemy. When we went in, I was in the extreme right flank, first wave, and we swung around to the right, right up past the Boat Basin. There was an old rusty boat up there that had been abandoned and the

Japs had an artillery spotter in there. I tried to nail him and I may have. When we went up along the Boat Basin, a machine gun nest was along the edge of the airfield mostly obscured by planes and parts of planes that had been blown up in the bombing. The Japs were camouflaged in there. The thing that mystified me the most was that they had smokeless ammunition. There would be machine guns rattling off at us and we couldn't see where it was coming from. There was a lot of dust in the explosions and shell holes and we were just moving from shell hole to shell hole. It wasn't long after that that I got nailed and they carried me out. I'm a lucky guy. I have no complaints. I'd do it all over again.

The Japanese would call mortar shells in, in different coordinates, when they saw overly aggressive Marines like myself and try to knock us out. Eventually one of them did. I lost a lot of very good friends and had very good friends killed the first day. Lt. Frank Urso was killed right on the beach with a chain of machine gun bullets, nearly cut him right in half. Another good buddy, Joseph Henry Kelly, an Irishman from Providence, Rhode Island, had a mortar shell land right on him. He was killed instantly. I saw the horrors of war. It was no picnic.

You cry and you try to maintain your composure so you can kill the son of a bitch before he comes to get you. Determination drives you and Marine Corps training. We were trained killers, and we were trained to kill. We knew what we were doing, and we knew what we were doing was right. I cried a little bit, I'm not ashamed of it, and I was just mad as hell. I wanted to kill them until they got me and I got out. And I was lucky because they dragged me over dead bodies to get me out. No regrets, I'd do it all over again.

When I got wounded a corpsman cut most of my clothes off and patched me up. I was wounded in the right hip and the right buttocks, and the corpsman put sulfa and bandages all over me then pumped me with morphine. I've got some of the black sand of Iwo Jima still in my hand. They carried me down to the beach and I laid there for a while until I got evacuated. The war was over for me. I had been on Iwo less than a day, but there had already been over a thousand Marines killed by then. It was a slaughter, but the only way we could go at it was straight up, right at them.

Guys were laying there, some of them were alive, some of them were dead, but we were pumped up with morphine. A doctor looked at me and tagged me to be evacuated. I went out to a hospital ship and laid on the ship for about five days until they got a load of casualties. Then they took us to Guam where I was a couple of days in the hospital. From there they took us to Pearl Harbor where I had surgery at the Army hospital because the Navy hospital was full with casualties. We were also liberating the Philippines at the time. So many casualties flowed in that they loaded us on planes and flew us out to other hospitals. After six months of being hospitalized, I was finally discharged. My hero, President Harry Truman, who had said something like, "Drop the damn bomb, if they had it, they would use it," saved me from having to go back overseas again and join my outfit because they were scheduled to go into Japan itself.

I didn't want to go. I would've gone, but I didn't want to. I still had a little shrapnel in me and got a little disability in my right leg but that wouldn't stop me. It was that kind of atmosphere during World War II, we just wanted to fight, and we wanted to serve our country. I don't believe in heroes. In my opinion, the heroes died. The rest of us were just Marines doing our job and trying to kill the enemy and keep from being killed ourselves. I still carry the sand with me every day. And I got holes back here on the prettiest right buttock you'd ever hope to see.

I have five kids, ten grandkids, and now four great grandkids. I have a grandson in the Marines, a granddaughter in the Marines, a son-in-law in the Marines. My son-in-law was in the first Iraqi war.

* * *

Sgt. Maj. Joe Parrish, USMC (Ret.)
Cpl., C Company, 1st Battalion,
24th Marines, 4th Division

Joe Parrish, 2006

I wanted to join when I was 17 years old but my dad told me to stick around one more year to help him on the farm then I could go where I wanted. I always kept seeing pictures of Marines in their dress blues, and I thought they looked good. I waited until I was 18. I got out of high school to help on the farm, and I didn't finish high school until a year later in the Marines. I got my high school diploma in the Marine Corps. I was infantry, and I went through the whole combat over there with a BAR. I was an expert with that.

I always said I was the best BAR man in the Pacific because I always thought I was. You know, you got to be proud of yourself whatever you do, and if you can't be the best, don't be nothing. I got a nickname of "twenty-round Parrish." A magazine holds twenty rounds and I didn't want to pull the trigger unless I had a target and if I had a target, he got twenty rounds. If there was one Jap or fifty, he got twenty rounds. I got a couple of ones in there where there was just one man and he got twenty rounds. I said, "Well, I ain't gonna shoot a Jap and him be able to shoot me in the back."

My first battle was on Roi-Namur and it wasn't so bad. I was 19. We were out there on an Amtrac floating for several hours. I never did get seasick but this time we were floating around for a long time and some people got sick. The wind was blowing and when they got sick, it flew up and hit me in the face. That made me a little sick. We got on the island and you could almost see across the other side but it was loaded with Japanese. The Japanese tracers were green and ours, red. At nighttime there is all kinds of tracers flying all over the place, close enough you could feel the wind go by with the bullets…that close.

The old company commander said to me, "Parrish, I want you to go back to the battalion and tell the battalion commander I want Amtracs up on the right flanks tomorrow morning because we're going to jump off."

So I took off. It was nighttime and I tried to get anybody to go with me.

"Hell, I ain't going," they said.

So I went alone. I found the battalion commander and told him.

"OK, you stay here tonight. Don't you go back," he said.

I thought, how in the hell is that company commander going to know that I got the message back. I went on back, found my company commander and told him. Amtracs came up the next morning and helped us out.

Our battalion commander, Colonel Dyess, a gung-ho man, got him a weapon and said, "Hey come on, we're going to jump off."

He got killed, but he got the Congressional Medal of Honor posthumously.* He lived in Georgia, I think. So we did all right. When we secured the island, I was the first man of the working party to go back aboard ship. I got up there standing guard duty and a plane came in and bombed the island.

Some civilian, we were on a merchant marine ship, came out and says, "Hey what's going on?"

"They're bombing the island." I answer.

"Oh that's good, that's another $500 in my pocket."

"That's a hell of a way to fight a war," I said.

We loaded up and went back to Maui to get ready for Saipan. On Saipan, I was a really good BAR man. One time we had to go up and secure a hill. We went up and found a cave. We threw a concussion grenade in it, an explosive type of grenade not much shrapnel, and dust comes flying out of the cave. I was only about 15 feet away kneeling down with my BAR and here comes a Jap out of there with his rifle, his bayonet and helmet, and all that. He was dusting the dust off him and he looked up and saw me and he grabbed his rifle ready to shoot me. I was kneeling down and had a grin on my face, and I gave him twenty rounds. He hit the deck and rolled down a little ways but was still kicking. By that time, I had a new magazine in there so I gave him twenty more rounds.

Later on, they had a patrol going out with this platoon sergeant with the 1st Platoon. I was in the 3rd Platoon; he's picking a bunch of people to go on patrol and he chooses me. We always wondered why he didn't get his own BAR man out of his own platoon instead of coming to the 3rd Platoon and get me. I talked to him several times; he's a retired Sgt. Major, too. Elmo Burns was his name.

"Well I'm the best BAR man so that's why you came down to the 3rd Platoon and got me," I laughed.

We went out on the patrol and we were standing there talking. He had his back to this side of the cliff over there, and out came a Nip and I gave him twenty rounds. So Elmo, he's always talking about that.

We got through Tinian after Saipan. When we hit the beach, they only had a beach that was 65 yards wide. The Amtrac that I was in hit the beach and came up on its side and we had to jump off. Well, when you have a BAR with thirteen magazines, it's kinda heavy. I went all the way to the bottom of the water. I had to walk on the bottom to get up there on the edge so I could breathe. But the fight on Tinian wasn't too bad. Nighttime banzai attacks—they'd just jump up and come running in there and we'd mow them down.

We went back to Maui and trained and then on to Iwo. I'll never forget when we were on the way in. I had been promoted up to squad leader. Lt. Manning, a platoon leader on his first operation, says to me, "What am I supposed to do?"

"I'll tell you what, if I was you I'd let the platoon sergeant handle it, you just stay with him."

"OK, I'll remember that."

But you know what's funny is that platoon leader, every night when we'd dig in on Iwo, he was in the foxhole with me.

You know Iwo was different than the rest of them. I remember one time we were going to see what's in this cave. I took a satchel charge and walked in the cave and went down in it a little way and set my satchel down and came back out and it went off. Hardly anything came out this end of the cave, but about 100 yards down there was an opening and it all came out down there. It blew it away.

One night we were up a little ridge and we heard somebody say, "Marines gonna die tonight."

We listened and he must have been in a cave right over the edge of this cliff. So we got a mortar round and taped a grenade to it. I tied a piece of com wire to the mortar round.

"Now I'll pull the pin," I told this guy, (you know the pin on a hand grenade is 3-5 seconds delay), I'll hold the com wire, and you throw the mortar round over the edge of this cliff. I'll give it slack and then I'll stop it."

The mortar round with the grenade on it went right over the cliff and BOOM! We don't know if we killed him or not but there was no more talking.

On March 2 we got hit and a mortar round hit my foxhole. It must have been a delayed fuse because I didn't get any shrapnel but it ignited my illumination grenade and my white phosphorus grenade and all that stuff set me afire. I jumped up and I started running, but my buddies threw me down. You know white phosphorus can't be put out with water you got to dig it out. And illumination is just like jelly and that was on my face and my hands. It was all over. It was around my eyes and I couldn't see. They took me back to the aid station, and the corpsman gave me a shot of morphine and boy that eased the pain. I kinda dozed off but I woke up burning like hell again.

"Hey corpsman," I yelled, "give me another shot. Boy that felt good."

They got us aboard a jeep ambulance and we're dodging the incoming rounds. I guess they were trying to hit the jeep on the way back to the beach. We got back there and they were loading us aboard the DUKW to take us to the hospital ship. Because I was burnt in the face, they had my poncho over my head. We get to the ship and they load me up on the stretcher on the back of the ship.

I got to the top and I heard somebody say, "Is this one still with us?"

I heard people say when you go back aboard ship and if you were dead you would go to the freezer locker and if you are alive you'd go to the medical ward. "You're God-damn right I'm still here," I said.

My arms and hands swelled up inside the bandages and it was hurting something fierce. I yelled for somebody, it must have been another wounded Marine.

"Find something and cut these bandages loose," I ordered.

"I'm not supposed to do that."

"Hell with that, do it anyway. Find some scissors or knife." He found something to cut them a little bit. They were so tight I could hear them kinda cracking.

By Dammit, We're Marines!

When I went to the hospital ship I could walk and I was there I think about seven days. I heard the doctor tell this nurse, "I want you every morning to take the bandages off and make sure there are no scabs forming around the eyes." The bandage they put on was Vaseline gauze, and they put that on and put bandages over the top of that. When they'd take it off, it stuck to the Vaseline gauze and they had to tear it off. That hurt worse than the original hurt did. I often wondered why they wanted to make sure no scab formed. I always figured if the scab stayed on, that wouldn't cause scars. The nurse done good because she was at my rack all the time.

One time I heard this doctor say, "I don't know if you'll ever see out of this eye or not, but with this one I think you'll be able to see." I was 20 years old.

I thought about back home and seeing the blind people sitting on the street selling pencils and apples just to make some money. One morning they took the bandages off and I could see out of one eye. They sent me back to the hospital in Honolulu and I stayed there for a while. We got back to Maui and they put the orders out—If anybody had been wounded and med evac'd out, they weren't going to go on the next operation. So they sent us to TAD, Temporary Additional Duty and I went to the Marine Barracks.

After I was discharged I went back to North Carolina for a while and I thought I don't want to end up on a tobacco farm so I went back and reenlisted. I raised my right hand and they sent me to Quantico to train troops. I made Tech Sergeant and went to Korea in a weapons company. All I had to do was dodge the incoming! I had a tour of duty in Viet Nam in the regular infantry. I was a company gunnery sergeant.

Combat never did bother me because of two little things in the Bible. That's Psalm 23 and Psalm 91. Sometime read them. Psalm 91 says 10,000 arrows flying to your right, 10,000 to the left, and they are all missing you. I always went with that. It was men and bullets instead of arrows. I didn't think about getting zapped. I just read that before I'd go in. I still have that little testament, and I got notes all the way through it.

I got along good with the Japanese when I was stationed in Japan. At Marines Barracks, Atsugi, Japan, we had a Japanese security platoon. Some of them big wheels were in the Japanese army but I talked to them just like you. It didn't bother me a bit and it seemed like it didn't bother them. I drank with them and every time they would have a big celebration with that platoon, I was invited. I could talk to them, but I would have to be careful what'd I say. See, in my type of war, you go to war to kill or be killed.

And this Iraq war, you're going to war to be killed. If you shoot somebody, you don't know if it's the right person now and you'd better sit back and let him shoot at you first. If he didn't kill you and you got a couple of witnesses, you can kill him and get by with it. Otherwise you don't know what's going to happen.

I always wanted to go back to Iwo and visit the caves. I almost went one time and then I got to thinking, well they have Japanese there at these reunions and I'd be sitting there thinking, how in the hell did I miss you?

I met my wife Ruby in a sweet shop in Winston-Salem, North Carolina, before I went into service. We have been married sixty something years and have three children, five grandchildren, and four great grandchildren. I retired in 1974 as a Sergeant Major after 32 years of service and was awarded three Purple Hearts and a Navy Unit Citation.

*Affectionately known as 'Big Red,' Lt. Col Aquilla Dyess posthumously received the Medal of Honor for his actions on Namur Island on February 1 and 2, 1944. In 1945, a Navy destroyer was named after him.

* * *

PFC Ken Stevens
E Company, 1st Battalion, 21st Marines, 3rd Division

I was deferred from service because I was on a farm before the war started. They kept telling me I should stay on the farm and kept sending me deferments. I didn't fill them out. I stayed on the farm for one summer so they finally sent me notice that I could go into the service. I entered the Marine Corps February 29, 1944. I was married when I was in the service. My oldest boy was a year old before I'd seen him.

I went to boot camp in San Diego. I got through boot camp pretty good. I didn't mind it because I had bounced around the country since I was 14. I worked on the threshing crews, farms and ranches, so they weren't getting a kid fresh off his mama's knee. In boot camp they gave us a choice of the branch we wanted to get in. I told them I wanted to get into the Fleet Marine Force. That's the outfit that does the beach landings.

The sergeant in charge told me, "In six months you're gonna be dead."

But I told him, "I don't want to come back and have to ask somebody 'how do you fight a war?'"

When I finished boot camp, they sent me to Camp Elliott, California, for combat training. Then I went to BAR school, Scout and Sniper school. The instructor told me overseas there are two kinds of BAR men—the quick and the dead. So I really practiced with the BAR every chance I got. I tried to compare myself with the gun fighters of the Old West because that's how they stayed alive.

The first day we were out there in Poway Valley we killed fourteen rattlesnakes. We slept on the ground and I could hear them buggers rattling all night. We moved to Camp Pendleton and did some amphibious training before we went overseas. We shipped out to Hawaii then to the Marshall Islands and stayed aboard ship a week waiting for the 3rd Division to land on Guam. We then joined them on Guam. After they finished the main resistance, they sent the 2nd Battalion to the north end of the island.

We set up a perimeter camp and we patrolled every day hunting for stray Japs. We had to stand guard on that perimeter fence. One day I was walking guard duty when a stray Jap took two shots at me and missed. Most of the Jap troops couldn't shoot very good. Most of them wore thick glasses. We did these patrols until November when they finally declared the island secure.

211

The Army sent a bunch of guys from New York City to man a radar station that they set up on the north end of the island. Our guys were mostly from the central states all the way from Montana to Texas, Tennessee, Oklahoma and Iowa. One day we were coming from patrol when we met some New York guys and they had about an eight hundred pound heifer on a rope. We asked them what they were gonna do with her. They told us they wanted to keep her for a pet but their CO wouldn't let them keep her. I told them we would take her over to our camp and they could come and see her. That was about 4 o'clock. By 5 o'clock we were eating steak. We all knew what a steak looked like on the hoof, and we hadn't had meat to eat for months.

About the 1st of November they moved us back to Base Camp across from Agana where we trained steady until we went to Iwo Jima. When we finished training, we started loading the ship, but we still didn't know where we were going. I was 19 years old and I never heard of Iwo Jima.

We loaded on the USS President Jackson. They put me in charge on the dock of hooking the cables to the machinery and supplies that went on the ship. I lived on the ship a week before we left. I had two close calls on the ship. One time I went to the head which was one deck above the sleeping compartment. When I came out of the doorway, I saw sparks fly. It was dark in there, black. When I went down in our compartment, it was full of smoke. I asked those guys what happened, and they told me that god damn Leach shot himself in his hand with a BAR. I looked up and I saw three holes in the deck right where I stepped out of the head. They couldn't have missed my feet by a couple of inches. I never saw Leach again. The day before we landed on Iwo Jima I was going up the stairs to the top deck when I heard a loud blast. A bunch of guys came a flying down the stairs. The Japs dropped a shell right on the deck from a shore battery. The next day we landed. I was glad to get off the ship.

We were supposed to be in floating reserve, but they lost so many people in the initial landing that they started unloading us the first afternoon. The beach was so crowded that they couldn't get us ashore so they started putting the Marines back aboard ship. But the Higgins boat I was in made it to the beach. I started just a ways up the beach when the Japs hit a big ammunition dump on the water's edge and blew it up. It blew mud and sand all over the guys right behind me. I could have walked all the way up the beach on dead bodies. I dug a foxhole next to the 5th Division and spent the night. The next morning the rest of the 21st Marines came ashore.

By Dammit, We're Marines!

That day we started moving up to the second airfield. We ran into some Jap pillbox. Two guys, Venezuela and Lerma got hit. They were both in my fire team. We got four Japs out of the pillbox. The third day we watched them put the flags up on Mt. Suribachi. It gave us a good feeling to see the flag go up.

General Holland M. Smith said we had to take that airfield that day at all costs, so we tried to take the airfield from the end of the runway. About every time we tried to get on the airfield, we got heavy small arms fire. Our bazooka man's name was Stagsdale. He put one bazooka shell in one pillbox, but the shell didn't go off because of the loose sand. So I reloaded the bazooka for him and he raised up to fire again and the Japs hit him and split his scalp just like you would cut it with a knife. I grabbed the bazooka so it wouldn't go off and he rolled over and sat up. He told me he just had a little headache but he had a perfect part in his hair. He had wavy blond hair and the cut was dead center. The Jap troops on Iwo Jima were excellent shooters. I never saw one wearing glasses.

They sent the 5th Division up the west side of the airfield and the 4th Division up the eastside. We went in behind the 4th Division to where the runways cross. Then we all crossed the airfield. Going across the runway was like going through a swarm of bees with the bullets buzzing by. I was in the lead fire team.

We were on the left side of the company so my fire team jumped down off the runway and jumped in the big shell hole. We ended up right in front of the big heavy machine gun bunker and they were firing rounds all around us. The fire team leader told us to take off for a ditch along the airfield. So PFC Bumps took off first, he got about half way and they killed him with a machine gun. Then Cpl. Rearden took off and they killed him. Then it was my turn. I grabbed the BAR by the sling and went out of there like a bat out of hell. I did a somersault into the ditch and they kicked up the dirt right underneath me. Then PFC Grobe came next and just hesitated a second before he jumped in the ditch. They hit him about seven times right through the chest. I reached up and caught him by the jacket and laid him in the ditch. He was from Iowa and only about 17 years old. I got into a small ditch where I could see the machine gun. They couldn't get the machine gun low enough to hit me. But I could shoot into the gun until I put it out of action. Then I crawled along the ditch until I could see the entrance to the bunker. The Japs kept coming out of the entrance trying to get at the rear of the company. I put the BAR on single shot and picked them off all afternoon. After dark, I got out of there and looked for my company. When I found the company, there were 22 of us left.

Lt. McCann came along and seen what I was doing and told me that he was going to see that I would get a Medal of Honor. He told me to cover him, then he went to check on the rest of the company. Minutes later he got shot right through the head they told me. So there went my medal.

I was told that K Company 9th Marines had only 2 guys left after we took the airfield. The 22 guys left in my company dug in on a little rise on the edge of the airfield. We were cut off from any other outfit and were by ourselves. I had one magazine of ammunition left. I laid my fighting knife in front of me and said a prayer and got ready to go down fighting.

I know that every man in that group would have fought to their death. We were surprised. The Japs never bothered us all night. We could hear them all around us but I don't think they knew how few there were of us. The next morning they sent a bunch of tanks right up behind us and they had a big tank and artillery battle right up above our heads. The Japs had an anti-tank gun 37mm, a high velocity shell that would about split your ear drums. After the tank battle, we were taken back to a rear area and given some chow, the first we ate. There were some guys in the 5th Division who told me I had 74 dead Japs in front of that bunker. We thought we were all done fighting. I was wandering around the area and I didn't know where I was. The corpsman got a hold of me and gave me a couple of pills and it snapped me right out of it. He told me I had a blast concussion.

That same afternoon they sent us right back on the front line. They put us in different outfits in different units because there weren't enough guys left to make a company. I spent another 30 days on the front lines. I fought with the 3rd Division but also with the 4th and 5th Division. Our company commander was a corporal when we landed and they made him a second lieutenant. His name was Robert Swaine from Pennsylvania. He later got hit on the side of the head by enemy rifle fire, but he came back to the outfit and stayed until the end of the campaign.

We moved to Airfield No. 3, then to sulfur flats. One morning I was sitting alone out on those stinking sulfur flats and as far as I could see all around laid dead Marines and Japs. When I was looking at this horrible scene, surprised to still be alive, the most beautiful sunrise I've ever seen came up out of the ocean. At that moment I could feel God's hand on my shoulder. I will never forget the feeling.

We crossed the sulfur flats to the rocks and caves into the north side of the island. One night I was kneeling on the edge of my foxhole when something hit me on the back, knocking me face down in the dirt.

Everything felt numb. Ken Sullivan was in the hole next to me. I told him to feel the back of me to see if there's any blood.

"No blood," he said, "but it really raised hell with your jacket."

It was a piece of shell fragment about 4 inches by 12 inches. Hit me flat. If it would have come sideways, it would have probably cut me in half. Those close calls happened all through the campaign.

Some night later on, a Jap came at me from in front and I seen him coming. I let him get about 25 yards from me then I let him have a round in the belly. He was carrying a Molotov cocktail that was a quart size bottle filled with aviation gas with a fuse in it. They'd throw it at you and burn everything but he never got to throw it. He laid there and burned all night. He had a watch on his wrist that didn't burn so I stuck the watch in my pocket and traded it for a quart of whiskey when I got back to Guam.

One night me and Ken Sullivan were in a foxhole right next to a steep bank. I was sitting with the BAR across my knees when I looked around over my left shoulder, and a Jap was sitting on his knees on the edge of the bank. He had a bayonet about a foot from my face. I jerked the trigger and fired three rounds with a BAR and he disappeared. I couldn't see him in the dark. So Ken threw two grenades but threw them too far.

"He's gone now," I said.

But the next morning when it got daylight Ken asked me if that's the Nip I was talking about in the night. He laid face down on the edge of my foxhole, and I lifted up his helmet and he had three holes over his left eye that you could have covered with a half dollar. He had a cavalry carbine with a fold over bayonet. I gave it to a guy in headquarters and he took it back to Guam and traded it to a Navy officer for seven quarts of whiskey. Whiskey was worth $100 a quart. He gave me one quart.

The next day I was standing up on a ridge and there were some tanks down below. They were shooting at some caves and I was picking the Japs off when they came out of the caves. Our battalion major came up and asked me what I was doing up there by myself. I told him to watch. About that time some Japs came out of the cave and I let go with the BAR.

He just shook his head and said, "You've got to be the coolest son-of-a-bitch I ever saw," then turned around and went back down the hill.

The next few days we made it towards the north end of the island, and General Smith put out the word that he wanted to give two cans of beer for every man in the unit who reached the north end of the island. So me and 11 or 12 other guys went on patrol out to Kitano point. I was sitting with my shoes off and feet in the water. That's the first time I had my shoes off since I landed.

Someone said, "How are they gonna know we are here?"

I took off my canteen and filled it with water and we put a piece of tape on it and wrote "for inspection not consumption."

Then we sent a runner to Division Command Post with it. That night we had our two cans of beer. Tasted pretty damn good. First beer we had since we left Guam.

They took us back to the rear areas where the Seabees had showers set up. It felt good since we hadn't showered since we landed. They sent in a bunch of replacements and reformed the 21st Regiment. Most of these guys were pretty green. One of them was souvenir hunting and put on a Jap helmet and Jap raincoat and a Jap rifle and he came through some brush right in front of me. When he heard me cock the BAR he threw that helmet off.

One of the officers saw that and really gave him heck. He told that kid, "Sonny, you don't know how close you came to being dead."

We dug foxholes and stood guard on every other foxhole, two guys in each hole. When that two got done then they would wake up the guys in the other foxhole. One of those guys came to wake me up and kicked my helmet that was on the edge of the hole. When the helmet fell down on my feet, I was out of that hole with my BAR sticking it in that kid's belly before he could even move.

We left Iwo Jima on Easter Sunday, 1945. They took us back to Guam where they trained us to land on Japan. We were about two weeks from invading Japan when the war ended. We heard about it over the radio. There was no celebration, in fact right afterwards we fell out for training. Didn't even get the day off. When we got home, we saw all the pictures of the guys kissing all the girls in New York. We got none of that. I left Guam the 1st of December 1945. They dumped us on the dock at San Diego then we went to Camp Pendleton. Just the high point troops in the 3rd Division got sent home. The guys who didn't have enough points to get out went to Japan. I would have liked to go over there, too, but I went home. I got discharged January 2, 1946. I was married for 51 years when my wife passed away. We had nine children, five boys and four girls. My present wife and I have been married for nine years. She had six girls and two boys. We have quite a family get-together.

* * *

Communications

Pvt. Gus Anastole
B Company, 24th Regiment, 4th Division

Gus Anastole, right, with friends

I joined the Marines the later part of 1943. I had three buddies: one joined the Navy, one joined the Coast Guard, and one joined the Army. I just wanted to be different. I was 17 when I joined. I lied about my age but by the time they caught on, I was 18. I didn't stay long in the states. After a few months of boot camp and maybe a couple or three liberties in Los Angeles, they shipped us overseas and the rest of our training was over on Maui. Mostly I trained for communications, but there was some infantry because we had a lot of infantry training in boot camp.

I was taught how to climb telephone poles and string wire for communication. When we got to Iwo there wasn't a pole, there wasn't a tree, there was nothing. That shows you just how things don't go the same way they're supposed to. Originally I was with the Headquarters

Company but I ended up with the 24th Infantry Regiment in the infantry. My specialty was communication but I didn't do much of it.

Iwo was my first and only battle. I was a private on Iwo and I stayed a private the whole time I was in the service. Two days before I was discharged in July of 1946, I was promoted to corporal. I never was a PFC, but I also never got corporal pay.

Nobody knew where we were going. Nobody even heard about the place. They invited us in this little room with a map and the captain started to tell us this is Red Beach, Blue Beach, this is where we are going to land. If we can't make it there, then he turned the map over, he said we'll land on the other side of the beach. Anyway, everything depended on the conditions. While they were talking, we all looked at each other ·

"Do you have any questions?" the captain asked.

Somebody asked, "Where IS this place?"

"About 700 miles from Japan."

There isn't anything between Iwo and Japan.

The reason why we were taking this island is because of its two airstrips. I think I heard about it more from an Air Force man I met at a Marine Corps party later. He says he was on a B-29 coming back from Japan and two of their engines were shot. They were flying on two engines and the pilot noticed this island and recognized it as Iwo Jima and the Marines had already secured it. He said that the plane landed there and saved their lives. He said when he got off the plane for a few hours to do repairs, he kissed the ground because he was so happy the Marines took that island. If we hadn't, they would have been in the sea. That made me feel better. I didn't know why we were there. There were so many of us who died and what were we going to do from a small island? We couldn't shoot from there to Japan. We were just kids then so we didn't know. We heard stories afterwards what had happened. It saved many, many lives. The Marines died to save people like that.

We arrived at Iwo and landed a half a mile away. From aboard ship the island just looked like a peaceful little island, nothing going on. I heard some shots, but no big thing. The Navy brought us in on LCVPs, and the front of them would open up. Once that was down you would run out into the water if you made it to the land. A lot of time the Navy guys wouldn't go all the way into the shore because they were getting fired upon. Wherever they stopped we had to get out. Luckily I did pretty good. I didn't get too wet, maybe just up to my knees. I got there on the second day at 9:00 in the morning. I saw everybody all spread out and so we all spread out and just started digging and putting our heads in the ground. That's the only thing you didn't want to get hit. You didn't care if you got hit in the butt or a leg but you didn't want to get hit in the head. An officer came over to me sometime later and asked what I was doing. I told him I was waiting for orders.

"You come with me," he said.

That's when I went with the 24th Regiment. I wasn't communications any more. There was always some confusion. They even didn't tell me where I was, I had to ask. When we were in Headquarters, we were on top of the 3rd, 4th and 5th Divisions. I wasn't on the front lines, but I was behind them. All of a sudden I'm in the 4th Marine Division. They asked me what my specialty was and I told them communications. On Iwo, my main job was communications though I didn't do much of that but I always had my rifle, you've got to have that. That's where I stayed the whole time until we left Iwo and I went back to my Headquarters Battalion.

I had been on Iwo for a couple of days when the flag was raised. I looked up there and saw the flag, but I don't remember it specifically going up because we weren't looking up there all the time. I thought it was great, but I knew the battle wasn't over with. It gives you a good feeling. They did that more or less to keep the morale going.

One time when we were camped out in foxholes, somebody in a foxhole right next to mine nudged me and said, "Get up, get up."

"I'm already up, what is it?"

"There something stirring up over there."

We had to wait real quiet until daylight and then we saw a bunch of Japanese crawling in the mud. I guess they were looking for food. We all got up and started shooting at them. There were 27 Japanese that we counted dead. We knew they were Japanese, because we knew no Marines would crawl like that. That was the only time that I really had enemy fire.

You feel scared, really scared. I don't want to hear one guy tell me he was never scared. You are really scared. When it's all over you don't mention scared any more…now they call you brave. What a brave Marine! If they only knew down deep you're scared to death. Gung ho is when you are in boot camp and training to be a Marine.

We had plenty to eat, but I wouldn't call it food. It was packaged C-rations and K-rations. They had a can of vegetables and beans and another can was beans and vegetables. Same thing, only a different name. Also, it had three cigarettes with each meal. Men who never smoked in their lives smoked those cigarettes. I never smoked in my life until I was on Iwo, but I figured it's there so I might as well light up. We didn't have hot food. Everything came out of a can. We never had milk; only water. I remember not having a bath for 35 days until I got aboard ship then the bathwater was salt water. But at least we ate a little warm food. We never ate warm food on Iwo, at least my outfit didn't. The same clothes I wore on the February 19 were the same clothes I left in on March 25.

When the battle was over, we didn't think it was over. We still kept hearing shots even as we were leaving. But they said that there was a ship waiting and we were supposed to go on this ship. We marched down to the beach and waited and walked on a gangplank and got aboard ship and left. No one ever said, "Hey this thing is over with." The Army came in when we were leaving. They took over because there was a lot of the enemy still in caves.

When I left, I went by the cemetery. It was March 25, my 19th birthday. I saw a bunch of names but I couldn't see any of my friends' names. You are still kind of weary and you don't know who is around so you don't want to be walking around a cemetery. That's all it took, the last day you're there and some guy picks you off. When we were ready to leave, we were gone. They were making those grave markers aboard ship and brought them in on a small boat. I used to see a lot of guys carrying those crosses.

Iwo was a terrible place. I had a lot of opportunities to go and visit but I will not go back. I have nothing there.

We were aboard ship heading for Maui. "I have news," the captain said, "President Franklin D. Roosevelt has passed away."

I didn't know who our new president was. Somebody said it was Harry Truman.

"Who's Harry Truman?" I asked. Thank God for him because he is the one who got us home.

So many men were aboard ship that I never saw any of my friends. I saw a guy with a name on his fatigues, Antonopolis.

I went over, tapped him on the shoulder and said, "You must be Greek."

"I am, how did you know?"

"I could tell because your name starts on one shoulder and it ends up on the other one!"

We became friends. Through him I met my first wife. I lost a lot of friends, about 11 that I know of. The saddest part was when I came home and went to visit my friend Bill's mother. She was living in Michigan, I believe, and she had word that her son was killed. I hitchhiked from San Francisco back there because I didn't have any money. I kept my uniform on so I could get a ride. It was a warm day in September.

By Dammit, We're Marines!

She was in her kitchen and she looked out and saw this Marine in uniform. When I knocked on the door, the poor thing almost fainted because she probably thought that I was her son. There were a lot of mistakes during the war and maybe she thought he didn't die. That was really sad for me. All she wanted to know was what his last words were but I couldn't tell her because it was a swear word. I just couldn't tell her that. I told her that he died peacefully which he really didn't. But I didn't want to worry her all the more because if you tell her he was in agony then the poor thing will live the rest of her life thinking about that. It's awfully hard to tell her the truth. She invited me to stay as long as I wanted but I told her I couldn't because I had to go back. We wrote to each other for a long, long time. I'm sure Bill would have done the same thing for me. I didn't hear from her so I guess she passed away. She didn't have any other children. Nobody wrote to tell me that she died.

Years later when I got married again, we traveled around the country and I'd visit my friends from the Marines. This time we hugged each other, we never had before. It was 20 years later, but we all looked the same. We didn't talk much about the war. There wasn't much to say. A lot of us had bad memories, and we didn't want to talk about that.

My first wife died in childbirth in 1950. I had a baby and no wife. My mother-in-law took care of the baby for a couple of years until I remarried. Then I married a gal and we had two boys. After 18 years we divorced. Sometimes things happen for the best. Then I met the best and most beautiful girl I ever married. She had five girls. Together we have eight children, 24 grandchildren and six great-grandchildren. My wife passed away a few years ago so I'm back to being a widower again.

* * *

Acting Sgt. John A. Holle
H Battery, 3rd Battalion, 14th Marines, 4th Division

John 'Beans' Holle, wartime photo

I joined the Marines because of the rifle shooting. It was all about the rifle shooting for me. Since I was 12 years old, I was involved with rifle shooting, small bore .22. I used to go all around the country and shoot at different rifle matches, and the Marine Corps were noted for their rifle shooting. I joined the Marine Corps because of that and, of course, to be a Marine. I liked the Marines. I thought that would be the best part of the service to be in for one thing. When I joined, I received $5 extra a month for making expert with a rifle. Five dollars extra — that was big money. I was straight out of high school.

I had two buddies and we grew up together since the fifth grade. We were all a year apart. David Brown was the oldest one of the group, Robert Hartman was in the middle, and I was the baby. One night we were down in Newark, New Jersey, I don't know if we went to a movie or something, but we all decided we were going to join together, the three of us. David and Bob worked at the Kearney Ship Yards at the time. David was drafted the next day into the Army and he ended up in Guadalcanal. Bob worked in the shipyards but they wouldn't let him go.

By Dammit, We're Marines!

Finally he got out of the shipyards and got into the Navy. I met him in Oahu during the war and we got liberty together. They managed to survive the war, but they are both gone now.

I was a tall skinny kid, so I was a string bean, but I also ate Van Camp beans by the can. I got them at the PX. While other guys were going for chow, I'd get a couple of cans and eat the beans with crackers. So my buddy, Charlie Troy, may he rest in peace he was killed on Iwo, came up with that idea of calling me 'Beans.' I still eat beans.

I was in all four battles of my outfit: Roi-Namur, Saipan, Tinian and Iwo Jima. On Iwo I was designated as head of the communication personnel and the liaison between the battery and the forward observers.

We went in the first day in the first wave, second wave, whatever. We were on LSTs with DUKWs. The first DUKW went off and sank, went right down with the gun and everything on it, a 105 howitzer, splash! Right under the water. One guy on there couldn't swim; he was all right, everybody was all right, and nobody drowned but the whole DUKW was gone.

It wasn't what we expected at all. Because we were bombing, we blew that island apart so we thought. There was one thing the Japs always made a mistake about. They'd let us land before they opened up on us. And once we are on land, we aren't going to leave, you know.

One night I was delivering a radio up to the forward observers with another Marine, I can't think of his name, that's what bothers me quite a bit, not remembering his name. We were in a foxhole or a crater, a shell came through right between the two of us and buried itself in and threw dirt and everything all over us but it never exploded. That was very close. Another time I was in a hole and on the radio. I was talking to a couple of Navy guys who were batting the breeze back and forth on the radio and I was telling them to get off the radios because we were using them to direct fire power. A shell landed in the hole along side of us and killed quite a few Marines, I don't know how many Marines were in there, but I got hit with a big piece of flesh right in the back of the neck. It was terrible. I managed to survive everything but it was quite an experience.

The only time you don't sleep is when it's your turn to sleep. You can't sleep. There are usually two of you in a hole and you try to have a buddy system and take turns. It's not that you don't trust your buddy, but you don't sleep. It was noisy, all right, with those shells dropping in around you.

I can see where you'd have bad dreams and somebody touches you and you just jump. I still have dreams like that, crazy dreams, unbelievable. I'm a great dreamer for some reason and they don't make sense half of them. I'd dream about the war then I dream about some stuff around here now.

It was a strange way I got injured later on. After almost getting killed a couple of times, I was sitting back at the battery with a Priest, Father Druffle. I forget who else was around there, but out of the clear blue sky I got shot in the leg. A sniper. Evidently I yelled out a couple of crazy words and all and asked the priest to excuse my language. They took me to an aid station and patched me up. It wasn't anything that serious. Never evacuated; I was the walking wounded. I still have the bullet at home. I was out hardly at all, just a couple of days, that's all. I was there on Iwo right until the end.

It was unbelievable when I found out all the guys who were killed. I took a little tour around the 4th Division Cemetery, and I was really surprised about the fellas who were killed there. Bob Merrick, Eddie Murphy, Charlie Troy. We brought Charlie back here and we had a funeral for him. He's buried in a military cemetery in New Jersey. I understand Robert Merrick from Newark, New Jersey, is buried in Oahu. I don't know for sure about Murphy. Yeah, they were all my buddies.

Only three of us from our tent came back from Iwo. We were tent buddies on Maui. We had a real racket there. After Iwo, it was back to Maui where they read us the articles of war. The war was over and you weren't allowed to skip out or something.

I came home, married a girl I knew from 4th grade in grammar school. I didn't go with her from the 4th grade, I had a few other girlfriends, but I married my sweetheart and we had four children. We've been married 60 years and have two grandchildren, too.

I keep trying to remember all my buddies...the ones who are gone and all. It seems the older you get the more it seems to affect you for some reason. I go to the VA for psychiatric treatments. The memories come back. I had plenty of nightmares when I first returned and it was surprising sometimes. I didn't talk to anybody about the war. On the Fourth of July, the fireworks sounded just like war. The VA offered help and I'm still going to the shrink now. I get depressed or something. They ask me questions, we talk. That's about the size of it. It's a funny thing, when I first got out, I guess you're just so happy you got out of it that it doesn't seem to affect you so much. It's later on when you start thinking about it. My advice is to get psychological help if you need it. I often was a little leery of that but I don't know if it really works or what.

* * *

For his service during World War II, Corporal Holle received the Bronze Star Medal. His citation reads in part:

"Volunteering as a radio operator for his battery commander's liaison party, Corporal Holle frequently traveled over rugged terrain and under intense mortar and small-arms fire to maintain communication with rear units. On one occasion, when a hidden hostile machine gun opened fire, wounding the officer in charge of his unit and killing or wounding several men who were occupying a position of the crest of a hill, he refused to withdraw and, advancing in the direction of fire, led his comrades forward to destroy the enemy position. His courage, devotion to duty and leadership were in keeping with the highest traditions of the United States Naval Service."

Corporal Holle is authorized to wear the Combat "V"

* * *

Cpl. Jack Leahy
Radar Technician, HQ Company, 3rd Battalion,
24th Marines, 4th Division

Jack Leahy, wartime photo

I enlisted in the Marines in April 1943 when I was 18 years old. When I came out of boot camp, I took a few tests and they decided to send me to Radar Technicians School. Radar was brand new at that time. It's a ten month course and the deal was that if we went through it, we would come out with a staff sergeant rating. We studied Navy radar in San Francisco. I took the course and got my corporal rating in about six months. In the final months of the program, we didn't receive the promotions we were promised. They decided to give the promotions that were set aside for us to the Fleet Marines. That's fine, but that kind of made me give up as far as the schooling was concerned. I lost interest in it and just got through it.

They sent me down to Camp Pendleton and I ended up in a carpentry shop. I didn't know the first thing about wood, made a mess of it, but from there I volunteered to go overseas. You had to volunteer to go overseas, I don't know why. I was attached to the 4th Marine Division from that time on.

In January we pulled out and were aboard ship before we found out where we were going. They had maps and showed us Iwo Jima. We could see it was a pretty insignificant piece of land and the word was we should be in and out of there in about a week because we had been bombing it and that supposedly neutralized the island.

On Iwo Jima, where I did not make the initial landing, a friend of mine who had gotten hit in the head with shrapnel his first day on the beach told me later, "I got off the island the first day and I'm glad I got hit!" He figured he had it made. Different people had different ideas.

We stayed aboard the attack transport while the infantry troops of the first and second wave went into the beach. The attack transports are usually hospitals ships as well as transport and supply vessels. It wasn't long before they started bringing bodies off the beach pretty badly beat up, pretty gruesome.

Our assignment was to unload the vessel. We had a lot of cargo in there that was to be brought up so we were the stevedores doing the operation. After about two or three days, we had it completely empty. They then transferred us from an APA to a LST. An LST is a flat platform type of vessel, open, with a conning tower and structures on one side of the vessel. It's primarily used for landing equipment and tanks. I remember being on the LST when we saw the flag going up on Suribachi. We could see from the water. We thought this was terrific. A lot of weapons were being fired up in the air, cheering, because we thought this is it, all done already, day four, we won.

It rained one night on the LST. We were all soaking wet and they put us down below and we hung all our gear out. I had my weapon, a carbine hanging next to some of my clothing. Someone came along and stole the damn carbine so when I finally hit Iwo Jima I had no weapon. Our LST pulled in at the north end of the island at night. If you know anything about the island, the beachhead was down south, the north was still under Japanese control. It's a wonder we didn't get blown up. I guess the skipper came in and thought, look here's a beach, so he opened the bow doors and dropped the landing ramp down.

I started to get off and someone hollered, "No, get back in."

So we scrambled back in and they pulled the ramp back up again and closed the bow doors. I think the only reason we made it out of there was that the Japanese probably had everything aimed south down towards the beach end. Boy, what a great place to be. The skipper doesn't know where he's going.

When I finally got off the LST, a sergeant grabbed me and asks, "Where's your weapon?"

"Some guy stole it."

"Go get another one. There's a pile of them over there."

He pointed to a lot of weapons from dead Marines. So I grabbed an M-1. I had a carbine before and it was a nice light weapon. Some place along the island I picked up a Springfield '03, a weapon with better accuracy than the M-1.

They assigned us to duties on the beach unloading any other vessels that came to the beach and putting wounded back on vessels to go to hospital ships. I don't remember how long we did that. We found a backward cave there that had its opening away from the beach. I remember staying in this cave two or three days. Out of the cave during the daytime, but in it at night.

A friend of mine, Carl Greymore, whom I went to radar schooling with, ended up with the 3rd Marine Division. I heard he was on the beach and found out where he was. He was a very resourceful farm boy, and he had constructed himself the most elaborate foxhole I had ever seen in my life. He stripped the battery and the lights out of a jeep and put the battery and the lights inside his foxhole. He had a cover over it, I forget what it was made of, and made a beautiful foxhole on the beach.

They had bodies stacked up like cordwood in the area we were in. This is one sight I will never forget. The bodies were all Marines stacked up. I don't know how high, my recollection was three or four feet. They couldn't bury them because the Japanese were shelling so much that the burial details couldn't get down there without getting killed, too, so the bodies were just left there. I was there when they started bulldozing the huge hole and temporarily covering the bodies up with sand. Even to this day I get choked up when I think of that scene. I get choked up every time I think of a dead Marine.

I was then assigned to a communication platoon of the 3rd Battalion, 24th Marines. I was responsible for getting replacement gear for front line communicators such as batteries for their equipment, radios, wire, or whatever else they needed. I wasn't with them for long because we started moving up the line and taking over from other Marines of the 4th Division.

One night four Japanese got in behind us. They were doing this continuously to rip off food, water, supplies or whatever that was set up all over the beach. They were coming back from the beach early one morning and someone spotted them and hollered so those poor guys jumped in a shell hole in our CP area. The Japs were not surrounded but they were covered on at least three sides by Marines, the other side was the road we came in on. There was no place to go. They were trapped and we had to goose them out. We were told to grab our weapons. Didn't know where we were going. This occurred towards the north end of the island which I always thought looked like a miniature Grand Canyon. We were just at the start of that area, just past an airfield. There was a guy slightly behind me carrying a Thompson sub machine gun.

I'm not familiar with how they fire but when you pull the trigger they rise right up in the air. That's not an infantry weapon but a weapon normally used in the tanks. Apparently this guy got one from a tank that was knocked out. He was a medical driver taking guys from where they were hit back to the aid station, so he didn't know anything about the damn weapon. Just as we started to advance towards the shell hole, one of the Japanese stood up and threw a hand grenade in our direction. I don't think it ever got very far when this guy with the sub machine gun cut loose on the Jap. A couple of grenades later thrown in by Marines was the end of the story. But this guy had gotten so excited when he saw the Jap jumping up he pulled the trigger. Bullets were dancing around everyone's feet and we're thinking that we're going to get shot in the rear end by this guy!

From then on it became kind of perfunctory. Some guys were walking through our area and stepped on a land mine. The land mine was not too far from where we set up our CP. These were two wiremen one of whom was killed and the other was seriously injured in the blast. It was gory. The wiremen had a tough job walking in unknown territory a lot of times. They were required to string wire from the forward observation post back to a CP or some other command or communication area. As they move forward to set up the next site to hook up the portable phones, wiremen would run wire back to tie into the wire at the previous command area. They would walk through territory that was unmapped and uncharted. We didn't expect land mines. That was a surprise. It surprised those two wiremen who had been doing this obviously for a long time as this was probably day 25 or 26.

I developed an interesting technique. Guys would bring in hand grenades from the Japanese as souvenirs. They were very colorful, red and black as I recall. They looked like a small version of what the Germans had that was called the potato masher because it had a long handle. The Japanese had a smaller version of that. The grenade body was a cylindrical shape about two to three inches in diameter and two inches deep and that's where all the powder was. I learned how to take those apart without killing myself. So I became a very popular fellow there taking them apart and deactivating them for souvenirs. Someone brought in a mortar shell. I had never taken a shell apart before so I gave it a try. What's the worst that could happen? But I took it apart. It was nothing, unscrew the cap, take it apart, dump the powder out. It's crazy what you do as a young kid. You wouldn't do it now. But I had just turned 20.

I thought this combat stuff was great because I didn't have to get up and march any more. This is a piece of cake. No one is on my tail for 30 some odd days. Of course I wasn't on the front lines. At HQ it's different than infantry. We were back behind the lines.

There was another interesting weapon that was used. I called them rocket jeeps. There was a rocket assembly with a number of rockets on the back of a jeep. They'd pull those rocket jeeps right into our area and ignite them however they did that and the rockets would fire towards the Japanese lines. As soon as the last one would fire, these guys would take that jeep and high tail it.

"Why are they doing that?" I asked.

"Because they know damn well the Japanese are going to shell that position," this guy says.

"Why the hell did they do it right next to us?"

No answer.

I had no infantry training. I often mention the fact that I was a radar technician and people ask, "What was a radar technician doing on Iwo Jima?" I didn't do anything with radar I'll tell you that. I didn't even do anything with the radios over there except replace parts for them. These guys would bring a radio in all shot up and ask, "Can you repair this for me?" I'd say, "You've got to be kidding," and give them another radio if I had one and I didn't have them very often.

When it was over, I packed up all the gear and got aboard the transport ships. We went back to base camp. And showers! I didn't have a shower on Iwo until I got back aboard the ship and then it was a salt water shower. You're sticky all the time but at least you felt you were getting a little cleaner. It was better than nothing. But I got that far and I didn't get hit. I was pretty thankful for that. I brought back to Maui the Springfield '03 that I found on Iwo. They had a shake down. You couldn't have weapons in any of the tents. If caught, you could go to the brig. So where do you think I dumped it? Down the latrine. It was the only place I could find.

"You never told me some of these things," my wife said.

"What do you want to talk about? There is not much to tell."

Some events were colorful and some were pretty gruesome. It was life. At least it was life there. I had no reason to talk about it. There was nothing I wanted to volunteer to talk about. I was just doing my job. I wasn't on the front lines. Everyone has their job, it's all necessary. But again you don't think about the potential for danger, I know I didn't.

"This is what they want me to do, I'll do it," I said.

All those souvenir grenades I made, and some that were given to me, I could have taken home. I had no desire to do that. I have very little memorabilia. I think I still have a flyer that was dropped by the Americans on the island about surrendering.* It's all in Japanese. It showed a Japanese soldier facing off against an American tank. They were dropped after the bombing. It didn't do any good. I had a Japanese translate it for me one time. I have since gotten sand from Iwo.

I left the Marines in '46. I went to college and finished a five-year engineering course. In 1949 I signed up for the Reserves because I wanted to go to Quantico the following year and become an officer. Trouble was 1950 was the start of the Korean War so they pulled me out of school with no opportunity to go to Quantico. They sent me back to radar school like they did in '43. This time I didn't goof off in my studies. I was number one in my class and got a promotion even though I wasn't promised one. I ended up as a buck sergeant.

*General Kuribayashi ordered instant death for any Japanese soldier caught with one of these surrender passes.

* * *

DUKWs and AMPHIBS

"The development of the amphibian tractor, or LVT, which began in the middle 1930's, provided the solution and was one of the most important modern technical contributions to ship to shore operations. Without these landing vehicles our amphibious offensive in the Pacific would have been impossible."
- Lieutenant General Holland M. Smith, USMC

Sgt. Maj. Lon White USMC (Ret.)
PFC, C Battery, 1st Battalion,
14th Marines, 4th Division

I was working in Ft. Lauderdale with my uncle and I was in the movies downtown when Pearl Harbor happened. When I came out, the news people were hawking the bombing of Pearl Harbor. So I grabbed a newspaper and I ran all the way home because I knew the lives of the guys in my age group were going to change. I was 18 at the time. I continued working for a while with my uncle but the war intensified. So in March of 1942 I left Ft. Lauderdale and went back to my home in Dooly County, Georgia, and registered for the draft. In my considered opinion, anybody who had to be drafted were not patriotic Americans. I joined the Marine Corps on August 12, 1942, and went to Parris Island then to New River, North Carolina, which is now called Camp Lejeune. We were in fact the first group to fire on the new rifle range at Camp Lejeune and the last group to fire the '03 rifle. The next group coming through had the M-1, and naturally we weren't too much impressed with those guys.

In those days, boot camp was seven weeks. So in seven weeks time we were out and I was put in the artillery. We were really very, very green and so was the whole expansion relative to the Marine Corps in those days. We had orders to go to Norfolk, Virginia. They asked me if I knew how to drive.

"Sure," I said.

"Go down to the motor pool and check out a jeep."

If you had a background of farming or anything like that, they immediately put you in the motor pool. That's how well we were organized. I went down, took this jeep and drove round and round. The next day we took out to Norfolk, Virginia. I didn't know nothing about convoy or convoy patrols, so here I was driving a sergeant and tailgating the jeep right in front of me.

By Dammit, We're Marines!

"White, you don't know anything about convoys, do you?" he asked.

"No."

"Well I'll tell you how to do it. Stay one telephone pole behind the other guy."

So that was my deal. I did that for a while then I went back into the artillery section and I did that on the Marshall Islands, Saipan, and Tinian. Saipan was quite a battle. We were continuously trying to be overrun by the Japanese because we were in 75 Pack Howitzers which means we were right behind the infantry. I always managed to pick up a pump shot gun because as a young boy I was a hunter. In fact one of my hunting buddies was Jimmy Carter. We lived in Plains, Georgia, in 1937 and Jimmy and I were boyhood buddies. Jimmy and I used to go hunting together and we always had shotguns. MPs carry pump shot guns and they'd always be MPs that were killed on the beaches so I picked up this pump shot gun with the double-aught buck shot. One night we were just about to get overrun in the middle part of Saipan when these little carbines weren't stopping those guys. They would get high as a kite on sake and whatever else and you couldn't stop them with those M-1 carbines. When we were about to get overrun my section leader grabbed my pump shot gun and that stopped them. That is how I spent my 21st birthday by stopping the Japs from killing us.

For my 21st birthday my mom sent me a huge birthday cake. We were cold and miserable. It was raining cats and dogs and we were shooting our guns and knee deep in mud. They were unable to feed us because of the weather and we were tired of eating K-rations so my mom's birthday cake fed my whole section. Those guys were so impressed with that cake. It was a coconut layer cake, a big, big huge thing. I was the king of the walk for that day.

When we landed in Tinian, we had a narrow entranceway to go into the island. There were coral reefs between the boats and the beach so we had to go in with amphibian trucks called DUKWs that were driven by the Army. A DUKW is a 2 1/2 ton truck with a boat body around it. The Army guys would never in the hell have been Marines, I tell you. We got hung up on the reef going into Tinian and the Army guys abandoned the DUKWs and took off over the hood of the thing. So Volillenger, our gun section chief, jumped up, got into the cab and took control, backed her off the reef, darted around the edge of that reef and we got off and got into position with our guns. Then he just drove that thing back down to the beach. I guess the Army guys came and got it. When we got back from there, the Marine Corps saw that they needed a DUKW company so we had to answer the same questions:

"Did you ever drive a truck or anything like that as a farm boy?"
They went through the whole Division getting guys who had that background to put together a DUKW company. The Marine Corps got it primarily to haul artillery into the beaches. That thing at Tinian showed us that we needed our own DUKW Company. On Tinian, I was a yardbird, a PFC, but a pretty capable PFC because I was assistant section leader of this gun section; in those days you didn't get promotions much. We had 85 DUKWs and I was an assistant driver.

We got to Iwo and we started off-loading. We were the last DUKW off the LST. As we backed out, I think the driver froze to the wheel, so consequently I am on the back telling him to come on, come on. The next thing I knew that DUKW was sinking to the bottom so I dove off and came up underneath that LST. I thought oops, I better head west, so I swam out and I yelled to the guys up on the LST to throw me a life jacket. They threw it behind me and the tide was going the other way so they threw another life jacket and I drifted into that one. Then the company commander come around and picked me up. If they hadn't I probably would have drifted back to Saipan.

I went ashore D-Day; we were probably wave six or seven. When we went ashore, I had no helmet, no pack, no nothing. I'm not trying to be a hero, I didn't have these things; but did have a .38 six-shooter. That's all because my rifle and all my other stuff went down with the DUKW.

As we're going in, naturally you couldn't miss Suribachi on the left, and we saw all the infantry guys struggling to advance enough to get up to where the first airport was. We were amazed that we weren't getting any fire from the shore. No mortar rounds and very, very quiet. What the Japanese were doing was waiting for us to get a foothold on the shore and then they would blast us off of it. But that didn't happen. We got ashore, they clobbered the heck out of us with their ammo but the Japanese didn't reckon with the type of ammo they had. The Japanese, if they had timed fire like we did, would have killed us all. Just wiped us out. We would never in the heck have taken that island. Timed fired means you could set the projectile before you put it into the tube of the piece of artillery and you can set it where it will go off before it goes into the ground. But the Japanese had point-detonating timers and with that volcanic ash, it had to go all the way down in before it reached enough resistance to make it go off. Hell, when it did, the volcanic ash would absorb the shrapnel. In fact I saw a corpsman carry this stretcher down with this wounded guy laying on the stretcher, and one of those rounds went right underneath that stretcher. It blew the guy off the stretcher but it didn't hurt anybody. The corpsman got up and grabbed both ends of the stretcher and the wounded man got back on the stretcher and went on down to the evacuation area. Timed fire was one of the effective things we had in the battle of Saipan, the battle of Tinian, and that helped too in the Marshall Islands. But they didn't, so consequently the volcanic ash absorbed all the shrapnel. That's why we had such a hard time taking the north end of the island. The north end of the island didn't have the volcanic ash, it was regular old rough terrain and when the rounds would hit in there with that point detonator — POW!

I was issued another DUKW as a driver and so for five days my job was to go out and haul the wounded out to the hospital ships and various sundry places where they tell me to take the wounded. I'll never forget one guy, he said, "I'm going home now. I'm going home now." His whole stomach was eaten up with automatic bullets. "This is my third time I got hit and I'm going home."

I hope the boy made it. You had to get shot three times before you could go home in those days. Coming from the evac station, they loaded them up with brandy and he was loaded up with brandy. I hauled him off and they pulled him up on a hoist to put him in the hospital ship. Then I'd pick up a load of ammunition and bring it in. Three or four times a day I'd do this.

On about the fourth day, I had just come in from a round trip when I looked up on Mt. Suribachi and the flag was going up. The flag never went up on any of the other islands we were on until we had secured the island and there right on top of Mt. Suribachi this flag was flying. I thought, oh boy, we'll be getting out of here in a hurry! Wrong. We went about 32 more days fighting this thing and more and more guys got killed. But we continued to do it and finally we got to where we could go all the way around Suribachi and come in on the other beach for supplies which was absolutely a better beach. That volcanic ash that we had to land on! We had a deal on the amphibian truck where you'd pull a little lever up or down and the tires would deflate. Sometimes we had to get down to where it just showed 2 lbs before we could climb up that volcanic ash. But when we went around to the other side, it was a lot easier.

At night time we'd stop and I slept in the corner of an old Japanese pillbox but in that pillbox was a Japanese soldier. It was down a ways from my battery that I had been with all the time in the other campaigns, Charlie Battery, 1st Battalion, 14th Marines. He was very, very quiet because I never heard him and I was in there eating and drinking and all this. On the fifth day this Japanese soldier came out and he said, "mizoo" which means water in Japanese. The rear echelon grunts shot him to death and that infuriated me because only poor men's sons fight wars in the enlisted deal. You have to be a poor man's son but very patriotic. I figured this poor Japanese guy was in the same capacity as me. He may have been on a rice paddy farm where I was on a farm in Dooly County, Georgia, but for them to kill him like that was just absolutely beyond my thoughts on life.

My cousin from Florida enlisted in the Marines one month before I did, and he was on Iwo. He was with the 3rd Marine Division in the Raider Battalion. I was a PFC and went up to see him up around the airport. "Do you have a Marine here by the name of Hickman maybe a corporal or a PFC?" I asked.

"No, we don't have a corporal, but we have a Master Sgt. Harry Hickman."

"Master Sergeant?" I grinned. Someway or another, he walked around the corner and there he was, my cousin, a Master Sergeant. Needless to say you can imagine what my impression was of him.

I was all the way out at sea one time and my DUKW was heading from one of the ships to the next and I got hit up side the head with my helmet on by a hunk of shrapnel….way out at sea. I picked up that piece of shrapnel, it was hot and I dropped it in the sea, this time I was sitting on the assistant driver's side.

A guy by the name of Alan H. West drove with me and asks, "What the heck is a matter with you?"

"That dad blame hunk of shrapnel hit me up side the helmet and I reached down and picked it up and burnt my hand!"

"Idiot," naturally he said.

I've talked to him quite a few times since then over the phone, he was fantastic. We selected each other because we had the same type of personality. We were about as organized an amphibian truck company after we hit Iwo as a Chinese fire drill. Consequently you just picked your own thing.

It was so screwed up that me and West said, "We'll take this DUKW," so we did our own deal.

I fought sixteen battles for this nation in World War II, Korea, and two tours in Vietnam. I retired from the Marine Corps in August 1974 as a Sergeant Major. I'm an Irishman and my great-great-great grandma used to sit on my shoulder. "Don't go there!" she'd say and I would duck. I landed D-Day on every operation and I don't have one single Purple Heart. Not one Purple Heart. She took care of me.

I went back to the 20th anniversary of the Iwo Jima battle. We flew in and out of Japan, and at that time I had some rank and we went up on Suribachi. We were entertained by our garrison group on the island, which was the Air Force, and they really rolled out the red carpet. I mean we were lavishly entertained, lavishly fed. The guys who welcomed us to come aboard, it gave them a little outlet that they were missing. The Americans are no longer there. With one of those treaties, we gave it back to Japan.

* * *

Tech Sgt. Earle W. Davis

Artillery Specialist, 2nd Armor Amphibian
Tractor Battalion, 5th Division

Earle Davis, left, in Hawaii 1942.

I joined the CCC (Civilian Conservation Corps) camps when I was 18 years old. My commanding officer was Sgt. York, the World War I hero, and I knew him real well. He would pick me up every morning for work and take me home. I went into the Marine Corps in 1939 when I was 19 years old. I think the Marines happened to be the only recruiters who were in Crossville, Tennessee. Me and my brother decided to enlist, and we went into the Marine Corps together.

I was in Sea-Coast Artillery at Guantanamo Bay as part of a gun crew. We manned 5-inch guns to sink any ships coming in to attack us. On Guantanamo Bay I got appendicitis and went to the hospital. When I come out of the hospital, I was put on what they called light duty working in the bake shop. Later, they decided to promote me to artillery specialist because I knew artillery and I got $5 a month extra for that.

Me and my brother were in Pearl Harbor and Guadalcanal together. I was still on light duty from Guantanamo, so I was at Marine barracks over at the Navy yard at Pearl Harbor and so was my brother.

By Dammit, We're Marines!

He was doing guard duty that day down on the docks when the Japanese bombed them.

The blasts threw him into the water and a sailor threw a rope and pulled him on board. When the captain of the ship found out his job in the Marine Corps was on the anti-aircraft guns, he put my brother in charge of the guns on the ship and wouldn't let him off for three days. They had lost most of their sailors. We thought he was dead. He finally came in three days later when they let him off the ship. He was all right.

I wasn't asleep on the morning of December 7 because it was my brother's birthday. Our plan was to go to Honolulu to celebrate his birthday when he got off duty at 7:30 that morning. I got up early and was standing outside the barracks on the parade ground when I saw the Japanese planes coming in. I knew what they were because I knew a little more about it than anyone else.

Back in August of 1941 when I was at Guantanamo Bay, we were put aboard ship one night about midnight. We only had about two hours notice before we had to board that ship. We had been at Guantanamo nearly 18 months and back then you went home from overseas after 18 months. Instead of going home, they sent us to Pearl Harbor. The idea was, at that time, to defend the islands. But they wouldn't let us set up the guns or nothing to defend the island. They pulled every ship into the harbor that Saturday night before the Japanese planes came. They wouldn't do anything like that in wartime, but we were in peace time we thought. The speculation was they wanted the Japanese to attack so we could get into the war. That was the idea but they probably didn't realize that things were going to happen bad as they did. That is the only thing I ever heard that made any sense to me.

After Pearl Harbor, my outfit was sent to Guadalcanal. They never needed our 5-inch guns because the Japanese never counter attacked us by ship. The only counter attacking they ever did on Guadalcanal was by airplane and we had anti-aircraft guns we'd use. The Marines in my battalion have the record for shooting down enemy aircraft on Guadalcanal. After Guadalcanal the Japanese were basically done for. They were always on the defensive. If the Japanese were to counter attack by ship and try to reinvade, then our outfit would be needed; but that never happened during the war, never. When we secured Guadalcanal, the Army was brought in to relieve the Marines and we went to New Zealand.

Me and my brother came back to the States in 1943; it was the first time I'd been home in three years, him either. They sent him to Portsmouth, New Hampshire, and me to San Diego. They said he couldn't go back overseas because he had already served three years over there. I didn't expect to go back either but then they put me in the 2nd Armor Amphibian in Oceanside, a new amphibian tank they developed for the war, and sent me to Maui. From there we invaded Saipan, and from Saipan we went to Iwo.

We sat out there on the ships off Iwo and watched them bomb that island. You wouldn't think there was anything alive on a little ol' two mile island. We went in at the beginning in case we were needed in the amphibs. The amphibs weren't just land tanks. They would load those tanks on the ships and when they are about half a mile out of Iwo, they'd go off the end of a LST ship and sink to the bottom of the ocean. The tanks would come up out of the bottom of the ocean like the waves come up. That's the first time the Japanese see them and by that time the tanks are right on top of them. There was a bluff about 100 yards in and about 20 foot high where the Japs were in concrete emplacements. The amphibs knew exactly where they had to go so they'd run right up to the emplacement and stick the barrel of the cannon in the hole and shoot. Then the infantry came in and they did their specialty job over the bluff. The infantry couldn't dislodge the Japanese. They were about to conquer us when our tanks went in. We had 100 tanks and they blasted the Japanese out of there. I don't think we would have ever defeated the Japanese, well maybe six months later, but not quick like we did without those tanks.

When we went ashore, the first thing we did was dig foxholes in the sand. I guess we were there about 4 or 5 days in the hole. We were in danger all the time because the Japanese, and our troops too, were firing all around. I could see men running all over carrying dead and wounded Marines. I don't think I had enough sense to be scared.

After a while, we moved our camp across the island by the hot springs where we could take a shower. I was in the Headquarters Division by that time. That's the people who drive the trucks, the mailmen who deliver the mail, but then I also had my other job. Let's say if one of the gunners got killed in the tank but the tank could still operate, I would have to take his place. But that never happened. The Japanese eventually knocked the tanks out and killed the guys, but there wasn't any tank for me to go in so I basically had nothing to do except do guard duty at night. Same with the mailmen. When you are in the battalion, you have to go where the battalion goes and you got to take the violence like anyone else.

I shot one Jap while I was on guard duty. He came down out of the mountain at night. They had no food or nothing to eat and starving to death. I told him to halt but he didn't, so I had no option but to shoot him. I always felt kind of bad about that because he was just starving to death, but we knew you can't play pretty with the Japanese because they would have some kind of a trick up their sleeve, bomb us or something, if we did anything like that. One time when we still had to travel back and forth across the island, me and another guy were going across right on top where one of the 16 inch guns had hit. It blew a hole that you could put a house in. It must have been 40 feet deep but right in the bottom of that, well, you could see a Japanese lying down there with his sword, rifle, pistol and whatever he carried. My partner said he's going to get that rifle as a souvenir.

"Don't do it," I said. "He's booby trapped and he will blow you all to pieces."

"I'm going to get it anyway," he says, so down he went.

Sure enough he grabbed that rifle and off went a bomb and blew him to pieces. You couldn't take pity on any of them. It just didn't work that way.

My outfit stayed there about 17 days and then we left. By that time, they had pushed the Japanese over the end of the island on the other side and captured Suribachi. We lost all but two of our 100 tanks.

We had rations in the beginning so we survived on that for a while. Me and this guy in the foxhole, we found a chicken. I don't know where it came from. We didn't kill the chicken, but it laid an egg and we fried the egg I remember. But of course you have all the ships out there with all the supplies. When it was safe enough, they started bringing in the food and setting up chow lines. When it comes time to eat then you eat the same as you do if you are in Oceanside. The eggs were powdered but they would put water with them and they stunk like crazy but they'd keep you alive. No one was firing back at us after we captured Suribachi and pushed the Japanese down the other side of the island. The Japanese didn't have planes. On Guadalcanal, every single day the Japanese bombed us so you had to spend most of your night in a hole. But on Iwo Jima there wasn't any thing like that, so there was nothing to keep the ships from bringing the food to us.

I think Iwo Jima was the worst battle. It was three times worse than Pearl Harbor. The Japanese were stupid; they wouldn't give up. They wouldn't even give up in their homeland until they got the atomic bomb dropped on them.

We went back to Maui after Iwo. For ten miles there, we had nothing but solid tents. I went back there years later, bought a condo timeshare and tried to find the camps but there is no sign of the camp … now it's all condos and big hotels.

* * *

241

Forward Observers & Topographical Draftsman

Cpl. James Francavilla

Forward Observer, Field Artillery, Fire Control Man, Draftsman, Topographer, 3rd Battalion, 10th Marines, 2nd Division

James Francavilla, wartime photo.

I was going to art school and working at a gas station for a buck a day. I was never broke. I met this artist from the Los Angeles Times who lived a little ways down, across the street from the gas station. He saw my drawings in the station.

"Do you do these little sketches?" he asked.

"Oh yeah," I said, "I do them all the time when I'm sitting here and there is not much to do." You know gas stations weren't busy like they are today. He got me a job as a copy boy at the Times. I loved the people at the Times.

When the war broke out, I told the Managing Editor, "I'm going into the Marines and I want to know if my job will be here."

"Don't worry, Jim, it'll be waiting for you," he said.

By Dammit, We're Marines!

I wanted to be a Marine because I liked the way they dressed. I saw a couple of Marine movies at the theaters, so I went into the Marines and the first thing I knew I was on Guadalcanal. I remember going over the International Date Line, that was a rough thing, you know, they stripped us, threw water on us and everything for crossing the International Date Line.

When we went overseas, we had the same rifles the World War I guys had, the '03. I tell ya, I never shot a rifle before but the Marines made a marksman out of me. I was a good shot.

I was on a survey team. They would send me and three or four guys to an atoll, or an island, or wherever. They wanted a panoramic sketch of everything in a 360 degree circle. We went there to get all the heights, depths, how big the islands were, how far apart, to make the maps they'd use later. We also surveyed for the artillery. I was a corporal and we had a sergeant in the survey team. We'd split up to go to different parts of the island. I'd go to one side and dig my hole and start spotting and looking for the enemy as well.

I came upon a camp on Guadalcanal away from everything, and I saw these Japanese sitting down like they were eating. They had all their food on the ground, but they were all dead. I don't know how they killed themselves but they were dead. It was strange. I don't know why they had this big suicide thing.

They told us we'd be going to Iwo Jima. On board ship we'd have a chart talk about the island and they said how the Japanese have been on this island for 40 years and had years to build up defenses. We didn't know what kind. I know I saw diagram drawings after the war in Time magazine, and I saw how it was. It was like a building. They had profile shots of it and they showed all the levels of caves.

I thought it was going to be a breeze, but it wasn't a breeze, they were killing Marines like hell. They probably knew they'd get killed if they had heard about all the other invasions. The Marines would go right though them again, we were not going to leave. I don't know about the Japanese. They are either going to die first or sacrifice themselves. Every island I was on, I saw so much suicide.

Iwo Jima was a bare little island, very small. When we landed, the first thing I saw was a bunch of Marines just laying there with their rifles beside them all lined up about 20 or 30 of them. I looked at them and I looked at them again and they never even moved or anything. They were all dead. The Japanese would pop up with a machine gun and spray the whole damn area, killing everybody in front of them and then disappear. I had one come up in front of me. God, I zig-zagged out of there because I didn't have my rifle with me. I was surveying or

243

something but you always got to take that rifle. I'm not used to it because I'm a forward observer and I never carry much stuff but my equipment--scared the living daylights out of me.

We were artillery. When we went ashore, I remember the officer saying we were going to have one place to put our big guns down so we can hit everything on the island. We were told when we got ashore to dig a hole and get protection from the night because there was going to be Japs swarming all over the island. I remember I dug a hole about six foot, nice and deep and carved a platform in there to keep my gear. That's when I saw my first Negro Marine. He was bringing ammo for the guns and on his way back he had one of these big ammo sleds.

"Hey, can I have that sled to put over my hole?" I asked.

"Sure, I'll move it in there."

He helped me with the sled and helped save my life. He put it on there and left a little hole for me to get inside. In those days, I was pretty thin. Anyhow, then I saw this tractor moving some sand.

I said, "Hey, over here."

He moved a couple of tons of sand on top of it and just left my little opening. That was what I used to crawl in every night.

When you'd go to sleep, you'd hear all these picks and shovels under you. I mean to tell you it was spooky. Nobody said a word for about a week and then we were around a fire or cooking something.

"Any you guys hear anything below you?" I asked. "You hear it, too?" someone said and then they all said, "Yeah!"

"There are Japs all underneath us!"

They got us surrounded but none of them came up. I figured one of them was going to come up in my hole. They were sons of guns; they'd just come out of a hole when they got an opening someplace, kill Marines and disappear.

One night the ammo dump close to us blew up. Boy, I tell you, I flipped over like a hot cake in that hole. I was on my stomach when I came to. I got up and flames and stuff were flying over and I just got back down in my hole. Next morning I found pieces of shrapnel about two feet long, sharp as a razor, some of it right over my hole. It was lying all over the place. Lucky the old man said to dig in. The guys that didn't were in bad shape.

For a while, you lose your hearing but after a while you get used to all the noise and you almost always knew what shell was coming. You hear all the familiar sounds of all the shells. There was always something firing at you, a sniper, or whatever. I remember going into Guam. I peeked around the Higgins boat for a look and I felt a bullet, it almost touched my ear as it went by. If I had my head out any more…BOOM! I guess I was the luckiest guy in the world. I had a lot of close calls.

I'm a very relaxed person, even in a hole I would shake for awhile but I would settle down. When you're in a hole and a lot of stuff is hitting all around you, you kind of worry because you know one of them is going to hit close. You're happy to be in that hole but a direct hit or even one on the side would kill you. We lucked out.

We kept busy. We could hit any place on the island. We'd have a marker out there for accuracy and boy we were accurate. When they needed us, they just called us and we'd let 'em go. I didn't have as much to do there as I did on the other islands. It was a small island. The flamethrowers did the biggest job, I think. When they came to a hole they just blasted it. Give them a hot foot. That's the only way we cleared them off. As far as I'm concerned, Iwo Jima was a big coffin.

I saw the flag raising. Nobody said a word when it happened. It was strange. We were out there on a survey job and this one guy looked up and then another guy, but nobody said a word. It made us all happy because we knew the war was going our way. We all looked up there and you've just got to cry. Every time I see Old Glory, I want to cry.

We went clear to the other side of the island to start our survey work and every once in a while we'd get a raid and we'd get armed but nothing happened. I never did fire my rifle. I'd have two bandoliers of ammo and other stuff wrapped around my neck, four grenades, and then I'd have this 60 lb big, black bag with all my equipment, papers, BZ scope, aiming circle and all that stuff and I was loaded for bear. In my back pack, I always had little cans of food or fruit. I didn't want to go hungry. It tasted good, and I knew we were going to be on the island a long time.

We had a lucky outfit but we lost a few boys. We lost a couple of replacements. One guy on Iwo went looking for souvenirs and he walked into a bunker. The Japs made mincemeat out of him and they put him up on the outside of the bunker. It took a whole company to take that bunker. Jesus, I've seen terrible things. One of my best friends was killed taking that bunker. Ol' Mitchell, I miss him to this day. He was a nice guy. He loved kids. He worked in the office at the base when we were on these missions.

"I want to do something. I want to get out there with the boys," he said. And so they made him an explosives man. When you saw Mitchell run and yell, "Fire in the hole," you'd get the hell out of there! One time he blew a whole side of a mountain down. A real bruiser and tough kid, he was having a ball. He finally got the job he wanted, blowing up things. And then this gol' darn kid walks into this bunker. Mitchell got ticked off when the Japs put the kid's body in front of the bunker all shot up. He got his bag and ran towards that gol' darn bunker alone; he was going to blow it up. They cut him in two before he got halfway there. That's the one guy I really missed the most because I really liked him. He finally got to fight, but he didn't last long.

Mitchell was buried next to John Basilone. Basilone shouldn't have gone back over, he should have stayed home. He already did his duty. I guess he got the urge. That was me. I didn't want to miss one of those invasions. You've got to be with your outfit. I got a photo of Mitchell's grave. We had a guy with a camera in there. If the Marines caught you with a camera, it was a general court marshal or something. But the gol' darn Army guys, they all had cameras. That's unfair, but of course, we always went on secret missions and stuff like that. They didn't want anything to get out.

I'm not a tough, rough guy; I was just doing my job. It was the greatest adventure of my life. I wouldn't have got it if I didn't go into the Marine Corps. We moved all the time. We were on ships, hitting islands, and I thought that was neat. I was very proud to be a Marine and people respected that. After the war, I returned to work for the L.A. Times as an editorial artist and retired after 46 years. I have been married for 57 years to the most beautiful girl in the world.

* * *

Cpl. Jim Gagne
I Company, 3rd Battalion, 21st Marines, 3rd Division

Jim Gagne, wartime photo.

I enlisted on August 7, 1942. The military was always something I had admired. I liked all the ceremony of the parades and bands. My friends, Louis Vincent, Jean Bellamare and I all joined at the same time. We were known as the Three Musketeers. We went to grammar school and high school together and we all left before our junior year.

We went to boot camp together at Parris Island and went to Camp Lejeune together. Louis went to the 1st Division, Jean went to the 4th, and I went to the 3rd. The only time we were unknowingly on the same island was on Iwo Jima. Jean was awarded the Silver Star on Iwo Jima. He led a flamethrower team that assaulted an enemy strongpoint. When the demolition man was killed trying to place his demolition charge, Jean rushed to the man, picked up the charge and pushed it into the bunker destroying the strongpoint. We all came back, all three of us.

I was assigned to camouflage school at Lejeune. We did camouflage netting over gun emplacements and camouflage uniforms. At the time, we had what they called leopard suits which stood out like a flare. We were taught how to make our own. We'd take burlap bags and loosely sew them in roughly the shape of a jacket and pants. We had Max Factor makeup tubes in ochre, browns, blacks, greens. We would

247

take a shaving brush and cut it short to about a half inch long bristle. We'd squeeze the tube on a piece of cardboard and take the brush and, according to the foliage of the surrounding area, stipple the burlap with different colors of the Max Factor makeup. I think I was preordained to this for an assignment at a later date.

We boarded the ship Lurline in San Diego for Auckland, New Zealand. Before the war it was a luxury ship that went from Los Angeles to the Hawaiian Islands but was converted into a wartime troop ship. When the ship came into dock in Auckland, it listed to one side because of all the men looking over the side at all the women. Of course this is an exaggeration, but there were hundreds of good looking girls on the docks, singing, "Bless them all, bless them all."

The New Zealand men were in Singapore, Malaysia, and Tunisia. We all looked at each other and said that this is going to be wonderful duty. We got there in January and left in July. We were there basically for defense in case New Zealand was attacked. The Japanese had tried to invade Australia, and the Coral Sea was a huge battle. New Zealand needed some kind of support.

We used to do 60 mile hikes with full combat gear, combat packs, two canteens, ammo belt, two bandoliers of ammo and an M-1 rifle. I don't know how much weight it was but it was a lot for someone who weighed 130 lbs, which was all I weighed at the time. It was grueling...thirty miles the first day, twenty the second day. The last ten miles was a semi trot. The battalion commander would drive up in his jeep, get out and say, "OK you guys, follow me." He had been riding for two days. The whole bottom of our feet would be blood blisters.

We went to Guadalcanal in July after New Zealand. I was on Guadalcanal for three days when the cargo ship John Penn contacted our CO to get our company to help them unload. We unloaded mail bags from the front hold and were walking towards the galley to get a cup of coffee when general quarters sounded. The officer of the deck told us to go to the bow and when all clear was sounded he'd take us down to the galley. Gunfire from two destroyers around Talagi Island started opening up with cross fire. The firing got closer and closer and actually crossed over us. Then the torpedo hit the ship. The destroyers had been firing at a Japanese torpedo plane. The Japanese Long Lance torpedo is the most potent torpedo bar none. The ship broke in half and sunk in about five minutes. Fortunately we were all on the bow when it hit mid-ship. I remember the deck plates buckled and we shot up in the air. I was ready to jump overboard when an older sailor came up to me, pulled me back and asked if I heard orders to abandon ship. I said we probably wouldn't since the bridge was destroyed. But the sailor said we had to wait until there were orders to abandon ship. The order came and I jumped off the bow as it rose up in the air.

I thought I would never hit the water. Most of the crew were killed in that attack. Since we were just a mile out, landing boats were immediately sent out for the survivors. I remember being hooked by the back of my garment and being pulled up into the boat. I couldn't help myself up, my muscles were just weak because I had tried to stay afloat for quite a while. They took us on shore and I sat there, soaking wet. One guy came up and asked if I wanted a cigarette and I said yes and he put it in my left hand. Another guy came up on my right and asks if I want a cigarette and puts one in my right hand. I had two cigarettes going. Then a B-24 came in for a landing at Anderson Field. When I heard the roar of the engines, I tossed those cigarettes and ran and jumped in the gutter. I heard a guy say, "It's one of ours!"

I was barely 17 years old.

There was no combat at the time we were on Guadalcanal. We were bombed all the time but no actual combat. There was a fellow who was situation map keeper, and I liked his job because I was always artistically inclined. He drew contour maps, and I used to watch over his shoulder. He was transferred to battalion intelligence and I asked my CO if I could apply for his job, which I did. I was pleased to get the job and a step up in rank.

On Guadalcanal we had battalion inspection by the colonel. Of course we couldn't press our khakis, but we could use Brasso for our belt buckles. We had Kiwi for our shoes. We slept in folding bunks so we used to put our trousers and shirts folded a certain way in them and it would kind of give them a crease. At inspection, we're all dressed up, our buckles were shiny, our canteens were full of water. The colonel marched in front of us with the lieutenant and a pad of paper. If you had something wrong, they'd write down your name. They walked behind you and checked if your canteen was full of water. One of the guys, Davis, was spic and span except he had mud on the back of his shoes. The colonel comes up and looks and says, "Corporal, about face." Davis about faces. "You're a sharp looking Marine from the front but you look like hell from the back; what's this mud on the heel of your shoes?"

"Sir, a good Marine never looks at the rear, Sir!" He had a little grin on his face.

"Carry on," the Colonel says.

On November 9, we invaded Empress Augusta Bay, Bougainville. That was a 3rd Marine Division operation. The CO called me in and asked me to take my map out. He said he wanted me to go on an azimuth of so many degrees and form a triangulation. He said take two men of a lower rank. That's where my knowledge of burlap uniforms came in handy because I insisted we all wear those. You can be in a bush five feet away and you couldn't even see us.

I told my captain, "Sir, an azimuth of 160 degrees at 2,000 yards is in back of enemy territory."

"I know what's behind us. I want to know what's in front of us!"

At that time I was wondering if there was another job I could apply for. We were reconnaissance. Our job was to bring back information and use weapons only if a matter of life or death. On Bougainville, the only map we had was an aerial photo and in jungle they can't tell if there is a cliff or what. I mapped behind enemy lines a couple of times on Bougainville, but on Guam and Iwo there was no need because they were well mapped.

Our battalion was at what is known as Hellzapoppin' Ridge on Bougainville.* That's Hill 1000 and 1000A. I remember we used to remind each other that they say the Marine Corps is an assault force, you hit and 72 hours later they take you off. We found that's not the case after all. We were on Bougainville for about four months.

We went back to Guadalcanal for replacements and restructuring. From there we invaded Guam. I Company was on Yellow Beach 1 which was the right flank of the invasion. I remember that afternoon on D-Day or D-Day+1 when we were pinned down. They landed a couple of Sherman tanks and when we saw those tanks we were happier. We got low on ammunition. The captain selected 18 of us again as volunteers to wade out to the boats to get re-supplied. The boats couldn't come in because of the coral and low tides so we had to go out there and bring in ammunition, hand grenades, mortar shells, whatever we were using. While we are doing that, the enemy shelled the beaches and the water pretty heavily. We felt much safer in the water because when a shell hits the water it sinks and it doesn't spray like it does on sand. You are actually safer unless you get a direct hit. A direct hit in any circumstances and you can say 'good bye, Charlie.' For doing that the Captain gave us a personal letter of commendation; it's a green and white ribbon, low down on the list of decorations.

After we secured Guam, I started my first business. We took 55 gallon drums and had them cut in half. We put them on rocks and built a fire underneath them, filled them full of water and we had our little laundry. We charged, I don't know, maybe 25 cents for a pair of shorts, 15 cents for a pair of socks. We had clothes lines from tree to tree and we looked out on a beautiful view of the ocean.

By Dammit, We're Marines!

Crazy enough, Hellzapoppin' Ridge was the worst battle in Bougainville, and our battalion was assigned to take that hill. Then on Guam we were told that the beachhead we were going to be involved in was going to be a piece of cake. It wasn't. So to make it up to us they put us on the reserve ship for Iwo. They said the chances are you won't even land because we won't need you. They can't predict. They didn't think there'd be a scorpion alive on the island after all the shelling from the 16s on the battleship. We landed about three or four days after the initial landing because they needed us. If those 16,000 or so men from the 3rd Division had not been there, we would have lost the island. The Japanese would have pushed the 4th and 5th out to sea.

I was still aboard ship when they raised the flag. We were far enough away so we couldn't see it. They announced it on deck. It was like your team scored a touchdown. Landing wasn't bad for us because they had the beach somewhat secure so it wasn't like an initial landing facing enemy resistance. Immediately, our assignment was to go take Airfield No. 2 and there we met a tremendous amount of resistance. I remember the incident very well because we took some friendly artillery fire from our own gun positions, and we had to retreat from the airfield. That sometimes happens.

We went towards the center and then moved to the end of the island. As it turned out, Japanese General Kuribayashi was at the other end of the island with his staff. He said as long as you can take ten Marines for every one of us you have done your duty. We didn't give them that privilege.

I and K Companies were ambushed at Meat Grinder Valley** and I remember that very well. We got in the valley and ended up getting ambushed from three sides, both flanks and the front. We had no choice but to fight our way out. The Japanese charged at us with hand to hand combat. By that time there were not too many of us, maybe half strength. We were taking a lot of casualties. For the Japanese, it's an honor to challenge you with fixed bayonets and they want you to return the challenge. Their bayonet was designed for challenging because of the hook on the handle part. They would engage your bayonet in that hook and with a certain twist it would break your bayonet. For them it was a kind of pride. But as long as I had anything in my rifle called bullets, that was my way of challenging them.

We had so much experience with the Japanese and their cruelty that we didn't even look at them as human beings. Things have changed now, of course. I witnessed a horrible sight on patrol on Bougainville. We were alerted to be on the look out for a missing American reconnaissance patrol consisting of three men. We found one guy and

251

he was strung by his hands on a branch with his feet about a foot above the ground. He was naked, he had bayonet pricks all over his body, and they cut off his private parts and stuffed them in his mouth. When you see something like that, the enemy ceases to be human. Monkeys wouldn't do that. Your attitude towards the Japanese changed dramatically on how you would treat them.

It's amazing how they changed after the war. A friend of mine went to Japan as the occupation force and he said the Japanese bowed and said, "So sorry, so sorry." They were polite and there was never any incidence of guerilla warfare or killing. They immediately changed.

I didn't do any map work on Iwo because there was nothing to map. An aerial photo gave all the information needed. They also called us topographical draftsman, but under combat time if you meet a lot of opposition you become infantry. You get yourself a rifle and you forget about your pencils and paper. I stayed on the island until it was secured.

War was pretty much what I expected. There were no surprises. Right after boot camp, the first movie they showed us was *Wake Island* with William Bendix, where none of them survived. I guess it was to get us angry. I was so young that to me war was a wide screen movie. I had friends who were 22, 23 years old and were married with a family back in the states. As far as I was concerned, they were real old men. I noticed those guys were much more careful, much more protective of themselves in combat. The younger you were it was the nothing-can-touch-me attitude.

After Iwo we were sent back to the states. When I heard the war was over, I was at Camp Pendleton in my bunk awaiting our orders to go aboard ship to go to Eniwetok for the invasion of Japan. Part of our division was already in route. The announcement came that an atomic bomb was dropped, and a couple of days later the war was over. I read later in released documents that our division was scheduled to invade Tokyo Bay. There was not too much left of Tokyo, but I wasn't ready to go. I remember when Admiral Halsey announced to the fleet that the war was over. He said something like, "The Japanese have surrendered so from now on if you see a Japanese plane above, shoot 'em down in a friendly manner." He was a good admiral. Highly respected.

I was discharged in November 1945. I went back to high school and completed my junior and senior years in 6 months. There were only three of us returned vets in high school. The other students kind of looked up to us as stars, heroes. I took flying lessons, got a private pilot's license and then I went to art school which is what I always wanted to do. I went to school in Boston and New York and then I worked in an advertising agency as a commercial artist. I was an art director for a couple of years and then went into business for myself. The next thing I knew I had 42 employees.

*Hellzapoppin' Ridge is also known as Fry's Ridge for the battalion commander whose unit finally took it.

**The Meat Grinder was in the northern portion of the island which included three distinct terrain features. Hill 382 was the highest point; the Amphitheater was a southeastern extension of Hill 382 and Turkey Knob was home to a large enemy communications center and had been reinforced with concrete.

* * *

Lt. Col. Frank McCarthy USMC (Ret.)
Cpl, 2nd Battalion, 14th Marines, HQ Fox Battery
4th Division, in direct support of the 23rd Marines

Frank McCarthy, wartime photo.

I joined the Marines at 18 because there was a war on. I had a cousin who had been in the Marines in World War I and had earned the Navy Cross at Belleau Wood, and he was a great influence. I went in again for the Korean War and stayed in the military for 23 years total.

I landed on Iwo the first day in a free boat. We were a reconnaissance team that was supposed to go ashore and locate positions for the guns of the 2nd Battalion when they came in later on. We left our transport in an LCM, then went over to the control boat to report in and get their permission to go in. I looked over and on the control boat was a radio operator I knew. I put my hands up like 'how does it look?' and he put his thumb down. It didn't look good at all so I thought, Oh boy! The head of our team was a fella named Haines and they called him Commando Haines. Boy, he was a tough guy. We headed off towards the line of departure, just past the control boat. We got there and I remember Haines had a .45 pistol. He pulled it out and he pointed it at the coxswain and said, "Coxswain when I tell you to go, you will go and you will not change course."

By Dammit, We're Marines!

The coxswain is looking at this brute of a man with a pistol. I laughed. I had been with him on Saipan and Tinian so I was used to his humor. I looked up over the bow and about that time the Japanese laid a barrage over the beach right where we were going. I thought, that's it, we are just going to get chewed up...just do your part as long as you can.

But it was horrible. We got up towards the beach there when Haines says, "Coxswain, turn around!"

We were a free boat so we could do that and the coxswain happily obliged. There was a sunken Japanese destroyer on the edge of the beach so we went down in that direction. Then Haines saw a spot that wasn't being shelled constantly, so we turned and landed there. We took some fire; in fact the fella beside me got killed. But we charged out and went up the beach, and I was with Haines. I was his only contact with the guns so I was important to him and he was important to me because I wanted to know what he was doing. We went further up the beach and began to lay out. On Saipan, I went ashore with a carbine and chucked it and picked up a rifle because the carbine jammed all the time. On Iwo, because of the way things were, I had a .45 and a submachine gun. It was vital that you had a personal arm.

I landed with a recon team and we got positions all staked out. After dark our guns, which were 105 Howitzers, started to come ashore slowly. I say slowly because they had to be carried by DUKWs and then they had to get them off and had to get them in position. Our first battalion and the first battalion of the 5th Division 13th Marines had 75 Packs and they could be carried in pieces so they came in and were set up real fast. Our communications officer captain said, "Frank, I want you to carry supplies up to the forward Marine observers of the 23rd Marine line." He said, "I'll give two men and another Marine in Com to go with you." We went up onto the airfield and across but we got shelled and the two kids with me were killed. We got to the front lines and dropped off what we had carried, supplies, extra radio batteries, stuff like that. I was about to go back when I got word that one of the forward observers in the Fox Battery had been lost so I had to go up and take his place. That was OK with me, so I went up and took his place. We were driving in the center of the island after the right turn and we took turns as forward observer, radio man, and wireman. I do believe we were just a really strong gung ho group of guys, and we didn't take much leadership. We had already fought in three other battles and knew the job. Oh, there might be a lieutenant who came around you and he might give you an order or two but generally it didn't happen. I think that means that they were excellent leaders. They knew when to lead and when to shut up.

Any time we could, we laid ground wire. We had a radio but when you broadcast everybody hears. I would say almost half the time we were on wire. It was more private, less formality and you didn't have to share the wire with anybody else. The danger was you get the wire all set up and you're talking and a god-damn tank would come along and grind the wire up or a shell would come down, whack! and the wire would go. You had to patch it, and we all did it, it's not just the wire men, even our infantry men would come in and fix it. I tried to keep wire as much as possible but not if you were moving all day or if they were moving tanks through the area.

I switched over from wire man. I had my glasses and I was looking at the terrain ahead of us for targets.

Somebody, I'm not sure who it was, said, "You can see people on Suribachi."

I had the glasses so I rolled over, turned around and looked up. "My God," I said, "they're Marines, they're Marines!"

I watched them raise the first flag, and we didn't know there was going to be two. We celebrated raising the flag. Boy that was good news... no longer was there somebody right behind us looking down at us. I stayed with Fox FO but hardly knew anybody in the outfit. I did know the company commander's name was McCarthy and he used to laugh at me all the time, "All right, McCarthy," as a joke. He received the Congressional Medal of Honor.

It's funny; you went along and rarely saw the Japanese. They were dug in. They would be firing right at you and your ears would hurt from the muzzle blast, but you didn't see them because they fired out of slots. You tried to second guess them...this is good visibility, this is good coverage. Were we always right? No, but we tried to second guess them.

It was my turn to look for targets one time and with my glasses, I picked out Marines in front of me sitting with their backs to a ledge. Their rifles are there and they're smoking a cigarette and talking. They were obviously on the front lines. I mean on the very front lines. I looked at them and laughed. I thought it was funny that they were sitting there shooting the breeze. All of a sudden two people crawling on the ledge caught my eye. They were Japanese. It was unusual to see them in the open like that. So I grabbed my radio and I was going to call the fire base but thought how can I fire a mission with guys so close to them? These Japanese were going to throw hand grenades down on them. Over to my right was a heavy 30, which can lay down a heavy fire.

I rolled over, grabbed the guys and said, "Can you see them right there?"

They had glasses too and they saw them and spun around and brrt—brrt—brrt right over the heads of the two guys sitting there talking and right into the Japanese.

"Oh boy, what a good cover that is," I said.

I rolled back to where I was and I looked and the two guys are still sitting there while those bullets with tracers and all must have gone right over their heads!

The FO team I was with got relieved and I went back to the guns and took over in the fire direction. This was up from the beach, not too far, you never get too far from the beach there. I worked at that but then I made one more trip up to FO. More supply trips. Days wore into days.

When I went by the cemetery, the battle was still on. There were some crosses the 4th Division had put up but guys were still either stacked there or laying in open rows. It was sad, but it's war. Some of the guys were blown to pieces, and it was just the pieces there. They were laid out with a poncho over them. I have since gone back to the cemetery in the crater in Oahu. A whole bunch of guys from our outfit are up there and some other friends I knew from other outfits. It is really a place of beauty; where the original cemetery wasn't a place of beauty at all.

The 4th Division hit the ocean at the north end of the island first then the 3rd Division hit the ocean. The 5th Division was the last. That was almost the end. I say almost because you got to realize that this place was still a mass of confusion. They decided to get the combat troops off the island and our artillery units no longer had anything to shoot at. Infantry regiments and the artillery slowly came down to the beach. There was one regiment of the 4th left and a little artillery. We got on boats out to the transports and climbed up. By that time it was night. You wanted to sleep and eat with a sense of relief, but you missed a lot of your friends who are not there. It was nice to know you made it and you're heading back to rest camp.

All of a sudden a big firefight broke out right up on Motoyama Airfield No. 1. The Japanese, maybe 200 of them, came out from underground on probably what was a last minute banzai with the idea of going after the planes. The Army Air Corps suffered the most casualties on that episode because they lost ground personnel. It was a mess. The regiment mowed the Japanese down. It's so sad. We stood on the deck on the ship at nighttime and tracers were going off all over the place.

We thought, what in God's name? We thought we secured the island. It was a bitter, dirty fight, right down to the end.

I would like to mention a group of heroes in my estimation. Most all the guys were. We had one 1st lieutenant named John Alden, and he was wild as they come. He was a FO with the company and a liaison with the battalion. He got wounded, badly, and was taken on a plane and flown back to Guam. He stayed on Guam for about two weeks until he got healed a little bit. He hopped on a plane and flew back to Iwo and he took over again. We all laughed at this. You had to know Alden. He was just gung ho and was going to do it. Here's a guy who was gone with good reason, good excuse and he came back and did his job again. Beautiful guy.

We had one liaison officer of the battalion, 1st Lt. Larry Graham. He came up to us on Hill 382 and we asked, "What the hell are you doing here?"

"Oh, I just came up to see how you were doing; I brought you this can of fruit juice."

He was a crazy guy, crazy in a good sense, like Alden, because what he did was right and he did it. Even though I was a corporal, I was very proud of them.

These were your friends and they depended on you like you depended on them. You felt somehow like you were shirking your duty if you were wounded and not a part of it. So you really did feel the obligation when the outfit was in combat to get back doing your job and not loaf around the hospital somewhere. I'm sure Alden carried it to the extreme, but I'm sure he felt that way, too. There was a strong camaraderie if you want to call it that. It wasn't just extended to your guys but extended to the other outfits that were good. Replacements, that was always kind of sad. They're new and scared and confused. They're actually more vulnerable for a few days until they got a little combat savvy.

War is horrible. War is stupid, but it's real. I'm sure it was for the Romans, the Greeks and it will be for whomever in the future is involved. But when you hit 17, 18, 19, 20, 21, 22, it's just the right time physically and mentally to go to war. For us at that time, we didn't consider ourselves too young. In fact we had a couple of sergeants who were 25 and we thought "old guy." I think most of the guys around me were about my age and it was our time to be ready. I have never met a bunch of people better than the Marines and Army folks I've gotten to know in my career.

If you sat back and thought about the whole thing, the Japanese were absolutely stupid to take on the United States. There was no way they could match us in supply, ammunition, or force. They had to know we were one of the greatest industrial powers in the world. They were good fighters, and they would have been our equal. They were well armed, but they had no control of the sea nor of the air. Those are two vital things particularly when you are on an island. They couldn't maneuver. We had them out gunned, and they had to stay in place to fight. After about the third day, there was no question about who was going to win. We just assumed that from the very beginning, always. The question was what was the price you pay? If they didn't knock us out the first day or so, then everything was going to get worse for them. That confidence comes from Marine Corps training and the mental attitude to go out there. Iwo had a reason for us. It was good military strategy.

* * *

Chaplains

Almighty God, who turnest our evil into thy good and maketh over our imperfection into Thy perfection; even as we perform the stern duties of war, free us from any base delight in destruction for its own sake.

Make us destroyers of the works of tyranny and hate, only that we may become creators of the things of peace and righteousness.

And may we so do our duty, that when the battle is over we may stand unashamed before our shipmates, our loved ones and Thee. Amen.

--Prayer given aboard ship by Chaplain John D. Wolf the night before the invasion of Leyte.

Lt. (j.g.) W. Charles Goe, Chaplain USNR

HQ, H and S Company, 23rd Regiment, 4th Division

Chaplain Goe, wartime photo.

I graduated from Seminary and joined the Navy as a chaplain when I was 23 years old. I had also applied to Yale University to work on a PhD, but then there was such a need for chaplains that I felt I needed to go in the Navy and serve as a chaplain. Before being accepted as a chaplain though, we had to go to Dallas to appear before key leaders from Washington who were chaplains and preach a sermon. Out of the twelve of us who went, they only accepted five. I was accepted and went

By Dammit, We're Marines!

to Navy Chaplain School at William and Mary College in Williamsburg, Virginia. There were some beautiful girls there and that was one of the privileges. I dated some of them when I was there. Of course I wasn't married at that time.

Chaplain training included knowing all the Navy regulations and doing a lot of physical training. You had to crawl through tunnels, get over cliffs, had to do all that. Then they sent us for two, two-week periods serving different places. After that, they asked us where we wanted to go. I said to the Atlantic so I could go to the Holy Land, but they sent me to Camp Pendleton. I bought a car there in Williamsburg, a Chevrolet, and drove it across country with another chaplain who rode with me. At Camp Pendleton, I was trained with a carbine and a pistol but with the understanding that I wouldn't use them because chaplains are not supposed to carry arms even in combat. Some of my friends who were chaplains carried a pistol, but I never did. I never felt that I should.

On October 31 I had a friend invite me to meet some folks, particularly a girl in San Diego. We had a bivouac that weekend. It gets cold at night out there in California! We slept out in the cold on cots with just one little blanket, and I turned over 30 revolutions a minute trying to keep warm. We freed up early Sunday morning so my friend invited me and another chaplain to lunch. During that lunch, a young lady named Grace and I started talking. She was from Texas and a WAVE, Pharmacist Mate 3rd Class, at the San Diego Naval Hospital. We were married on December 2, 1943, at Camp Pendleton, 33 days after we met. We were married a little over 60 years. We had a boy and a girl and each of them have three children, and altogether we have 11 great grandchildren.

In March, I had orders to go to the 2nd Marine Division. I caught a ship from San Francisco to Honolulu. When I arrived out there they said they needed a chaplain at Camp Catlin. That was a military base of about 13,000 men right between Pearl Harbor and Honolulu. They said I'd be the only chaplain. I preached on Palm Sunday and on Easter. I was Protestant but I ministered to all the men. A few weeks later, the 4th Marine Division had landed on Kwajelein and Roi-Namur. They said they needed me with the 4th over on Maui and would I be willing to go? I said that I came out here to serve and will go wherever needed. I walked in the colonel's office in Maui and gave him a brisk salute.

He waved his cigar at me and said, "I hope you're not like the last chaplain we had."

He had kicked out the chaplain and sent him back to Pearl Harbor. I don't know all the ramifications of it. He told me to get acquainted with the men so I started going tent to tent meeting the men. They had only been having half a tent filled for the worship services, but the first Sunday I was there, they overflowed the tent. The tent would hold about a hundred men, I guess. The next Sunday, we had two services. That Sunday we sat out on sort of a hillside when we heard some test firing of mortar shells. The shells went right over the heads of our whole group. A couple of the shells went astray and killed two of our men. It was just an accident. I had their funerals there on Maui. The third Sunday, we couldn't hold them in the tents so we met out at the boxing area for our service.

We boarded ships in May not knowing where we were going but knew we were going into combat. We found out where from Tokyo Rose. She knew things we didn't. A lot of times we wouldn't learn where we were going from our commanding officers, but we'd walk down the street in Honolulu and from her radio broadcasts, we could find out what was happening.

From Maui we stopped by Pearl Harbor. On Sunday May 24, I was in a small boat headed across Pearl Harbor to a group of six LSTs to hold services on at least one of them. We would invite the other men to come over because they didn't have a chaplain on the LSTs. All of a sudden we heard an explosion and we saw the LSTs on fire. We found out later that ammunition accidentally exploded and caught other ammunition on fire. It sank most of those LSTs. If I had been there 30 minutes earlier, I would have been on one of those LSTs.

They brought us back to the shore and instead of holding services they wanted me to visit some of those who had been injured in the hospitals. A lot of them were taken to the morgue because scores of men had been killed. That was called the Second Pearl Harbor. *

We left for Saipan about a week later. I had regular preaching services aboard the ship. Later I started a discussion service on the mess deck where I would open up with a statement and ask the men to respond to that statement and ask questions. We went from 30 to 40 in attendance up to 300 on the ship going into combat. Some of the men stayed up all night and discussed the subjects we had talked about that day.

The Normandy invasion was on June 6, 1944. We landed on Saipan on June 15, just a week later. About 20 of us were transferred to an amphibious tractor and we started ashore in the late afternoon of D-Day.

Of course the chaplain doesn't go in with the first barrage. As we got close to shore, the Japanese started firing at us from the beach so we had to pull out back towards the ship. Our ships then fired back at the

Japanese. We were caught in the middle with the shells flying overhead from both directions. Shells landed all around us during the night, but none of them hit us.

Navy chaplains, doctors, and dentists all serve the Marine Corps. The Navy said they picked the best men to go to the Marines. So when we were with the Marines and being shot at we could say, "Ah boy, if I hadn't been such a good man I wouldn't be here!"

We moved north up the island after we landed and were there 39 days. I would hitchhike up to the combat zone since I didn't have a jeep assigned to me. The men were out a little bit further, but they came back and met with me so I could have a service for them. I had a suitcase I carried with the sacraments to have communion for them, along with bibles and hymnals. I preached and I held communion for those who wanted it. Communion was usually the intinction method with wafer and a little juice that I carried. I had that with me on the front line. I held other services, too, but you couldn't have many services in combat.

I stayed with the troops and ministered to them. Usually I'd go to the sick bay, and when the wounded came in, I talked with them and prayed with them and encouraged them. Some of the men killed were very close friends of mine. I had a number of men that I was able to stay right there with until the end. Of course we had to deal with all sorts of things. It's a wonderful ministry and it's very much needed. During that time in combat, several men accepted Christ. Now they used to say that there are no atheists in foxholes but that wasn't true. Some of the men would tell me, "Chaplain, I never accepted Christ before and I'm not going to be a sissy and accept Him now."

But there were some who were injured and some who were not who accepted Christ, and I would have an opportunity to talk to them about the Lord.

In the beginning there were several men who committed suicide. They would go right into combat and walk right into machine gun fire. That has never been published much and it shouldn't be, but it did happen. Some of them had lost their wives back home. They would receive a letter saying that she had gone out with somebody else. It happened. It's hard for people to imagine the strain the men were under there. There was quite a bit of combat fatigue. A number of men suffering from combat fatigue were evacuated from the combat zone and taken to a hospital back on the ships for treatment of one kind or another. By being wounded on Tinian and taken aboard ship, I saw a lot of combat fatigue where men were just out of their heads really. We would try to minister to them with some success but not always. A friend of mine was evacuated from Iwo with combat fatigue, and he did get to go back for a while afterwards. We didn't have many psychiatrists available at the time. There were some available in the large hospitals, but very few available in combat. There was rest and some medical treatment. The men always kid about taking it to the chaplain if you have a problem to get a "tears and sympathy slip." TNS they called it. I was prepared pretty well to talk with people and counsel with them. I had been a pastor of two churches in north Missouri my last year in college when I was only 19 or 20 years old so I had experience.

Of course, every one of us needed to know that the Lord watched over us. Many of the men had problems at home and faced them. Many had a real desire to serve their country and wanted to do the best they could even if it cost them being injured or cost them their life. Most of them were of that category but there were a few who really sort of flunked out on their own, and combat fatigue was one of the things that happened.

The second day after we landed on Saipan two Chamorros, a baby and an adult, were killed. Chamorros were the natives on the island. A Catholic chaplain and I had a brief service for them. One of the old Chamorros said, "Chamorros waited a long time for Americans to come." They had been under the control of the Japanese for quite a while.**

We captured a house the Japanese had used and found a bunch of chickens there. Our cooks fixed them for us to eat. The house had been a commanding officer's place for the Japanese. We looked up on the wall and there were full-scale wall maps with the planned conquests of the United States, printed, not sketched, so we knew there had to be other copies made. The maps detailed the conquest of the U.S. beginning on the west coast with San Francisco and Los Angeles, making their way across the country planning to control the United States. This was the Japanese plan. We actually saw it. We knew God had a purpose for us when we were there because we just couldn't put up with what the Japanese had actually planned to do.

I remember when two naval air pilots landed on Saipan and Colonel Jones says to me, "Chaplain, go get a jeep and take them around and show them some of the things."

Do you know what banzai means? 'Blood for the emperor.' We passed a whole bunch of dead Japanese that had run a banzai charge. They were lying along the road there. Nobody had buried them yet. I showed the pilots some of the caves on the island and told them how we had to go to the caves with flamethrowers to get some of the Japanese out.

By Dammit, We're Marines!

They said, "Chaplain Goe, it's certainly a different thing down here in combat on the ground than it is up there where we fly."

And of course it was.

After Saipan, we went aboard ship for one night and landed on Tinian on July 24. I was pinned down by machine gun fire within minutes of landing about 4 o'clock in the afternoon. The initial landing was on three unsuspecting beaches with very few casualties. The Japanese were expecting us at other places and prepared for us there but by afternoon they found out where we were. By that time we had made quite a big advance already. By the time I landed on the beach, the Japanese had found us, and I was pinned down with machine gun fire within minutes. I lay on the ground and pulled a notebook out of my pocket and wrote a letter to my wife. I wrote to her almost every day.

By that night we were at a command post of the 23rd Regiment and we dug our foxholes. The Japanese discovered where we were and started to really fire at us. The next morning I was talking to this young dentist, Stu Cates was his name, while we were eating K-rations. He had come along for the ride really. He was not scheduled to be in combat, but he wanted to help out so he functioned as a corpsman.

He said, "Padre, you have an awful lot to tell when you get back to the States."

We were standing close together and I said, "Yes I do, that's right."

He said, "You can tell them we Marines and Navy men did a lot of praying out here."

"Yes, that's true," I said. Just at that time an artillery shell hit and we were both knocked to the ground. My arm was shot and the bone was sticking up with blood pouring out. Another piece of shrapnel, just a small piece, hit me in the chest and another one hit me in the ear. I looked at Cates and blood streamed from his neck. He died 15 minutes later of a severed jugular vein. That was July 25, 1944. I was evacuated to a ship and Cates was taken to be buried. A Navy doctor was on that ship and I'm told he must have been one of the best orthopedic surgeons in the Navy because he put my arm back together and it works just fine.

They transferred me to New Hebrides, and it took some time to get to Espiritu Santo. When we pulled into that harbor, it was the most beautiful thing I'd ever seen, you can imagine, after being in combat all that time. I did not make it to Iwo Jima. According to a book I read by two Catholic chaplains some time ago, there were 54 chaplains on Iwo and not a one was seriously injured or killed.

265

Gail Chatfield

* The West Loch disaster, as it is called, occurred on May 21, 1944, at 1500 hours. Sailors and Marines were loading 29 LSTs in Pearl Harbor in preparation for the invasion of Saipan. During the loading of fuel and ordnance, one of the LSTs exploded for a reason never definitely determined. Six LSTs and 3 LCTs were destroyed. There were 163 dead and 396 injured during the catastrophe.

**Japan took over Saipan as a mandated territory after World War I and by 1938 the Japanese represented 90% of the population.

* * *

Lt. (j.g.) Gage Hotaling, USNR
Chaplain, HQ Battalion and HQ Company, 4th Division

Chaplain Hotaling presiding over the last service on Iwo Jima.
Official USMC photo.

I joined the Navy in September 1944. I had been a pastor for four and half years, and I saw about thirty of the young people of my church going into military service. Gradually I began to feel they would need a pastor in their military life just as much as they did in their civilian life. I also felt that God was calling me.

I was 29 years old, about 10 years older than the average Marine. Every chaplain is older because we have to be a college graduate and a seminary graduate which takes you up to the age of 24 or 25. Most of us had some kind of parish work after seminary before we joined the Navy. My four and a half years set me in good stead because a young fellow who never had any pastoral experience might really find himself in a lot of difficulty.

We had eight weeks of Chaplain School at the College of William and Mary in Williamsburg, Virginia. We had a class of twenty one. We learned the history, the tradition, and the customs of the Navy and we had lectures and examinations. One or two lectures would be on the Marines.

They would usually point to the big, rugged, husky fellows in the class and say, "You're likely to get Marine duty." They never pointed to me because I was one of the smaller men in the class. When we received our orders, we lined up and our names were called out. They said E.G. Hotaling, Fleet Marine Force Pacific. So it was quite a shock when I got Marine duty. Now some of the others went to a Naval station here in the States or went to a Marine base like Camp Lejeune. I was the only one of the class who was sent directly overseas to the Marines. Normally that is not done. Normally you have a chance to have five or six months of training and experience with either a Navy or Marine unit right here in the States, but I never had that. I went straight out to Pearl Harbor.

I had no training about the Marines until I actually got overseas. During the two and a half weeks that I was at Pearl Harbor, I had instruction from chaplains who had been with the Marines and who had come back from combat. That was a great help to know what I was going to face. While at Pearl Harbor, we were given liberty about every other day so we could go ashore on Honolulu. That, of course, is something that was very enjoyable. Usually I went up to the chaplain's office to see if there was any mail. When you get transferred around like that, it takes a while for mail to follow you and almost always there would be some mail from my wife or from my mother or from some of my friends. Of course, it was always nice to walk around Honolulu with your friends. Sometimes we would go down to Waikiki and go swimming; sometimes we would just visit the stores and do a little shopping before we went back to the ship.

I was then assigned to the 4th Marine Division training on the island of Maui. I arrived there three days before Christmas in 1944. In the Marines there is a Protestant and Catholic chaplain with each regiment. They had already been assigned by the time I got to Maui, so I went and talked to my Division Chaplain.

"Where are you going to put me?" I asked.

"Well for now you are going to be my assistant."

"What happens when I get into combat?"

That's when he told me I was to be the chaplain at the cemetery. In previous operations when they had a chance to bury some men there was not always a chaplain available and they had to hunt around and find one. It was agreed that the best thing to do was to have a chaplain right there on duty at the cemetery.

Three days after Christmas I went on board ship. It was that quick. The entire Division of 15-20,000 men was loaded on board ship ready for combat. Of course, none of us knew where combat was going to be.

268

By Dammit, We're Marines!

I was on board ship from December 28 until D-Day, February 19. I was on Iwo Jima just five months after I left my parish in Massachusetts.

Aboard ship on the way to Iwo, I found a group of Marines who I could meet with every day for what we called fellowship. It was on the open deck of the ship and we would exchange bible verses, experiences that meant a great deal to us, and we would sing some songs. I taught them a few little songs that I knew and they taught me some I didn't. We sort of prepared each other for going into combat. You prepare men going into battle the way you are taught in seminary and in chaplain school. Faith is the one thing that carries you through any of those experiences, faith and prayer.

We had guys on board who had already been in combat in some of those early battles at Guadalcanal, Bougainville, Tarawa and so on. Those battles took place in the South Pacific where it was very, very hot. They told us that there would be all kinds of mosquitoes, bugs and other insects that would bother us and we were likely to get malaria or some other kind of disease. They really laid it on thick. If you weren't scared before you heard those lectures, you were scared afterwards. Fortunately Iwo Jima didn't have mosquitoes, bugs or insects so that was one thing we didn't have to face. Furthermore, it was not that hot on Iwo. Most of the nights were pretty cold.

The day before the invasion was Sunday and we had two Protestant services. There were probably an equal number of Masses. Every man who wanted to go to church that day could do so. I preached the afternoon service the day before D-Day.

I often say that probably the most unusual place I ever gave a sermon was the day before D-Day aboard ship. I compared our landing to that of Saint Paul going to Europe for the first time. I said he made an amphibious landing in Europe, and that is exactly what we are going to do here. I tried to point out the faith and courage of Saint Paul and that we should have the same kind of faith and courage.

We expected to go ashore on D+1, not D-Day, because there would be too much fighting on the beach. We knew that. And you can't do anything about a cemetery when there is fighting right there on the beach. When we heard how fierce the fighting was, the word was passed to us that it would be at least D+2. By that time the units had moved off shore and they were probably several hundred yards inland.

We went ashore on D+2. Twelve of us came ashore in a Higgins boat, and we were told that we were supposed to pick up casualities by an ammunition dump. We had taken off our knapsacks and all of our gear, and the men who had rifles stacked them all in one corner of the Higgins boat before we all ran ashore looking for casualties. When we got there, we couldn't find any casualties. The coxswain of the boat got scared standing there so he pulled away with all our equipment. The twelve of us had nothing but the clothes on our backs. I voluntarily decided that after we found out where the cemetery was going to be that I would scour the beach and pick up blankets, ponchos, mess kits and all kinds of equipment the men would need. I did that for a couple of days until we were all pretty much in order again. Our equipment finally came ashore 10 days later.

The men who are in the fighting units were moving up and are not staying in the same foxhole every day. But at the cemetery, we stayed in our own foxhole the whole time and were able to make them as comfortable as possible. I don't know how they decided on the location of the cemetery, other than it had to be a fairly level spot.

There were a few times that I am sure a Japanese sniper was trying to hit us, but nobody was killed in our outfit. We had between 40 and 50 men who were doing the cemetery work. Six of us were officers and there were several corpsmen and the rest of them are what you would call gravediggers. Not only were they gravediggers, they went out to bring the bodies back.

We went ashore as a graves registration unit, and the first burials were done about three days later. We then had burials every day right up until our Division left to go back to Maui. With each burial we had four Marines, two at the head and two at the body of each grave, and they knelt while I said the committal service. Then we would move on to the next one because we would usually have a number of burials at one time. We very seldom just buried one or two at a time. It was generally anywhere from 20 or 30 or 40 or maybe more. The largest number we ever had in one day was 238 and of course that meant several services during the day. The bodies were laid in rows of 50.

When a large number of bodies were brought back, they were laid right near the cemetery and my job was to count the bodies twice a day. Usually there were two or three hundred lying there. I have often said this is the only time I ever smoked. It was necessary as you walked among those bodies because the stench was terrible. The only way I could do it was to smoke. I often say there is one good thing about smoking. If you are counting the dead in combat, smoking is a help. But I can't see that it is a help any other time.

I don't remember the first man I buried because we buried a whole group at a time. I would say that I was a little unsure of myself because I had never done anything like that before. I know that it took several days to get used to doing it. After I had been at it for three weeks, it was just like any other job. This is what I was assigned to do, and I did my duty. Somebody had to do it. This is the way we often felt. All the guys there would say, "Well, somebody has to do it, and we were the ones who were picked to do it."

It's hard to say if they identified every body. In some cases, I know that there were only parts of bodies not the full body. However, they did have a marker set up at every grave. We did have a very unusual situation once. The corpsmen were supposed to go around to check each body and to write a death report to indicate the cause of death. One corpsman was making his rounds one day and he heard a fella moaning. The minute he heard that he checked him and found the man was still alive. He was taken immediately to the first aid station at the beach and taken out to the ship as quickly as possible and was saved. I don't remember the fella's name but I heard he later became a dentist in Houston.

I saw the flag raising from a distance. You could see Mt. Suribachi from everywhere on the island. I would say we were probably about two miles away at the time the flag went up. Somebody in our outfit had a pair of field glass and when they saw the flag up there, they passed the glasses around so we all had a chance to see it. Now today I can't tell you if it was the first flag raising or the second. We knew nothing about the fact that there were two flag raisings. When we saw the flag, we all cheered. It was a great feeling. At that point we knew for sure that we were going to capture the island. We still did not know it was going to take 36 days altogether.

As the cemetery chaplain for the 4th Division on Iwo, I held the burials of 1800 men. The cemetery was dedicated on March 15. We had a general service for the entire Division and separate Protestant, Catholic and Jewish services were held afterwards. The 4th Division was the first to leave Iwo and I think I left on March 19. I was ashore for 26 days.

I was married and had a six month old baby when I went into the service. He had his first birthday on March 15, 1945. I still have the letter I wrote to him on that day from Iwo. My wife and I have been married for 66 years and we have three children and five grandchildren.

I was released from the chaplaincy in April of 1946. By July, I had a church in Hyannis on Cape Cod. I happen to be the only living chaplain of the 4th Marine Division who was on Iwo. I just happened to have lived longer, I'm 90. I was 29 at the time, but that was 62 years ago.

* * *

Lt. Commander John D. Wolf, USNR (Ret.)
Lieutenant, Chaplain, USS Frederick Funston

Chaplain Wolf, 1944.

I graduated from Oberlin College in 1939 and majored in history. At that time the major topic on campus was whether we were going into war or staying neutral. In 1942, I graduated Union Theological Seminary in New York City and majored in Christian ethics. I had some professors who were pacifists who wanted to stay out of the war entirely and some who felt that it was our obligation to be a part of that generation in stopping Hitler.

I was a student under Reinhold Niebuhr who was the leading theologian at the time. I had become a pacifist but was influenced by Niebuhr who pointed out that the war was the lesser of two evils. I came to agree with him that war itself is a terrible catastrophe but not as evil as Hitler. I had to reconcile war with the Christian faith.

Niebuhr and Paul Tillich, who came to teach at Union from Germany, were constantly in touch with the underground in Germany and that included Dietrich Bonhoeffer who was a major martyr of the period. They had been aware of all the atrocities that were perpetrated by Hitler's camps. The war debate was a very heavy one. When Pearl

Harbor was attacked in December of '41, that too became part of the debate because we were now in a defensive position.

When I went into the Chaplain Corps in July of 1942, they told me that, at twenty-three years old, I was the youngest chaplain in the Navy. My first assignment was the Naval Training Station in Newport, Rhode Island. I was there nine months and edited "The Newport Recruit." I was then assigned to the USS Frederick Funston. It was one of the first Navy ships built on a large scale for amphibious landings. Originally its hull was designed for a cruiser but it was converted to a transport because of the changing picture of the war. We carried 35 LCVPs, the landing craft that you see in all the pictures of the South Pacific. We had 550 Navy personnel on our ship and carried anywhere between 1200 and 1400 Marines. We had nothing but compliments from the Marines because our ship had more room and it had fresh water for showers.

Aboard ship, I gave talks every night over the PA system to the men during general quarters before we went into an invasion. Very unique thing because, as far as I know, no other ship in the Navy was doing this. I had a captain who was very anxious that the men understand when we left port what the operation was all about.

Once we got out of Pearl Harbor, the captain opened up the classified data and allowed me the privilege of reading that material which had to do with where we were headed, where the battle is going to be, how long it is going to take, and what areas we were going through. I had prepared myself with books from libraries in Hawaii to know general types of things. I had, for example, the history of Saipan, the Philippines, and Guam. I communicated this information every night to the men which was really quite remarkable. The men knew less about what was going on than people back home. They didn't know where we were going. They had never heard of Saipan. They knew probably nothing about the world outside of fifty miles from their hometown. We gave them as much information as we could about the natives, the customs, and the history of the area. It wasn't military alone, it was education. Of course I could slip in a lot of things like what was going on with the fleet and clear up any scuttlebutt. If we received a sub warning from our destroyers who were escorting us or if we had warning of an attack that was nearby, the captain would let me have all of that and I would pass the news to the men. I'd also give baseball scores, hold contests, discuss the system of passwords, relay the sanitary conditions on the islands and answer the men's questions about the G.I. Bill of Rights.

The men were very attentive because they were at their battle stations as part of the training that went on at sunrise and sunset everyday. I spoke from the bridge and reached everybody, particularly the men below decks in the engine room. They don't know what is going on topside. For instance, if there was a bomb dropped from a plane, as there was occasionally, the concussion may be a mile away but when it hits the side of the ship it sounds like a hammer. The sailors down in the engine room didn't know how far away it was. Those shipmates were most appreciative of knowing what was going on topside with the fleet.

I buried a lot of men at sea. After landing troops, the ship was transformed almost immediately into an auxiliary hospital ship. Those same LCVPs brought the wounded back to us. We carried extra doctors. Ordinarily a ship would carry one doctor and maybe a dentist. I think we had six doctors to tend the wounded. We were a hospital ship until we could get back to Pearl, about two weeks away.

My best friend became Peter Brooks, a young doctor just out of Yale residency and a year older than me. Brooks often called on me to assist him because he was short handed when too many casualties came at once. They tried to space them by assigning the returning boats to other ships that had also become auxiliary hospital ships, but we had our share of wounded. We turned the recreation room into a hospital and used the metal tables for surgical tables. We even set up one right outside the ship's office near my own office. The quarters that had been occupied by the Army or Marine officers were on the main deck and they became the main hospital quarters for the wounded. The wounded were under my care as chaplain all the way back to Pearl.

I made the rounds several times a day to get acquainted with the wounded particularly at night after the doctors had done their work. Sometimes the doctor would call me to talk to one of the men to let him know in the best way I could that he was to lose his arm or his leg. I remember one time in particular Peter Brooks said, "Chaplain, I need some help here, hold his leg."

So I did while Brooks amputated it.

"What shall I do with it?" I asked.

"Wrap it in cloth, wait until night, and drop it overboard."

I learned quickly that's what you did with amputated legs. One of the main things we had was sulfa powder which prevented infections in the wounds and that meant we saved a lot of men who in other wars would not have been saved.

I could tell from their dog tags, marked P, C or J, whether they were Protestant, Catholic, or Jewish and I was prepared with prayers for whatever religion that particular soldier or Marine was. If they wished, I would talk to them at night when they were getting ready to sleep about

274

their faith and pray with them. Their main concern was how they were going to face the future especially if their wound required an amputation.

They'd ask, "How am I going to survive this?—What will my girl think when I get back home with just one arm?—Can I get a job?"

Some became depressed about their future. Others were not because they had what I called spiritual fortitude or faith.

Every Sunday, of course, whether at sea or wherever we were, I conducted services. I also conducted services the night before an invasion. The Divine Services we held were well attended going into battle. We always had a service right after the battle called a Service of Gratitude. It was an important expression of thanks to God for surviving not only individually but as a ship. The ship was vulnerable as well as the individual. The service was always well attended particularly if the captain was there. In the case of Capt. Anderson he was always there on the front row. That made a difference with the officers and the men. He would go through officers' country and would ask some of the officers he met in the passageway, "Are you going to services?"

If they said, "No I hadn't planned to," he would ask, "Why, aren't you grateful?"

By golly they would show up. Often times we had more than one service because of attendance.

I always served Holy Communion before an invasion and had announced ahead of time that if anyone wished to talk about baptism I'd be available. We had quite a few baptisms. They were just young kids, and they were scared. I wouldn't give much credence if they weren't. If they were veterans and had been through a battle before, they knew what to expect. If they were recruits who had just been through amphibious training, they were scared and so were we. We didn't know what to expect. When those guys went down those rope ladders to their boats early in the morning, I was always there with them. But you could tell they were frightened kids.

There's a point to make; it was not "macho" to go see the chaplain. The guys who came to me were really troubled. My office quarters were convenient enough so that they would come to see me. It was in officers' territory but aboard the Funston it was not too hard to get to. If they came to the library, which I was in charge of as well, they could let me know that they'd like to talk to me so I would arrange for them to come to my cabin.

Every night we left our anchorage off Iwo Jima and went out to sea as a precaution against night attacks and came back in the morning to load more casualties. I think at Iwo we had 138 wounded Marines aboard ship. We wanted to get those boys back on Pearl as soon as possible where they could get better care. We weren't full but there were other ships that were coming in to load.

I was only ashore on Iwo twice and that was to take bodies in. I buried two boys, one was Sgt. Anderson. After that, any other casualties who died aboard ship before we got back to Pearl, I buried them at sea. Sgt. Anderson's burial was so spectacular because I had personally known him. His father, Capt. Charles Carter Anderson, took command of our ship at Saipan. His only son was named Charles Carter Anderson, Jr. and was a Marine with the 4th Division. Through the scuttlebutt, he was able to keep track of his father's ship. When we were in an atoll in the rendezvous of the ships that were going into an invasion, young Charles would maneuver and somehow find a way to get over to his dad's ship. There and back at Pearl I got to know him quite well. He spent time with me playing cribbage, talking about his life. We became friends. A chaplain is in the position where he can do that. That's one of the characteristics of a chaplain. He is an officer but he's not an officer. He's a chaplain to everybody aboard ship. I think the officer's rank sometimes gets in the way of what I call a pastoral relationship with the men.

Sgt. Anderson came aboard his dad's ship at Iwo on D+8. He was a sniper with the 4th Division going up the east coast and saw his father's ship out there in the harbor. The ships have huge numbers on the bow, ours was APA 89 and the 89 is so big you can see it from shore. He finagled a way from his commanding officer to go out to his father's ship while this battle was going on. He came aboard, passed me and said, "Hi, Chaplain."

I had to look twice to recognize who he was because he was covered with this volcanic black ash. He was in his battle gear and of course the first thing he wanted was a shower. He showered in his dad's cabin and had a good steak dinner. He got a night's rest and a chance to talk with his dad and then went back in the next morning.

A few days later he was wounded on Iwo and was taken to another ship by the shore officer who was doing the loading of the casualties. Knowing his father's ship was in the same area, he asked that a message be sent up to the ship's captain to notify his father that he was on this flat barge that was hauling casualties. I was with the captain up on the bridge when he got this signal from another ship's captain. He immediately called for his gig and went over there. I knew what was happening as soon as he was gone.

The captain didn't recognize his son. He was not just wounded, but mangled. He had stepped on a mine or a mortar had gone off at his feet and blew his legs and one arm off. The other arm was salvageable. When the captain arrived back at the ship with his son, the whole ship knew about it. Word passes fast. That was a bad night. Peter Brooks and I were with him all night. A corpsman was there, too. We had other casualties to take care of, and we did, but this was the captain's son. We went out to sea at night and the captain came down off the bridge whenever he could get relief. Young Carter only lived until the next morning. His death was such an unusual thing that it was reported in Time magazine on March 19, 1945. It read:

"On the transport cruising slowly back & forth off the sulfurous, bloody hulk of Iwo Jima, Navy doctors knew there was no chance for Sergeant Charles Carter Anderson Jr., U.S.M.C. He would never see the sun again. Sixteen hours after the young Marine had been brought aboard, he died. His death certificate was filled out and sent to the captain of the ship. Grimly the skipper signed it: Captain Charles Carter Anderson, U.S.N. Then Captain Anderson took his son's body back to the battlefield to be buried there in the cemetery of the 4th Division, U.S.M.C."

It was just one of those unusual things that happened in the war. You read these casualty lists of all the men who are killed on Iwo, and they are just numbers. But when you personalize it, when it is somebody you know, then that person represents the other casualties, too. Sgt. Anderson would be in his 80's now if he had lived, and he would have had a great contribution to make to his country. He had been a student at Georgetown University and had a lot of promise; there were a lot of things he wanted to do.

We named our second son after him as a reminder of war's sacrifice. But it's more than that. To me, Iwo Jima is something of a turning point because I began to realize how heavy a price was being paid. Iwo was a most unusual situation. The flag on Mt. Suribachi was not even noticed by us while we were there. Iwo became famous because of the picture and the monument in Washington. But that's not war. War is all those bodies I buried.

Later, I gathered together the talks I had given aboard ship and, encouraged by history professors, published them because the most important parts of the war record are usually diaries and memoirs that are written at the time. That's what I had.

I am not sympathetic to war but I am sympathetic to the veterans. If they have a faith commitment, you can deal with that because it has to do with adaptation and adjustment to the future, and there is a future for them regardless of their wounds. Some veterans just slink into alcoholism and drug abuse while others run for political office. Veterans need to sound a voice. They're citizens in a democracy, and they need to make their message known.

My message is peace is patriotic. Work for peace. That's the only solution to our problems. You can't live in this world in a nuclear age without finding solutions to problems. My son's name is a reminder that an Iwo Jima should not happen again. War is an enemy to our whole civilization.

After Iwo Jima I was assigned Navy Chaplains School Faculty, College of William and Mary, Williamsburg, Virginia to teach until the war ended.

* * *

Sgt. Charles Carter Anderson, Jr. USMC

Corpsmen

Pharmacist Mate 2nd Class
Maurice "Lib" Laliberte, USN
G Company, 3rd Battalion, 25th Marines, 4th Division

Maurice Laliberte

The only unusual thing about me that I mention as I get older was that I made D-Day in Normandy and D-Day in Iwo Jima. Not that I volunteered, but that's quite unusual for a guy to be attached with the 4th Marines and have done both. It's not that I have done anything interesting; it's just that I have done both.

I enlisted in the Navy in 1943. I wanted to join the Naval Air Corps but the schools were closed. After I got out of boot camp they were trying to figure out where I would be going. I hadn't done anything but graduate high school. They asked me what my dad did and I told them my dad was a pharmacist. I was told if I decided to go to pharmacy school that trains corpsmen, I could go home on a 33-day delayed leave. I went home and then went to corpsman school in Virginia. The most interesting thing is that as a young man I fainted at the sight of blood and I hated hospitals. The smell of ether made me sick. After the war, the family was getting together and someone asked why would Maurice ever join the medical corps. So I said that I told the

Navy that dad was a pharmacist and he owned a pharmacy; the Navy said that was a good place for me to be. Actually my dad was a taffy maker who owned a pharmacy, but I didn't find that out until after the war four years later.

Corpsman schooling is like any other schooling. I had to go to a hospital to be a bedpan commando as they used to call them. I ended up in this Collection Section Delivery, which I knew nothing about. Nobody knew about it. I got on a LST in Brooklyn, New York, and was sent to England.

They sent twelve of us and a doctor to all kinds of schools to learn what happened if certain types of gas were used. I went through all these different gas schools. It was in preparation for D-Day in Normandy in case the Germans used gas, but they didn't tell us that at the time. That's how I ended up being in D-Day on Normandy.

I slept on the way over and woke up on Normandy. I knew how I got there but it was really surprising what it looked like. So much going on! Daylight on Normandy was just unbelievable; we're talking about 400,000 people, and hundreds of different kinds of ships. We woke up and the LST had two big balloons, one on the rear and one on the front, hanging above so the planes couldn't strafe us. Now you are looking at 30 maybe 40 LSTs with two of those balloons hanging above them. Never in my right mind did I think I would wake up and see that in the morning. Then you are seeing everything you can imagine coming from England. They are bringing in landing strips, all kind of ships, cruisers, destroyers, battleships.

I really didn't know that much about my job, but I was to land on D-Day on Normandy at Omaha Beach. I would take the casualties that were on the beach and put them on the LST I was on, then bring them back to England, that is, the casualties who could be safely carried that long. That's really all I did. We'd load the patients on and take them back to a dock in England where they would be unloaded and taken to a hospital. Then we'd turn around and go back.

I made Pharmacist Mate 2nd Class pretty quick. It was no big deal. I didn't take any exams; I got meritorious promotions. I didn't do that much medical administering in France. The twelve of us plus the doctor were still attached, but we had other medical help for the patients we brought on the ship.

The second trip I made to Normandy the Americans were 28 miles in. Once they started moving, they just moved. I never went in more than 400 yards maybe. It ended up the third time we came we were taking wounded German prisoners. I had no idea how far in they were by then.

By Dammit, We're Marines!

I'm the kind of a guy that if I see a lot of stuff that's terrible or that I shouldn't remember, I don't remember it very well. It's like the things I did medically. If you asked me to do them now, I'd faint! It wasn't that I had seen so much, it was just the idea that I was there.

When I got home I got 33 days more delayed leave because of a survivors' leave. About a month before Normandy, we were in the middle of the channel and German U-boats came into our flotilla and shot the hell out of us. We were loaded down with the 40th Armor Division from Pennsylvania. The U-boat hit us but didn't sink us. We scuttled 20 miles away from England, but it took us 78 hours to get there because we were barely getting by.

After that leave, I could volunteer for a selected service in the Navy because of what I'd done, and I had four choices of what part of the Navy I would want to serve. The fourth choice was the FMS Fleet Marine Service. Nobody volunteers for that as a rule. I knew they wouldn't do that to me because I thought I was kind of a half ass hero. But that's the first thing they assigned me to, so I was put into the Marine Corps, went to boot camp on Parris Island, and I joined the 4th Division.

I was stationed on Maui and we simulated taking what would later be Iwo on Molokai, the leper island. I thought, I'm just a kid, I'm scared to get leprosy! Remember, I came from a small town in New Hampshire. I was not brought up in a big city. It's kind of hard the predicaments you get put in.

It's really an advantageous type position when you're a corpsman with the Marines. They treat you pretty darn good. The Marines want to be as close to you as can be. Maybe it's because we also carried twelve bottles of Lee John Brandy. The Marines knew you carried brandy, so it would be a nice thing to get down at night and somebody give you a shot of brandy.

We loaded on an APA just after Thanksgiving. We didn't know it was Iwo until about three days before we got there. We were told we had bombed it for so many days and nights, there was nothing alive there and no need for us to worry. They only gave us a password for three days. We would be off the island in three days. It was kind of a nothing deal.

I think it was about 4:30 in the morning when we loaded. We came off of an APA into a LCVP. I was supposed to land on H-Hour, which is the first wave but we had a little problem getting in so we started circling. When I landed it was only about 2 hours after it started. The first guy I treated was a Seabee officer. His name was Long...it was written on his shirt. They came in before H-Hour and laid the Marston mats so we could take the LCVPs off and could surface them. It's funny because you don't picture the Seabees being ahead of everybody.

In France, I had an armband with a red cross on it. On Iwo, I didn't or I would have been a target. I carried a weapon on Iwo from the day I landed until the day I left. In Europe I didn't have a weapon. Two different theaters of war.

What's different about Iwo is that you are always on the front lines when you are there. You never leave until you get relieved. We used to move maybe 200 yards and give them back 100 yards. Even though you are 200 yards behind the front lines, you are at the front lines. My job was at night. They would lay smoke and I'd go retrieve casualties that weren't able to come back by themselves. It was frightening at first. You're nervous and scared as hell, but you are assigned to do it. You have no choice unless you crack up in front of them. Even though I had been through Normandy, I didn't do any of that personal stuff. I got educated pretty quick and grew up pretty quick. It didn't take very long for me to get smart. A Marine would come back and tell how his buddy is wounded and can't come back unless somebody goes and gets him and treats him. He just figures somebody is going to assign a corpsman who will go up and get him. Well that's the way it worked for me. Somebody assigned me and I went.

After five or six days, I'd say to the Marine, "OK you and I are going."

"I'm not going; I just got back from there," he'd say.

"I'm not going alone; somebody has got to show me where he is and we're going."

I made it a more human thing between two people. When you go up on the front lines, the people there don't want to be disturbed. They are alive because nobody knows they are there. Marines have been sitting there for 24 hours and nobody's bothering them. But you are attracting attention getting up there and they just want to shoot you. It's a tough night.

The Japanese buried their dead so you never knew how many you killed. The only time you'd find a dead Jap is when you would come back at night to camp and you would dig out a foxhole. You might dig up a dead body they had buried the night before. You could smell them. That would ruin your evening.

Every night before it was dark, I would treat Marines who had cut their hands on can openers, or have bad athlete's foot, or other human problems.

Always the Marines want you to sleep near them, and they would say, "I got your foxhole dug out over here." No corpsman had to worry about digging a foxhole. And we were always better off with the Marines anyway. More protection.

When I got in with the foot Marines on Iwo, I saw quite a bit whether I wanted to or not. On Iwo I was just a corpsman, but by the time I left I was senior corpsman. There were so many casualties that I kept moving up without volunteering.

Each platoon had a corpsman and each company had six corpsmen and one senior corpsman. In the section of corpsmen I went in with, at least 30% got killed, and another 30% were casualties. We had about 20-25% survive. We had 120% casualties so you know we had to have about 80% replacements. It's a tough life for a corpsman.

I had to do it all. Suture, treat sucking chest wounds, and amputate as another corpsman who was smarter than me told me what to do. I was 19 years old. I was educated in units of plasma. I had so many syrettes of morphine, so much this so much that, a lot of battle dressings, sulfa benemide. We carried stuff that is probably obsolete today and medically they don't do anymore.

I tackled so many people who were critically injured. There is no particular injury that I wasn't supposed to treat. But the closer I was to a better facility, the better for the Marine. Surprisingly you can do things you know you shouldn't be doing but you are trained to do. When you learn it, you don't expect you'll ever use it.

I don't think I went to the bathroom for eight days. I never thought about sleeping, I know I must have slept. I know I never changed my clothes for 28 days. I brought a change of clothes but I never used them. When we got back aboard ship we threw everything away. They assigned us new clothes, new shoes.

Physically I didn't do anything heroic. I was there because I had to be and saw a lot more than I wanted to see. I never saw hand to hand combat with a German. I saw Germans wounded lying in a bunk. There was no such thing when you were with the Marines. I never had that combat man-to-man but I was just like a Marine. At night the Japanese would get drunk on sake, find courage, and try to invade us. We would have trip wire around us so it wasn't unusual to occasionally have Japanese in your hole, or close to your hole, firing.

We got to the end of the island in 28 days. It took us 28 days to go from one end to the other. Normally you could walk in three or four hours. When I physically saw Army generals and big staff people, it kind of floored me that the Army was there. I was at the end of the island and I hadn't seen any Army. Come to find out the Army would not relieve us until we policed our area and killed the bugs. You know when you have your bug guy come and spray once a month? My assignment was to give 20 Marines those tanks on their backs to walk their way back to the beach and lay that stuff down. Kill the bugs, dysentery, or anything else. I was so mad to think that we had lived through the bugs while we were getting shot at, but the Army wanted the bugs killed. Here's a Marine, he's got a gun in one arm and you give him a tank to wear on his back like a bug killer.

After the war I was stationed on Guam at the 5th Naval Service Depot because I didn't have enough points to get out. The Marine depot that I was at was in the capital, Agana. We used to have sick call for the city of Agana once a day and every other day I was in charge of duty for 24 hours. We had doctors but anything trivial had to be seen through a corpsman. I had a lot of good people around me.

I've talked about this more recently than I have in the past 20 years. I always used to say to people, you are lucky to be with me because I'll be the only guy you'll ever meet who hit D-Day on Normandy and D-Day on Iwo.

* * *

Hospital Apprentice 2nd Class
Herman "Doc" Rabeck, USN
HQ, L Company, 23rd Marines, 4th Division

"Doc" Rabeck, left, with wounded Marine on Iwo Jima.
Official USMC photo.

We were Navy Corpsmen and we were taken to the Marine Corps. I was number 28 out of a list of 27 to go into the Marines but one of the guys hid in the bathroom. He didn't want to go into the Marine Corps. Corpsmen were very much in demand; little did I know it was the toughest job in the Navy. The Navy Corpsmen with the Marine Corps have the highest losses of them all. A lot of the guys considered it a suicide job because we had to go out there and take care of them under fire. And there was no question you were going to go. If somebody hollers "corpsman," you went. Never even thought about it; it was second nature. You try to manipulate it so that you can be as safe as you can, but you're under fire. You have to get out in the open to take care of these guys who are hit and then drag them back to where they have a little safety. It's a rough job.

I went to Hospital Corps School in Brooklyn, New York, at the Brooklyn Navy Hospital. We did a normal six month course in two months. They kept us going from 8 o'clock in the morning to 9 o'clock at night. They were desperate for corpsmen and if you didn't pass, then Sunday you didn't get to go out on half day liberty. So you crammed up and passed your test. We learned anything that had to do with medicine. Aboard ship you had to check the mess hall that they were taking sanitary procedures. Field lavatories, you had to oversee all that. Everything had to be tip top or else you reported it. That was our job. In fact when it came to anything that had to do with the health of a Marine, we had the say over the officers.

The most important thing we had was sulfa drugs for infection and APC capsules. All Purpose Capsules...whatever you had, that's what you'd get. It's your everyday pain reliever like Tylenol with a little bit of aspirin in it and caffeine, the three of them mixed in together. We used to sit aboard ship or back at the base and grind them up with mortars and pestle and fill up gelatin capsules.

When I ran out of medical goods, I would go to the emergency kits and many times I had to take them off dead men. But I was a sly dog. Iwo was my fifth operation, and I got smart and started becoming a pack rat. I would go to the MASH unit wherever we were, and I would get bits and pieces I might need. I stole from every place.

I had an ammunition belt, it had no ammunition, but I had medical gear in it. I had all kinds of things you might need, you name it, it was in there. I even took a bottle of Vaseline, got it good and warm, and with a roll of bandage I made my own Vaseline gauze. On the battlefield I was putting Vaseline gauze on these guys so it wouldn't stick to the wound; when they got to whoever was taking care of them, they wouldn't rip the wound open again. It was something that I had learned. I think I was the only one on the battlefield who did that. I taught it to some of the other corpsman, but some were too damn lazy to do it. You used morphine sparingly. It was one thing you really held as a last resort. If the guy was really in bad pain, then you'd use it. If it was a head wound, you couldn't use it. A gut wound didn't matter because he was going to die anyway. If he wanted it, you gave it to him.

We had some characters, too. We had some really bigoted bastards, as well. I had one guy right on the battlefield that cussed me out and said it was because of the Jewish people that we were in the war.

My fault. I looked at him and said, "Yeah?" and let him have it. That was during the battle on Saipan, and I was in the midst of beating the hell out of him when they pulled me off to take care of the gunny who had been shot. The funniest part of it is that three months later he had to have a circumcision. He had an infection. When it was all done and he was walking bowlegged around the camp, I said to him, "Hi buddy, joined our ranks, right?" I really razzed him.

My first experience as a corpsman was aboard ship to North Africa. We landed Patton's guys safely, but we took the brunt of it. Out of the eight ships that sailed, five of them were sunk, only three of them got back. I was luckily on the flag ship and we were protected by the other ships. We shot out of there after we picked up as many injured as we could. We had to take care of all these burn patients because when you get torpedoed you get burned badly. We learned something very, very strange. Sometime before, the Copacabana night club in Boston was burned down and hundreds of people were burned. They started a process of doing different things to treat burns. They took sulfa drugs, mashed them up and made a solution then put those burned into a rubberized bucket more or less in the bed and covered them with cotton batting and this wet sulfa combination. It worked perfectly for us because it healed 90% of the people we treated. We spent hours sitting there with a pair of tweezers and pulling off skin. One of the guys I was pulling skin off said, "Rabeck, don't you know me?"

"Arnheim?" I said, but almost choked. The guy had been in the bunk above me at corpsman school and I couldn't recognize him his face was so burned, but boy by the time we got back to the states he was back to normal, like he had sunburn. Only six of the burned had to be carried off. The rest were able to walk, and they just looked like they were sunburned.

After that, I didn't care about ranks. It didn't mean anything to me. Doing your job and staying alive was the most important thing. We never wore any insignias. That they learned on Guadalcanal. The Japanese picked off the corpsmen and the officers first to kill morale. We learned a lot of their tricks.

I think the most important thing I ever did was on Roi-Namur. A little two by nothing island, two little halves split in the middle and a causeway in between. I'm in there with some of my men and we had been told by the intelligence people to watch out for documents that have black edges and red lined edges, they're secret and top secret. Well here we come to one booby-trapped character and we diffuse the booby trap. We move on over and look down in a shell hole and see these guys lying on top of papers. Everything is smoldering and right on top there is a Japanese officer with his sword out and pistol in his hands. They had committed hara-kiri and he had given them the coup de grace. They set the fire and it was going nicely but their bodies fell on top of the papers and covered them. Now I saw the black and red edges and I grabbed hold of two Marines who were with me and we threw sand on the fire. We put it out and I had the radio man call back to G2 to send up people to get the documents. There were thousands of papers there, some were burned but most were intact because their bodies were on top of them. A few weeks later we got some kind of an acknowledgment thanking us for the very important documents that were uncovered. It seems that these documents gave information on all the other islands the Japanese had. Things like where the charges were around perimeters, all the important details that stop an invasion. So I say that is the most important thing I did because look at all the people who were saved by that information.

I remember every detail of Iwo from the day they got us on the top deck and they laid out a miniature of the island. A whole bunch of us who had been in action before took one look at the island and we all said the same thing—suicide mission. The worse thing I remember was just before we hit the island they put DDT on us. We had to stand there and they covered our whole body with this crap. That was on our bodies before we went. I don't care what it was, that DDT killed anything. Iwo Jima was the only place we got DDT; we had never gotten it before. Stupid idea!

First thing I remember hitting the island was that there was just one little embankment with black soil that peaked up and it was the only thing to cover you. Shells dropped behind us, on the sides of us, all over the place. Now for the first time we were in what we thought was a great wave, we were the 12th wave. We had always been in the first, second or third. Twelfth wave is great, but the Japs didn't open upuntil the sixth and by the time we got there, bodies were everywhere, pieces of bodies. When I came ashore the first thing I heard were guys screaming, "Corpsman."

I didn't even know it but there was a photographer there who took two shots of me, one just after I landed. I was coming back to get my gear, I had taken care of a guy who had gotten a blast in front of his eyes. The ash had gone into his eyes and he was completely blind and screaming. It must have been terrible this ash just graveling in his eyes, and I used up an extra canteen of water washing out his eyes and half of his canteen, leaving him a little water. I had some ophthalmic ointment in my ammunition belt, and I used that yellow oxide ointment. I squeezed it into his eyes, but I didn't have enough for both eyes so I went back to my pack, and I had to pull out the other tubes that I had to treat him again.

I covered his eyes and said, "Don't you dare touch them," and bandaged them up.

By Dammit, We're Marines!

As soon as a boat came in, we pushed him on it to go back out again. What happened to him from there I have no idea, but he had terrible scarring on his eyes, I'm sure, from the volcanic ash. I didn't even know that a combat photographer had taken a picture of me and that Marine until my nephew saw it in a magazine.

It was a couple of hours later, I was taking care of another guy when I started to feel my back going. A young corpsman, a replacement, didn't know much, called me over to take care of this guy. I was taking care of him, and shells started dropping all around us and the concussion of one of them must have hit me as I leaned forward over the body. Everybody else ducked for cover, but I didn't and then I couldn't get up. So I hollered to them to pull me up. They pulled me up and I finished off what I was doing. I thought nothing of it; I just kept going. I didn't realize that little by little my back was being beaten to hell by all those concussions.

I had 150 tags to write down what I did for the wounded, and I'd snap it on to them and go to the next. I ran out of those and went over to a dead corpsman and took 50 of his that were left and just kept going. It must have been about 200 the first couple of days that I treated. God knows I don't even remember half of what I took care of because you go with the flow whatever happens, whatever is needed, you did it. Then you go to the next one, you don't even think about it. I don't recall when it was but shortly after that I started running out of all kinds of supplies. I sent Marines out and I went out and we started taking the first aid packages off the backs of the dead men so I would have more equipment to use because I had nothing left outside of a couple of rolls of gauze and a piece of tape.

I took care of a guy in a foxhole who had a rump wound. I patched that up and sent him back. Another guy had an elbow wound, and I was in the midst of taking care of that when I heard the guys saying, "Look at that crazy guy out there. He's stumbling all over the place."

He was covered with bandages and must have been a hundred yards out and I said, "Why doesn't somebody pull him in and take cover?" Then, and only a corpsman would think this way, I'm thinking look at all that bandage material going to waste if he gets killed. So I run out there and grab him. I started coming back and this photographer who had been interviewing somebody else at that time stands in the middle of the foxhole there taking our picture. You can't see all the shells behind us blasting all over the place. He's blocking our way in, and I started to cuss the hell out of him.

"Get out of our way," I yell.

He jumps as I pulled the guy into the hole. Had he stayed there a little while longer, he would have been blown to bits. He was just like a drunk, running in between these mortar shells. I couldn't believe it, he never got hit.

On probably the third day on Iwo, we started getting those big tin cans flying. They were missiles actually. They were the Japanese version of a V-2 rocket. The Japs themselves didn't know where it was going to land and sometimes it shot off the island. This particular rocket dropped down, and I went over there to see who was hit. In the shell hole, right on the ridge there was one guy with a minor wound so I let that go for a minute. I walked over to the other guy laying on the other ridge and he's dead, mass concussion, not a mark on him, dead as a door nail. And then I went to the guy down at the base and his leg was blown apart, I mean it was just in shreds. All the muscles and sinew were still there and luckily it was a hot piece of metal so it sheared some of the vessels closed. He's out. I know he's alive, I hear him breathing. I got two Marines in the hole with me. I told them to hold him and I took out scissors and a knife the Marines themselves purchased for me, stainless steel for just this purpose. They bought it when they went on liberty in Tijuana and brought it back for me. I used that knife to sever through the leg and then I power packed it so it wouldn't bleed. I asked the two Marines to bury the foot and the two of them walked over to the side and vomited, both of them. I had to pick up the foot and bury it on the other side of the foxhole, just couldn't leave it there. I met him, it must have been 12 or 15 years later at a reunion in Philadelphia, when one of the guys at our table hit his leg by accident.

"That's all right I didn't feel a thing. It's fake," he said. Lambert was his name.

"I know, I took it off," I said.

"Where did you take it off?"

"Just above the ankle."

"Yeah, that's right but they took it off at the knee to prepare it for the prosthetic."

He didn't even know who had done it. He was out of it. A lot of the guys were out of it that I took care of. One of them says to me, that little guy took care of me, the little guy from L Company. One corpsman had been killed and one was injured so I was the only little guy there. That was the conversation that went on all the time.

I saw a lot of battle fatigue; you never knew what was coming. Battle fatigue can do a lot of things to people. One guy would lose the use of his legs, couldn't stand any more. When it comes down to all the other islands, they were deadly, they were horrible places and a lot of bad things happened there but nothing like Iwo Jima because Iwo Jima, the only way you can describe it, was pure slaughter.

The first night we laid in the sulfur fields and the heat from the sulfur was like hot water springs. You would sweat all night. When you left the sulfur fields, it became damp and cold. We didn't have the gear for it, we were freezing and we would lie in our ponchos and shiver. There was no happy medium there. It was a terrible island.

When I finally got hit, I had just waved to another corpsman, Matthew David, 50 feet from me in this little valley by Meatgrinder Hill. He spotted me and we waved to each other and he went down and I went down as we watched the tin can. And whack! He was right next to a 75 mm artillery, and it blew up the artillery weapon. When I got up to go to him, the sergeant waved me off. There was nothing I could do. They didn't even want me to see it. I stayed where I was and another was coming, I could see it. As I ducked in, we got the hit. One dropped about five feet from us. We were in the shell hole just behind a big sandstone rock and it pulverized the rock.

My wound was blast concussion. I couldn't stand, the pain was too gross. I had been hit by a lot of concussion. I had shells hit all around me on four different occasions before that so I suffered a lot with that, and this last one was a 700 lb missile. The guy who was sitting with me went way up in the air and I went up with him, but I came down first and he came down on top of me. I was completely buried in sand and all this volcanic ash was lying on top of us. The first thing I remember was people's hands coming to dig us out. They shoveled it out by hand. He was on top of me but his body left a pocket so I could breath otherwise I would have smothered. I was fortunate, but that did a lot of damage. They took me aboard the ship, but the doctors wouldn't touch me until the corpsman got scissors and cut off all my clothes and threw everything overboard, even my wallet, everything. They wouldn't touch me because I was so covered with blood. My uniform was starched with it. They scrubbed me clean and threw me naked in a bunk. I was totally out until morning.

I was lying in a cot below deck and a chaplain came over and gave me a toothbrush and some other things I needed, soap and all. One of the men came down with clothing and after I got dressed I went back to the unit where they put a body cast on me from just above my hips all the way up to under the arms. I had my arms up and out to the side. I stayed like that for six months. I got up in that contraption and I moved up to the top rail and I'm standing there looking toward the island. Mt. Suribachi is clear as a bell. We were not that far off shore, and all of a sudden all the ships started their horns going. We all turned to Mt. Suribachi and bingo the flag started to creep up.

I hollered, "There goes the flag everybody."

Another announcement came over the loud speaker. The ship was scheduled to go to Guam in the Marianas and anybody who wanted to go ashore on Iwo, go now. A bunch of Marines started to go down the side ramp and one of them looks up at me and hollers, "Hey Rabeck, come on."

I look at him with this big contraption on me. "What, are you kidding, I can't even bend! I'd be more hindrance than help out there."

"OK, Doc," and away they went.

You had guys there that just didn't know fear. You know how green Marines are, they're brash. I started cussing them out and saying, "We'll see what you're like in action."

They were damn good. They were well trained and they had a lot of guts. God forbid we should have any blacks in there. A lot of the guys said we should have some black Marines here.

I said, "Hell no, these rednecks will kill them, they're crazy."

Some of these guys were so prejudiced that they'd frag them left and right. Black Marines would unload the ship and do all kinds of duties, but they wouldn't go on the battle lines.

On Saipan, two black guys walked through our lines and I looked at them and asked, "Where are you going?"

They said they were going to get some souvenirs.

"You're crazy, you are going to get killed out there," I said.

They just kept going. I never saw them again. I don't know if they made it or not, I doubt it. But seeing black Marines would have scared the hell out of the Japanese.

When we left Iwo Jima, the crew had to give us their clothing. We had no clothing to wear, and mine were cut off me and thrown away. I was in Navy jeans with a Navy work shirt until we got to one of the islands and they got us khakis. But the food was good. When you are aboard ship one thing you get is good food. You appreciate it because in the Marine Corps they have the same material to work with but it doesn't taste the same! It's god-awful. In fact I remember for two months we ate nothing but spam; they called us the Spam Commandos. The cooks came up with all kinds of combinations to get us to eat the Spam....Spam and eggs, Spam and this, Spam and that.

We were a very close bunch and could count on each other for anything. We were together for almost three years. I saw so many things happen where guys deserved the Medal of Honor. Guys who actually gave their lives just to protect the other Marines. It is a shame that so many people went unrecognized for the things they did.

* * *

Navy doctor and medical corpsman treat a wounded Marine
on the Iwo Jima battlefield.

Official USMC photo/Silverthorn collection

Navy

Seaman 1st Class Bruce Hallett USN
USS LCI (G) 449

Bruce Hallett, 1946

I went into the Navy in June 1943 at the age of 18. I had tried to get my parents to sign the papers for me when I was 17, but they wouldn't so I had to wait until I was 18 to register for the draft and then volunteer for induction.

I reported to receiving station in San Diego and eventually wound up being assigned to the LCI(G) 449. I participated in the invasions of the Marshall Islands, Saipan, Guam, and Tinian in the Marianas. That was all in 1944 and eventually we wound up doing some more additional training with the Marines on landings in the UDT (Underwater Demolition Teams) outfits. The 449 was part of a group, Landing Craft Infantry (Gunboats) Group 8, and that consisted of about ten LCIs. Group 8 was part of LCI(G) Flotilla 3. We had two primary missions: one was to cover and to protect the underwater demolition swimmers when they went in to try and clear the beaches for the Marines to land. The Japanese built bunkers on the coral reefs surrounding the islands to deter and impale landing craft coming in to prevent the invasion. The Japanese would have gun turrets close to shore on the beach and the

294

swimmers were to go in and attempt to blow these up. Our other mission was getting into formation again and lead the first wave of Marines into the beach. On D-Day, we would go in and fire rockets off about 1,000 yards, move in fire another salvo, move in, reload, fire another salvo. Then we would withdraw and the Marines would go in on their landing craft. We tried to saturate the beach to keep the enemy down while the Marines were landing.

On February 17, 1945, two days before D-Day on Iwo Jima, Group 8 was assigned the mission of lining up abreast, 100 yards apart, and providing protection for the swimmers while they did their jobs. These LCI Gunboats had been converted from Landing Craft Infantry Large. The landing ramps had been removed and replaced with a large number of rocket launchers so we could throw, I can't recall exactly, but it was either 120 or 144 5-inch rockets in about 12 seconds. Each LCI had this fire power. The original Landing Craft Infantry Large were only equipped with five 20mm guns. We were equipped with three 40mm and four 20mm and in some instances extra 50 caliber machine guns that were clamped to the rails with brackets. A tremendous amount of fire power. Plus they had a mean draft of five feet and had twin screw and rudder which means you could operate in shallow water and get in through the reefs.

I was the trainer on the 40mm, which means I sit on the right hand side seat and I move the gun in a horizontal means. The pointer was Charles Banko. He sits on the left and operates it vertically. Between the two of us we bear in on our targets. The man who is the pointer does the firing. There were seven of us up there on the bow. There was the four man gun crew, including the second loader, plus the young ensign as the talker, and two extra ammo bearers to bring ammo up.

This is what I wrote in my diary on February 19, 1945. I was 20 years old:

"We arrived off Iwo Jima just as dawn was breaking on D-Day minus 2 and all hands were topside watching the wagons, cruisers, cans and planes pound the island with shells and bombs. It was cold and damp and I wore a dungaree jacket over my shirt and a pair of foul weather coveralls over my trousers. We moved in closer on the eastern side of the rock and laid to until about 10:20 a.m. when the LCIs moved into formation for the run into the beach. General Quarters was sounded and all hands went to battle stations. My gun position was No. 1, 40mm on the bow. Rocketeers loaded all rocket launchers with a full salvo and pulled out the safety wires. The entire group of LCIs executed a left flank movement and started in towards the beach. We opened fire at about 2,500 yards and my stomach muscles tied themselves into a knot and I had the usual funny feeling that I get when I go into battle. All gunners had been studying detailed photographs of the beach with all of the gun emplacements, machine gun nests and pill boxes marked out. We moved in slowly picking out the targets with care so as not to waste ammunition and heat the gun.

We were to move in to 1,000 yards of the beach and then fire rockets and lay to for 45 minutes and blast at predetermined targets. We reached the 1,000 yard line and I fired into three machine gun nests and had just brought the gun to bear on the large gun emplacement when all hell broke loose. There was a tremendous explosion and I seemed to be enveloped by a solid wall of flame. The explosion blew me completely out of the gun tub and out onto the small point on the bow just forward of the gun. I felt something on my left and looked down and saw blood running out of a wound in my leg. My first thought was my God, I've been hit! I then noticed another wound in my hip, two very small ones on my arm and slight flash burns on my legs and arms. The only reason I wasn't severely burned was because I had worn some extra clothing because of the cold and damp. As I lay there another large explosion rocked the ship and immediately after that one, another hit the conning tower and blew one entire side of it off. The ammunition on the bow was exploding from the fire so that I couldn't go aft to get my wounds treated nor could anyone get to me. It was the most horrible feeling I'd ever experienced; and as I lay there bleeding, I expected another shell to hit the bow where I was. I don't know why I felt that way but I thought that I was going to die and couldn't understand why I was still alive. Finally the ammunition stopped exploding and I stood to see what had happened. A terrible sight met my eyes as I looked into the gun tub. Where the deck had been was a hole about 7 feet in diameter and there were two bodies lying beside it. Both of them had been burned brown from the flash of the exploding shell and one of them had a stump where his head had been. The deck was covered with pieces of raw flesh and was slippery with blood. The head was found 50 feet aft by the starboard 20mm. Nothing could be found of two others except a portion of a leg, which was identified as one of theirs. I was sickened at what I saw. You couldn't move without having to pick your way over the dead and wounded. One guy had been shot in the back by about a 37mm shell and he was just hanging together at the waist by a few shreds of flesh. Another was lying on the deck in a pool of blood with both legs shot off.

When the conning tower was cleared out they picked up the men in pieces and carried them out in buckets, guts, arms, legs and pieces of raw flesh. It was enough to make anyone sick and some of the men who were new to the ship and hadn't seen action before went completely out of their heads. When the casualties were added up, we were told that out of our crew of 63 men, 21 were dead, 2 missing, and 21 wounded, which is about 70% of the crew. Casualties were then taken aboard the USS Terror, a cruiser minelayer where we were then given a check up and put to bed. One crew member died from shock and loss of blood an hour after he was brought aboard. Nothing much could be done for him as his arm and part of his shoulder had been blown off. Another guy died that same night at 10:30 and I was taken out on deck the next morning to watch the funeral services for my shipmates. I wish that they could have been buried on land with a marker over their grave instead of being buried at sea. Today is the 19th and we are leaving for the hospital at Saipan. I wish that the people in the states could realize that there is a war going on and that men are dying, but it is impossible to understand what war is like unless a person goes through it."

What saved my life and the life of the other man was the splinter shield which is the shield around the gun tub. It's about 3/16 maybe 1/4 of an inch steel and it surrounds the gun with an opening in the rear to get into your gun positions. When we were hit, the splinter shield had been picked up and blown loose of the deck and slapped right up against the back of my seat on the gun and that knocked me down, knocked me out. That splinter shield deflected a lot of the flame and shrapnel over on our left. We both came out alive, both wounded with burns and shrapnel.

They did not have hospital ships up at the scene of invasion until D-Day. All we had for medical personnel on our LCI was one pharmacist mate. And you could imagine what he was trying to do with 40 some casualties out of a sixty man crew. We were taken aboard the USS Terror and treated for our wounds. They had three or four doctors on board plus pharmacist mates. The skipper of our vessel was Lt. Rufus Herring and he was awarded the Medal of Honor for his actions that day. Four Silver Stars, three Bronze Stars and twenty Purple Hearts were awarded to crew members.

The USS Terror transported us back to Saipan to an Army hospital where we were put in for treatment. If your wounds were severe enough that you would not be fit enough to go back into combat again say within a month or whatever, you were air evac'd to Hawaii to the Navy hospital. I spent a total of six weeks hospitalization. In the meantime, the 449 had been taken to Saipan, repaired, and sent back to Iwo Jima. When I was released from the hospital, I was sitting there happily waiting for my orders to go back to the states as a survivor but they got my orders screwed up. I was sent right back to the 449 at Iwo Jima. It had a whole new crew, fresh right out of the states, not a one had ever seen a day of combat. I was extremely fortunate to be alive. The battle of Iwo was over and I was treated like a king when I came back. I was on Iwo about six or seven weeks when the skipper calls me up. At that time I was Seaman 1st Class striking for Gunners Mate.

The skipper says, "I just got word that I could rotate two senior men on the vessel back to the states so you have a choice. I will either promote you immediately to Gunners Mate 3rd Class or you can go home as a Seaman 1st Class."

I said, "Good bye."

It was a very simple choice because they were getting ready for the invasion of Japan. And after five invasions, I had enough. I remember having to find the dead and wounded. You don't get used to it. If I went in to combat today, I would be scared shitless like I was then.

I have the greatest admiration and respect for the US Marine Corps and their infantry men. They are the greatest. I don't think I could have handled their type of battle. We were in and out and we did suffer a lot of casualties, but those poor guys were in there sometimes for months, day in and day out. I had a lot of friends in the 2nd Marines. We got to know the Marines quite well, and I tell you they are the greatest.

I was discharged from the Navy in 1946. I joined the Army and went to Korea because I felt that was the right thing to do even though I was castigated by some of my ex-Navy buddies. I put in 20 years between the Navy and the Army, and I retired out in 1966 and then went to work for the US Customs as a criminal investigator. My wife and I were married for 50 years and we have two daughters and five grandchildren. My wife, Phyllis passed away in July 2006 after a two year battle with cancer. We had lost our firstborn and only son in 1961 in an accident in Germany.

* * *

Wilfred "Bud" MacGiffert
Motor Machinist Mate 2nd Class, Platoon 5,
Company D, 133rd NCB

Bud MacGiffert standing on step in front row, with Platoon 5 in
Gulfport, Mississippi, November 1944.

I joined the Seabees at the end of my third year high school at the
age of 17 and went into service August 16, 1943. I picked the Seabees so
I could work at my future trade. Boot training was at Camp Peary,
Virginia, for about one month. Next stop was Camp Endicott, Rhode
Island, for advanced training, lots of drilling. I attended motor school.
After six weeks we went to Gulfport, Mississippi, for two months of
training. We were then sent to Port Hueneme, California, by train which
took about four boring days with no bunks, just hard seats. While there,
it rained a lot but the liberty was great! We shipped out to Pearl Harbor
later and were stationed at the Naval Air Station near the airport. While
there I worked on a pipe line that went way out in the bay. It was a
future sewer line. After that I worked on a barge driving piles for sea
plane lights on a model 78 crane as an oiler, that was the pile driver, and
later I learned to run it. Some of the Seabees were along in years when

they went in the battalion because most of them had experience with the various trades. A lot of them were already in their 30's or so.

Before we left Pearl Harbor, we took jungle training and amphibious landings on Maui. We then went to Camp Maui and joined up with the 4 th Marines. There I helped load ships for the Iwo trip. The ship I was on took approximately 54 days to Iwo with stops at Eniwetok and Saipan. The first night out we learned we were going to Iwo when Tokyo Rose came on at 11 p.m. She told us we would be wiped out the first day of the invasion. Life aboard the ship was boring with a lot of sub scares. I got to be friends with some of the Marines on board and one from my home town. The night before we landed we were briefed with our orders and fed a steak dinner.

On D-Day we headed for shore in a Higgins boat. Almost 1100 of the 133rd landed on D-Day. My group landed on Blue Beach 2, later known as Blew to Hell Beach.

When landing on shore a Marine yelled at us, "Damn, you Seabees are going to draw fire."

We had just gotten ashore when all hell broke loose. The Japs hit us with mortars and artillery fire and we were pinned down at the first shelf a very short way from the ocean. I had my rifle lying across my hips when a large piece of steel hit the stock of my rifle and glanced off my leg. My gun saved me from getting badly injured. My first impression of Iwo Jima was that this is going to be hell, and it was for weeks to come. I was 19 years old.

When we landed we were supposed to work our way up to Airfield No. 1. It wasn't operational because the Japs and our outfits had been shelling it so bad. It was full of shrapnel and a lot of big holes. They wanted to get that into operation for the Mustang fighter planes to come in and land so they could go out and drop bombs on the front lines. We were supposed to get there the first day but things were so bad that it was quite a while before anyone got up there. They changed our orders two or three times. Then they had us stay on the beach and unload supplies and lay the Marston mats from the LSTs when they finally could come in. We unloaded the steel matting and made a place for the amphibious tractors and the DUKWs to be able to go up to the front with the supplies. We got shelled really badly for the first two weeks. In fact, I couldn't find any of the men from the squad I landed with. After five days I could only find a few.

I was in a 14 man squad; each man had to be able to do two things. My job was being a mechanic and able to operate a crane. The 133rd moved to the other side of the island where we set up our camp. I was assigned to the garage as a mechanic. I learned a lot for future use from the older fellows in the shops. Our battalion did a huge amount of construction while we were there.

Our mission was to get the airstrips ready for the B-29s. We had two 12-hour shifts. Vehicles were running all the time, and we had a lot of work to do to keep them running. That was my job anyway. There were a lot of skilled mechanics and men running equipment. There was a quarry that had been bombed out, and we got the quarry going and then got the black top plant going. The Japs flew over and destroyed it, but we got it back working again. We laid tons and tons of blacktop for those airstrips. When we got that done, it was the longest air strip in the Pacific. The fighter planes used to come back pretty beat up, too. We got to know a lot of the fighter plane pilots who were stationed there, and they were real nice guys; they were officers but they didn't act like it. We tried to do things for them, and they sometimes gave us stuff we couldn't get. For some of the guys who drank, the pilots would bring them down a bottle and we would put some blacktop in front of their tents or something to help them out. Those pilots told us that they were in the cockpit on an average of 14 straight hours when they had to go to Japan and back. They were really going through an awful lot. We used to get some visitors from Japan who would come over and bomb us a little bit and strafe us when they got a chance. But later on our Black Widow fighter planes would go up, especially at night, and would either knock them down or scare them away.

I had some pretty ambitious guys in my tent and they confiscated a radio out of a disabled tank. They put that radio in the foxhole we built just outside our tent. As soon as we got the air raid alarm, no matter where we were working, we would head down to our tent and climb in that foxhole and turn the radio on. We'd hear how many fighters or bombers, called bogies, were coming from Japan and what direction they were coming from. That was quite handy for us.

We had some casualties after the Marines left. A lot of those caves still had Japs in them even after the island was secured. We had groups that had to go check the caves every day for stragglers. We put bars in there so they couldn't get out. Sometimes if you were dumb enough to let them out with their clothes on, they would come out with a hand grenade and blow everybody up. It got so that we wouldn't let them out at all unless they took all their clothes off.

We had a real nice theater, a chow hall that could feed a thousand people and a lot of small shops. The garage I worked in had a large shop, parts room and machine shop. We also had a beautiful church. I was up to Mt. Suribachi quite a few times but never explored any of the

301

caves. When we could, we toured the cemeteries looking for our comrades. The 133rd lost one third of our outfit.

We played volleyball and went to the movies in our spare time. We worked 12-hour shifts and sometimes more so there was not too much spare time. We left Iwo in November 1945 for Guam. After approximately a two week wait, we boarded the ship White Plains for Seattle, Washington. We were given a 30 day leave from Seattle. It was Christmas time so we had to use some "CB Can Do" to get a train back east and home. I arrived home on Christmas night.

I think we had 370 casualties on that one invasion, and that was more than any Seabee group in the history of World War II. We lost a lot of our men and it took me a long time to get over it. The 133rd is still looking for the Presidential Unit Citation.* The Marines got it, and the ones we worked with got it, but we never got it. The Seabees seem to be an outfit nobody ever heard of. We never got much recognition and it doesn't look like the 133rd will ever get the Presidential Unit Citation.

I was discharged March 31, 1946. At home later my brother and I built a service station and opened an auto repair shop that we ran for 40 years.

I liked the Marines because we were with them a long time and I got so I knew them well. In fact, there was quite a few from my hometown. One lived not far from me. We were on the same ship on the way to Iwo from Maui.

He kept telling me, "Don't worry, we'll have it all secured when you land."

On D-Day, I'm getting in the Higgins boat and he's up there waving at me. He was in water distillation so they couldn't land his equipment early. He came in about 4 or 5 days later and the first thing he did was to see if I was still alive. I still see him occasionally, and it makes me quite happy to see someone who landed with me.

*The 133rd Seabees continue to petition for the Presidential Unit Citation that the 4th Marine Division was awarded. The 133rd became part of the 4th on November 1, 1944, and was used as a Marine Pioneer Battalion on Iwo Jima. Members of the 133rd wore Marine uniforms and were subject to Marine rules and regulations. Both the 133rd and the Marine 4th Pioneer Battalion became shore parties for the 23rd and 25th Regimental Combat Teams of the 4th Marine Division. The entire 133rd landed in the first waves and suffered 40% casualties, more than any other Seabee Battalion in history. Six other Seabee Battalions received the PUC during World War II.

Petty Officer First Class Robert J. Steinmetz, USNR
USS Gear ARS 34 (Auxiliary Rescue and Salvage)

Robert J. Steinmetz, 1943

I enlisted on the night of Pearl Harbor to join the Army Air Force. I wasn't 21, and my parents wouldn't sign for me. You had to be 21 in those days. Later, I joined the Navy and brought the papers home for my parents to sign. My father liked the Navy so he signed. I was 19 going into the Navy on October 17, 1942.

The Navy wanted volunteers to go to deep sea diving school. That's when they used the hard hats. I volunteered. Every test they gave me in the deep sea diving I accomplished. I made a dive in San Francisco Bay picking up some Spam that a barge had sunk at the dock. The Navy didn't need any more divers, so I never finished that school. I was sent out to Mare Island Navy Yard. I went to welding schools and fire fighting school while we were waiting for our ship, ARS 34, to be built. It went into commission in September 1943. Salvage ships were named after some sort of equipment on the ship. Before the war these ships were being built for the British and entitled BARS. When the war started, they had to grind the 'B' off the ship.

On the ship we weren't allowed any electric razors. They brought us on the fantail and saw that we threw those electric razors overboard. A submarine could pick up that sound better than our engines.

After the Tinian invasion, we were pulled away and towed some ships to Pearl Harbor for repair. We dropped them off and came over to a dock where the naval yard must have been waiting for us because they immediately started working on our ship.*

They took off the 1.1 anti-aircraft guns we had, the best guns we had, and installed two 40mms port and starboard. Then they installed sixteen 50 caliber machine guns on our ship, and I wondered where we were going now. They got everything done and we picked up a brand new captain, the best one I ever worked under. With him, we hit Iwo.

We rounded up at Saipan and we were the ship that was in the lead of the attack transports to Iwo. Our code name at Iwo and Okinawa was Sob Story. Our command's name was Wiseman. I was ordered to raise the anchor. When it left the ground I signaled to the Captain and, as usual, I could hear him say, "Head one" and we were on our way.

We zigzagged towards Iwo. A couple of days out, one of the attack transports broke down. Wiseman radioed us to come about and to take it in tow.

We had it in tow and were moving when we radioed back to Wiseman, "Where to?"

We hoped to go back to Saipan with it. That's the way you get when you've been in five previous engagements seeing bullets.

"Straight ahead. Marines don't turn back," replied Wiseman. That remark should be embedded in the history of the Marine Corps. So we towed that ship full of Marines to Iwo.

We couldn't zigzag so we went straight ahead and got to Iwo way ahead of the other attack transports. We arrived at Iwo at 2300 the night before they were supposed to hit the beaches at 0900. We were trying to anchor this ship off Iwo but there was so much depth there you couldn't find the bottom. We found a spot and had the ship anchored.

While we're doing that, as usual, we heard, "Can you move?"

That was the message to us. They gave us a man overboard location and what a man overboard meant in this war for us was that something was hit. We traveled a long way to get to the location and we picked them up in daylight. We pulled alongside APD 48. **

The reason I know this is because we came in portside to portside, bow to bow. When we got along side I jumped on board the APD and it had a pretty good list on it. I went around to the starboard side forward of the front gun turret. I saw an officer and an enlisted man, the only ones left on the ship. The rest of the crew must have been picked up. I spoke to the officer who said they had just successfully picked up the Marine frogmen and they were in the mess hall celebrating the good job they did and that's where the bomb hit. Right in the mess hall. When I spoke to him, he had them all ready to push into the water to bury. There were so many. This officer and one man stayed on board to bury their gang.

Then we got, "Can you move?" and we moved to another location.

The LCTs couldn't get ashore, couldn't grab the ground so the Seabees placed two portable docks across the landing beach at an angle and thought they may help get the tractors on. But it was worse. We got orders to pull the docks off. When you get a stable landing, you lay down docks so you can just unload on the docks, you don't have to go up on the beach with the tractors. Ships can come in close and just unload. These things must have been 100 feet long or longer each one of them. They are made, I recall, in 6 x 6 foot cubicles, all separate and all bolted and welded together. You almost have to shoot each one of the bolts out to make them sink. They were made to take a hit. We were told to come about to the portable docks. We had a special boat that picked us up off our ship. I had never seen anything like it. It was a speed boat. I looked at that freshly painted, freshly made boat and I thought we're going to hell on this! That bow was up out of the water, that guy had it going. There were four of us who went in to hook the docks up. We always worked together on the tough stuff, Basil Kaphart, Fred Stead, John Skinner and me. We didn't even have a gun. All we had were Marine knives. As soon as I hit the beach, I grabbed a weapon from a dead guy lying there. I got myself a .45 caliber Thompson sub-machine gun. We lay there on the ground while we waited for our ship to shoot us a line. Our carrier planes were strafing the ground in front of us to protect us from the Japanese. Anyway, our ship was good at this from doing it over and over.

We had a line firing gun that shot a big piece of lead that carried a line into the beach from our ship way off shore. And I'm telling you our boatswain mates put that lead right in my back pocket. That's how good we were. We pulled that line in and another line in and another one in and we finally got a line that was strong enough to pull this thing off the beach. You couldn't pull a heavy line in right away. We hooked it up and pulled the dock off. While we are doing this the Japanese are shooting the shit out of us but they didn't hit us. We pulled one of the docks off and were ordered to take it to the right and sink it. The way they are built you just can't sink them with 40mm. We had to have another destroyer with 5 inch guns to sink it. By the time they sunk that one, another ship had gone in to pick up the other dock. Every ship had their job to do.

We went in again to pull out the LCTs that were loading up the beach. The LCTs were trying to get in but were hit. There were Marines in the water, and we picked them up with our whale boat. The operators of the LCTs were dead and the tractors ran amuck. There were dead Marines in the bottom of the landing craft. One of our machinist mates jumped aboard and cut their engines. We picked about six of the tractors up and towed them to an LST and they took care of the dead.

We were assigned to Iwo for nine days and never slept. We were in the war before the other guys were. We were there as long as it took to make a stable landing, which is when the ground troops have their own artillery on shore. Before that happened, they used the battleships, cruisers and destroyers for artillery.

We were involved in seven stable landings. Iwo Jima was the sixth and Okinawa was the seventh. Sob Story never took a hit in seven engagements. From Iwo we went to the Philippines to get ready to hit Okinawa. We hit Okinawa on Easter Sunday. It was also April Fools Day, April 1st. Iwo Jima was a picnic to what we did on Okinawa. Okinawa was the worst I've ever seen. It was dead, dead, dead, and more dead. There were 5,000 Navy dead on Okinawa on the picket line. The Marines and Army walked into hell. After Okinawa, we went back to Portland, Oregon, to get a major repair done. I went out early in the day with my friend Gerald to a movie. At the end of the movie, the newsreels started and the first thing that came on was a picture of me working on the Newcombe, a destroyer that was hit in Okinawa. It had a title of "The Ship That Wouldn't Die."

When the war was over I was in Portland, Oregon, waiting for the ship to be overhauled. I found out later that we were going to hit Kyushu, Japan, on November 1, 1945.

*The USS Gear returned to Pearl Harbor on December 6, 1944, for overhaul and departed on January 29, 1945, with an amphibious assault force bound for Iwo Jima.

**APD 48, named Blessman, scored a direct hit from a "Betty" bomber at 2121 on February 18 sustaining heavy damage with 42 men killed and 29 wounded.

* * *

Army Air Corps

By March 3, the Marines had captured all three air fields on Iwo Jima and transport planes were now operating on Motoyama No. 1, or South Field, evacuating the wounded and bringing in much needed supplies. P-51 Mustangs and P-61 Black Widow night fighters stationed there flew combat air patrols over the island. Cub planes from VMO squadrons flew daily artillery spotting and observation missions. B-29s returning from bombing raids on Tokyo made emergency landings on this small field, but the 5,225 foot air strip on Motoyama No. 2, or Central Field, was soon repaired and provided a better runway. Thomas Neff and Vic Chalker were crew members on B-29s that made emergency landings on Iwo Jima and recall the importance of the Marines' hard-fought efforts in securing the island.

Tech Sgt Thomas A. Neff, U.S. Army Air Corps
Central Fire Control Gunner, "Little Jeff,"
40th Squadron, 6th Bomb Group

Crew of Little Jeff on Tinian before flying 31st mission, July 1945.
Tom Neff, top row, third from right.

Gail Chatfield

I finished my first college degree and graduated in 1942. The forest service put out a call that they needed some help for the summer. I came out to Northern California to the Siskiyou National Forest. The Japanese had sunk a freighter across the entrance to the harbor in Crescent City. The reason I think the Japanese wanted to close off that harbor was that Highway 199 went from Crescent City over to Grant's Pass and that was the only way through the mountains. The Japanese had a big submarine out there with a plane on it. I was sent out to be a lookout, and I saw that plane several times flying around. The Japanese at that time were sending balloons way up into the jet stream and they were coming all the way across the Pacific. The balloons were armed with a timer. When they'd get over what they figured was land, the timer went off and they would drop incendiary material down on the forest. Some of these balloons got as far as Idaho and started fires.

I got injured on a fire and was laid up for about six months. As soon as I got well, I went to the draft board and enlisted in May 1943. I said I wanted to go to the Air Force and came in as an aviation cadet. When they separated us all out, they didn't need pilots, but they needed bombardiers and navigators. So I went to bombardier school down in Texas. The next thing I knew I was up in Denver and into the B-29 program. From Denver I went to Grand Island, Nebraska, where they put this whole group together in the spring of 1944. We trained first with the B-17 because we didn't have the B-29 then; they were just starting to come out. We didn't get our first B-29 until August 1944. We flew planes all over the place...Puerto Rico, Belem just off the coast of Brazil for navigation purposes. We flew to Newfoundland and to Alaska on training flights and we thought we were going to fly into Japan from the north. When we got our orders, the orders were to fly to Hawaii, from Hawaii to Kwajalein, and from Kwajalein to Tinian. That's when we found out we were going to be in the South Seas.

The Marines took Saipan and Tinian in '44 and the Seabees built the big airfields there. Japanese were still on the island and every once in a while they would set off some explosives. The Seabees were building roads and the airfields while this is all going on. The Marines stayed on the island until they finally cleaned out the Japanese. We were flying practice raids off of there by January. For our first raid into combat we flew down to Truk which was near Australia and I remember when we went over that big Japanese naval base.

"Gee, look at the flak!" the fellas said.

I watched that and made the comment, "Boy, we could get hurt here!"

By Dammit, We're Marines!

We flew that practice raid mainly for the navigator more than anything else to be sure he knew where he was going.

We had a B-29 group on Saipan, two groups on Tinian and one down in Guam. Guys from Guam, they had the job of flying the farthest. They were 100 miles more south of us. If we flew from Tinian, it was 1500 miles up to the coast of Japan. In the middle was Iwo Jima. The Japanese had a fighter group there. Not only were they warning Japan that we were coming, but they worked on our planes when we came back. We lost more planes on the way back than we did over the target. When the Marines came in and took over Iwo Jima, we were really glad to see them. We eventually made six landings on Iwo.

When we first got into Tinian, they put us in a tent. We didn't have Quonset huts. On the radio that night we listened to Tokyo Rose.

"We understand that crew 40-15 came in today," she said. "We want you to know we'll have a warm welcome for you when you come up to Japan."

How she found out, I have no idea. That was kind of a shock, indeed. Then we flew up to Iwo Jima and we bombed Iwo and we also bombed one of the Northern Marianas Islands. The end of January is when we started going up to the island of Japan

The 6th Bomb Group consisted of the 24th, the 29th, the 39th and the 40th squadrons. We were the last plane in the last squadron, 40-15. The plane was called Little Jeff and was the only ship I was in. Jeff was the name of the pilot's son. He was about a month old when we flew overseas. I got a call from Little Jeff last Christmas time saying that his dad passed away. Little Jeff retired as a full colonel in the Air Force and his son now is in the Air Force. I call him Little Jeff the third, his name is William Jefferson Christie III. Christie was our pilot and at 29, the oldest man on the ship.

Our youngest boy, a kid from Chicago, Johnny Olinger, was the right side gunner. He came in when he was 17, and he was only 19 on Tinian. I was the oldest enlisted man at 24. The flight engineer was 23, the tail gunner was 22 and the copilot, Tom Kenny was only 21 or 22. I used to correspond with several of them at Christmas time but they all gradually passed away. I'm the last man on the crew. That's what the pilot's son, Little Jeff, told me, "You're the last man."

Tinian was a nice island, very few beaches, it was all cliffs. The only town was at the south end. The Seabees built everything. The trucks and bulldozers ran 24 hours a day building the airfields. I remember in March they brought in a whole new batch of trucks, and by May they were practically shot from the work they were doing. The coral was used to make asphalt roads. The island was laid out almost like Manhattan. I always tell the kids, we lived on Riverside Drive just about where Grant's tomb is. There were two big airfields, North Field was the biggest and the West Field was where the group from China was based. Each bomb group contained 45 planes and we had four bomb groups just in our wing, the 313th wing. Plus there were wings on Guam and Saipan. I don't know how many planes we had altogether, but I remember one raid that we had over 300 B-29s.

Eleven people were on the B-29. Pilot, copilot, bombardier, and navigator were the four officers. There was a flight engineer, a radar man, two blister gunners, a tail gunner, and I was the central fire control gunner in charge of all the guns. We flew VFR. The B-29 was the first ship with computers. I had a control and could switch the turrets of each gun and give the gunners as many as they wanted. Gunners sat by a gun site, not in the turret. Information went through a computer controlled by the navigator who plugged in the elevation, the air speed, any windage and things like that. In the tail we had two 50 calibers and a 20mm canon but the 20mm couldn't be tracked like the 50s, the computer wouldn't separate it out, so we took the 20mm out and put in another 50 caliber. The system was pretty accurate. It was developed by General Electric. A man from G.E. was there all the time to help us. I remember talking to him at one time about it.

"Don't ask me why it works," he said, "I don't know how, but it works!"

The comfort level of the B-29 was a lot better than the B-17 because it was padded on the inside and pressurized. We never flew above 8,000 feet actually until we got over a target area and we depressurized because if we had been hit with anything good, the whole plane would have exploded. The engines were big, we used super fuels, 135 octane, I think it was. They called it volatile fuel. It stunk. You had to get used to it. The plane's engines were turbo charged for high elevation flying, but after March we didn't fly high elevations any more; we never flew above 15,000 feet.

We found out the Japanese had sonic radar. They listened to sounds. When we would go over a target, we would set two of the engines at a certain RPM and the other two at another RPM so it sounded like two planes coming. Every plane did this. You could tell the search lights were tied into the radar and were hunting for you. You got used to the noise level after a while. No ear protection, it wouldn't have done any good. Of course you had the constant vibration, too. When you took off, you had an extension of the wing to make it wider so it would get better lift. When you came in, you'd pull these extensions out and pull them down to slow the plane. But there wasn't anything to tell the pilot if they were out or up or what and from the cockpit he couldn't see anything. The blister gunners had to tell him.

We had a little electric heater on board to heat up the food they gave us. But some of the food we got was really something. I'll never forget one time we had sandwiches that were made with tongue. We put them in the heater and when they came out the tongue was all curled up. Awful! We each had a map, a mirror to signal, that's all we had. We didn't have anything else except a one man life raft. If you ditched, you had a chance of using that. If you had to bail out, you were in trouble.

For a daytime raid, we would leave about 2 o'clock in the morning. For a nighttime raid we would leave about 5 o'clock in the afternoon, around sunset. Eighteen, nineteen hours was an average raid. We were tired, yes, and we napped as much as we could. I was trained also as a flight engineer and would relieve him on the way back so he could crawl up in the tunnel and get an hour or so nap. Then I would go back in the other end of the tunnel and get a nap. Even with the noise, you'd sleep. If you were lucky, you could get a mission in about every 3 or 4 days. The plane had to be worked over, all four engines, and then they would try to figure out what the weather was going to be like. It was all long distance stuff. Planes were sent up to take pictures and check the weather out. One time we broke through a storm front. I counted 17 waterspouts, tornados, along the front of this weather front, but we didn't have a camera to take a picture of it

We were the second plane to land on Iwo and that was on the 4th of March, 1945. The first plane that landed was named Dinah Might from Saipan. They didn't survive the war. After a big raid over Tokyo, we had one engine out and a broken oil line. With adverse winds, we were using too much gas so we had to set down.

We called Iwo and they said, "Yeah, we can repair it. We got fuel, just be sure you come in and stop as quick as you can."

The island was only about half taken at that time. I remember when we landed we managed to stop at the end of the strip. We tried to turn around and Marines popped out of the ground all around hollering, "Get out of here. We've been under mortar attack. Get out of here."

We got down back to the other end of the airfield, and out came a big truck full of barrels of gasoline with one of these little pumps but the hose wasn't long enough to reach the wings. They brought out big funnels and put them in the two wing tanks and the flight engineer says, "Geez, where's your filters?"

They didn't have any filters and the wind was blowing that black sand everywhere.

The pilot said, "Well, we've got to have something to filter."

So me and the tail gunner were detailed to take off our coveralls and put them over the funnels. The gas was poured through that so there wouldn't be any sand or anything going in the tanks. There we were up on the wings filtering gas while the cannons were going off. We could hear machine guns and we were in our underwear! The fellas brought the gas up to us in five gallon cans and we needed 600 gallons in each wing. We poured it in while we got the engine repaired. We took off through a mortar barrage but got back and were the last plane in. I still remember we had to go to a debriefing and the tail gunner and I went in there in our shorts. Some lieutenant bawled us out, "You're out of uniform!"

We jumped up and told them what had happened on Iwo.

We were one of the lucky ones. We never had an injury. We had a couple of shells come through the compartment, and I can still remember hearing that stuff whiz around but none of us were ever hurt. We flew 38 raids. Three of them were practice raids. The tail gunner and I each got a plane. He got one of the Bakas which was a flying torpedo with a man in it. They would be launched from a Betty bomber and only at night. All we could see was this big ball of fire flying around. Everybody was shooting at the ball of fire. Actually the ball of fire was the exhaust, the rocket was ahead. We were scared of them because we didn't know what they were. They just seemed to dart around our formations. One of them hit a plane heading back to Saipan, went into it, but didn't explode. They landed with it on Iwo Jima, and that was the first time we found out what they were and that we were shooting at the wrong end of it.

Late in May in '45, one of them came down on us and the tail gunner got it. As a result of that, the Betty dive bombed at us and I was able to knock that one down. I got a certificate for that. They were the only two that actually threatened us.

When the Okinawa invasion came along in April, the Japanese were using kamikazes. The Navy was really taking a beating. The Navy wanted us to bomb every airfield on Kyushu because that's where all the kamikazes were coming from. We spent probably all of April bombing Kyushu. Every airfield we could hit, we bombed. I don't know whether we wiped out a lot of those planes or not. On one trip, in the F bomb bay, the lower tier of bombs didn't release and all our other bombs dropped down on them. The bombs always had a little prop on the front with a wire coming back. When the bomb went out, the wire was pulled off so the props were turning. They would turn so many times, fall off and the bomb was armed and ready to go. That was the thing we were worried about when all those bombs dropped inside because the props were turning. They were ready to go; we were sitting ducks. It was a madhouse, just like a jigsaw puzzle. I was sent to see if I could do something. On either side of the bomb bay there is a switch called a salvo switch which you can turn with a screwdriver and release all the bombs. I couldn't get the bombs away with the switch. We were at 15,000 feet and I was running out of steam because there was little oxygen at that altitude. The pilot came back. How he got over the mid-wing section I don't know but he says, "I think I can get this one over here. Give me your screwdriver." And then he said, "If you can grab hold of this one tail piece and pull…"

I hung across the bomb bay, grabbed hold of that, and managed to move it about six inches.

He said, "That'll do it. That'll do it. Just one more thing. Let go of that tail piece!"

When the bombs went out, they scattered and hit our bomb bay doors and bent them. We couldn't close our bomb bay doors so we had to land on Iwo to get that done because they were slowing the plane down. They couldn't get the doors straightened to close so we took two of the cables from the hoist in the bomb bay and hooked them around a broom handle and pulled that piece of broom handle up to hold the door shut. That's how we got back to Tinian.

I can remember the last time we bombed Tokyo in May. We were one of ten ships that went in and dropped bombs to outline the target area. Three of us came back. That was the last big raid over Tokyo, we never went back. There wasn't anything left. Tokyo was burned out. In the meantime we hit cities to burn them out. There was a factory town a little south and east of Tokyo and if you had any trouble getting rid of your bombs over Tokyo, you'd fly down to Hamamatsu. Hamamatsu had a piano factory that was making all kinds of airplane stuff. Hamamatsu at the end of the war had nothing but a fringe of homes around it.

We had to land on Iwo after a massive raid over Osaka and Kobe in June of '45. I don't know how many planes were on that raid, but there must have been a hundred planes land on Iwo Jima on the way back. We were in a formation and a Japanese plane blew up right in front of us. I can still see the engine with the prop turning go through our formation. Something hit one of our props and it was thrown out of balance and the engine was shaking. We landed on Iwo again to have our propeller repaired. I saw three B-29s come over the island. The crews bailed out of two of them because the pilot and co-pilot had been killed and nobody could land the planes. Fighter planes were sent out to shoot the B-29s down. One plane had ditched on the east side of the island right where the Marines made the big landing. They rescued that team there. They had good mechanics on Iwo. They could take care of you. Over 1200 B-29s sat down on Iwo Jima for repairs of some kind. It was needed. It would have wiped out the B-29 groups if we didn't have it. When we first started without Iwo, as I recall, for every plane that went down over the target there were at least five or six planes downed in the ocean on the way back. It was that high. And that was just from Saipan. Most of the losses were on the mining raid; we had to fly down so low to mine the harbors in the Shimonoseki Straits. When you had to fly through there, which was between Honshu and Kyushu, the Japanese were shooting down at you from the peaks.

In July 1945 we were picked for some reason to fly the longest raid of the war. We flew up to North Korea and mined a little town up there I think it was called Rashin. We dropped our mines and flew off to the northeast. Two Russian planes came out and lined up on us because we were flying across the entrance to the Bay of Vladivostok. Our pilot said to let them have it and we did. We chased them away. The interesting thing was they were lend-lease planes that the Russians had gotten from us. We identified them as King Cobras. That raid was 22 hours I recall. It was 2,000 miles one way. We landed on Iwo Jima first to gas up and take on the mines. On the way back we had to land on Iwo Jima again to refuel. They had the gas tanks buried by this time. Iwo is a volcanic island and the ground is hot so the gas would expand and burst out of the hoses.

During July I remember we used to crack the entrances to the bomb bays to get a breeze into the plane. It was hot. In the wintertime, if you went through a storm, it was chilly. We didn't wear a jacket; you didn't want anything to interfere with getting that parachute harness on. The harness was always ready to snap on as quick as you could.

We made the last raid of the war over the Awakuni rail yards about 50 miles southwest of Hiroshima. Just after we dropped the bombs, the code word came through: Utah, repeated three times.

The radio man hollered, "It's all over, it's all over!"

The pilot said, "Let's go down and take a look at Hiroshima."

So we did, we flew over Hiroshima about 2,000 feet. Nobody had a camera! But everything looked fuzzy. I remember the whole town of Hiroshima was built on a river delta kind of a triangle with hills in the center. That bomb must have been dropped south of the hills because there was a little spot north of the hills where nothing was touched but the rest of the city was just devastated.

The group that dropped the atomic bomb was moved in with our group. They only had about 6-7 planes. Their planes were modified.

They only had one bomb bay because the atomic bomb was so large. They didn't have any gunners or anything like that, they had observers. The night they loaded the atomic bomb they called a lot of us fellas down there to stand guard and we stood there until they came back. I remember seeing the first bomb. It looked like a great big lemon up close. The other one was different shaped. That was the only two they had. They hit Hiroshima first and then Nagasaki. The Enola Gay was the plane they used over Hiroshima and Bockscar over Nagasaki. They never let the Japanese know at all. I talked with the tail gunner of the Enola Gay and he's the one who took some of the pictures. He said they could see the explosive wave coming through the air.

"When it reached us," he said, "it was just like somebody hit you. The whole plane reeled over."

He and I went back and took a look at the tail and it was twisted just slightly from the impact from the explosive wave. I'll never forget when we came back on that last raid. We told them what we had done and the medic sent us over to the hospital.

"You guys might be radioactive," he said. "You might light up the barracks tonight!"

They didn't find a thing wrong.

I met one of the Marines who was on the airfield at Iwo Jima when we landed that first time. He came from Chicago and just happened to attend an Iwo reunion at Pendleton the time I spoke. When I made my talk, I said I couldn't tell them what the Marines yelled at us because there are ladies present.

He came up after and I asked him, "Did I tell the story right?"

"Right," he says, "and I'm glad you didn't tell them what I told you!"

For his service during World War II, Neff received the Distinguished Flying Cross, the Air Medal plus four Oak Leaf clusters, and three Battle Stars. He was married for 55 years, has three children and six grandchildren.

* * *

Staff Sgt. Victor Chalker, U. S. Army Air Corps
871st Squadron, 497th Bomb Group,
73rd Wing, 20th Air Force

Victor Chalker, 22, Flying School, Hicks Field,
Ft. Worth, Texas, Spring 1943

I was in the New York National Guard and was called up in 1940. I eventually wound up being in an armored unit. In 1942 I got in the aviation cadet program. I was in pilot training for four months but washed out because I got an upper respiratory infection. They desperately needed air crew members because we were losing so many in Europe. I already knew Morse code, and I wanted out of the hot weather in Texas. Radio schools were up north so I opted to go to radio school in Sioux Falls, South Dakota. Three of my buddies and I were top of the class and were offered deals of going to Communications Officer School at Yale or to a very secret, hush, hush deal, which happened to be the B-29 program. We chose the hush, hush. We trained in Kansas but as we started training they couldn't keep it hush, hush because everyone could see us flying in these fields in Kansas. We were the second wing to go overseas. The first was the 58th that went to China, but that didn't work out because they had to fly everything from India over the hump, the Himalayas, to get to China. It took a long time to fly the bombs and gasoline over because it took a lot of gasoline to fly this stuff, too. Eventually the 58th Wing was sent to Tinian about three months or so after we were there on Saipan. We were based on Saipan in late 1944 and were the first B-29 unit in the Pacific. We started operations in October, our first B-29 raid on Tokyo was somewhere around Thanksgiving 1944.

In the beginning the engines were very poor on the B-29. They were brand new, the biggest radial engine in the world at the time, but they never took the time to get the bugs out of them before they made us fly them. I guess they were anxious to get the 29 over Japan. The engines overheated very rapidly. If you are in the tropics and taking off you had to be very careful. Even in the states we had trouble from the overheating engines. The B-29 was the first aircraft ever made that had computer controlled gunnery. That was a quantum leap forward. As far as I can remember, the computers worked pretty well. We also had Loran radar so we could do radar bombing. Even the communications equipment was state of the art and completely different than they had on the standard bombers of the day, the B-17 and the B-24. It was pressurized and heated, too.

I was a Staff Sergeant Radio Operator and the cryptographer in charge of all the codes. Anything that had to be sent was encoded. We changed the codes everyday. The code then was letters, certain 4 or 5 letter groups that could mean anything from one letter, to a paragraph. It could be a word or a sentence. They were fitted so it would pertain to what we were doing. Even if the Japs caught one of our code books, it wouldn't do them any good because in 24 hours it would change. That was only when we used Morse code, otherwise it was voice. When we took off and on the way to the target, there was radio silence. We could receive messages but not send them so the Japs wouldn't pick it up. An average mission was 13-15 hours. If you got battle damage, lost an engine, it might even run into 16 hours. We'd have certain times we had to listen for any emergencies where somebody who got shot down might have an emergency transmitter and we could pick it up.

The Marines took Saipan and it was secured in so far as there was no organized resistance, but we had an Army unit that hunted down Jap stragglers who were still hanging around. Every week they would come out with a body count of whoever was captured or killed. The Japs really didn't bother us. We were quite sure when we built our own outdoor movie theater that the Japanese were in the bushes watching the movies. The Japs who were there could have done a lot of damage with sabotage but they didn't. I don't know why. I think once their resistance was broken and without leaders, they were content to live and let live so to speak.

Saipan was warm and had dry and wet seasons. We slept in Quonset huts. The food was horrible because we didn't have refrigeration in the beginning. We were eating powdered potatoes and powdered eggs which came out looking like foam rubber. They had a meat that looked like a big bologna loaf that wouldn't rot or go bad. You can imagine what that tasted like—shoe leather! We had butter that wouldn't melt, and we called it axle grease. When we went on missions they gave us special food. We had heaters and cookers on the plane. There might be a ham steak, some corn, soup, bread, coffee, but when you're in combat your stomach gets all knotted up. We'd mainly use the coffee, the bread and the soup. When we landed, we would give the food we didn't eat to the ground crew who really appreciated it. It was something they wouldn't get. The only thing that was good on the ground was the bread. The Army baked good bread, and we did have jam. Bread and jam. I have pictures and we all looked so skinny!

Eventually we got refrigeration. Our group exec was some kind of an electrical engineer, and he found some Jap diesels and power parts and built a mini power station and wired up our area so eventually we got refrigeration. The cargo ships went down to New Zealand and picked up lamb and mutton and butter. When we first tasted that New Zealand butter, we thought we were in heaven. I don't know what they were giving us to eat, but I know that they weren't taking care of diets like they do for people now in the service. We never had fish. We weren't allowed to fish ourselves because we didn't know which fish were poisonous and which were not. One time they got some of the natives there, the Chamorros, to go out in the bay, and they got the fish that was fresh and not poisonous. Once we got ice cream off a visiting ship, and we'd get packages from home. One of my bunkmates came from New Jersey and his mother made pepperoni. It would take three months to get out there in the hold of a ship. Even with the heat, it would still come in perfectly OK. That was my first experience with pepperoni and I loved it.

In the beginning there was a lot of time between missions because we didn't have that many aircraft and we were sustaining a lot of casualties. After a month or two, they told us that we would have to fly 30 missions before we were rotated and sent home. According to our figures, we had 100 percent casualties in 16 missions. It didn't auger too well for us to finish 30 missions. Then we started getting a better flight plan. We discovered the jet stream. On the bomb run we indicated an air speed of 215 but our ground speed was 522 miles per hour due to the jet stream. Our bomb release line was eight miles before the target so you couldn't be too accurate with that because of the altitude and ground speed. The bomb was really traveling in a wide arc. When the bomb leaves the plane, it is traveling at the same speed as the plane and then it decreases exponentially the closer it gets to the ground. As you're releasing it at 30,000 feet, the air is thin so that is another factor. When the bomb gets closer to the ground, the air gets denser so it changes the ballistics of the bomb. General LeMay, head of the 21st Bomber Command, made a decision that we are going to go in at low altitudes and burn the cities out. I remember when they briefed us for the first fire raid on Tokyo, we were aghast at flying 5,000 feet, saying they could shoot us down with a fire hose. They usually gave us 30,000 feet plus to fly out. The number of Japanese casualties on our first fire raid to Tokyo was quite drastic. We heard the casualties were about 150,000 people killed and 390,000 injured and 700,000 left homeless in one raid. I think those figures were downgraded a little bit since then but it was still a tremendous raid. After that we started bombing the other cities like Nagoya, Osaka and Kobe and back to Tokyo. We were not getting a lot of rest in between missions. If your airplane was down because of the frequent engine changes, it might be a week before you flew another mission. During the blitz, we were flying one right after another.

The Japanese were trying to knock us down not only with anti-aircraft fire, but they would send up a Betty, a twin engine bomber that would release a rocket called a Baka. It was a manned bomb so to speak. It had little stubby wings and a warhead of anywhere from 500-1000 lbs. A Betty would drop the Baka to pick up a 29 that might be caught in search lights. The trouble with the Baka was he had primitive controls. He definitely knew it was a suicide mission because once he made his pass and if didn't make it, he had no power to land or go anywhere and he couldn't bail out. He would just drop from the sky, hit the ground and explode.

Our plane landed three times on Iwo. The first time was when the fighting was going on. The last two the island was secure. Our first emergency landing on Iwo Jima was after a raid over Tokyo. We knew we weren't going to make it back to Saipan. Iwo was about half way between so the pilot decided to go into Iwo. It was not a good thing because the B-29 was the biggest aircraft in the world and Iwo had this little runway, the first one they captured near Mt. Suribachi. It would have been hard to land on that under normal conditions. The basic thing in our favor was that the aircraft was light. We had burned off most of the fuel and all of the bombs so it was lighter and easier to handle. We passed air traffic control when we got in the traffic pattern.

Gail Chatfield

"Don't go past the end of the runway. It's not ours yet," they said.

We landed and were inside a barbed wire enclosure. We stayed in tents, really just a few tarps they put up to keep the rain off.

The fellow who was in charge of the area said, "Don't move at night."

I said, "What if we have to go to the bathroom? Are the Japs going to come up out of the ground?"

We knew the Japs were still underground.

"No," he says, "the main thing is we have guards all along the barbed wire enclosure here. They are young Seabees manning 50 caliber machine guns and they'll fire at anything!"

We were more afraid of our friendly fire than we were about the Japs! That was quite a thing to think about but I could understand, too. These kids were young and nervous. And on Iwo, you just never knew who was out there.

We fixed the aircraft ourselves which was basically the bomb bay doors all blown up and flopping in the breeze. We were able to get them fastened up, jury rigged because once airborne the air pressure alone will keep the bomb bay doors closed. We took off the next morning and picked up another crew from our group who had bailed out over the southern tip of Iwo. Thank God they bailed out over the southern tip that was in our hands. A couple of them went in the water but they got them too so we took them back with us. Once the Seabees got ashore, they were in charge of the airstrip. They knew it was going to be used, so they were prepared to bring the stuff in that was needed.

Around the first of May 1945 the 21st Bomber Command no longer considered Tokyo a target area. There was nothing there worthwhile to go after. At that time and up until the time I left, they were bombing little cities all over Japan, 30-40,000 in population.

I flew my thirtieth mission in the middle of June. We were very fortunate. Of the 29 original crews of our group that left the states, we lost 19. We set a record in our crew to be the first ones who finished all of our missions without ever aborting or turning back, particularly with the engine failures in the beginning. Only one man was ever wounded and not seriously. A piece of flak came through his Plexiglas blister, hit his gun site and went off the top of his head.

There was a B-24 outfit right next to us on Saipan, I think from the 7th Air Force. They bombed Iwo 70 days straight before the invasion and it didn't do a thing. Once in a while a B-29 would go up and have a practice mission for bombing Japan on Iwo, but it did no good.

I owe my being alive to the Marines who took Iwo. In a way we repaid the Marines. With the bombing that we did of Japan, they didn't have to invade it. They didn't have to lose anybody invading Japan. The Marines on Iwo Jima took a terrible licking. It is a terrible price to pay for eight square miles.

* * *

Symbolic of America's power in the Pacific is this Marine at a battered Japanese anti-aircraft position outlined against the Motoyama Airfield No. 1 on which rests the first B-29 that landed on the island. Official USMC photo/Silverthorn collection

Army

The battle for Iwo Jima ended and the decimated Marines left to regroup for the invasion of Japan. By late March, Iwo Jima had become an Army island as Army Engineer battalions replaced the Seabees and finished repairing the airfields. By July 1945 the Central Field had been paved to 8,500 feet and during the day over 100 B-29s returning from bombing raids on Japan landed there. Iwo Jima was now a front line air base with aviation fuel tank farms, repair areas, and a radar station on top of Mt. Suribachi. To support the base, the Army built roads, a water-distribution system, storage areas, waterfront facilities, and three hospitals with 1,250 beds. Housing and mess facilities for 37,000 officers and men were erected in addition to the individual battalion camps on the island.

PFC Joe Taverna, U. S. Army
483rd AAA Automatic Weapons Battalion

I was born in Italy and came to the United States in 1939 before the war. I was 19 years old when I was drafted in September 1943. When I got the letter from the government I remember there was a part that read something like "I may or may not be subject to the draft."

I could have put "I may not" because I wasn't a citizen at the time. All my buddies were going in so I checked "I may." I didn't say anything to my parents. When I went in they asked me where I wanted to go. I said the Marines or the Coast Guard so they put me down for the Coast Guard. Then the guy starts stamping the paper and says I can't go into the Marines, the Coast Guard or the Navy because I am not a citizen. The only place I could go was into the Army. I had visions of marching in the mud. The Army was looking for volunteers as interpreters, so I submitted my name but nothing ever came of it.

I went into the service in San Francisco and was sent to Camp Callen which was just north of La Jolla, California. It happened to be an anti-aircraft basic training camp. During basic training, there were several of us who were non-citizens, so they took us to San Diego Superior Court and swore us in and made us all citizens. I must have trained at Camp Callen for three months and then they sent me to the 483rd AAA A/W Battalion, which happened to be a 40mm anti-aircraft battalion. I was on 90mm in training and they put me in 40mm when I transferred out of there. They gave us summer clothing so we knew we were going to go to the Pacific. They transported us up to Seattle and from there to Hawaii. I think it was early August 1944 when we were attached to the 81st Infantry Division who had invaded the island of Anguar which was just across the straight from Peleliu where the Marines were.* We went to another island group, the Ulithi group** and were there for 3 to 4 months. After that we shipped out to places unknown. We had no idea. Fortunately or unfortunately I came down with appendicitis, so they took me off the ship and put me back on the island. I went into surgery and stayed there for another month. Meanwhile my outfit took off and come to find out they went to Iwo Jima. The convoy got in there February 25, beached on Iwo at 8:45. The ship I should have been on, LST 224, apparently was hit by some darn thing and the steering went out so it went back and forth in the tide and landed March 2. I think I got to Iwo about the 19th of March or so. As soon as the Marines took the air strip, that's when my unit went in and surrounded it with anti-aircraft guns.

I arrived on Iwo and promptly joined my unit which had already set up their anti-aircraft guns and 40mm guns. We were at the end of the air strip not really close to it but maybe 300 or 400 yards away. We pulled guard every night. One night we did have a raid. It was a moonlit, clear night, you could see the Japanese planes. I remember the 90mm shot at one plane and my particular gun shot at it and then the next thing we know we saw the plane catch fire. It finally ended up falling into the ocean. That same night one of the unit batteries on the other side of the airfield also knocked down a plane. In any event my unit got credit for one and a half kills.

We saw a lot of B-29 bombers and Black Widow fighters come in. We saw a few B-29s fall into the ocean because they were so shot up they couldn't land. They would put the plane on automatic pilot, the men would bail out over the land, and the plane would go down in the water. I was by the airstrip one time when a B-29 came in. I guess he caught the edge of the airstrip with his landing gear and he slid all the way down from one end to the other end. It caught fire but the men got out.

We had P-51s and P-38s there on the island that would pick up the B-29s coming from Guam as they were going to Japan and be their fighter escort and then return to Iwo Jima. The 29s that couldn't make it back to Guam would land there on Iwo. When these fighter pilots came back and were over the island, if they shot anybody down they would fly over the airfield, go straight up in the air, and do a victory roll. This one B-29 bomber guy, I guess he thought he was being funny or maybe he was an ex-gunfighter guy, I don't know, but he did the same thing right on the last day of the war. I'm over there watching him and two guys fell out of the bomb bay doors. They were there playing cards, the bomb bay opens up and these two guys splat right on the airfield.

They had an NCO club on Iwo and held a contest on the island to name the club. My entry was the 345th, as in the 3rd, 4th, 5th Marine Divisions. It won. Another suggestion was FBI, Forgotten Boys of Iwo. I remember seeing the cemetery. It was impressive but you look at the crosses and wonder who was underneath there. It was sad for me. We were on guard on Iwo when we heard the war was over. We jumped up and down. We didn't shoot any rifles. We just patted each other on the back and thanked God that we came through it.

I was on Iwo for 10 months when the rest of my unit went home. I had to stay there another month because I didn't have enough points to come home. About two months later they called my name, put me on an aircraft carrier, and I went home.

*The 81st invaded Anguar on 17 September 1944.

** The Ulithi Group is located 460 nautical miles southwest of Guam.

* * *

Sgt. John J. Herman, U. S. Army
E Company, 2nd Battalion, 147th Infantry Regiment

John Herman with his Bronze Star.

I enlisted in the Army in 1944. I was 21 years old and had been married for two years. I had a farm deferment but every time I went to town for groceries or repairs or something, somebody was on my fanny for not being in the service. It got on my nerves so bad that I just told my wife and my father, who I was farming with, that I was going to go into the Army.

I spent 17 weeks in Camp Roberts for basic training and then went to Fort Ord for probably 10 days or 2 weeks before we went overseas. We left Ft. Ord and were aboard ship for two weeks or so going to New Caledonia where we had 30 days advance infantry combat training. I was assigned to 147th Infantry Regiment which they called a bastard regiment. It was originally part of the 37th Division. When they broke that up from a four regiment division to a three regiment division, the 147th was left out so it was a single regiment by itself. There were three battalions in the regiment.

After New Caledonia, we were put on a ship; we didn't know for sure where it was going. I can't remember the name of the island now but we were to spend a few days there until we knew where we were going for sure. It was after the invasion of Iwo Jima. Just as we got off the ship we got an SOS to proceed to Iwo Jima immediately because the

Marines had got beat up pretty bad. I think we got there around the middle of March. We were attached to the 3rd Marine Division for a week or ten days and went on different patrols with them. We had to bring the Japanese out of their caves...dynamite them out, or blow them out. We were then to seal the caves so the Japanese eventually had to die in there. There were an awful lot of caves.

It was terrible on Iwo. It was an awful mess when we got there. There were so many dead bodies lying around on the ground. It got really bad before they could get the dead all taken care of, American and Japanese. The blow flies came in, and it was terrible. They had to start fumigating, flying over with pesticides to kill the blow flies.

After the island was pretty well secured, we still kept having patrols during the day and the night. We guarded the water points and things like that at night, too. There was a bad suicide attack one night on the air strip.* The Japanese killed a lot of our troops and pilots.

The Marines left and we finished the mopping up on Iwo Jima. I went along as a guard. I was more or less a mortar man in the mortar part of our company but I was a rifle man, too. I can't remember the figures, but we took quite a few prisoners. We tried to talk the Japanese out with interpreters. Some we did and some we didn't. They still had weapons and there were still lots of Japanese back in the caves even when we left for Okinawa. Some of the Japanese were tickled to death to surrender. Others it was more or less bred into them or beaten into them that they were Japanese troops and they wouldn't surrender. There was a holding area for prisoners but I don't remember where it was on the island. We didn't see them anymore after we took them prisoner. The island wasn't very big. We always called it '2 x 4' island; eight square miles

One of the major problems was fresh water. There were so many sulfur mines the water wasn't any good. We had to purify the water before we could even drink it or use it for cooking. We all ate a lot of K-rations and finally we came into some C-rations which were a lot better than the K-rations. We took good care of the prisoners with food and water.

The Coast Guard was there and the Signal Corps came in later. We left in June or July to go to Okinawa. It wasn't nearly as bad there any more because the biggest part of the battle was over. There was just a lot of mopping up and going on patrols and guarding a lot of things. The war was over in September and my outfit came home but you had to have 80 or 85 points to come home if I remember right. I didn't have enough points because I served as a replacement in this outfit. I went in on the 25th of April '44 and I got discharged on the 10th of April '46 so

By Dammit, We're Marines!

I lacked two weeks from serving two years. I left Iwo Jima as a buck sergeant and left Okinawa as a staff sergeant.

I was awarded a combat infantry badge on Iwo Jima, and I also received a Bronze Star because of actions we went through but I never received it until 45 years later. I didn't even know I had it coming until I started going to some of these reunions. They asked me if I ever received the Bronze Star. I said, "What Bronze Star?" He said, "You are eligible because of what you did on Iwo." One of the members had been to Washington, D.C to the archives. He went through what troops were eligible, and he brought the original order back to the reunion and gave it to us. I don't remember how many there was who were entitled to the Bronze Star. I had to get my congressman to get it for me. Our battalion, as a group, was given an award from General Erskine, Commanding General of the 3rd Marine Division on Iwo.

* March 26, D plus 35, Japanese overran the bivouac area of the Army Air Corps, Seabees, and 5th Pioneer Battalion in a well coordinated nighttime raid. After bitter fighting, 223 enemy soldiers lay dead. The morning revealed that 44 airmen were killed and 88 were wounded; 9 Marines were killed and 31 were wounded.

* * *

Gail Chatfield

Remembrance

"Iwo Jima was the most savage and the most costly battle in the history of the Marine Corps," Lt. General Holland M. Smith later acknowledged. Nearly 75,000 Marines fought an estimated 22,000 Japanese troops on that eight square miles of volcanic hell. When the battle ended,. 6,821 Americans had been killed and 19,000 wounded. A little over 1,000 Japanese survived and were taken prisoner. Both sides paid an enormous price.

At the base of Mt. Suribachi, a little south of Motoyama Airfield No. 1, thousands of young men lay buried in the cemeteries of the 3rd, 4th, and 5th Marine Divisions. Row upon row of white crosses and stars were seen by the troops as they regrouped to leave the island. Some walked among the grave markers in search of their fallen buddies while others could only turn to look and pause for a moment of silence as they boarded their ships.

Joe Rosenthal's photograph of the raising of the American flag on Mt. Suribachi provided the image of that horrible battle, but the words of Lt. Roland Gittelsohn, CHC, USNR, furnished its meaning. Lt. Gittelsohn was the first Jewish rabbi assigned to the Marine Corps and he, like his fellow chaplains, ministered to all faiths in combat. The rabbi knew the horrors of war and the toll it took on the men.

At the 5th Marine Division Cemetery dedication on March 21, 1945, Division Chaplain Warren Cuthriell asked Rabbi Gittelsohn to deliver the memorial sermon at a combined Protestant, Catholic and Jewish service. Chaplain Cuthriell wanted a single, nondenominational ceremony to honor the men of different races and religions united as Marines. It was not to be; the Protestant and Catholic chaplains objected to the idea of a combined service and a rabbi preaching over mostly Christian graves.

Rabbi Gittelsohn gave the eulogy he originally wrote for that ceremony at a separate Jewish service. Several Protestant chaplains, angered at the attitudes of their colleagues, attended the service. Unknown to the rabbi, thousands of copies of the sermon were circulated among the troops who then sent them home for their families to read. Coverage of Gittelsohn's eulogy spread even further when excerpts were published in Time magazine. The entire sermon was later inserted into the Congressional Record.*

Rabbi Gittelsohn's words remain powerful and timeless:

"This is perhaps the grimmest, and surely the holiest task we have faced since D-Day. Here before us lie the bodies of comrades and friends. Men who until yesterday or last week laughed with us, joked with us, trained with us. Men who were on the same ships with us, and went over the sides with us as we prepared to hit the beaches of this island. Men who fought with us and feared with us.

Somewhere in this plot of ground there may lie the man who could have discovered the cure for cancer. Under one of these Christian crosses, or beneath a Jewish Star of David, there may rest now a man who was destined to be a great prophet... to find the way, perhaps, for all to live in plenty, with poverty and hardship for none. Now they lie here silently in this sacred soil, and we gather to consecrate this earth in their memory.

It is not easy to do so. Some of us have buried our closest friends here. We saw these men killed before our very eyes. Any one of us might have died in their places. Indeed, some of us are alive and breathing at this very moment only because men who lie here beneath us had the courage and strength to give their lives for ours. To speak in memory of such men as these is not easy. Of them, too, it can be said with utter truth: 'The world will little note or long remember what we say here. It can never forget what they did here.'

No, our poor power of speech can add nothing to what these men and the other dead of our Division who are not here have already done. All that we can even hope to do is follow their example. To show the same selfless courage in peace that they did in war. To swear that by the grace of God and the stubborn strength and power of human will, their sons and ours shall never suffer these pains again. These men have done their job well. They have paid the ghastly price of freedom. If that freedom be once again lost, as it was after the last war, the unforgivable blame will be ours, not theirs. So it is we, the living, who are here to be dedicated and consecrated.

We dedicate ourselves, first to live together in peace the way they fought and are buried in war. Here lie men who loved America because their ancestors generations ago helped in her founding, and other men who loved her with equal passion because they themselves or their own fathers escaped from oppression to her blessed shores. Here lie officers and men. Negroes and whites, rich men and poor...together. Here are Protestants, Catholics, and Jews...together. Here no man prefers another because of his faith or despises him because of his color. Here there are no quotas of how many from each group are admitted or allowed. Among these men there is no discrimination. No prejudice. No hatred. Theirs is the highest and purest democracy.

Gail Chatfield

Any man among us, the living, who fails to understand that will thereby betray those who lie here dead. Whoever of us lifts his hand in hate against a brother, or thinks himself superior to those who happen to be in the minority, makes of this ceremony and of the bloody sacrifice it commemorates, an empty, hollow mockery. To this, then, as our solemn, sacred duty, do we the living now dedicate ourselves: to the right of Protestants, Catholics, and Jews, of white men and Negroes alike, to enjoy the democracy for which all of them have here paid the price.

To one thing more do we consecrate ourselves in memory of those who sleep beneath these crosses and stars. We shall not foolishly suppose, as did the last generation of America's fighting men, that victory on the battlefield will automatically guarantee the triumph of democracy at home. This war, with all its frightful heartache and suffering, is but the beginning of our generation's struggle for democracy. When the last battle has been won, there will be those at home, as there were last time, who will want us to turn our backs in selfish isolation on the rest of organized humanity, and thus to sabotage the very peace for which we fight. We promise you who lie here: we will not do that! We will join hands with Britain, China, Russia in peace, even as we have in war, to build the kind of world for which you died.

When the last shot has been fired, there will still be those whose eyes are turned backward, not forward, who will be satisfied with those wide extremes of poverty and wealth in which the seeds of another war can breed. We promise you, our departed comrades: This, too, we will not permit. This war has been fought by the common man; its fruits of peace must be enjoyed by the common man! We promise, by all that is sacred and holy, that your sons, the sons of miners and millers, the sons of farmers and workers, will inherit from your death the right to a living that is decent and secure.

When the final cross has been placed in the last cemetery, once again there will be those to whom profit is more important than peace, who will insist with the voice of sweet reasonableness and appeasement that it is better to trade with the enemies of mankind than, by crushing them, to lose their profit. To you who sleep here silently, we give our promise: We will not listen! We will not forget that some of you were burnt with oil that came from American wells, that many of you were killed by shells fashioned from American steel. We promise that when once again men seek profit at your expense, we shall remember how you looked when we placed you reverently, lovingly, in the ground.

Thus do we memorialize those who, having ceased living with us, now live within us. Thus do we consecrate ourselves, the living, to carry

330

on the struggle they began. Too much blood has gone into this soil for us to let it lie barren. Too much pain and heartache have fertilized the earth on which we stand. We here solemnly swear: This shall not be in vain! Out of this, and from the suffering and sorrow of those who mourn this, will come—we promise—the birth of a new freedom for the sons of men everywhere. AMEN"

The cemeteries are no longer on Iwo Jima. The return of the American dead buried in foreign cemeteries was provided for by Congress in 1947. Those buried on Iwo Jima were either re-interred at the National Memorial Cemetery of the Pacific at Punchbowl, Hawaii, or returned to their families for burial. While the American Graves Registration Service recovered most servicemen killed in the campaign, an estimated 250 servicemen are still listed as missing.

In 1968, the United States returned Iwo Jima to Japanese jurisdiction. In June, 2007, at the urging of its original inhabitants, Japan changed the island's name back to its prewar Iwo To. The 48-star flag raised on Mt. Suribachi is on display at the United States Marine Corps Museum at Quantico, Virginia.

*United States Congress. House. *Address at Dedication of Fifth Marine Division Cemetery on Iwo Jima.* 79th Cong., 1st Sess., 1945.

Dedication of the 5th Marine Division Cemetery, March 21, 1945.
Official Marine Corps photo/Silverthorn Collection

Gail Chatfield

BIBLIOGRAPHY
and suggested reading

Aurthur, R.A., Cohlmia, K., & Vance, R.T. (Ed.). *The Third Marine Division*. Washington: Infantry Journal Press, 1948.

Bevan, Denys. *United States Forces in New Zealand* 1942-1945. New Zealand: Macpherson Publishing, 1992.

Burrus, L. D. The Ninth Marines: *A Brief History of the Ninth Marine Regiment*. Washington: Infantry Journal Press, 1946.

Conner, Howard M. *The Spearhead: The World War II History of the 5th Marine Division*. Nashville: The Battery Press, 1950.

Dickenson, James R. *We Few: The Marine Corps 400 in the War Against Japan*. Annapolis, Maryland: U.S. Naval Institute Press, 2001.

Gailey, Harry A. *Bougainville 1943-1945: The Forgotten Campaign*. Lexington, Kentucky: The University Press of Kentucky, 1991.

Proehl, Carl W. (Ed.). *The Fourth Marine Division in World War II*. *Nashville*: The Battery Press, 1988.

Ross, Bill D. *Iwo Jima: Legacy of Valor*. New York: Vanguard Press, 1985.

Wolf, John D. *Amen! Until Tomorrow: Retaking the Pacific after Pearl Harbor*. Lima, Ohio: Fairway Press, 1990.

MARINE CORPS TERMS AND SLANG
As Defined By The Marines Themselves

AMTRAC:	Landing craft for going over coral reefs.
APC Pill:	All Purpose Capsule; Sick Bay's answer to your problem.
B.A.R.:	Browning Automatic Rifle
Betty:	Japanese light bomber plane
Boondockers:	Field shoes
Bouncing Betty:	Nasty type of land mine.
Brig:	Correctional facility
Brown bagger:	Married Marine
C-4:	Plastique explosives, forms like hard putty.
C-ration:	Hash or stew in small cans for field use, also called C-rats
Captain of the Head:	Your turn to clean the latrine
Chow:	Food or meals
Chow Call:	Head for the mess hall or whatever
Close it up:	Keep together; don't straggle
Combat fatigue:	Can't take it anymore
Corpsman (Doc):	Navy Medic attached to a Marine unit, or a call for medical help
Cruise:	A tour of duty or one enlistment period
D-Day:	Invasion Day
D-ration:	Rough chocolate bar (lunch if and when)
Daisy Cutter:	Shell or bomb that explodes just above the ground
Defilade:	A depression or area that somewhat protects from direct fire while still open to high trajectory shelling or air bursts.
D.I.:	Drill instructor
Dig In:	Get below ground (dig a foxhole)
Disembark:	Leave a ship by nets, or ramp, or gangway
Ditty Bag:	Small cloth bag for personal items often supplied by the Red Cross
Dog Face:	U.S. Soldier (slang)
Dog Tag:	Metal I.D. worn around neck
Down the Nets:	Leave a ship by landing net
DUKW:	Amphibious truck used to transport light artillery
Dump:	Area for storing ammo or supplies
Dungarees:	Our combat and work uniforms

Embark:	Board ship by nets, or ramp, or gangway
Fire in the Hole:	Explosion imminent
FO:	Forward Observer
Foot Slogger:	One who walks or crawls into battle (an Infantryman)
Foxhole:	The Infantryman's home in combat
Foxhole Buddy:	One who shares life and miseries on the frontlines
G.I.:	Government Issue (men or equipment)
Gear:	Any item
Geedunk:	Ice Cream; snack bar; slop shute
782 Gear:	Pack, cartridge belt and related items
General Quarters:	Prepare for action aboard ship
Get Yer Gear On:	Don helmet, cartridge belt, pack and prepare to move out. Saddle up.
Gizmo:	The perfect word. Covers the unknown as well as the forgotten
Going Asiatic:	Acting strange
Grinder:	Parade deck
Grunt:	Infantry, foot Marine
Gung Ho:	Chinese meaning to 'work together' adopted by Marines
Gunny:	Gunnery or maybe First Sergeant
Gyrene:	Slang for Marine (among Marines)
H-Hour:	Invasion hour
Hash Mark:	Stripe on dress uniform indicating length of service (hitch)
Head:	Latrine
Heavy:	30 caliber water cooled machine gun
Higgins Boat:	Landing Craft for personnel
Hitch:	Four years in the Corps
Hold:	Below deck area for troops or cargo
HQ:	Headquarters
Hubba Hubba:	Get with it, hurry up
IFF:	Identification friend or foe
I Got Mine Mac:	But if yer hurting I'll share, Semper Fi.
Iron Bottom Sound:	Area around Guadalcanal with many sunken ships; also referred to as Iron Bound Bay
Joe:	Coffee
K.I.A.:	Killed in action
K-ration:	Light weight meal for field use
K-Bar:	Marine Corps sheath knife

Land Mine:	Step on it and you'll never be the same
Landing Net:	Used to climb down into or up from a Higgins Boat
LCI:	Landing Craft Infantry
LCM:	Landing Craft, Mechanized
LCVP:	Landing Craft, Vehicle and Personnel (Higgins Boat)
Liberty:	Allowed time away from camp (rare)
Light:	30 caliber air cooled machine gun
Line of Departure:	Point at which the invasion run to the beach begins (no turning back now)
Lister Bag:	Device for holding drinking water in camp
Lock and Load:	Push ammo clip into rifle and put safety on
Long Tom:	Long barreled 155mm artillery piece
LSD:	Landing Ship, Dock
LSM:	Landing Ship, Medium
LST:	Landing Ship, Troop
LVT:	Landing Vehicle, Tracked
LVT(A):	Landing Vehicle, Tracked Armored
M-1:	The Garand semi-automatic rifle. A rifleman's delight, single deadly shot, clip fed, 8 rounds of .30 caliber ammo
Maggie's Drawers:	Red flag indicating a shot completely missing the target
Mac:	Slang for any Marine (Hey, Mac)
Marston Matting:	Long sheets of corrugated metal designed to lie flat and can be put together to provide a 'road' for tanks and equipment, as well as aircraft landing strips
Mess Hall:	Eating place (chow hall)
MIA:	Missing in action
Million Dollar Wound:	Non crippling wound generally to the legs
Move Out:	Could mean either a walk in the park or a walk in hell
Nambu:	Any Japanese light machine gun
Nervous in the Service:	Showing signs of strain
New Man:	Replacement
Officer's Country:	Area aboard ship reserved for Commissioned Officers
Old Man:	Been through at least one campaign; someone 22 or older

Overhead Cover:	Anything to make your foxhole somewhat secure from air bursts
Patrol:	The eyes of the company. A rather nasty but important way of keeping the enemy from mounting a surprise attack
Paramarines:	Marine parachute units. Disbanded in 1944
Pistol Pete:	A particularly accurate Japanese artilleryman on Guadalcanal
Pogey Bait:	Candy, soft drinks, fast food
Pole Charge:	Explosive fixed to a long pole
Police the Area:	Clean the damn place up
Poncho:	Rain gear seldom used for its original purpose but found to be invaluable in many ways (one of the last items to be discarded)
Pot:	Our steel helmet
Problem:	Marine lingo for a training maneuver
Raisin Jack:	Alcoholic beverage made in the camp on the sly
Rear Area:	Everything behind the Front Lines
Rear Echelon:	Those to the rear of where you are
Red Lead:	Ketchup
Reserve:	Off line for a bit
Reverse Slope:	The side of a mountain away from the enemy
Reveille:	You gotta get up
Rotation:	Going home (in your dreams)
Sack:	Bed, cot, bunk or whatever
Salt:	A Marine who has been in the Corps a long time or experienced a lot of combat
Scuttlebutt:	Rumor; also drinking fountain on ship
Sea Bag:	Large canvas bag for storing clothing and personal gear
Semaphore:	Arm signals with flags that the Navy uses
Semper Fi:	Always Faithful
Ship Over:	Sign up for another hitch
Short round:	One of ours landing too close
Short Timer:	One going stateside or getting out soon
Side Arms:	Salt, pepper and condiments in the Mess Hall; Hand gun in the field
Skivvies:	Underwear
Slop Chute:	Enlisted Men's "club"
Smoking Lamp is Lit or Out:	You can when lit, you cannot when out

SNAFU:	Situation normal, all 'fouled' up
S.O.S.:	Creamed something or another on toast
Spit Shine:	Just like it says, the ultimate for dress shoes
Stand watch:	Your turn to stay awake or pull guard duty
Stateside:	Where those who are not would like to be
Straddle trenches:	Instead of today's porta-potties or porta-johns.
Straight Scoop:	I got it from the General's Orderly
Survey:	Turning in used equipment for new gear; also used to describe a man being discharged, i.e. 'surveyed out of the Corps'
Swabbie:	U.S. Sailor (slang)
The Island:	Could mean any island but usually Guadalcanal
The Old Corps:	The way it was way back when or perhaps last week
The Point:	Front man on a patrol
The Word:	Find out what's going on (get the word)
Tropical Ulcers:	Deep, painful hard-to-heal sores
UDT:	Underwater demolition team
WIA:	Wounded in action
Wait a minute vines:	Strong, dangling, jungle vines with sharp thorns that catch the unwary
Washing machine Charlie:	Name given to Japanese planes making nightly bombing raids on Guadalcanal
Willie Peter:	White phosphorous round that explodes into a mushroom cloud that's used for targeting and inflicting casualties
Yard Bird:	One not with it (often on or being the clean-up detail)
Zeke:	Japanese fighter aircraft
Zero:	Single engine Japanese fighter plane: light, fast, and maneuverable

About The Author

Gail Chatfield is a native of Southern California and received her Bachelor's Degree from San Diego State University courtesy of the G.I. Bill.

A degree in Anthropology, the study of man and the role that culture exerts on individuals or groups, thoroughly prepared her for working in the exotic, fertile fields of the entertainment industry in Los Angeles. Positions at AFTRA, the William Morris Agency and for nearly a decade as the personal assistant to Farrah Fawcett, confirmed the theory that nothing beats reality for a good story.

Currently living in San Diego, Gail is a freelance writer and an opinion columnist for the North County Times. She is an associate member of the Third Marine Division Association.